Prentice Hall LITERATURE

PENGUIN EDITION

Reading Kit

Reading and Literacy Intervention

Grade Nine

PEARSON

Upper Saddle River, New Jersey
Boston, Massachusetts
Chandler, Arizona
Glenview, Illinois
Shoreview, Minnesota

Copyright© by Pearson Education, Inc., or its affiliates. All rights reserved. Printed in the United States of America. This publication is protected by copyright, and permission should be obtained from the publisher prior to any prohibited reproduction, storage in a retrieval system, or transmission in any form or by any means, electronic, mechanical, photocopying, recording, or likewise. The publisher hereby grants permission to reproduce these pages, in part or in whole, for classroom use only, the number not to exceed the number of students in each class. For information regarding permission(s), write to Pearson School Rights and Permissions Department, One Lake Street, Upper Saddle River, New Jersey 07458.

Prentice Hall® is a trademark, in the U.S. and/or in other countries, of Pearson Education, Inc., or its affiliates.

13-digit ISBN: 978-0-13-366703-5
10-digit ISBN: 0-13-366703-0

1 2 3 4 5 6 7 8 9 10   12 11 10 9 8

PEARSON

Contents

PART 1: PRACTICE AND ASSESS

BENCHMARK 1 SKILLS

BENCHMARK 2 SKILLS

BENCHMARK 3 SKILLS

BENCHMARK 4 SKILLS

BENCHMARK 11 SKILLS

BENCHMARK 12 SKILLS

PART 2: LITERATURE-BASED STRATEGIES

PART 3: CLASSROOM MANAGEMENT FOR DIFFERENTIATED INSTRUCTION

ALPHABETICAL LIST OF SKILLS

The *Reading Kit* has four parts, each designed to help you address the needs of students with varying ability levels.

- Use Part 1 to reteach and reassess unmastered skills
- Use Part 2 to develop independent application of active reading strategies
- Use Part 3 to ensure that students of all ability levels actively participate in learning activities and class discussions.
- Use Part 4 to devise strategies for addressing the special needs of diverse learners.

Part 1 Practice and Assess

Part 1 is organized around the skills taught in the student edition and is organized in the order in which the skills are taught and assessed. These *Practice* pages are designed to reteach skills targeted by the benchmark, but you can use them at any time that you feel reteaching is needed. All *Practice* and *Assess* pages are also available electronically on Success Tracker.

- After administering a benchmark test, use the Interpretation Chart that accompanies the tests to determine which *Practice* pages should be assigned to students.
- After students complete the *Practice* assignments, use the *Assess* pages to check mastery of the specific skills that have been retaught.

Part 2 Everyday Reading Strategies

Part 2 provides teacher and student pages for teaching reading strategies that develop active, thoughtful reading practices in *all* students. In addition, by giving direct instruction in these strategies, you will provide struggling readers with the tools they need to improve their comprehension and interpretation. These strategies can be used with any literature selection.

- Introduce the strategy, using the strategy plan and the graphic organizer.
- Once students are familiar with the strategy, encourage them to use the strategy independently with other selections.

Part 3 Classroom Management for Differentiated Instruction

Part 3 describes practical, effective strategies for engaging students of all ability levels in learning activities and class discussions. These research-based, classroom-tested techniques allow you to support your struggling students and challenge your advanced students in the same discussion or activity. These frameworks can be used with any literature selection or discussion topic.

Part 4 Language Arts Instruction—Professional Articles

Part 4 gives an overview of the diverse classroom. It also provides an analysis of the reading process, identifying the four aspects that need to be addressed to fully support diverse learners. Sections dedicated to specific characteristics of and challenges posed by three groups follow, along with discussion of strategies and resources for each: English language learners, less proficient learners, and special needs students.

Practice and Assess

Literary Analysis: Narrative Essay

Practice

A **narrative essay** is a short piece of nonfiction. It has these characteristics:

- It tells a true story about a real person or event.

- It includes **significant details** that help move the story forward or that help make the writer's point about the subject.

For each question, circle the letter of the best answer.

1. In a short work, a writer describes a friend of hers, Kayla Jeffers, who became a champion gymnast. If the work is a narrative essay, then which of the following must be true?

   A. Kayla Jeffers has broken many world records.

   B. The writer has written best-selling biographies.

   C. Kayla Jeffers is a real person.

   D. The characters in the essay are fictitious.

2. The essay about Kayla includes this significant detail: Kayla once helped the writer by lifting a log that had rolled onto the writer's foot. What point might this detail help the writer make?

   A. Kayla is friendly.

   B. Kayla is strong.

   C. Kayla is smart.

   D. Kayla is famous.

3. Which of these details is likeliest to help move the story of Kayla forward?

   A. Kayla has brown eyes.

   B. Kayla was born in October.

   C. A college coach comes to watch Kayla at a gymnastics meet.

   D. Kayla's grandmother is from North Carolina.

4. Why might the writer include a detail about Kayla's father's athletic achievements?

   A. to tell the complete story of his life
   B. to compare his achievements with those of professional athletes
   C. to show that he works hard
   D. to show that athletic ability runs in the family

Literary Analysis: Narrative Essay

Assess

For each question, circle the letter of the best answer.

1. Which of the following works is a narrative essay?

   A. a true story showing how the writer's grandfather inspired the writer
   B. a book giving the complete history of a family
   C. a made-up story with a character like the writer's grandfather
   D. a true explanation of the difference between snakes and lizards

2. George is a successful writer. In a narrative essay, he explains how his grandfather inspired him as a writer. The essay includes this significant detail: George's grandfather often told funny stories at dinner. Why might George include this detail?

   A. to explain what it was like having dinner at George's house
   B. to show that his grandfather's stories inspired him to tell stories himself
   C. to prove that he knew his grandfather well
   D. to show that older people have much to offer the world

3. Which of these details is likeliest to help move the story of George and his grandfather forward?

   A. George and his grandfather argue about their favorite baseball teams.
   B. George's grandfather was born in 1927.
   C. George's grandfather came to the United States in 1938.
   D. George's grandfather urged George to send his story to a magazine.

4. Why might George include a detail about the books his grandfather read?

   A. to show how his grandfather's preference for books influenced his own
   B. to show that his grandfather is a great writer
   C. to show that his grandfather still has good eyesight
   D. to show that his grandfather spends money on books

Literary Analysis: Plot and Conflict

Practice

A **plot** is the sequence of events in a story. It involves a **conflict,** or struggle between two opposing forces. A plot can be divided into these parts:

- the **rising action** is where you first learn about the conflict in the story
- the **climax,** or the most exciting moment in the story, is the moment just before you find out how the story ends
- the **falling action** is the part of the story after the climax, when the excitement grows less
- the **resolution** is the part of the story where the writer explains many details readers might still be curious about

A   For each question, choose the letter of the best answer.

1. At the beginning of a story, you read that Ashley Jones is trying to defeat a powerful criminal, Paula Smith. What is this part of the story called?

   A. the rising action   **C.** the falling action
   B. the climax   **D.** the resolution

2. In the middle of the same story, Paula traps Ashley in a building. The building is about to collapse, and Ashley has only seconds to escape. What is this part of the story called?

   A. the rising action   **C.** the falling action
   B. the climax   **D.** the resolution

3. Ashley escapes and arrests Paula. At the very end the story, Ashley decides to retire from fighting crime. What is this part of the story called?

   A. the rising action   **C.** the falling action
   B. the climax   **D.** the resolution

B   The following item describes a conflict between two characters or a character and a force. Tell who is involved in the conflict.

Julie wants to be captain of the softball team. Debbie is telling lies about her, though, to make sure Julie is not picked as the captain.

The conflict is between _____ **and** _____ .

Literary Analysis: Plot and Conflict

Assess

A For each question, choose the letter of the best answer.

1. At the beginning of a story, you read that a veterinarian went into a forest to help a wounded bear. What is this part of the story called?

   A. the rising action   **C.** the falling action
   B. the climax   **D.** the resolution

2. In the middle of the same story, the veterinarian slips on wet leaves as she approaches the bear. The frightened bear turns to attack. What is this part of the story called?

   A. the rising action   **C.** the falling action
   B. the climax   **D.** the resolution

3. After fooling the attacking bear, the veterinarian puts the bear to sleep and treats it. What is this part of the story called?

   A. the rising action   **C.** the falling action
   B. the climax   **D.** the resolution

4. The treatment is successful. The veterinarian calls in a helicopter and flies back to her home. What is this part of the story called?

   A. the rising action   **C.** the falling action
   B. the climax   **D.** the resolution

B Each item describes a conflict between two characters or a character and a force. For each item, tell who is involved in the conflict.

1. Sal has been friends with James since they were young. Now, though, James has found some new friends. He thinks he is too good to be friends with Sal anymore. Sal is hurt, and he tries to figure out what to do.

   The conflict is between _____ **and** _____.

2. Isabel is traveling through a rain forest. In the middle of the trip, she is bitten by a poisonous snake. She must do her best to treat the wound so that she will be able to walk back to civilization and find a doctor. She wonders, "Who will win, me or the poison?"

   The conflict is between _____ **and** _____.

Literary Analysis: Point of View

Practice

Point of view is the perspective from which a story is told.

- **First-person point of view:** The narrator is a character in the story. This character uses the first-person pronouns *I* and *me* to tell the story.

- **Third-person point of view:** The narrator is not a character in the story. This narrator uses third-person pronouns such as *he, she, they*, and *them* to refer to all the characters in the story.

Writers can use different types of third-person point of view. In **third-person omniscient point of view,** the narrator knows everything and can describe the thoughts of each character. In **third-person limited point of view,** the narrator reveals the thoughts of just one character.

A Complete each sentence.

1. In _____ point of view, the narrator is a character.

2. In third-person _____ point of view, readers learn what more than one character thinks and feels.

3. In third-person _____ point of view, readers learn the thoughts of just one character.

B Read the paragraph. Then, answer the questions that follow.

Chris got to the mall early. As he looked around for his friends, he caught sight of himself in a mirror. *Won't my hair ever lie flat?* he thought. He wondered whether Bob and Dean were as self-conscious as he was. Just then, he saw Dean waving to him across the food court. When Chris waved back, Dean started doing his gorilla imitation, jumping around and hooting. *No,* thought Chris, *Dean has too much fun to stop and think about how he looks.*

1. Who tells the story—one of the characters or a narrator outside the story?

_____

2. Do you learn as much about Dean's thoughts as about Chris's? Explain.

_____

3. What is the exact name for the point of view in the paragraph?

_____

Literary Analysis: Point of View

Assess

A Read each item. Identify the point of view in each, writing either *first person* or *third person* on the first blank. Then, explain how you know.

1. I really like Jerry. He is easy to get along with and is always willing to help out.

Point of view _____

How I know _____

2. Kathy seemed angry, but Samantha did not know why. She wished Kathy would just tell her what was wrong.

Point of view _____

How I know _____

B Read each paragraph. Then, answer the questions that follow.

Marla walked across the crowded dance floor. A spy was stealing secrets from the government, and Marla had figured out who he was. Now, her job was to make friends with him. Marla would then trick the spy into telling who sent him. That part could be hard. *It all depends*, Marla thought, *on whether he likes to dance.* Marla reached the corner where the spy was standing. She walked up to him and said, "Care to dance?" He looked surprised, but then he smiled.

1. _____ Whose thoughts do you learn in the paragraph?

2. _____ Whose thoughts do you NOT learn in the paragraph?

3. _____ Is the point of view in this paragraph third-person limited or third-person omniscient?

Marla walked toward the enemy spy. *I wonder whether I can get him to trust me*, she thought. Marla did not realize that the spy knew who she was. As the spy watched her walking toward him, he thought, *I will pretend to help her—but then I will double-cross her!*

4. _____ Whose thoughts do you learn in this paragraph?

5. _____ Is the point of view in this paragraph third-person limited or third-person omniscient?

Reading: Make Predictions

When you use what you *know* to explain what you *think* is going to happen in a selection, you are making a **prediction.** Predictions are based on information from the selection and knowledge from your own experience.

You can make predictions by using the following three steps as you read:

1. Ask yourself what you know about the story and the characters. Look for descriptions and clues in the text and make notes about these details.

2. Ask yourself what your own personal experiences have taught you about the details you wrote in your notes.

3. Based on what you discovered in steps 1 and 2, ask yourself what you think will happen. Write your predictions down on a piece of paper.

Read the selection. Then, answer the questions that follow.

    Kurt had finally finished restoring his grandfather's old truck. After months of repairing rust, searching for replacement parts, and rebuilding the engine, the truck was ready. The town was having a big parade to celebrate its centennial, and Kurt's truck was scheduled to follow the school band.
    Parade day began with a dark, overcast sky but no rain. Kurt went to the barn to put the finishing touches on the truck's decorations and give the gleaming bumpers a final polish. Finishing with little time to spare, Kurt started the engine and made his way into town. As he pulled the truck into position before the parade began, he heard a strange rumbling noise coming from under the engine. He stopped the truck, got out, and looked under the hood. Small dots of a dark fluid had begun to drip. Kurt took a deep breath and thought about what he might have in his toolbox to fix the leak.

1. What do you think will happen in the next few paragraphs of the story?

_____

_____

2. What details in the passage helped you make this prediction?

_____

_____

Reading: Make Predictions

Assess

Read the selection. For each question, circle the letter of the correct answer.

How Andrew's Summer Job "Paid" Off

Last summer, Andrew got the perfect job—right in his own front yard. Andrew's mother had suggested that he could earn money and help improve the appearance of the family home by cleaning up fallen branches and pulling weeds in the front yard. Andrew had helped neighbors with similar projects, so he knew he would be the perfect choice for the job.

As Andrew pulled on his work clothes for the first day of work, he thought how best to tackle the overgrown jungle in the front yard. He knew if he got rid of the large branches first, he would be able to see how many weeds he would have to pull. He went to the tool shed and took out the saw, rake, and hoe. Pulling on his heavy work gloves, Andrew began his first day of work.

After lunch, the sun was hot and high in the sky. Sweat began running down Andrew's face as he cut and stacked branches. As he put the last section of cut wood on the pile, Andrew noticed something glittering on the ground next to his left foot. He reached down and loosened the dirt around it. His fingers grasped the metal object—a gold coin and obviously one that was very old and valuable!

1. What does the title lead you to predict about the story?

   A. Andrew's summer job will be unrewarding.

   B. Andrew's summer job will prove to be valuable.

2. After reading the first paragraph, what might you predict?

   A. Andrew will do a good job cleaning the yard.

   B. Andrew will not finish the job that summer.

3. Which event could happen next in the story?

   A. Andrew throws the coin down the sewer.

   B. Andrew gets his picture in the paper with his historic coin.

4. Which prediction for the future is most likely to be true?

   A. Andrew sells the coin for a lot of money.

   B. Andrew goes to summer camp and forgets about the coin.

Reading: Reading to Perform a Task

When you **read to perform a task,** you read instructions carefully before or as you follow them. Here are some things you need to pay attention to when reading to perform a task:

- **The order of steps:** The steps in instructions are frequently numbered. Plan to follow the steps in numerical order. When the steps are not numbered, or when the parts of an individual step are not numbered, look for signal words such as: *first, next,* and *finally.*

- **Signal words:** Pay close attention to signal words that indicate *how* to perform a step ("*Gradually* add the flour"), *how much* of an ingredient to add ("Add *one spoonful*"), *what kind* of tool to use ("a *Phillips* screwdriver"), and so on.

Read the instructions. Then, answer the questions that follow.

Assembling the Dresser

1. Check to make sure you have all of the pieces listed under "Contents" (page 2) and all of the tools listed under "Required Tools" (page 3).

2. Carefully squirt a small amount of wood glue into each of the small holes in the corners of the Left Side Piece. Wipe off any excess glue.

3. Insert four Dowels in the holes on the corners of the Left Side Piece.

4. Squirt a small amount of wood glue in each of the two holes on the left side of the Front Face (the side marked "L"). Wipe off any excess glue.

5. Join the Left Side Piece to the left side of the Front Face. First, turn the Left Side piece so that the side marked "F" rests on your work surface. Then insert the mounted Dowels into the holes on the Front Face. Gently push the bottom of the Left Side Piece until it is flush with the Front.

1. _____ Which task should you perform first: Squirting glue in the holes on the Left Side Piece or inserting the Dowels in the Left Side Piece?

2. _____ In step 2, which signal word tells you how to squirt the glue?

3. _____ In step 5, which signal word tells you which is the first step in joining the Left Side Piece and the Front Face?

4. Why does it make sense to perform step 1 before performing any of the other steps?

Reading: Reading to Perform a Task

Read the instruction sheet. Then, answer the questions that follow.

Installing a New Car Radio

Parts Required

- Radio Mounting Unit
- Snap-on Wiring Unit

First Step. Uninstalling the Old Radio

1. Using a Phillips screwdriver, remove the four screws that hold the Center Dashboard Panel in place. (See diagram 1.)

2. Using your fingertips, locate the flexible tabs on either side of the Center Dashboard Panel. Squeeze the tabs inward. Gently pull the panel loose. Caution: Do NOT use sudden force, or the tabs may break.

3. After the Center Dashboard Panel is removed, you will be able to look underneath the place where the radio fits into the dashboard. Find and unscrew the screws that hold the Radio Panel in place. (The Radio Panel is the panel that holds the car radio, the air conditioner controls, and the center air vents. See diagram 2.)

4. Locate the black and the white plastic wiring connectors that attach wires to the Radio Panel. Disconnect the wires.

5. Pull the Radio Panel free from the dashboard.

6. Unscrew the old radio from the Radio Panel and disconnect it from the Wiring Unit. (See diagram 3.)

1. _____ To complete step 1, what tool should you have ready?

2. _____ In step 2, which signal word tells you how to pull the panel loose?

3. Why is it important to follow the signal word in step 2?

_____

4. In step 3, which phrase tells you when to look underneath the dashboard?

_____

5. Why does it make sense to perform step 2 before performing any of the other steps?

_____

Vocabulary: Prefixes *fore-* and *con-* and suffixes *-tion* and *-ate*

Practice

A **prefix** is added to the beginning of a word or word root to change its meaning. The prefix *fore-* means "earlier" or "in front of." The prefix *con-* means "with" or "together."

> fore- + see = foresee: "to predict, to see something before it happens"
> con- + join = conjoin: "to join two things together for a common purpose"

A **suffix** is added to the end of a word to change its meaning or part of speech. The suffix *–tion*, meaning "the act of," is often used to change verbs to nouns. The suffix *-ate* means "to become or form." It can change other word forms to verbs.

> reflect + -tion = reflection: "a reflected image"
> motive + -ate = motivate: "to give someone a motive"

A   Circle the letter of the answer that completes each sentence correctly.

1. If you <u>confide</u> in someone, you

   A. keep secrets from that person.   **B.** share your thoughts with that person.

2. If something has been <u>foretold</u>, that means it was

   A. predicted before it happened.   **B.** explained after it happened.

3. If you show <u>consideration</u> for someone, you

   A. treat the person with care.   **B.** ignore the person's needs.

B   Match each word with the sentence in which it fits best.

1. The firefighter did not _____ before rushing into the flames.

2. I tried to get an even _____ of sprinkles across the cake.

3. So far, no one has come up with a _____ to the problem.

4. This year, I hope to _____ in more sports activities.

distribution

hesitate

participate

solution

Vocabulary: Prefixes *fore-* and *con-* and suffixes *-tion* and *-ate*

Assess

A Circle T if the statement is true or F if the statement is false. Then, write a sentence to explain your answer.

1. T/F In a book, <u>foreshadowing</u> can help the reader guess how the story will end.

_____

2. T/F If a story is <u>consistent</u>, it does not make sense.

_____

3. T/F You would offer <u>condolences</u> to someone who has just heard some good news.

_____

4. T/F Someone who has <u>foresight</u> tends to act rashly.

_____

B Choose the correct word to complete each sentence. Write the word on the line.

1. conversation   conversed

I _____ with the professor after her lecture.

We had a very interesting _____.

2. captivated   captive

I was absolutely _____ by the singer's performance.

I was held _____ throughout the entire concert.

3. locate   location

I could not _____ the town of Springfield.

I could not find its _____ on the map.

4. distract   distraction

A ringing cell phone can be a _____ during a movie.

Please do not _____ other people with your conversation.

Reading Kit **13**

Grammar: Common and Proper Nouns

Practice

A **common noun** names a class of people, places, or things. A **proper noun** names a specific person, place, or thing. Proper nouns are capitalized.

A Each of the following sentences contains one noun. Write each noun in the first column and indicate whether it is common or proper in the second column.

Noun	Type
1. _____	_____	Steamy clouds rose up and nearly suffocated us.
2. _____	_____	We plan to visit Utah sooner or later.
3. _____	_____	Once I visited the White House.
4. _____	_____	Uncle Henry became increasingly nervous.
5. _____	_____	Before they moved, they located a new apartment.

B Fill in each blank with a proper noun.

1. The musician she likes the most is _____.

2. I enjoyed traveling to _____ on my vacation.

3. _____ is usually the busiest time of the year.

4. We attended Ryan's graduation from _____.

5. Jane bought a wonderful birthday gift for _____.

6. The airplane flew over the _____.

Grammar: Common and Proper Nouns

Assess

A For each sentence, write the proper noun it contains in the blank, adding the missing capitalization.

Example: She greatly misses uncle earl. _____Uncle Earl_____

1. Jasper's favorite author is margaret atwood. _____

2. When we were in ireland, we saw many castles. _____

3. My favorite pizza parlor is on pine street. _____

4. Where did you learn to speak japanese so fluently? _____

5. They eagerly climbed to the top of the empire state building.

_____

6. We spotted several dolphins off the coast of florida. _____

B Add nouns to the following sentences according to the directions in parentheses beneath each blank.

1. _____ was a famous _____.
   (proper)   (common)

2. We saw many _____ in _____.
              (common)   (proper)

3. _____ bought a _____ for me.
   (proper)   (common)

4. We visited _____ sometime last _____.
              (proper)   (common)

5. When she left the _____ and moved to _____,
                    (common)   (proper)

she was happier.

Grammar: Abstract and Concrete Nouns

Practice

Concrete nouns name things you can see, feel, hear, taste, or smell—for example, *apple, wind, John Loew, automobile*. You can directly experience concrete nouns through your senses.

Abstract nouns name feelings, ideas, and beliefs. You cannot directly experience abstract nouns through your senses. Words such as *happiness, guilt, pride*, and *faith* are abstract nouns.

Compare the following examples of abstract and concrete nouns.

Examples of Abstract Nouns	Examples of Concrete Nouns
annoyance, beauty, courage, fear, love	burglar, explorer, mosquito, mother, rose

Underline the nouns in the following sentences. The number in parentheses indicates how many nouns are in each sentence.

Example: <u>Planets</u> like <u>Uranus</u> and <u>Pluto</u> are still a <u>mystery</u> to <u>scientists</u>. (5)

1. Helen broke her wrist and her hand in the accident. (4)

2. Peas and carrots are the only vegetables José likes. (4)

3. The boy was impressed by the kindness of the coach. (3)

4. According to his mother, Gus walked at an early age. (3)

5. Ricardo practices many hours a day so he can be the best vaulter on the gymnastics team. (5)

6. The old clock on the mantel chimes every fifteen minutes. (3)

7. When fishing season begins, Jennifer and David will drive to the lake. (4)

8. Australia exports a large quantity of fine wool. (3)

9. Marblehead, a small town in Massachusetts, is sometimes called the birthplace of the navy. (5)

10. The carpenters made many improvements in the old building. (3)

Grammar: Abstract and Concrete Nouns

Assess

Write each noun and whether it is concrete or abstract on the line provided.

Example: Because our class has been studying civics this year, a representative from Congress will come and speak to us.

class—concrete; civics—abstract; representative—concrete;

Congress—concrete

1. Your car was towed to the garage down the street.

_____

2. Gideon and Shulamit study mathematics at the college.

_____

_____

3. Nana felt great joy when we sang our song for her.

_____

_____

4. Joey was filled with disappointment when the college rejected him.

_____

_____

5. Bill and Sue wear helmets whenever they ride motorcycles.

_____

_____

6. He bought a ticket to a town where he could enjoy peace and quiet.

_____

_____

7. The movie filled Linda with hope and happiness.

_____

_____

Grammar: Possessive Nouns

Practice

Possessive nouns show ownership. A possessive noun is most often formed by adding an apostrophe (') or an apostrophe and an *s* ('s) to a noun.

A Combine the phrases in each item to form one possessive phrase. Write your new phrase on the line after each item.

Example: driveways   the neighbors __the neighbors' driveways__

1. garden   the Smiths _____

2. furnishings   men _____

3. sons   the Davises _____

4. rules   Monopoly _____

5. great strength   Hercules _____

6. cards and dice   the games _____

7. soccer team   Lawrence High _____

8. contact lenses   Kris and Sara _____

9. news reports   TV stations _____

10. locker room   the women _____

B In the following sentences, the nouns inside the parentheses should be possessive. Write the possessive form on the line after each sentence.

Example: (Doris) attitude is that her problems are (Beth). __Doris's; Beth's__

1. (Columbus) destination wasn't North America. _____

2. (Hercules) coat was the skin of the Nemean lion. _____

3. Use (Phyllis) microwave oven, not (Barbara). _____

4. (Rome) army was defeated by (Hannibal) cavalry. _____

Grammar: Possessive Nouns

Assess

A Circle the letter of the form that correctly completes each sentence.

1. The _____ roars frightened the children.

    A. lions'   **B.** lions   **C.** lion

2. Have you seen _____ new house?

    A. Jack's and Joyce's   **B.** Jack and Joyce's   **C.** Jack's and Joyce'

3. _____ wish is to become a concert pianist.

    A. Karen Tomas   **B.** Karen Tomas'   **C.** Karen Tomas's

4. The _____ clothing section is upstairs.

    A. men's   **B.** mens'   **C.** mans'

5. Is this _____ classroom?

    A. Mr. Joneses'   **B.** Mr. Jones's   **C.** Mr. Jone's

6. Canada and the United States export many of the same products. The

    _____ include wheat, processed food, and paper.

    A. countries exports   **B.** country's exports   **C.** countries' exports

7. The _____ cheers could be heard from afar.

    A. crowds   **B.** crowd's   **C.** crowd

8. _____ decision to move so far away surprised us.

    A. Jim's   **B.** Jims'   **C.** Jims's

B In the following sentences, the nouns inside the parentheses should be possessive. Write the possessive form on the line after each sentence.

1. (Water) three states are solid, liquid, and gas. _____

2. (Wells) novel *The Time Machine* is a classic. _____

3. (Julius) stopwatch clocked Jo at a record speed. _____

4. The (people) choice for mayor was Tom Meyers. _____

5. The (dog) barking kept us awake. _____

Writing: Anecdote

An **anecdote** is a brief narrative about an interesting, amusing, or strange event told to entertain or to make a point. A well-written anecdote includes these features:

- It is directed to a particular audience, such as friends or classmates.
- It is about a single topic, which is usually stated in a topic sentence.
- It includes descriptive details that appeal to the senses.

Read the paragraph. Then, answer the questions and complete the activities that follow.

It was on my tenth birthday that I received the best birthday present ever. That morning I woke up and saw a large box sitting next to my bed. The box had a big, red bow on top. I could hear something whining inside the box. I jumped out of bed and tore off the lid. Inside was a wiggling ball of fur—a puppy! I had always wanted a puppy, but my mom said they were too much trouble. I picked up the fuzzy bundle, and it began licking me with its warm, wet tongue. I knew then that I had found the best friend I would ever have. I have had five birthdays since then, but my dog Charlie is still the best birthday present I have ever received.

1. Explain to what audience this anecdote might appeal. _____

2. What is the topic of the anecdote? _____

3. List three details that appeal to the senses. Identify the sense to which each detail appeals.

_____

_____

_____

4. Write a one-paragraph anecdote telling about a birthday gift that you received.

_____

_____

_____

Writing: Anecdote

Assess

Circle one of the following topics. Then, complete the activities that follow.

A case of mistaken identity   A craving for some food

Backstage at a recital   Planning a camping trip

A birthday surprise   Finding a missing pet

1. Identify your audience. _____

2. Write a topic sentence. _____

_____

3. List three events you would use. _____

_____

_____

_____

4. Tell what point of view you would use. _____

5. List two action verbs and two sensory impressions you might use.

_____

_____

6. Write the first paragraph of your anecdote on the following lines.

_____

_____

_____

_____

_____

_____

Writing: Critique

A **critique** is a written evaluation of a piece of writing. A well-written critique has these features:

- It lists the standards by which the piece of writing is judged. These standards might require writing to include characteristics such as vivid sensory details, character development, and an interesting story.

- It gives specific examples or explanations of why these characteristics are present or absent in the writing being judged.

- It includes a clear statement of the evaluation of the piece of writing.

A Circle the letter of the best answer for each of the following questions.

1. Which of the following might you include in a critique of a short story?

   A. It is the right length.

   B. It has an interesting story line.

   C. It contains many rhymes.

   D. It has the right number of characters.

2. Which of the following might be applied to the following passage?

   The trees had turned orange and gold. I could see the frosty cloud of my breath in the crisp morning air.

   A. use of vivid descriptions

   B. interesting setting

   C. well-developed characters

   D. good story line

B Read the critique. Then, complete the activity that follows.

The main character of the old man in this story is well developed. The writer explains how he worked hard all his life and how he loved the land. The writer uses vivid descriptions to help the reader "see" the old man. Details such as the old man's rough, work-worn hands, his worn and shiny cane, and his careful planting of vegetables help the reader understand and sympathize with the old man.

1. What are two standards that the writer uses to evaluate the story?

_____

2. Underline examples from the critique that support your answer to question 1.

Writing: Critique

Read the passage. Then, complete the activities that follow.

The sky was turning dark. Heavy rain clouds were rushing toward us from the west. I knew we were really in trouble. A thunderstorm over the desert could be dangerous, with deadly lightning and flash floods that washed down the deep gullies. I looked out over the rocky, barren landscape, searching for something that might provide shelter from the storm. I spotted a group of large rocks about a quarter of a mile away that might provide some shelter. Rain was already starting to pour. As Jack and I ran toward the rocks, thunder was pounding, and lightning was flashing all around us.

Both of us huddled under a rock outcropping as the thunderstorm pounded around us. I looked at Jack and saw that his face was twisted with fear. Jack is my younger brother, and I felt that I had failed him. It was not enough that I had gotten us both lost in the desert. Now we were in the middle of a terrible thunderstorm. I put my arm around him and hugged him close. I knew I had to take care of him, no matter what.

1. What are three characteristics or standards that you would use to critique this passage?

_____

_____

_____

2. Write a short critique of this passage based on the standards you listed in question 1.

_____

_____

_____

_____

_____

_____

_____

_____

Writing: Autobiographical Narrative

Practice

An **autobiographical narrative** describes real events in the writer's life and shares the wisdom the writer gained from the experience. A well-written autobiographical narrative includes a clearly identified span of time and descriptive details about the setting and the characters. Autobiographical narratives may include a conflict or problem that the writer faces. They can include characters in addition to the writer.

A   Read the paragraph. Then, answer the questions that follow.

When I was six years old, we lived on the outskirts of town. Our backyard backed up to a thick forest. Often in the morning I looked out the window and saw deer in our yard. One morning I decided I wanted to see where the deer went when they left our yard. My mother did not notice when I sneaked out of the house, barefoot and still in my pajamas, to follow the deer into the forest. I had not gone far when they disappeared from sight. When I turned to go home, I realized I did not know which way to go. I walked for a long time, getting more and more scared. The forest seemed to get thicker and thicker. I was hungry and just wanted to go home. I walked for what seemed like hours until I got too tired. I sat under a tree and fell asleep. When I awoke, the sun was going down and the forest was getting darker. I could feel the cold air through my thin pajamas. I began to cry. Then, through the darkness, I saw lights flashing and voices calling. I began yelling, calling for help. Soon I felt myself being picked up in the strong arms of my dad. I was safe at last!

1. What time span does the narrative cover? What details support your

   answer? _____

   _____

2. Write two details that tell about the setting. _____

   _____

3. Write three details that tell about the character. _____

   _____

4. Explain the problem or conflict the writer faces in this narrative. _____

   _____

B   Imagine you are the writer of this narrative. On a separate sheet of paper, write a few sentences that tell what happens next. Include a description of one or more other characters.

Writing: Autobiographical Narrative

Assess

A Use the following prompts to help you prepare your autobiographical narrative.

1. What time period will your autobiographical narrative cover? _____

2. Identify the setting. _____

3. List the events and a problem or conflict that you want to include.

_____

_____

_____

4. Identify the characters you want to include. Include details describing them.

_____

_____

5. Arrange the events in the order you will present them. How is the problem solved?

_____

_____

_____

6. Select some descriptive details about the setting you have chosen that will help you to visualize what you are writing about.

_____

_____

B On a separate sheet of paper, write the first two paragraphs of your autobiographical narrative.

Literary Analysis: Author's Voice

Practice

The writer's **voice** is the way the writer "sounds." It is the personality the writer expresses in his or her words. A writer's voice can have qualities such as the following:

- **smooth:** The employees at the library appreciate the special effort volunteers make. That is why they are offering volunteers free snacks on Wednesdays and Saturdays. You know something? They just made volunteering a little easier.
- **blunt or direct:** The community wanted a new high school gym, but they voted against paying extra taxes to build it. I say, quit complaining. Face the facts—you get what you pay for.

Writers create voice by choosing words and including details of the right type. They also create voice through the length and kind of sentences they write.

A For each paragraph, circle the letter of the phrase that best describes the writer's voice.

1. Let me say it in plain English. The mayor's idea is ridiculous. He calls it a great plan. Sure—a great plan to make the mayor rich!

   A. blunt and sarcastic   **B.** sad and thoughtful

2. The longer we wait to solve the problem of global warming, the greater the problem will become in the future. We need to face this problem now, not for our own sake, but for the sake of our children.

   A. serious and formal   **B.** friendly and informal

B Read the following paragraph. Then, answer the questions.

When my man takes a solo on his sax, look out! The notes pour out of his horn in a joyful jumble. He is so hot, he sizzles!

1. List two words or phrases that give the writer's voice a casual or informal

   quality. _____

2. List two words or phrases that give the writer's voice an energetic quality.

   _____

3. The first sentence ends in an exclamation, "look out!" What quality does

   this sentence ending add to the writer's voice? _____

Literary Analysis: Author's Voice

Assess

A For each selection, circle the letter of the phrase that best describes the author's voice.

1. I turned for one last look at the house where I had grown up. I remembered skipping up the front steps when I was happy. I remembered stomping on them when I was mad. Angry, sad, happy, glad—I had climbed those steps every day of my childhood. I would never set foot on them again.

    A. blunt and sarcastic   **B.** sad and thoughtful

2. Okay, so you are about to bake your first apple pie. You're worried that it will be a disaster, and you stayed up late reading the recipe. You now have dark circles under your eyes, and all your friends are worried about you. Relax! I remember my first pie. I worried and worried, and it *still* turned out terrible. The *fourth* apple pie I baked, though, was perfect!

    A. serious and formal   **B.** friendly and informal

B Read the following paragraph. Then, answer the questions.

     Rain drummed on the car. I watched the drops of water as they drizzled down the windows. They made lines that looked like a map—a crazy map of roads that led nowhere. I could still see my brother's yellow raincoat where he waited on the train platform. Soon, the train would come and take him away to college. We would wait there in the car until he boarded. The train took him away into the rain and the fog and the dark. It made me sad, so I tried not to think about it. Instead, I watched the rain fall.

1. List two phrases that give the author's voice a poetic quality. _____

_____

2. List three details that create a sad feeling in the paragraph. _____

_____

3. By saying just a little about his or her own feelings, does the writer create a chatty, friendly voice or a quiet, thoughtful one? Explain.

_____

_____

Literary Analysis: Character

A **character** is a person or an animal who takes part in the action of a literary work. Characters can be divided into four types:

- A **round character** is complex. A round character might have a mix of good and bad qualities. A **flat character** has only one main characteristic.

- A **dynamic character** changes as the story goes on. A **static character** stays the same from beginning to end.

A Identify each character as *round* or *flat*. Write your answer in the blank.

1. _____ Bob is too lazy to help his brother clean up. He is too lazy to make breakfast. He is too lazy to get up and see who is at the door.

2. _____ Linda works hard at her job after school. She also loves playing soccer. She is trying to decide whether to give up her job to join the soccer team.

3. _____ Max usually follows the rules. His friends decide to go skateboarding in an outdoor mall. Skateboarding is not allowed there. Max does not want to be left out, so he decides to go with his friends.

B Identify each character as *static* or *dynamic*.

1. ***Beginning of the story:*** Bob is too lazy to help his brother clean up.

   Ending: Bob is too lazy to see who is at the door. _____

2. ***Beginning of the story:*** Superguy believes he can solve most problems using his special powers.
   Ending: Superguy is unable to save his friend from an illness. Superguy realizes he cannot solve every problem.

3. ***Beginning of the story:*** Max lets his friends talk him into skateboarding where it is not allowed.
   Ending: Max's friends see someone coming. They run away and let Max get caught. Max realizes he should not let his friends lead him to break the rules—especially because they will not save him from trouble.

Literary Analysis: Character

Assess

A Identify each character as *round* or *flat*. Write your answer in the blank.

1. _____ At school, Samantha is shy and does not talk much. On the weekends, she leads a group of hikers on difficult trails. She explains safety rules to the group. She also gives orders to the group as they hike to prevent hikers from getting into danger.

2. _____ Joe is a friendly fellow. He greets people with a big smile. He often tells good jokes and leaves people laughing. He belongs to a few clubs. Other people often comment on how friendly he is.

3. _____ Dr. Bad plans to rule the world one day. He does wrong whenever he can. He has no friends and has never been seen smiling.

4. _____ Lateesha finds much to do in her city. She goes to plays, concerts, and museums. She volunteers for a neighborhood organization and helped organize a "Keep Our Block Beautiful" day. When she rides the bus, she daydreams about moving to the country and living on a farm.

B Identify each character as *static* or *dynamic*.

1. ***Beginning of the story:*** At school, Samantha is shy and does not talk much.
Ending: Samantha makes new friends. She speaks up more in class.

_____

2. ***Beginning of the story:*** Joe greets people with a big smile. He belongs to a few clubs.
Ending: Joe joins another club. He makes a new friend at work.

_____

3. ***Beginning of the story:*** Dr. Bad plans to take over the world. He does wrong whenever he can.
Ending: Dr. Bad finds a stray kitten. He is filled with pity. He adopts the kitten and spends millions to build a shelter for homeless animals.

_____

Literary Analysis: Theme

A **theme** is the message or insight that a writer presents in a work. Sometimes, the writer states the theme of the work directly. For instance, a writer might begin an essay with this sentence: "Honesty is the best policy."

In a short story, the writer may imply a message without directly stating it. Readers must figure out the theme by noticing what happens in the story.

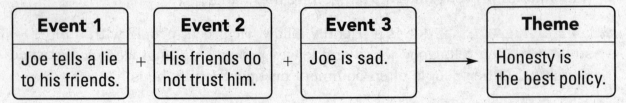

Event 1		Event 2		Event 3		Theme
Joe tells a lie to his friends.	+	His friends do not trust him.	+	Joe is sad.	⟶	Honesty is the best policy.

A   For each paragraph, circle the words that directly state the theme.

1. You can find Nature's beauty in the strangest places. Deep in the ocean, miles below the surface, groups of giant tube worms attach themselves to the ocean floor. Their feathery red heads wave in the current.

2. As I brought the spaceship in for a landing, I started to whistle. With just one spaceship and a simple electronic device, we had destroyed the Fangon fleet. I turned to Bob and said, "Courage and quick thinking can help you can get any job done—even the impossible!"

B   Read the following story. Then, answer the questions.

    When my cousin Keesha said she did not like my new necklace, I decided I would never talk to her again. As it turned out, I did not talk to her for three days. On the fourth day, I was in the store on the corner buying an orange. Suddenly, I heard a voice. "Young lady, if you eat too much fruit, you will swell up like a balloon!" I started to laugh. I turned around. It was Keesha.
    "You do not have to talk to me," said Keesha. "I know how mad you are."
    "Well," I said. "I have decided that just because you do not know anything about necklaces, it does not mean we cannot be friends."

1. The narrator has an easy time making up with Keesha. What does this fact show about their quarrel?

_____

2. What theme about friendship does the story express?

_____

Literary Analysis: Theme

A   For each paragraph, circle the words that directly state the theme.

1. The main reason to explore outer space is to keep our curiosity and our courage alive. We cannot say what good things will come from sending a mission to Mars. There may be many, or there may be few. What is most important is that once again, we leap into the unknown.

2. Once, my sister and I ran into a visitor in the woods behind our house—a black bear! We had to think fast, and I almost made a big mistake. I learned a lesson, though. Always treat wild animals with caution.

B   Each of the following paragraphs tells a story with an implied theme. For each paragraph, circle the letter of the answer that correctly states the theme.

1. Some criminals told Karen that she would make a lot of money if she invested in their crooked plan. Karen was greedy, so she gave them her money. In the end, Karen lost the money and was almost arrested. She realized that money is not as important to her as her freedom.

   A. The most important thing in life is making money.
   B. Honesty is the best policy.
   C. Greed can lead people to forget what is important and to do foolish things.
   D. Never invest money.

2. An old fisherman and a young fisherman went fishing. Near the end of the day, the old fisherman hooked a huge fish. The two struggled for an hour to get the fish in their boat. The fish was too strong, though, and it got away. The young fisherman was upset that they did not catch the fish after so much work. The old fisherman laughed and said, "Now you have a reason to go fishing tomorrow—to catch that big fish!"

   A. It is better to catch many small fish than one big fish.
   B. If you do not succeed at first, give up.
   C. Never go fishing alone.
   D. If you do not succeed at first, keep trying.

Reading: Author's Purpose

Practice

An **author's purpose** is his or her reason for writing. There are four general purposes for writing: to entertain, to inform, to describe, and to persuade.

Read the selection. Then circle the letter of the best answer for each question.

The Fun They Had
by Isaac Asimov

Margie even wrote about it that night in her diary. On the page headed May 17, 2155, she wrote, "Today Tommy found a real book."

It was a very old book. Margie's grandfather once said that when he was a little boy, *his* grandfather told him there was a time when all stories were printed on paper.

They turned the pages, which were yellow and crinkly, and it was awfully funny to read words that stood still instead of moving the way they were supposed to—on-screen, you know. And then, when they turned back to the page before, it had the same words on it that it had when they read it the first time.

1. In this story, what is the author's purpose?

   A. to inform readers about the past   **C.** to entertain readers with a tale of the future

   B. to inform readers about the future   **D.** to persuade readers to read more

2. What is the author's purpose for including the detail about Margie's diary?

   A. to present events and Margie's reactions in a realistic way
   B. to persuade readers that books are in danger of dying out
   C. to explain what a diary is
   D. to inform readers of today's date

3. What is the author's purpose for including details about Margie's grandfather and her great-great-grandfather?

   A. to show readers how long it has been since people read books
   B. to show readers how silly Margie's family is
   C. to show readers how popular computers will become
   D. to show readers how close Margie's family is

Reading: Author's Purpose

Assess

Read the passage. Then circle the letter of the best answer for each question.

"The Man to Send Rain Clouds"
by Leslie Marmon

Silko is a story that explores the traditions of the Pueblo Indians. The Pueblos have lived in the southwestern United States for nearly 3,000 years. They first came into contact with Europeans when the Spanish arrived in the 1500s. During the twentieth century, the Pueblos have incorporated many aspects of the modern world into their lives. Nevertheless, they have tried to hold on to their ancient traditions and beliefs. These beliefs include the view that if they stay in harmony with the natural world, nature will give them what they need, such as enough rainfall for their crops. The Pueblos' combination of modern ways with their own customs provides a central conflict in Silko's story. Her description of a funeral service shows an important moment in which a Native American tradition is combined with other traditions.

1. Which word best describes the author's presentation of information about the Pueblo Indians?

    A. hostile   **C.** factual

    B. sympathetic   **D.** biased

2. Why did the author probably write the passage?

    A. to express an opinion about the Pueblo Indians

    B. to persuade people to read Leslie Marmon's story

    C. to entertain readers with the history of the Pueblo Indians

    D. to inform readers about the Pueblo Indians

3. Why does the author mention the funeral?

    A. to give an example of the combination of traditions

    B. to show that the Pueblo culture is dying

    C. to show that the Pueblos refuse to change

    D. to show that all people die, whatever their tradition

4. What does the author seem to suggest about the Pueblos?

    A. The modern Pueblo funeral should be changed.

    B. The Pueblos control the rain.

    C. Traditions help the Pueblo see themselves as part of the natural world.

    D. The Pueblos should not combine Native American traditions with others.

Reading: Analyze Structure and Format

Practice

Reference works such as dictionaries have a certain structure and format. Analyzing the structure and format can help readers find and understand information.

Dictionaries and other reference works include sections explaining their organizational features. These guides appear at the beginning or the end of the book. They can help you recognize and use organizational features.

Study the guide to dictionary entries. Then, answer the questions that follow

Each entry in the dictionary begins with a main entry word in bold print.

apple (ap´əl) *n.* [ME *appel* < OE *æppel*, fruit, apple] **1** a round, firm fruit with red, green, or yellow skin **2** any of the trees that bear this fruit **3** any of various plants bearing applelike fruits or growths, such as the May apple and the love apple.

The main entry word is followed by its pronunciation. To understand the special characters used in the pronunciation, see page xiii.

Each separate meaning of the main entry word has its own numbered definition.

The part of speech of the main entry word appears as an abbreviation.

An explanation of which languages the main entry word originally came from appears in brackets.

1. What information do you expect to find after number 2 in the sample entry?

_____

2. What is the abbreviation for the part of speech of the main entry word?

_____

3. To which page in the dictionary would you turn to understand the symbols in a pronunciation? _____

4. What type of information appears in brackets in this sample entry?

_____

5. Give the number of the definition that is closest to the meaning of *apple* in this sentence: "To make space for a new shed, we chopped down the <u>apple</u> tree in the corner of the yard."

_____

Reading: Analyze Structure and Format

Assess

Study the guide to dictionary entries. Then, answer the questions that follow.

Each entry in the dictionary begins with a main entry word in bold print.

guffaw (gu fô´, gə-) **n.** [echoic] **1** a loud burst of laughter— **v.** to laugh in a loud burst— **SYN.** LAUGH

There may be more than one correct way to pronounce a word. Different pronunciations are separated by a comma. If the only difference is in the first or last syllable, then only that syllable will follow the comma.

To find synonyms for a word, look for a dash followed by the abbreviation "SYN." Then look up the word that follows. At the end of the definition for that word will appear a number of synonyms and an explanation of the differences in their meanings.

An explanation of the source of the main entry word appears in brackets. For an explanation of the terms and abbreviations used here, see page xiv.

Some words can be used as different parts of speech. After the first definition, each additional part of speech is marked by a dash, followed by the part of speech and a definition.

1. What is the main entry word in this entry? _____

2. How many different ways can you pronounce *guffaw*? Explain how you know. _____

_____

3. To which page in the dictionary would you turn to understand the term *echoic*? _____

4. How many parts of speech can *guffaw* function as? Explain how you know.

_____

_____

5. To figure out the difference between a "guffaw" and a "chortle" (another kind of laughter), what word should you look up? Explain how you know.

_____

_____

Vocabulary: Word roots -*fin*- and -*term*- and suffixes -*able*- and -*ive*

Practice

A **root** is the basic unit of meaning of a word. A **suffix** is one or more syllables added to added to the end of a word to change its meaning or part of speech. Study these examples.

Example:

Root or Prefix	Meaning	Words with the Root
-fin- (root)	end	final, finish, confined, infinite
-term- (root)	limit, end, boundary	terminal, determined, exterminate
-able (suffix)	capable of being	remarkable, portable, reliable
-ive (suffix)	of, belonging to, quality of	collective, cooperative, instinctive

A Replace the underlined word or phrase in each sentence with a word from the chart above containing the root -*fin*- or -*term*-.

1. _____ The patient was <u>restricted</u> to her bed during her illness.

2. _____ I tried to talk him out of his decision, but he was absolutely <u>firm</u>.

3. _____ I plan to <u>wipe out</u> the weeds that have taken over my garden.

4. _____ The student spent hours preparing for his <u>end-of-year</u> examinations.

B Match each word with the sentence in which it fits best.

1. She seems to have an _____ sense of direction.

2. I'd rather have a _____ car than a flashy one that breaks often.

3. These folding chairs are very handy because they're _____.

4. Organizing the school fundraiser was a _____ project.

cooperative

instinctive

portable

reliable

Vocabulary: Word roots -*fin*- and -*term*- and suffixes -*able*- and -*ive*

Assess

A Circle the root in each word, and think about its meaning. Then, write the word's meaning on the first line. Use a dictionary to check the meaning. Finally, use each word in a new sentence.

1. infinite _____

_____

2. determine _____

_____

3. terminal _____

_____

4. refined _____

_____

5. terminate _____

_____

B Revise each sentence so that the underlined vocabulary word is used logically. Be sure not to change the vocabulary word.

1. As a criminal, he was a <u>respectable</u> figure in the community.

_____

2. She has an <u>active</u> lifestyle and spends a lot of time watching TV.

_____

3. The dirt and dim lighting gave the room a <u>festive</u> atmosphere.

_____

4. The book was so <u>predictable</u> that I had no idea what would happen next.

_____

5. I found his kindness and generosity toward others <u>despicable</u>.

_____

Grammar: Personal and Reflexive Pronouns

Practice

A **personal pronoun** refers to the person speaking, the person spoken to, or the person, place, or thing spoken about. **Reflexive pronouns** end in *-self* or *-selves* and are used to indicate that someone or something performs an action to, for, or upon itself.

A Underline the personal and reflexive pronouns in each of the following sentences. The number in parentheses tells how many pronouns are in the sentence.

Example: Joan did not have a tent, so <u>she</u> borrowed one from <u>us</u>. (2)

1. Tony said, "We will help you, Paul." (2)

2. We want you to do the experiment yourself. (3)

3. He and Pat helped us rebuild the car. (2)

4. Sharon made herself a delicious dinner. (1)

5. I found the books very dull, and only two of them interested me. (3)

6. The survivors cried with joy when they were rescued. (1)

7. Mr. Takata read the poem aloud to himself and his wife. (2)

8. She promised mom she would never listen to him again. (3)

9. We looked at the exhibits but did not like them. (2)

10. The salesman asked if he could help us. (2)

B Read each sentence. Indicate whether the italicized pronoun is personal or reflexive.

1. _____ Phillip squeezed *himself* onto the crowded bus.

2. _____ Does the hat belong to *you* or to Danielle?

3. _____ He washed the dishes and left *them* to dry in the rack.

4. _____ Mom said I should learn how to do the laundry *myself*.

5. _____ Carlo and Dinah said *they* would bring food to the class picnic.

Grammar: Personal and Reflexive Pronouns

Assess

A Underline the pronoun in each sentence. Then, indicate whether the pronoun is personal or reflexive.

1. Tina saw the cat clean itself. _____

2. Lindsay unlocked her car. _____

3. Phyllis bought herself new earrings. _____

4. Anna whistled to herself. _____

5. Please bring your sister to the dentist. _____

6. When he was very young, John collected rocks. _____

7. During the storm, the house lost its antenna. _____

8. Nirav taught himself how to ski. _____

B Fill in each blank with a personal pronoun.

Example: Julia never remembers to bring _____*her*_____ lunch.

1. Jennifer's friends congratulated _____ for winning the contest.

2. Did you bring _____ camera with you?

3. In spite of _____ flaws, the movie was still enjoyable.

4. The mice escaped from _____ cage.

5. With _____ money ready, Timothy entered the bank.

6. George, would _____ please help me carry this box?

7. We want _____ to learn how to do it herself.

8. He washed his pants and shirts and put _____ in the dryer.

Grammar: Relative, Interrogative, and Indefinite Pronouns

Practice

A **relative pronoun** begins a subordinate clause and connects it to another idea in the sentence. Relative pronouns include *that, which, who, whom,* and *whose.*

An **interrogative pronoun** is used to begin a question. Interrogative pronouns include *what, which, who, whom,* and *whose.*

Indefinite pronouns refer to people, places, or things, often without specifying which ones. Indefinite pronouns include *all, both, few, much,* and *none.*

A Write whether each underlined word is a relative pronoun or an interrogative pronoun.

1. Is he the man <u>whom</u> you danced with at the wedding? _____

2. <u>Whom</u> did you call in Canada? _____

3. It is a story <u>that</u> we all enjoyed reading. _____

4. <u>Which</u> of the children will be coming on the school trip? _____

5. <u>What</u> can we do to help you find your keys? _____

6. Maya Angelou is an author <u>whose</u> work I admire. _____

B Underline each indefinite pronoun in the following sentences.

1. Each of the musicians practiced the new orchestral piece.

2. Everyone enjoyed the beautiful weather over the weekend.

3. Many of us were unable to bring guests to the party.

4. Few of the speakers had anything new to add.

5. No one was able to complete all of the tasks.

6. Some of the tenants chose to move to another apartment complex.

Name _____ Date _____

Grammar: Relative, Interrogative, and Indefinite Pronouns

Assess

A Fill in each blank with an appropriate relative or interrogative pronoun.

1. Did you find the video _____ you were looking for?

2. Rebecca is a friend _____ I have known since grade school.

3. _____ do you predict will win tonight's baseball game?

4. Is there any way in _____ we can help you with your chores?

5. _____ is the quickest route to get back on the highway?

6. _____ should I ask to go to the dance with me?

B Fill in each blank with an indefinite pronoun that makes sense.

1. _____ of us were able to attend her birthday party.

2. The librarian asked _____ of the new patrons to fill out an application.

3. When can we have _____ to eat?

4. Kate brushes her teeth _____ times a day.

5. _____ of the test questions were easy.

6. When _____ is ready, the plane will depart.

7. Only a select _____ are able to climb such a tall mountain.

8. _____ of the customers were disappointed with the service.

Grammar: Pronoun-Antecedent Agreement

Practice

A **pronoun** is a word used to take the place of a noun. The noun it substitutes for is called an **antecedent.** A pronoun should agree with its antecedent in person, number, and gender.

Pronoun-Antecedent Agreement

Elizebeth likes *her* new car.
John, Garrett, and *Mike* wore *their* suits.

A Underline the pronoun in each sentence. Then, circle its antecedent.

1. Victoria, can you show George how to fix the computer?

2. When Lydia sang, everyone was amazed by her voice.

3. Roberto said that he had learned how to speak Spanish at an early age.

4. "I will practice my flute more often," Sheila promised.

5. Why are you so upset, David?

6. Since their commute was similar, Gina and Trey decided to carpool.

B Fill in each blank with a pronoun.

1. "How are _____ enjoying your new school, Mark?"

2. Many stores have _____ hours posted on the door.

3. The tree dropped _____ acorns on the ground below.

4. Jacob promised his parents that _____ would never lie again.

5. Mildred brought _____ broken watch to the repair shop.

6. The actors did such a great job that _____ were nominated for awards.

Grammar: Pronoun-Antecedent Agreement

Assess

A Assume that each item is an antecedent for a personal pronoun. After each item, write *his, her, its,* or *their* to show which pronoun you would use.

Example: Jane and Rachel ___*their*___

1. my kitten _____   6. a robot _____

2. Jim and Allen _____   7. each niece _____

3. the boy _____   8. Janet, Annie, or Wendy _____

4. many authors _____   9. the stewardess _____

5. only one tractor _____ 10. either Kevin or Karl _____

B Write an appropriate personal pronoun to complete each sentence.

Example: Jasper's parents attended _____*his*_____ graduation last night.

1. Alicia or Kimberly will give you _____ sweater.

2. The squirrel built _____ nest high up in the trees.

3. I accidentally dropped _____ stack of papers on the floor.

4. Ever since Ted started _____ new job, he has been much happier.

5. Betsy and Lindsay decorated _____ new apartment.

6. Arthur, please remember to bring _____ towel.

7. The train sounded a horn as _____ rounded the corner.

8. Neither Ryan nor Henry had a watch with _____.

Reading Kit **43**

Spelling: Frequently Misspelled Words

Practice

Content area words are word that come from science, social studies, literature, and any other subject areas that you may study. Some content area words are tricky to spell because they have unusual letter combinations.

Math	parallel	Literature	metaphor
Social Studies	Arctic	Health	psychology
Science	muscles	Music	chord

To learn how to spell these words, identify the difficult letter combination in each and memorize it. You might make up a reminder to help you remember the correct combination. Here are some examples:

All l's are parallel.

You can see the frozen sea in the Arctic.

Musical muscles sing a silent c.

A For each misspelled word, find the correct spelling in the box. Write the correct spelling on the line.

1. musels _____

2. metafor _____

3. cord _____

4. sycology _____

5. Artic _____

6. paralell _____

B Circle the three misspelled words in the paragraph. Give the correct spelling for each on the lines that follow.

I took a long trip to the Arctic. I went to study the psichology of seals. Afterward, my muscles were sore. The problem was that I did not keep my skis parellel when I went skiing. Before I go to the Artic again, I will practice skiing more.

1. _____ **2.** _____ **3.** _____

Name _____ Date _____

Spelling: Frequently Misspelled Words

Assess

A Write *correct* next to each correctly spelled word. If the word is incorrectly spelled, write the correct spelling.

1. metefor _____

2. chord _____

3. psychology _____

4. musuls _____

5. Artic _____

6. paralell _____

B Circle the three misspelled words in each paragraph. Give the correct spelling for each on the lines that follow.

In my English class today, we learned that a metaphor is a figure of speech. A metaphor can help you understand someone's psycology. For example, I could say, "My friend Fred is a playful puppy." You can tell that I am saying that Fred is full of energy and is friendly. A metafor can sometimes be hard to understand. If I say, "He lives in the Artic of her heart," I am using a metaphor. I am saying that her feelings for him are cold, just like the Arctic.

1. _____ **2.** _____ **3.** _____

In Music class today, we learned that a cord is a group of notes played at the same time. My friend Janet told the class that she practices chords on the piano. Sometimes she has to stretch her fingers to play all the notes in a chord. Some chords make the mussles in her hand hurt! Our teacher explained that one chord can change to another in something called parelell motion. He also said that each chord has its own personality. Some are full of joy and contentment. Others are gloomy and dissatisfied.

1. _____ **2.** _____ **3.** _____

Writing: Journal Entry

A **journal** is an ongoing record of important events and personal observations. Journals record events and ideas in chronological order and include vivid, significant details.

Read the journal entry. Then, answer the questions that follow.

Yesterday we arrived at our new house in a new town. It is really not a new house but a very old house, which is surrounded by fir trees that darken the downstairs windows. They were dripping with rain for our arrival. I just wanted to get into bed and forget where I was. But this morning the sun woke me, shining in the half circle of windows where my room rounds out into the tower. I got up to look out, and across the long green stretch of lawn I saw the blue waters of the lake dancing in the sunlight. And there at the end of the lawn is the boathouse and jetty, just as Dad promised. I suddenly feel that I cannot wait to go outside and start exploring.

1. How often do you think the author makes entries in this journal?

_____

2. Why do you think the author wrote this entry?

_____

3. What details in the passage set up the descriptive tone?

_____

_____

4. What personal observations does the author include?

_____

_____

_____

5. What is the important event in this passage?

_____

_____

Name _____ Date _____

Writing: Journal Entry

Choose one of the following topics or a topic of your own. Then, answer the questions to plan a journal entry.

Your feelings about a friendship　　Your reactions to a happy surprise

Your reactions to a current event　　Your feelings about moving to a new place

1. When? _____

2. Who? _____

_____

_____

3. Where? _____

4. What? _____

_____

_____

_____

_____

5. Your reactions: _____

_____

_____

_____

_____

_____

_____

_____

_____

_____

_____

Writing: Character Profile

Practice

A **character profile** is a form of descriptive writing in which a writer creates a picture in words of a person. Character profiles contain vivid language and sensory details that capture a character's appearance and personality.

A Read the paragraph. Then, answer the questions that follow.

Dani smiled as he brushed his horse's black coat. His own hair was the same color. He looked into his horse's big, brown eyes and saw his own brown eyes reflected there. His horse, Rob Roy, was his favorite thing in the world. He whistled a soft tune as he combed Rob Roy's mane. He hummed a song as he put the blanket and saddle on. It was time to ride! He felt free as the wind when he rode across the meadow; no problems followed him here. He rode easily and well, and he was strong from years of practice. Dani wished that everything in life—especially math and French—were as easy and as satisfying as riding.

1. Write two details about Dani's appearance.

_____

2. List at least two adjectives that describe Dani's personality.

_____

3. What is the one impression that the writer gives about Dani?

_____

4. What are Dani's achievements?

_____

5. What are Dani's problems?

_____

B Choose one of the following: a character from fiction or the movies, a famous person, or someone you know. List important details about the appearance, personality, and achievements of your character.

_____

_____

_____

Name _____ Date _____

Writing: Character Profile

A   Use the following prompts to help create a character profile of an original fictional character.

1. Character's name and age: _____

2. Physical characteristics (hair color, height, clothing): _____

_____

_____

_____

3. Personality traits: _____

_____

_____

_____

4. Interests and hobbies: _____

_____

_____

5. Education or work history: _____

_____

_____

6. Family or friends: _____

_____

_____

B   Use the details from Exercise A to create a character profile. Focus on a single event that demonstrates the character's personality. Write your profile on a separate sheet of paper.

Writing: Problem-and-Solution Essay

Practice

A **problem-and-solution essay** identifies and explains a problem and proposes a practical solution. Problem-and-solution essays include the following:

- a clear statement of the problem
- a suggestion for a solution to the problem
- facts, statistics, and details that explain the problem and how it might be solved

---

A Circle the letter of the best answer to each question.

1. Which of the following types of details would help explain the problem of crowded schools?

   A. statistics about the average number of students in a classroom
   B. a discussion of the writer's feelings about school
   C. a discussion of how people feel about crowded schools
   D. facts about the history of public education

2. Which of the following would help explain a solution to the problem of crowded schools?

   A. discussion about how people would like to help schools
   B. statistics about how much money would be needed to build additional classrooms
   C. facts about the number of students in school
   D. a discussion of how students feel in a crowded school

B Answer the following questions.

1. What is an important problem in the world or in your school?

   _____

2. What is a possible solution to the problem?

   _____

3. What are two types of details that you would use to explain a solution to the problem?

   _____

Name _____ Date _____

Writing: Problem-and-Solution Essay

Assess

Read the following prompt. Then, use the exercises that follow to help you plan a response.

> Raising money for extracurricular activities often presents a problem for high-school students. For example, while a Spanish club's trip to Spain or the marching band's involvement in a nationally televised parade can be rewarding, raising enough money for these trips can be a daunting task.
>
> Choose an activity that you believe your school should help sponsor. Write a letter to your principal in which you clearly state the problem you are facing and offer possible solutions to fundraising for your activity. Use details to support your response.

Who is the audience for your response? _____

_____

What is the purpose of your response? _____

_____

To brainstorm for the best possible solution, fill in the cluster diagram with at least four ways to raise money for the school activity. Then, underline the two strongest solutions.

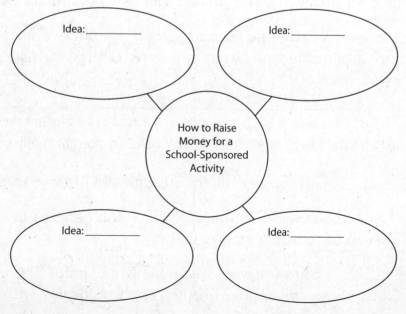

Literary Analysis: Conflict

Practice

Conflict is a struggle between a character and a force that is against the character. The opposing force might be another character, a force of nature, or the character's own mixed-up feelings.

A car chase in a movie is a simple example of a conflict. In the car chase, the hero tries as hard as he or she can to catch the villain. The villain tries as hard as he or she can to get away. Only one of them can win. At the end, their conflict reaches a **resolution,** or final outcome—the hero captures the villain, or the villain gets away. There are two types of conflict:

- **external conflict:** the struggle between a character and an outside force, such as another character, a natural disaster, and so on.
- **internal conflict:** a character's struggle with his or her own feelings or beliefs.

A Write *conflict* on each blank that describes or suggests a conflict. Write *resolution* on each blank that describes a resolution.

1. A. _____ Linda is about to solve the energy crisis. She discovers that someone has broken into her lab and stolen her files.

B. _____ The FBI arrest the man who took Linda's files. He is another scientist. It turns out he took the files so that he could take credit for her discovery.

2. A. _____ George takes a risk. He uses most of his air to blow the submarine free. He reaches the surface just as the submarine runs out of air.

B. _____ George goes in search of underwater treasure. His one-person submarine gets stuck in a cave. George struggles to free it before his air runs out.

B Write *external conflict* before each sentence that describes an external conflict. Write *internal conflict* before each sentence that describes an internal conflict.

1. _____ A group of hikers struggles to survive in a snowstorm.

2. _____ Devon is afraid Keesha will laugh at him if he asks her out. He works up his courage and calls her.

3. _____ Sara is trying to decide what to do. She wants to go to the movies, but she promised her brother she would play with him.

Literary Analysis: Conflict

Assess

A Write *Conflict* on each blank that describes or suggests a conflict. Write *resolution* on each blank that describes a resolution.

1. A. _____ Jill is chased by criminals who believe that she has photographs of them committing a crime.

B. _____ Jill tricks the criminals into meeting with her at a train station surrounded by police. The criminals are arrested, and Jill is safe at last.

2. A. _____ Nat and Jen spot a Coast Guard boat heading their way. They signal the boat and are soon rescued.

B. _____ Nat and Jen are sailing in shark-infested waters. They hit a rock, and their boat begins to leak.

3. A. _____ Rudi fights for freedom in his country. His struggle comes to an end when he is captured and sent to prison.

B. _____ In the dark of night, Rudi and his fellow freedom fighters stage a raid against the enemy.

B Write *external conflict* before each sentence that describes an external conflict. Write *internal conflict* before each sentence that describes an internal conflict.

1. _____ Michael's doctor tells him he should not eat sweet things. Michael wants to follow his doctor's advice, but he keeps thinking about eating pastry.

2. _____ A flood threatens the village where Robin lives.

3. _____ Ashley's birthday is coming up. Michael decides to impress her with an expensive gift. Daniel hears about Michael's plan. Daniel wants to be the one who impresses Ashley, so he decides to get her an even more expensive gift.

4. _____ A coach realizes that one of the players is no longer good enough to be a starting player. That player is also the coach's friend. Each day, the coach decides to bench the player, but each day the coach finds an excuse not to.

Literary Analysis: Irony

Practice

Irony can be the difference between what happens and what you or a character expects or wants. This kind of irony is called **situational irony**.

What the Character Wants		What Actually Happens
Jack wants to score high on the test. He stays up all night studying for it.	vs.	The next day, Jack is so tired that he falls asleep during the test.

A Write *irony* on each blank that describes an ironic situation. Write *no irony* on each blank that does not contain irony.

1. _____ Susan works hard at her job. Her boss gives her a raise. A few months later, Susan gets a promotion and another raise.

2. _____ William works hard at his job. His boss never gives him a raise. William decides he will not work so hard. A few months later, his boss says, "Good work, William. I'm going to give you a raise."

3. _____ Aisha wakes up late. She is so worried about being late for school that she calls her cousin for a ride. They arrive exactly on time, only to discover that school is closed for a holiday.

B For each example of irony, explain the difference between the expectation and the reality in the situation.

1. Robbers break into the bank, and the guard takes a great risk trying to stop them. Later, the guard learns that there was no money in the bank that day.

Expectation: _____

Reality: _____

2. Janice agrees to meet with Earl at the library to work on a school project. Earl is very popular at school. Janice is nervous about meeting him. When Earl arrives, he says, "I'm sorry I'm late. I was so nervous about meeting you that I left all my notes at home and had to go back to get them."

Expectation: _____

Reality: _____

Literary Analysis: Irony

A Write *irony* on each blank that describes an ironic situation. Write *no irony* on each blank that does not contain irony.

1. _____ Brittany saves up her money to buy a special kind of computer. Just when she has enough money, the company that makes the computer stops selling it.

2. _____ Lee tells his mother that he will pick her up at the airport when she arrives. On the way to the airport, he gets stuck in a huge traffic jam. He gets off the highway and takes a smaller road. He arrives just as his mother's plane lands.

3. _____ Bill hears on the radio that it is expected to rain heavily on Friday. Bill decides not to buy tickets to Friday's ballgame. On Friday, it rains heavily and the game is canceled.

4. _____ Sal buys a fancy car. He is worried that sap will fall on the car from the pine tree in his driveway. He thinks the sap may harm the car's paint job. Sal decides to get rid of the tree. As he chops it down, it falls the wrong way and smashes the roof of his car.

B For each example of irony, explain the difference between reality and expectation or desire in the situation.

1. Amy meets Stacy, who acts very adult. Amy decides she wants to be more adult, too, so she arranges a sidewalk sale to get rid of her old toys. Stacy stops by the sale and buys several dolls. "Don't tell anyone," Stacy says, "but I still keep all my old toys."

Expectation: _____

Reality: _____

2. Matt wants to show off to Sandy. As he drives her to her tennis lesson, he tells her a long story about how good a driver he is. He is talking so much that he misses their turn and gets lost. Sandy says, "Great driving, Matt!"

Expectation: _____

Reality: _____

Literary Analysis: Setting

Practice

The **setting** of a story is the time and place in which it occurs. In many stories that you read, time and place are not stated directly. The writer expects you to find clues and make inferences about where and when the story takes place.

Read the story and look for clues that will help you figure out the time and place of the events. Then, answer the questions that follow.

I looked at my military watch to check the time. Ever since my dad had given it to me a week earlier, I checked the time about every five minutes. It was a great watch. The hours were numbered in digits from 1 to 24, a whole day's worth.

The watch had one function I tried to ignore. It told the date. Even though I did not look, I knew it was June 16. Five more days, and my dad would be gone.

Miles of sand dotted with sagebrush skimmed past the car window. The sight of all that desert twisted my insides too, just the way the date on my watch did.

In five days we would reach Nellis Air Force Base, in Nevada, where I would say goodbye to my dad, perhaps forever. He was being sent on a Joint Armed Forces mission overseas. I did not know what the mission was, because it was top secret, but Dad had just finished two months of intensive training in desert survival.

1. In what part of the country does the story take place?

_____

_____

2. What clues did you use to figure out your answer to question 1?

_____

_____

3. When are the events probably taking place—the distant past, the present time, or the far-off future?

_____

_____

4. What clues did you use to figure out your answer to question 3?

_____

_____

Literary Analysis: Setting

Read the following story and look for clues about the time and place. Then, answer the questions that follow.

The cannons stopped firing, and the air became filled with the odor of burnt gunpowder. Aaron Dobson crouched low behind the wall and watched the yellow cloud of dust move slowly toward him. Across the creek he could see the Redcoats staggering back.

"Powder!" a voice called out.

Aaron turned from the embankment, picked up the powder keg at his feet, and hurried down the trench. "Right here, sir," he said, stopping beside a tall, thin New Englander who was busy reloading his musket.

"I guess we taught ol' fancy-pants Cornwallis a lesson he was not expectin'," the soldier said, grinning.

"Do you think they will try us again?" Aaron asked, helping the soldier draw powder from the keg. The New Englander sniffed at the air and glanced up at the darkening sky.

"Don't think so, boy. It is gettin' too late in the day. I am thinking the British will wait until mornin' before they try us again."

1. During what period of history are the events probably taking place?

_____

2. What clues did you use to figure out your answer to question 1?

_____

3. In what country does the selection take place?

_____

4. What clues did you use to figure out your answer to question 3?

_____

Reading: Make Inferences

Inferences are logical assumptions about information that is not directly stated.

Read the following story. Then, answer the questions that follow.

At 3 A.M. Honolulu time on July 12, 1959, Pan American Airways Flight 947 from San Francisco was well over the Pacific Ocean. It was a star-bright night, the air was calm, and all was quiet.

The pilot looked to his left, when suddenly a cluster of white lights sped across the sky toward the airliner at a fantastic rate of speed. The pilot, copilot, and flight engineer watched the lights for at least ten seconds before the lights disappeared.

"What was that?" the copilot exclaimed. All agreed the object could not have been a plane.

The pilot reported the sighting to the Air Traffic Control headquarters in Honolulu. He was the first of several pilots to call about the lights.

A second call came from Pan American Flight 942. Its pilot had seen the lights, too. He reported, "It could be a shooting star. The sighting lasted ten to fifteen seconds." Another report came in from a Slick Airways flight. The pilot said that what he saw "appeared to be one large light, with four smaller lights in the trail. It came right at us. It could have been a meteor."

When the flights landed in Honolulu, military intelligence personnel questioned the pilots and copilots. Reporters were also present. Half-jokingly, one reporter asked, "Could it have been a flying saucer?"

A pilot hesitated and then replied, "I have never believed that such foreign objects existed." Then he took a deep breath. "I am a believer now."

After the airmen were dismissed, the reporters dashed for telephones.

1. Why did one of the pilots infer that what he saw could not have been a plane?

_____

2. Why might the pilot of Pan American Flight 942 have inferred that the lights were a shooting star?

_____

3. What do you infer was the reason the reporters ran to telephones?

_____

Reading: Make Inferences

Assess

Read the story. Then, circle the letter of the best answer for each question.

A Backwoods Boy
by Russell Freedman

Abraham was growing fast, shooting up like a sunflower, a spindly youngster with big bony hands, unruly black hair, a dark complexion, and luminous gray eyes. He became an expert with the ax, working alongside his father, who also hired him out to work for others. For twenty-five cents a day, the boy dug wells, built pigpens, split fence rails, felled trees. "My how he could chop!" exclaimed a friend. "His ax would flash and bite into a sugar tree or a sycamore and down it would come. If you heard him felling trees in a clearing, you would say there were three men at work, the way the trees fell."

1. The writer compares Abraham to a sunflower. What can you infer from this?

   A. He grew tall quickly, like a sunflower.

   B. He is tiny, unlike a sunflower.

   C. He is a vine creeping along the ground.

   D. He is attractive, like a sunflower.

2. Abraham's father hires him out to work for others. What can you infer is the father's reason for hiring him out?

   A. His father did not want him to get an education.

   B. His father did not want to work himself.

   C. The family needed the money that Abraham earned.

   D. Abraham preferred working to going to school.

3. Abraham earned twenty-five cents working all day. What can you infer about the value of twenty-five cents when he was a boy?

   A. It was worth about the same as it is today.

   B. It was worth much more than it is today.

   C. It was more than most boys earned in a day.

   D. It was exactly what his father earned in a day.

4. Abraham's friend says that when Abraham worked chopping trees, it sounded as if three men were at work. What can you infer from this?

   A. Abraham was clumsy and made a lot of noise.

   B. Abraham was not good at chopping down trees.

   C. Abraham spent a lot of time in the forest.

   D. Abraham chopped down many trees quickly.

Reading: Critique the Logic of Functional Documents

When you read a sign, use instructions to change a tire, or bake a cake with a recipe, you are using functional documents. Functional documents help you perform everyday tasks, so when you **critique the logic of functional documents,** you look for the "hows" and the "whys" that will help you complete the task. Look for these features as you read and learn from functional documents:

Text Features	Functions
Subheads	Identify the main idea of a section.
Highlighted Text	Bold, italic, and uppercase type points out important information.
Charts, Graphs, and Maps	Call out and order information.
Illustrations and Diagrams	Show ideas described in the text in a visual way.
Captions	Call out and describe important information.

Read the sign and think about how it gives you information you can use. Then, answer the questions below.

1. What does this sign tell you?

_____

2. What text features helped you understand its message?

_____

3. Write a caption for the sign that points out its meaning.

_____

Name _____ Date _____

 Read the functional document below, which describes how to use a DVD player. Then, answer the questions that follow.

How to Use Your DVD Player
Step 1: Press *POWER* on the remote control.
Step 2: Press *DVD* to select the DVD mode.
Step 3: Press *OPEN/CLOSE* to open the disc tray. Place a disc on the tray.
Step 4: Press *OPEN/CLOSE* to close the disc tray.
Step 5: Press *PLAY* to start playing the DVD.
Step 6: Press *STOP* to stop the DVD.
Step 7: Press *OPEN/CLOSE* to open the tray and remove the disc.

1. How does the title help you understand the document?

_____

2. Why do you think the steps are numbered?

_____

3. What words are set in **bold** type? What words are set in ***bold, italic*** type? Why do you think the writer highlighted these words in this way?

_____

_____

4. Why do you think the company included a drawing of the remote control with the instructions?

_____

_____

5. Who is the audience for these instructions? How do you know?

_____

_____

6. Why would it be important for the writer to know the audience before writing directions?

_____

_____

Vocabulary: Suffixes -ant and -esque and prefixes de- and ac-

Practice

A **suffix** is added to the end of a word to change its meaning or part of speech. The suffixes -*ant* and -*esque* are used to form adjectives. The suffix -*ant* means "performing an action," while -*esque*, means "in the style or manner of."

ß

defi + -ant = defiant: "defying, resisting"

picture + -esque = picturesque: "looking like a picture; charming"

A **prefix** is added to the beginning of a word or word root to change its meaning. The prefix *de*- has various meanings, including "down." The prefix *ac*- means "to" or "toward."

de- + press = depress: "to press down or lower; to sadden"

ac- + cept = accept: "to agree to, to take willingly"

Circle the letter of the word that is closest in meaning to the underlined word or phrase.

1. She felt <u>sorry</u> for the crimes she had committed.
   A. compliant   **B.** reliant   **C.** repentant

2. She was widely admired for her <u>shapely</u> figure.
   A. arabesque   **B.** Lincolnesque   **C.** statuesque

3. I first became <u>familiar</u> with him at school.
   A. acclaimed   **B.** acquainted   **C.** acquired

4. He had to quit work because of his <u>failing</u> health.
   A. declining   **B.** depending   **C.** deposing

5. I <u>walked down</u> the stairs.
   A. decreased   **B.** demolished   **C.** descended

Vocabulary: Suffixes -ant and -esque and prefixes de- and ac-

Practice

A Add the suffix indicated to each underlined word to form a new word. Write this word on the line. Then rewrite the original sentence to use the new word.

1. _____ I have always <u>relied</u> on her advice. (add –ant)

   _____

2. _____ He was compared to <u>Lincoln</u> because of his way with words. (add -esque)

   _____

3. _____ I <u>complied</u> with all their demands. (add -ant)

   _____

4. _____ He had a gift for using body language like that of the actor Charlie <u>Chaplin</u>. (add -esque)

   _____

B Think about whether each sentence below makes sense, given the meaning of the underlined word. Circle "Y" if it makes sense and "N" if it does not. Then explain your answer. If the sentence does not make sense, write a new sentence using the word correctly.

1. Y/N After <u>demolishing</u> the old building, they gave it a fresh coat of paint.

   _____

   _____

2. Y/N At the trial, the prisoner was <u>acquitted</u> and sentenced to prison.

   _____

   _____

3. Y/N <u>Acknowledging</u> that a problem exists is often the first step toward solving it.

   _____

   _____

4. Y/N The car <u>decelerated</u> as the driver approached the red light.

   _____

   _____

Name _____ Date _____

Grammar: Regular Verbs

Regular verbs form the tenses following a regular, consistent pattern. The four parts used to form the tenses are **present, present participle, past,** and **past participle.** With regular verbs, the past and past participle are formed by adding -*ed* to the present tense form. Sometimes, before adding -*ed*, it is necessary to double the final consonant or drop a silent -*e*.

Principal Parts of Regular Verbs

Present	Present Participle	Past	Past Participle
paint	(is, was) painting	painted	(has, have) painted
return	(is, was) returning	returned	(has, have) returned
rub	(is, was) ru__bb__ing	ru__bb__ed	(has, have) ru__bb__ed
like	(is, was) li__k__ing	liked	(has, have) liked

A Write the principal parts of each regular verb. The first one is done for you.

Present	Present Participle	Past	Past Participle
1. fill	filling	filled	filled
2. stop	_____	_____	_____
3. play	_____	_____	_____
4. hire	_____	_____	_____
5. confuse	_____	_____	_____

B Write the *present, past, past participle,* or *present participle* to identify the principal part of the underlined verb in each sentence.

1. _____ The quarterback <u>calls</u> the plays.

2. _____ We *have* <u>replaced</u> the old porch with a new deck.

3. _____ Sally was <u>answering</u> the door when the phone rang.

4. _____ The defendant *has* <u>exercised</u> his right to remain silent.

5. _____ The parents <u>waited</u> eagerly for cards from their son.

Name _____   Date _____

Grammar: Regular Verbs

A Write the principal parts of each regular verb below.

Present	Present Participle	Past	Past Participle
1. contain	_____	_____	_____
2. clap	_____	_____	_____
3. whistle	_____	_____	_____
4. fold	_____	_____	_____
5. practice	_____	_____	_____
6. wiggle	_____	_____	_____

B Write *present, past, past participle,* or *present participle* to identify the principal part of the underlined verb in each sentence.

1. _____ Morgan always <u>changes</u> the channels.

2. _____ Mari is <u>holding</u> the tickets for the show.

3. _____ I *have* <u>studied</u> so hard for that exam!

4. _____ For her report, Karen <u>interviewed</u> the mayor.

5. _____ Are you <u>baking</u> cookies for the party?

6. _____ Carl *had* <u>scribbled</u> his name on the back of his paper.

C For each item, write a sentence using the word in parentheses in the form indicated.

1. (*exercise*/present) _____

2. (*bite*/present participle) _____

3. (*trip*/past) _____

4. (*rescue*/past participle) _____

Grammar: Irregular Verbs

Practice

An **irregular verb** is one whose past and past participle are not formed by adding *-ed* or *-d* to the present form. Instead, the past and past participle have various forms. Look at the following examples.

Present	Present Participle	Past	Past Participle
cost	(is, was) costing	cost	(has, have, had) cost
run	(is, was) running	ran	(has, have, had) run
rise	(is, was) rising	rose	(has, have, had) risen
bring	(is, was) bringing	brought	(has, have, had) brought
send	(is, was) sending	sent	(has, have, had) sent

A Complete each sentence with the correct form of the verb in parentheses.

1. (run) I was _____ home, when I _____ into Lee.

2. (bring) Tom had _____ her a CD, and she was

   _____ it to me.

3. (send) I _____ Tom a party invitation, but he hasn't

   _____ an answer.

4. (cost) In the old days a stamp _____ 10 cents; today it

   _____ 37 cents.

5. (rise) Prices usually _____; stamp prices have

   _____ almost every two years.

B Fill in each blank with the correct verb form from those given in parentheses.

1. I _____ the answer, so I raised my hand. (knowed, knew)

2. Were you _____ when you tripped on the step? (hurted, hurt)

3. Nancy _____ the concert early. (leaved, left)

Grammar: Irregular Verbs

Assess

A Underline the correct verb in each sentence. Hint: An auxiliary verb such as *has, have,* or *had* is a clue that the past participle form should be used.

Example: The guard (*threw*, thrown) a life preserver to the drowning man.

1. Joan has already (drew, drawn) the winning lottery ticket.

2. Couldn't Kiyoko have (wear, worn) her sister's gloves?

3. The survivors of the shipwreck all (swam, swum) to a nearby island.

4. Your canoe paddle has (sank, sunk) my model boat.

5. If you had (froze, frozen) the steak, it would have stayed fresher longer.

6. Everyone had (took, taken) a shower before going into the pool.

7. Mr. Baez (rode, ridden) the pinto down to the campsite.

8. Nancy must have (took, taken) out the books on her brother's library card.

9. Sales of subscriptions to the magazine (fell, fallen) off this past year.

10. Tom couldn't have (drank, drunk) all the soda by himself.

B Write the correct verb form on the line next to each sentence.

Example: What (lead) him to choose cake, not pie? _____led_____

1. Mitsuko (give) Kenya her birthday present early. _____

2. Have you ever been (sting) by a bee? _____

3. Naomi has (leave) the room five times today! _____

4. We would have (freeze) without a space heater. _____

5. Marisa (teach) piano to five children last year. _____

6. Mr. Reyes has (lend) me five dollars for lunch. _____

7. Moths have (eat) holes in all our sweaters. _____

8. Rey (break) three track records today. _____

Grammar: Verb Tenses

Practice

A **tense** is a form of a verb that expresses the time of an action. The six verb tenses are present, present perfect, past, past perfect, future, and future perfect. Inconsistent or unclear use of verb tenses can cause confusion in a story.

A Complete each sentence with the correct form of the verb in parentheses.

1. (remember) The author _____ some significant events in her life, so she decided to write about them.

2. (learn) As a child, Vincent _____ to greet his grandfather respectfully.

3. (live) I wonder whether I _____ in Oregon when I am older.

4. (cook) When Lucia finished her homework, she _____ herself an omelet.

5. (use) My brother always _____ my razor, but he never buys me any new blades.

B Underline the correct verb form in parentheses.

1. Although Liz entered the photo contest, she never really (expects, expected) to win.

2. Ed did not realize that we (are, were) on our way to a party.

3. The crew (is, was) tired because they had been painting all day.

4. I will have been sleeping for five hours when you finally (arrive, arrived).

5. Just as the flight attendant finished packing for a flight to Miami, she (gets, got) transferred to the Seattle-to-Rome run.

Grammar: Verb Tenses

Assess

A Read the passage and choose the word or group of words that belongs in each space.

On Tuesday, the Project 352 Team (1) ____ for an important meeting. After (2) ____ the issues, the team (3) ____ to change its approach in terms of planning. In the time since the meeting, the Project 352 Team (4) ____ to the conclusion that the new approach is working quite well. The team (5) ____ to apply the method in the future, and (6) ____ to many successful projects.

1. **A.** met
    B. did meet
    C. was meeting
    D. meet

2. **A.** having discuss
    B. discussed
    C. discuss
    D. discussing

3. **A.** did decide
    B. deciding
    C. decided
    D. decides

4. **A.** come
    B. has come
    C. have coming
    D. camed

5. **A.** hope
    B. hoping
    C. will hope
    D. hopes

6. **A.** looks forward
    B. have looked forward
    C. looking forward
    D. look forward

B Underline the appropriate verb in parentheses.

1. My science teacher says that the human eye (works, worked) like the lens of a camera.

2. Now, Tory wishes she (had gone, would have gone) on that blind date.

3. The tired hiker put down his pack, (had propped, propped) himself up under a tree, and promptly fell asleep.

4. Lynette (will fail, failed) the test if she does not study.

5. Bess (plans, planned) to make the same chicken dinner tonight that she made last week.

Writing: Alternative Ending

Practice

A **short story** is a brief, fictional narrative. An **alternative ending** to a story is an ending different from the writer's original ending. A good alternative ending has these qualities:

- It is logical based on the events of the story.
- It is something that might happen to the characters as they are described in the story.
- It gives a clear solution to the problem or conflict in the story.

In this story, an old farmer has lived all his life in the same house in a little village. He loved the land that he had farmed all his life. As he grew old and feeble, his sons insisted that he come to live with them in the city. Read the story ending. Then, answer the questions that follow.

The old man slowly pulled on his boots and stood up, taking a battered straw hat from the rack next to his easy chair. His roughened hands told the tale of his many years of labor in the garden, sowing seeds, pulling weeds, and planting rows of tomatoes and pepper plants. He picked up a cane leaning against his chair. Its handle was worn smooth and shiny from years of use. Leaning on his cane, the old man walked toward the back door that led out to his garden. He sat down beneath the peach tree that he had planted so many years before and closed his eyes. When his son arrived late that afternoon, he found the old man still sitting, eyes closed forever. He had died holding what he loved most—a handful of the dirt that he had farmed all his life.

1. Why is the ending of this story logical based on the character of the old man?

    A. He was tied to the land and could not live away from it.

    B. He did not like his son.

    C. He was stubborn.

    D. He was too old to make changes in his life.

2. Circle the letter of the logical alternative ending based on the character of the old man.

    A. The old man greets his son with affection and happily leaves with him.

    B. The old man marries a widow in the village and moves to another town.

    C. The old man moves with his son to the city and starts a new life there.

    D. The old man refuses to leave his home, and the last scene shows him sitting under a tree.

Name _____ Date _____

Writing: Alternative Ending

Read the following. Then, complete the activity.

In the story "The Interlopers" by Saki, two men whose families have feuded for generations find themselves face to face in the forest. As they are about to destroy each other, a tree crashes down and traps them. While they are trapped, they agree to settle their quarrel and become friends. Each promises the other that when his men come to rescue him, the other man will be the first to be rescued. This is how the story ends.

"I can see figures coming through the wood. They are following in the way I came down the hillside." . . .

"Are they your men?" asked Georg. "Are they your men?" he repeated impatiently as Ulrich did not answer.

"No," said Ulrich with a laugh, the idiotic chattering laugh of a man unstrung with hideous fear.

"Who are they?" asked Georg quickly, straining his eyes to see what the other would gladly not have seen.

"*Wolves.*"

Write an alternative ending for this story. Keep in mind the events that have occurred in the story and how the characters feel about each other.

_____

_____

_____

_____

_____

_____

_____

_____

_____

_____

_____

_____

_____

_____

Writing: News Story

A **news story** presents facts about events that have occurred. News stories answer the questions *Who? What? When? Where? Why?* and *How?* The opening sentence or paragraph of a news story should make the reader want to read more.

A   Read the news story. Then, complete the following activities.

Early Tuesday morning, the Carpenter family was saved from a possible tragedy by their family dog, Tommy. A spark from the fireplace had landed unnoticed on the carpet. After the family went to bed, the spark started a fire. The alert Tommy woke the family by barking and scratching at the bedroom doors. The Carpenters escaped and called firefighters, who quickly put out the fire. The family was safe, and their home suffered very little fire damage, thanks to Tommy. Mr. Carpenter said that Tommy has been a member of the family for nearly ten years and that he had always been protective of family members.

Write the answers to each of the following questions using the news story:

Who? _____

What? _____

When? _____

Where? _____

Why? _____

How? _____

B   Explain how the first sentence makes the reader want to read more.

_____

_____

_____

_____

Name _____ Date _____

Assess

A Think of a recent event that has occurred in your school or community. Based on the event, write an answer to each of the following questions.

Who? _____

What? _____

When? _____

Where? _____

Why? _____

How? _____

B Use your answers to the questions in Exercise A to write a news story about the event. Include an opening sentence that makes the reader want to continue reading the story.

_____

_____

_____

_____

_____

_____

_____

_____

_____

_____

_____

Writing: Short Story

Practice

A **short story** is a brief, fictional narrative composed of plot, setting, and characters. It is told from a consistent first-person or third-person point of view. It follows a chronological time order, and often includes dialogue.

A   Read the following passages. Then, write your answer to each question.

1. I entered the room quietly, hoping that I would not wake the sleeping dog.

   What is the point of view in this passage? _____

2. Angela slid into her desk before the bell rang. This was the first day at her new school. She was a year younger than her classmates, most of whom were 15. That made her feel even more shy. Her shyness made her blush as other students filed past her desk, looking at her. She stared down at her desktop, her long blond hair falling forward over her face.

   A. Write some key details about the character in this passage.

   _____

   B. What is the conflict or problem faced by the character in this passage?

   _____

3. I knew that somehow the time machine had gone out of control. I found myself in a dense forest of strange plants that appeared to be huge ferns. Little light penetrated the forest, and a thick fog covered the ground. Suddenly I felt the ground begin to tremble. At the same time, I heard an ear-splitting roar very near. It was the roar of an animal—a *very large* animal.

   Write the details of the setting described in this passage.

   _____

   _____

B   Choose one of the passages in Exercise A. Add one or more characters to the story. Then, create a brief dialogue between the characters. Make sure the dialogue is related to the story and adds to the action.

   _____

   _____

Writing: Short Story

Assess

Choose one of these topics to create a short story. Then, complete the activities.

the case of the missing soccer ball   two friends compete for a place on the team

why Mary Ann wanted to dance   a scientist discovers a strange new animal

1. Briefly summarize your idea for a story.

_____

_____

2. Identify your audience and keep it in mind as you write. _____

3. Identify the point of view you will use. _____

4. List the characters you will include in your story. _____

_____

5. Write the key details about each character: name, age, appearance, and personality traits.

_____

_____

6. Write some details of the setting, including time and place.

_____

7. Decide on a conflict or problem and state it in one or two sentences.

_____

_____

8. Create dialogue that uses words that suit each personality and moves the action of the story forward. Tell where in the plot you will use the dialogue.

_____

_____

Name _____ Date _____

Literary Analysis: Character and Characterization

Practice

A **character** is a person or an animal that takes part in the action of a literary work. A writer uses **characterization** to show what a character is like.

- **Direct characterization:** The writer tells you what the character is like. For example, the writer might say that the character is "mean" or "tall."

- **Indirect characterization:** The writer gives you clues about the character. For example, the writer tells you what the character does and says and shows how others react to the character. Using these clues, you form an idea of the character.

Clues	What Scrooge Is Like
Scrooge did not visit family on holidays. He stayed home and counted his money.	Scrooge is greedy and does not have warm feelings toward others.

A Write *Direct* for each item that uses mainly direct characterization. Write *Indirect* for each item that uses mainly indirect characterization.

1. _____ Evan has a good sense of humor.

2. _____ When Mai heard that Beth had been elected, she said, "Isn't that nice? I hope being president is good enough for Little Miss Perfect."

3. _____ Martha said that Janine was mean to her.

B Following are two examples of indirect characterization. Underline two clues that show what each character is like. Then, use the clues to describe the character directly.

1. **Roberto:** "Roberto has arrived," said Roberto loudly, stepping onto the basketball court. He handed his jacket to Rodney, the friend who followed him everywhere. Roberto was wearing a top-brand sports shirt. He flexed his arm muscles so that others could admire them. The other players looked at each other nervously.

What Roberto is like: _____

2. **Paula:** When Paula came over, Susan and Janet were sitting around being bored. Paula called the museum to find out what the hours were. Then, she found the bus schedule and got Susan and Janet out the door.

What Paula is like: _____

Literary Analysis: Character and Characterization

Assess

A Write *Direct* for each item that uses mainly direct characterization. Write *Indirect* for each item that uses mainly indirect characterization.

1. _____ Jessica is generous and shares many things with her friends.

2. _____ When Sam said, "I scored three touchdowns last game," Sid said, "I can beat that." When Eleanor said, "I got an 87 in Math," Sid said, "I can beat that."

3. _____ Many people think Sara is very smart. I heard one person say that Sara might be a genius.

4. _____ Most of the time, Emily is cheerful and talks a lot. Every now and then, though, she gets in a quiet mood and does not say much.

5. _____ When Brian heard that the storm was coming, he ran outside and brought his little brother and sister back into the house.

B Following is an example of indirect characterization. Underline two of the clues that show what the character is like. Then, use the clues to describe the character directly.

Jack: When Jack came home, his sister asked whether he had stopped to pick up milk. She suspected that, as usual, Jack had gotten distracted and had forgotten all about it.

"I tried, Sis, really, but the police wouldn't let me through to the store."

"Police!" she said.

"Sure," said Jack. "A tiger escaped from the zoo, and the police are out warning people."

"Jack," said his sister, "you aren't telling me one of your stories, by any chance?"

What Jack is like: _____

_____

Literary Analysis: Dialogue

Dialogue is the conversation of characters in a short story or play. Dialogue is set off by quotation marks. To show when one character stops talking and another begins, short story writers start a new paragraph:

> "What's going on?" asked Mary. She could tell John was excited. His face was flushed, and he was pacing rapidly.
> "I have just found the secret treasure," said John.
> "That's great news!" [The start of a new paragraph shows that Mary is speaking now.]

Writers use dialogue for a few reasons. In the example, the dialogue does these things:

- It informs readers about an important **event** in the story—John has found treasure.

- It shows something important about the **characters**—Mary and John are friends.

Underline each line of dialogue spoken by the characters in the paragraph. Then, in the numbered blanks, explain who is speaking each line and what the line adds to your understanding of the events or the characters.

> "I'm glad summer is coming," said Todd. "I need a break."
> "You told me last time I came home that you had a lot of homework," said Joe. "What else happened?"
> "I joined the basketball team."
> "Whoah, little brother. You have to make sure you pace yourself."
> "I know," said Todd. "It's probably even harder in college, right?"

1. **Speaker** _____ **What I Learned** _____

2. **Speaker** _____ **What I Learned** _____

3. **Speaker** _____ **What I Learned** _____

4. **Speaker** _____ **What I Learned** _____

Literary Analysis: Dialogue

Assess

A In each item, underline the dialogue, or words spoken by a character.

1. "You are doing a great job!" said Elaine to Anna. Anna thanked her.

2. When I saw Michelle's painting, I thought, What a mess! When I saw Michelle, though, I said, "Your painting is beautiful."

3. In front of the cave was a sign that said "Warning." Sam read the sign and said, "Let's go back."

4. When Gina told Kayla she wanted to go home, Kayla said, "Okay, I'll get the car."

5. I heard that Robert called Craig a grouch, so I asked Robert why. "Craig is always in a bad mood," said Robert.

B Underline each line of dialogue spoken by the characters in the paragraph. Then, in the numbered blanks, explain who is speaking each line and what the line adds to your understanding of the events or the characters.

"What was that noise?" Anna exclaimed.

"Shhh," hissed Elaine. "That was just your nerves. Do you want to wake up the guard?"

"Okay, Elaine, but I want you to know that I wouldn't be prowling around this museum basement if you were not my friend."

"I know, Anna," said Elaine, "and believe me, I appreciate your help."

"All right, ladies," said a voice from the stairs behind them, "and just what is it that brings you to the museum basement in the middle of the night, might I ask?"

1. **Speaker** _____ **What I Learned** _____

2. **Speaker** _____ **What I Learned** _____

3. **Speaker** _____ **What I Learned** _____

4. **Speaker** _____ **What I Learned** _____

5. **Speaker** _____ **What I Learned** _____

Literary Analysis: Symbolism and Allegory

Practice

A **symbol** is a person, place, or thing that stands for another thing or for an idea.

- The American flag is a *symbol* of the United States.
- In a story, a dog might be a *symbol* of friendship or loyalty.

An **allegory** is a story in which all characters and events are symbols.

A Each of the following items can be a symbol. For each symbol, name one thing that it is likely to stand for.

1. _____ a bald eagle

2. _____ a person's fist with the thumb sticking up

3. _____ a fancy white dress with a long veil

B For each question, choose the letter of the best answer.

1. In a story about two friends, Sally and Ashley, the friends share a portable CD player. Sally uses it one week, and Ashley uses it the next. Sally and Ashley have an argument. The next day, the CD player breaks. What is the CD player a symbol of?

   A. the girls' friendship   **C.** the girls' music
   B. the girls' argument   **D.** the girls' unhappiness

2. In story A, there is one main symbol and many realistic characters. In story B, all of the characters are symbols. Which of the following is true?

   A. Both stories are allegories.   **C.** Story A is an allegory, but story B is not.
   B. Neither story is an allegory.   **D.** Story B is an allegory, but story A is not.

3. In a story, Sue goes to the city to become an actress. Before she leaves, her mother gives her an old hairbrush. It first belonged to Sue's grandmother, who gave it to Sue's mother. In the city, Sue uses the brush whenever she needs good luck. What is the hairbrush a symbol of?

   A. family love and pride   **C.** acting
   B. the grandmother's hair   **D.** the city

Literary Analysis: Symbolism and Allegory

Assess

A Each of the following items can be a symbol. For each symbol, name one thing that it is likely to stand for.

1. _____ a red circle with a slanted red line through it

2. _____ a skull with two crossed bones beneath it

3. _____ a stork carrying a bundle in its beak

4. _____ a pumpkin

B For each question, circle the letter of the best answer.

1. In a story, a little boy's grandfather falls ill. The little boy is sad and worried. One day, the boy finds a bird with a broken wing outside his house. He takes the bird inside and helps it heal. A few weeks later, he learns that his grandfather is better. That same day, the bird flies away, its wing fully healed. What is the bird a symbol of?

   A. the boy's worries about his grandfather   **C.** the boy's father
   B. the grandfather's worries about the boy   **D.** the grandfather's doctor

2. You are reading an allegory. Which of the following do you expect to be true?

   A. None of the characters in the story are symbols.
   B. Most of the characters in the story are realistic, but one is a symbol.
   C. All of the characters in the story are symbols.
   D. There are no symbols in the story.

3. In a story, a young man is in love with a young woman. Every evening, he sits outside her home and plays songs for her on his guitar. She tells him that she likes his music. One day, the young man comes to her home and sees a wedding taking place. The young woman is getting married to another man. The young man goes home and puts his guitar away. He swears he will never play it again. What is the guitar a symbol of?

   A. the young woman's marriage   **C.** the young man's love for the young woman
   B. the young man's life   **D.** the young woman's love of music

Reading: Cause and Effect

Practice

A **cause** is an event or a situation that produces another event. An **effect** is the event produced.

A Write the letter of each effect in the blank next to its cause.

Cause	**Effect**
1. _____ The door was locked.	**A.** The flowers were drooping.
2. _____ The storm knocked down the power lines.	**B.** I could not get into the house.
3. _____ No one had watered the flowers for weeks.	**C.** The lights went out.

B In each sentence, circle the word or phrase that tells there is a cause or an effect. Then, underline the cause once and the effect twice.

1. Yusef couldn't ride his bike because it had a flat tire.

2. Maria missed the school bus because she got up late.

C Read the selection, and then answer the questions.

Why did the United States enter World War I to fight Germany and its allies? There was more than one cause. First, Americans were angry that German submarines sank a ship called the *Lusitania*. About 1,200 people on board died, including 128 Americans. Then, in 1917, the Germans sent a secret message to Mexico trying to get Mexico to fight with Germany against the United States. Finally, German submarines sank three American merchant ships. In April of 1917, Congress declared war against Germany.

1. List three causes for the United States to go to war with Germany.

_____

_____

2. Underline the sentence in the selection that names the specific effect of these causes.

Reading: Cause and Effect

Assess

Read the selection, and then circle the letter of the best answer for each question.

Life was hard for most people who lived in Russia in the 1800s. Until 1861, most Russians were serfs—people bound to the service of a small group of wealthy land-owning nobles. The czar, or ruler, of Russia declared emancipation of the serfs in 1861. As a result, the laws that bound serfs to masters came to an end. Still, most Russians lived lives of poverty and lacked freedom.

Some people challenged Russia's unfair social system. They were dealt with harshly, often being sent into icy exile in Siberia. Eventually, however, people's desire for reform led to the Revolution of 1905. The revolution forced the Russian czar to provide greater political freedom. A parliament, in which representatives of the people met, was founded. Change was not happening fast enough, and the people were still unhappy. In 1917, their discontent led to another revolution. Workers and peasants led by a man named Lenin fought against the czar. The czar lost. He was removed from power and was later killed.

1. According to the selection, which event or fact caused the Russian Revolution of 1905?

   A. Change was not happening fast enough.

   B. A parliament was founded.

   C. The czar was killed.

   D. People wanted to reform an unfair social system.

2. According to the selection, which event or fact was an effect of the czar's emancipation of the serfs?

   A. Most Russians lived in poverty.
   B. Serfs were bound to the service of landowners.
   C. The laws that bound serfs to masters came to an end.
   D. People wanted to reform an unfair social system.

3. According to the selection, what was a possible effect of a person's challenging the social system?

   A. being sent into exile in Siberia

   B. being bound to the service of a landowner

   C. unfair social conditions

   D. the rule of czars

Reading: Analyze Structure and Format

Signs, brochures, and other informational materials help people find information. To find specific information quickly, **analyze structure and format,** or figure out the visual clues. For example, a sign in a movie theater might include these three large headings.

- **"Show Times":** The heading printed in the largest type, "Show Times," gives information that most people are looking for: the time of the movie.

- **"Prices":** The cost is under the next largest heading, "Prices."

- **"Renting the Theater":** Only a few people need information about renting the movie theater, so it is under a smaller heading.

The heading size indicates the information that is needed most quickly.

Read this page from a brochure. Then, answer the questions that follow.

Visit the Colonial Parksburg Village!

See life in the thirteen colonies as it was actually lived!
Located just 40 minutes away from Petersville, Abbott's
Landing, and Frederickstown.
(See page 2 for detailed directions.)

Activities

Candle-making ■ Wool-carding
■ Thread-spinning ■ Animal rides

Seasons and Hours of Operation

Open daily, March 21 through November 30, from 8 A.M to 6 P.M.

Price of Admission

Adults: $20 ■ Children under 12: $10

---

1. Under which heading should you look to find the cost of tickets to Colonial Parksburg? _____

2. You want to know whether the village is open during the winter. Under which heading should you look? _____

3. Why do you think the heading for "Activities" is larger than the heading for "Price of Admission"? _____

Name _____ Date _____

Read this page from a brochure. Then, answer the questions that follow.

All Aboard the Music Cruise!

Dance to fine music under the stars ~ *Featuring the Hudson Hotshots!*

Spacious dance floor! ■ All-you-can-eat buffet!

Cruise Times and Locations

Boats depart from Pier 62 every two hours Thursdays through Sundays.

EARLY CRUISE: 6:00 P.M., daily

LAST CRUISE:

8:00 P.M., Thursdays and Sundays ■ 10:00 P.M., Fridays and Saturdays

Cruises Run Only When Weather Conditions Permit.

Music Cruise Management reserves the right to cancel or recall any cruise to protect its property and the safety of its passengers. Tickets may be refunded up to 15 minutes before cruise time but are nonrefundable thereafter.

Tickets: Call 811-77MUSIC for ticket prices and reservations.

---

1. Under which heading should you look to find the days of the week on which the cruise sails? _____

_____

2. On the day you planned to go on a Music Cruise, it is raining. Under which heading should you look to find out if the boat will sail? _____

3. Why is the list of activities in larger size type than the information about weather? _____

4. What do you need to do to learn the price of tickets for the Music Cruise?

_____

Vocabulary: Word roots -jec(t)- and bene- and suffixes -ity and -ous

Practice

A **root** is the basic unit of meaning of a word. A **suffix** is one or more syllables added to the end of a word to change its meaning or part of speech. Study these examples.

Examples:

Root or Prefix	Meaning	Words with the Root
-jec(t)- (root)	to throw	inject, projected, trajectory
bene- (root)	well, good	beneficial, benefactor, benediction
-ity (suffix)	the quality of	formality, intensity, gravity
-ous (suffix)	full of, having	anxious, curious, luxurious

A Replace the underlined word or phrase in each sentence with a word from the chart above containing the root -jec(t)- or bene-.

1. _____ Taking a daily walk has been very <u>helpful</u> to my health.

2. _____ The police tried to figure out the <u>path</u> of the car during the crash.

3. _____ The manager figured the company's <u>predicted</u> earnings for next year.

4. _____ Her simple words of kindness felt like a <u>blessing</u>.

B Add -ity or -ous to each underlined word to form a new word that fits the meaning of the sentence.

1. _____ The team won a <u>glory</u> victory over its chief rival.

2. _____ The <u>complex</u> of the problem made it hard to understand.

3. _____ Her sudden appearance in town was very <u>mystery</u>.

4. _____ I'm worried about the <u>possible</u> of failing this test.

Vocabulary: Word roots -jec(t)- and bene- and suffixes -ity and -ous

Practice

A Revise each sentence so that the underlined vocabulary word is used logically. Be sure not to change the vocabulary word.

1. I was willing to take a job with low pay because the <u>benefits</u> were terrible.

_____

2. I felt <u>dejected</u> because I was doing so well in school.

_____

3. I was thrilled to receive a <u>rejection</u> letter from the publisher who had read my book.

_____

4. He was universally hated for his <u>benevolence</u> to everybody.

_____

5. The <u>injection</u> removed blood from the patient's veins.

_____

B Add the suffix indicated to each underlined word to form a new word. Write this word on the line. Then rewrite the original sentence to use the new word.

1. _____ I need sunglasses because I am <u>sensitive</u> to bright light. (add –ity)

_____

2. _____ As a child, I dreamed of achieving <u>fame</u> as a movie star. (add -ous)

_____

3. _____ Their wedding was an event filled with <u>joy</u>. (add -ous)

_____

4. _____ I was surprised at how <u>intense</u> his anger was. (add -ity)

_____

5. _____ Her new hairdo deserved <u>ridicule</u>. (add -ous)

_____

6. _____ She is widely known for her <u>eccentric</u> behavior. (add –ity)

Grammar: Subjects and Predicates

Practice

Every sentence has two main parts, a subject and a predicate. The **subject** is the word or group of words in a sentence that tells whom or what the sentence is about. The **predicate** is the verb or verb phrase that tells what the subject of the sentence does or is.

                                           V

Example: <u>Lenore Smith</u> <u>bought a new house.</u>
              (SUBJECT)   (PREDICATE)

A In each sentence, underline the subject once and the predicate twice. Write **V** over the verb in the predicate.

1. The angry lion growled at its tamer.

2. Men and women worked side by side on the assembly line.

3. The soldiers were standing at strict attention.

4. Santa Catalina Island lies off the coast of California.

5. The plane landed safely on the runway.

6. Many in the audience laughed at the actor's mistake.

B Following the directions, add a **subject** or a **predicate** to complete each sentence.

1. (subject) _____ is a great place to go for a vacation.

2. (predicate) Most science fiction movies _____.

3. (predicate) The front page of today's paper _____.

4. (subject) _____ is the most exciting sports event.

5. (subject) _____ are delicious and good for your health.

6. (predicate) After leaving school, my friends and I _____.

Name _____ Date _____

Grammar: Subjects and Predicates

A In each sentence, underline the subject once and the predicate twice. Write *V* over the verb in the predicate.

Example: <u>The car in my friend's driveway</u> <u>belongs to her uncle</u>.

1. General Lee surrendered on April 9, 1865.

2. Joseph always stops at stop signs.

3. Deer and other animals roam freely through the San Diego Wild Animal Park.

4. Ernie and his brother often help around the house.

5. Lunch was served promptly at 1:00 P.M.

6. The lawyers in the group had been educated at Southern universities.

7. We climbed to the top of Mount Rainier in Washington.

8. Several huge boulders had fallen onto the highway and shattered.

B Add a complete subject or a complete predicate to each item.

1. The most interesting school club _____.

2. _____ raked the leaves yesterday afternoon.

3. A worker in a steel helmet _____.

4. _____ jumped into the swimming pool.

5. The class president _____.

Grammar: Active and Passive Voice

Practice

The **voice** of a verb tells whether the subject of the sentence performs the action or receives the action. When the subject performs the action, the verb is in the **active voice.** When the subject receives the action of the verb, the verb is in the **passive voice.**

> Active voice: Ted *repairs* all defective appliances.
>
> Passive voice: All defective appliances *are repaired* by Ted.

A Underline the verb in each sentence. Then, write **A** if the verb is in the active voice or **P** if the verb is in the passive voice.

1. _____ The kicker missed the point after the touchdown.

2. _____ Several people were arrested by the police.

3. _____ The wheat crop was ruined by a sudden storm.

4. _____ The guest speaker told the audience about the South Pole.

5. _____ Dan Angelo caught a ten-foot shark off Block Island.

6. _____ An urban renewal program will be organized by the town council.

7. _____ The code has been broken by the spies.

8. _____ Superb Foods, Inc., will build a new market in North Mall.

B Rewrite each sentence, using active verbs.

1. Eyeglasses with bifocal lenses were invented by Benjamin Franklin.

_____

2. Two bills and a letter were delivered by the mail carrier.

_____

3. A new sports car has just been bought by Ginny.

_____

Name _____ Date _____

Grammar: Active and Passive Voice

Assess

A Underline the verb in each sentence. Then, write **A** if the verb is in the active voice or **P** if the verb is in the passive voice.

1. _____ Recently, John read *Gulliver's Travels*.

2. _____ In Holland, dikes are maintained to prevent the sea from flooding the land.

3. _____ A committee chose the site for the monument.

4. _____ Four of the prize-winning essays were written by the students.

5. _____ Several valuable paintings were stolen from the Struther Art Museum.

6. _____ We grew tomatoes and cucumbers in our garden.

7. _____ All of the pizza pies were eaten by the guests at the party.

8. _____ The Dalai Lama visited the United States.

B Revise each sentence by changing the passive voice to the active voice or the active voice to the passive voice.

1. The old sofa was hauled down to the basement by Barney.

_____

2. The wild sea tossed and lifted the boat.

_____

3. The way an engine works has never been understood by David.

_____

4. The phone had been hung up suddenly by Rey.

_____

Grammar: Subject-Verb Agreement

Practice

In any sentence **the subject and its verb must agree,** or match, in number. A singular subject takes a singular verb; a plural subject takes a plural verb.

Singular	Plural
The **athlete** *trains* constantly.	The **athletes** *train* constantly.
The **horse** *runs* swiftly.	The **horses** *run* swiftly.

Errors in agreement often occur with compound subjects, with subjects joined by *or* or *nor*, and with indefinite pronouns serving as subjects.

Compound subject: The bride and groom look so happy together.

Subject joined by *or* or *nor*: Either the boys or Joe is receiving the prize.

Indefinite pronoun as subject: Each of the boys is going to get a turn at bat.

In the third example, *Each* is the subject, not *boys,* so the verb is singular.

Underline the verb form in parentheses that agrees with the subject.

1. Two strings on my electric guitar (is, are) out of tune.

2. Days in the summertime (seems, seem) to pass very quickly.

3. All stars, just like our sun, (has, have) a system of planets.

4. A bouquet of roses (was, were) thrown on the stage.

5. Mort's major worry (is, are) the four months of unpaid bills.

6. Both the defendant and the plaintiff (agrees, agree) to the terms of the settlement.

7. Pizza and soft drinks (makes, make) a cheap and popular dinner.

8. Pandas and orangutans (is, are) endangered mammals.

9. Cassie or Kevin usually (does, do) the supper dishes.

10. Neither the children nor Mrs. Ramirez (was, were) on the bus.

Grammar: Subject-Verb Agreement

Assess

A Underline the verb form in parentheses that agrees with the subject.

1. Neither the coach nor the team members (was, were) happy with the loss.

2. Breezes from the ocean (is, are) cooler this evening.

3. The mechanic who fixes transmissions (was, were) sick yesterday.

4. Either Mara or Tony (shovels, shovel) the snow off the sidewalk.

5. A plate of crackers (is, are) Sherri's favorite snack.

6. The lights of the cars in the valley below (shines, shine) brightly.

7. Neither the kittens nor the mother cat (likes, like) the rain.

8. A desk, a table, and a pile of books (is, are) needed for this scene.

9. Just thinking about those strong winds (scares, scare) her.

10. Everyone on the roller coaster (appear, appears) to be having fun.

B Add a verb in the space provided in each of the following sentences. Make sure the verb agrees with the subject of the sentence.

1. Neither Harold nor his siblings _____ feeling well today.

2. Stephanie and Uncle Stan _____ to water-ski when they get to Florida.

3. The students in Mrs. Lacey's class _____ learning the alphabet.

4. Tina, Yolanda, or Megan _____ the directions to my house.

5. Every one of the paintings _____ very valuable.

Spelling: Unusual Consonant Groupings

Practice

Some words are hard to spell because they contain **unusual groups of consonants.** They may contain unusual combinations of consonants, such as these: the **thm** in *rhythm,* the **rh** in *rhythm,* or the **sc** in *reminisce.* Generally, to learn to spell these words, you must memorize them. You might make up a reminder to help you; for example,

When we remini<u>sc</u>e, we often "C" the past in our minds.

Study these words with unusual consonant groupings. Then, complete the exercises.

bro<u>ch</u>ure	con<u>sci</u>entious	di<u>sc</u>ipline	e<u>xh</u>ilarating	non<u>ch</u>alant
remini<u>sc</u>e	<u>rhy</u>thm	si<u>lh</u>ouette	sub<u>tl</u>e	uncon<u>sci</u>ous

A   Write *correct* if the word is spelled correctly. If it is not spelled correctly, write the correct spelling on the line.

1. reminisse _____

2. rythym _____

3. unconscious _____

4. exilarating _____

B   Write *correct* if the underlined word is spelled correctly. If it is not, write the correct spelling of the underlined word.

1. _____ We obtained a four-page <u>broshure</u> from the Travel Office.

2. _____ Jana is a <u>consientious</u> student who always does her homework.

3. _____ The student showed good <u>dissipline</u> by following all the rules.

4. _____ The actress gave a <u>subtle</u> performance instead of an emotional one.

5. _____ The artist drew a <u>silouette</u> of the bird instead of showing its features.

Spelling: Unusual Consonant Groupings

Assess

A Write *correct* if the word is spelled correctly. If it is not spelled correctly, write the correct spelling on the line.

1. reminice _____

2. rythm _____

3. exsilarating _____

4. unconcious _____

5. nonchalant _____

B Write *correct* if the underlined word is spelled correctly. If it is not, write the correct spelling of the underlined word.

1. _____ The new museum has a colorful <u>broschure</u>.

2. _____ Kyle did not study before, but now he is trying to be more <u>concientious</u>.

3. _____ The black and white poster showed her profile in <u>silhouette</u>.

4. _____ The title gives a <u>suttle</u> hint about the meaning of the poem.

5. _____ Tom was forced to <u>dicipline</u> the puppy when it did not behave.

C Underline the three misspelled words in this paragraph. On the lines following the paragraph, give the correct spelling of each of the words you underlined.

   I am very consientious about walking at least one mile every day. It takes discipline to walk on really cold or hot days. A brisk walk can be very exilarating. As I walk, I try to maintain a steady rhythm. Often I reminise about the past.

1. _____ 2. _____ 3. _____

Writing: Written Presentation

A **written presentation** is a set of suggestions aimed at one person or group for solving a problem or making changes. It can take the form of an essay, a personal letter, or a short story that contains a moral. A written presentation has the following features:

- It is addressed to a specific audience.
- It focuses on a particular problem or desired change.
- It offers specific suggestions for solving the problem or making changes.

A Choose one of the following suggestions for a written presentation or choose one of your own. Then, answer the questions that follow.

> Suggest a wider variety of choices in the school cafeteria.
>
> Help the school football team overcome a long losing streak.

1. What issue or problem will you address? _____

2. Describe your audience. _____

3. A. What form will you use to make your presentation? _____

   B. Explain your choice. _____

4. List two specific suggestions you will make in your presentation.

_____

_____

B Read the following introductory paragraph to a written presentation. Then, answer the questions that follow.

> Many students in our school seem to lack school spirit. Football games are poorly attended. Those who do attend show little enthusiasm for our team. Even our cheerleaders seem to be just going through the motions. We have a great school, and it is time that we begin to show some spirit.

1. What issue does this presentation address? _____

2. Who do you think is the audience for this presentation? _____

3. Write one suggestion that you might include in this presentation.

_____

Writing: Written Presentation

Assess

A Imagine that a close friend is in danger of failing a class because he or she has trouble completing homework on time. You are going to prepare a written presentation to help your friend overcome this problem.

1. Describe the form that your presentation will take: an essay, a letter, or a

   short story with a moral. _____

2. **A.** If you choose a short story, explain the moral of the story.
   B. If you choose a letter or an essay, list two suggestions that you will make
   in your presentation.

   _____

   _____

B Using the information you completed in the activity above, write the introductory paragraph to your presentation.

_____

_____

_____

_____

_____

_____

_____

_____

_____

_____

_____

_____

_____

Writing: Informal Letter

Practice

An **informal letter** is usually addressed to a friend or family member. The purpose is to tell about the writer's feelings or about events the writer has experienced or witnessed. A well-written informal letter includes vivid descriptive details of events and people.

Read the following passage. Then, complete the activities that follow.

Dear Jack,

My visit with my Grandpa has been great. Yesterday we went fishing. He has a cabin right on the lake. We got up early that morning. There was mist over the water. It was so thick you couldn't see the other side of the lake.

We put the little flat-bottomed boat in the water. The boat is just big enough for two people. Grandpa likes to use an electric motor on the boat. He says it doesn't scare the fish, and besides, he likes the quiet. I see what he means. Even with the motor, it was really quiet on the lake.

Grandpa was right about not scaring away the fish. I had barely thrown my hook in the water when I felt a big jerk. It nearly bent my pole in half! It took about ten minutes to land the fish, a big bass. Grandpa says it weighed about seven pounds, a pretty good size for this lake. We kept the fish for a while, and then we threw it back in the lake. Grandpa says he always throws the fish back that he catches. He says it's so he can catch them again. But I think it's because he doesn't want to kill them.

I'll be home in a couple of days. I'm going to miss Grandpa, but we're already making plans for my visit next summer. I'll call you when I get home.

Jeremy

1. A. Describe to whom this letter is addressed. _____

   B. Describe who wrote the letter. _____

2. Give one descriptive detail about the place the writer is visiting.

_____

3. List two things that you learn about Grandpa from this letter.

_____

4. A. Explain how the writer feels about the event. _____

   B. List two details that support your answer. _____

Writing: Informal Letter

Assess

A You will be writing an informal letter based on one of the topics below. First, choose one of the topics below. Then, complete the following activities.

a trip to a rain forest   a visit to a relative's home in another town

a special holiday   a trip to an amusement park

1. List the topic you have chosen. _____

2. Describe an imaginary friend or relative to whom you will address the letter.

_____

_____

3. Explain what you want your reader to know about how you feel about the event.

_____

_____

_____

4. List two details you will include in the letter that will let your reader know how you feel.

_____

_____

B Use your answers to the above items to write an informal letter.

_____

_____

_____

_____

_____

_____

Writing: Cause-and-Effect Essay

Practice

A **cause-and-effect essay** shows the relation between events. It explains how one event or situation causes another. A good cause-and-effect essay has the following features:

- a description of the cause or event that produces a result
- an explanation of the effects or results
- facts and examples that support the relation between cause and effect

A Read the following passage. Then, answer the questions that follow.

Everywhere you go today, you see people using cell phones—in restaurants, in the supermarket, walking down the street, driving their cars. This widespread use of cell phones has had many effects on society.

One of the most important effects is on highway safety. Many people drive on the highway at high speeds while talking on their cell phones. Studies show that drivers did not perform as well or react as quickly while using cell phones. Drivers cannot give their full attention to driving. This can lead to serious automobile accidents. The problem of drivers using cell phones has become so great that some areas have passed laws against using cell phones while driving.

1. What is the cause described in this passage?

_____

2. What is an effect described in this passage?

_____

3. What facts or examples does the writer give to illustrate the causes and effects?

_____

_____

B List two or three more effects that you might include in the essay.

_____

_____

_____

Writing: Cause-and-Effect Essay

Assess

A Circle one of the following topics or choose a topic of your own. Then, complete the activities that follow.

why pets are good for children   the importance of vacations
how music affects people   the weather and people's moods

1. Write a description of a cause involved in the topic that you have chosen.

_____

_____

_____

2. List two or three effects involved in your chosen topic.

_____

_____

_____

B Use the answers to the activities above to write an introductory paragraph to a cause-and-effect essay describing the cause. Write a second paragraph describing one effect.

_____

_____

_____

_____

_____

_____

_____

_____

_____

_____

_____

Literary Analysis: Author's Style

Practice

An author's **style** is his or her special way of using words. It is made up of these elements:

- **Diction:** the words an author chooses. For example, a writer might call a musician "an *awesome* guitarist." The word *awesome* helps create an informal style. Writing in a formal style, the writer might call the same musician "a *gifted* guitarist."

- **Syntax:** the flow of sentences. Some writers write in short bursts: "That was that. The test was over, I had done my best." Others write long, flowing sentences: "Looking back on that long, hard test, I found a reason to be happy: I had done my best."

- **Tone:** the author's attitude toward the readers or the topic. For example, a writer might write an article to help beginning painters. Because the writer wants to encourage readers, the writer might use a cheerful, gentle style.

Read the paragraph and then answer the questions that follow.

I'm a plain, simple guy. I don't ask for much. I do have one rule, though. If you don't show respect when you talk to me, I stop listening. Period, the end. Nick should have remembered my rule. Poor guy, he really should have. He forgot, though. He showed me disrespect, and that's when the trouble started.

1. What type of syntax does this writer use?

   A. short, simple sentences   **C.** different types of sentences

   B. long, complicated sentences   **D.** long but simple sentences

2. What does this syntax add to the style?

   A. a beautiful flow   **C.** the sound of a tough guy talking

   B. a poetic sound   **D.** smooth connections between ideas

3. What type of words does the author's diction feature?

   A. many difficult words   **C.** many colorful, lively words

   B. mainly simple words   **D.** many slang words

4. What tone does the phrase *poor guy* add to the paragraph?

   A. a tone of kindness   **C.** a tone of anger or annoyance

   B. a tone of pity or regret   **D.** a tone of generosity

Literary Analysis: Author's Style

Assess

A For each question, circle the letter of the best answer.

1. What is the best definition of an author's style?

A. his or her special way of using words

B. a story the author tells

C. the type of nouns the author uses

D. a formal way of using language

2. What is the difference between diction and syntax?

A. Diction has to do with sentences, and syntax has to do with word choice.

B. Syntax has to do with sentences, and diction has to do with word choice.

C. Diction has to do with style, but syntax does not.

D. Syntax has to do with style, but diction does not.

B Read the following two paragraphs. Then, answer the questions.

1 What a weekend! Boy, am I beat! First, we went to the amusement park. As usual, the main amusement was Uncle Herman. He kept us laughing all the way there with his silly hip-hop don't-stop-till-you-drop rapping. Then, we went to see the new Magnet Man movie. I can't help it—I think Magnet Man rules!

2 Some weekends are dull, and some are filled with excitement. Last Saturday, I discovered a perfect recipe for weekend amusement: Fill the day with activity. Of course, the presence of Uncle Herman, who has his own unique brand of comedy, added greatly to the weekend's pleasures. The latest chapter in the adventures of Magnet Man rounded off the day's activities. Magnet Man combines extraordinary powers with human qualities, and I find I am fascinated by his character.

1. _____ Which paragraph is written in an informal or casual style?

2. _____ Give a word or phrase that is an example of this informal style.

3. _____ Give a more formal word or phrase from the other paragraph.

4. _____ What word would you use to describe the writer's tone, or attitude towards the topic, in the first paragraph?

5. _____ Which paragraph uses longer sentences?

Literary Analysis: Expository Essay

Practice

An **expository essay** is a short piece of nonfiction writing. A writer might write an expository essay for one or more of these reasons:

- to give readers information on a topic of general interest
- to explain how something works or why something happens
- to present an idea, such as a suggestion about how to reduce crime

Writers of expository essays may include writing of these types:

- **Description:** To help you imagine what something is like, writers use description, created with sensory language, such as "icy cold."

- **Comparison and contrast:** To explain a topic, writers may compare and contrast two or more things, showing their similarities and differences.

- **Cause and effect:** To explain how something happened, writers show the connections between causes and effects. A cause is a thing or event that makes something happen. An effect is the event or situation that comes from a cause.

For each question, circle the letter of the best answer.

1. Which of the following is an example of an expository essay?

A. a book about a famous person

B. a made-up story about dogs

C. a short article discussing reptiles

D. a poem full of descriptions

2. Which of the following is an example of description?

A. The melted iron ore flows in a red, fiery river.

B. Adding limestone helps clean out other materials

C. To make steel, workers add oxygen to the iron.

D. Steel is much stronger than iron.

3. Which of the following is an example of a comparison?

A. Both snakes and lizards have scales.

B. Snakes swallow prey whole.

C. Most snakes slither from side to side.

D. A heavy snake moves by expanding and contracting its body.

4. Which of the following is an example of a cause-and-effect relationship?

A. The king lied to the colonists.

B. The colonists did not have representatives in Parliament.

C. The colonists were taxed anyway.

D. When the British put a tax on tea, it caused the colonists to revolt.

Literary Analysis: Expository Essay

Assess

A For each question, write your answer in the appropriate blank.

1. Name a topic you would be interested in reading about in an expository

essay. _____

2. Read the three purposes below. Circle the main purpose of an expository
essay on your topic. Then, tell what the essay will inform readers about,
what it will explain, or what ideas it will discuss.

To give information about _____

To explain how _____

To present ideas about _____

B For each question, circle the letter of the best answer.

1. Which of the following would make the best topic for an expository essay?

   A. how I spent my summer vacation **C.** the complete history of America
   B. the story of a made-up hero **D.** the discovery of a new medicine

2. Which of the following is an example of a description?

   A. A fox looks like a reddish brown **C.** Red foxes use their sense of
      dog with a bushy tail.   smell to hunt small animals.
   B. Red foxes live in families.   **D.** Females dig dens.

3. Which of the following is an example of a comparison?

   A. Brazil is a country in the   **C.** A large part of Brazil is covered with
      northeast part of South America.   dense, lush green rainforests.
   B. Brazil is a little smaller in area **D.** Natural wealth such as timber
      than the United States.   brought settlers from Portugal.

4. Which of the following is an example of a cause-and-effect relationship?

   A. The Sun appears as a solid disk **C.** Sunspots are cooler and darker
      in Earth's sky.   than the rest of the Sun's surface.
   B. Different areas of the Sun's   **D.** Sunspots are formed by magnetic
      surface have different qualities.   fields below the surface of the Sun.

Literary Analysis: Biographical Writing

Practice

Biographical writing is nonfiction writing in which the writer tells the story of another person's life. Biographies contain the following:

- **Facts** Biographical writing presents facts about the person's accomplishments and the important events in his or life.

- **Interpretations** A good writer will tie together the facts in a biography with an interpretation of their meaning. For example, a biographer might report the *fact* that Dr. Martin Luther King, Jr., gave his memorable "I Have a Dream Speech" in 1963. The biographer might then give an *interpretation* of the meaning of this event: "With this speech, King clearly showed that he was a national, not just a southern, leader."

- **Support** Biographers provide support for interpretations by showing how the facts make the interpretation reasonable. For example, a biographer might explain that King was mainly active in the South at first. He then gave the "I Have a Dream" speech in Washington, D.C., the nation's capital. After the speech, he organized protests in the North. These facts support the idea that he had become a national, not just a southern, leader.

For each question, circle the letter of the best answer.

1. Which of the following is an example of biographical writing?

   A. a book giving facts about Dr. Martin Luther King, Jr.

   B. a made-up story about Dr. Martin Luther King, Jr.

   C. an essay that quotes the words of Dr. Martin Luther King, Jr.

   D. a poem dedicated to Dr. Martin Luther King, Jr.

2. Which of the following is a statement of fact about Albert Einstein?

   A. Albert Einstein was the greatest scientist of all time.

   B. I love Albert Einstein's crazy-looking hair.

   C. It is hard for me to understand Albert Einstein's theories.

   D. Albert Einstein was born on March 14, 1879.

3. Which of the following gives an interpretation of Albert Einstein's life?

   A. Einstein's theories changed the way we look at the world.

   B. Einstein came to live in the United States in 1933.

   C. For his ideas about light, Einstein was given the Nobel Prize in 1921.

   D. Some scientists were doubtful about Einstein's theories.

Name _____ Date _____

Assess

A For each question, write your answer in the appropriate blank.

1. Name a person you would be interested in reading a biography about.

_____

2. What is one question about the facts of the person's life that the biography could help you answer? _____

3. What interpretation might the biography give of the person's achievements?

_____

B For each question, circle the letter of the best answer.

1. Which of the following is an example of biographical writing?

A. a book about jazz in the 1940s

B. an essay on the life of singer Ella Fitzgerald

C. a made-up story about Ella Fitzgerald

D. a book about the songs sung by Ella Fitzgerald

2. Which is a statement of fact about saxophonist Wayne Shorter's life?

A. Shorter was the main reason jazz musicians started playing to a rock beat.

B. I love the mood of mystery in Shorter's pieces.

C. Shorter played in the Jazz Messengers, a band led by Art Blakey.

D. Shorter is the most original composer in jazz.

3. Which is an interpretation of pianist Thelonious Monk's life?

A. Monk was born in North Carolina on October 10, 1917.

B. Monk used notes, rhythms, and silences that startled listeners.

C. Through music, Monk celebrated the beauty that even ugliness can have.

D. For a while, Monk played with the famous saxophonist John Coltrane.

Reading: Main Idea and Supporting Details

Practice

The **main idea** is the central message, insight, or opinion in a work.
Supporting details are the pieces of evidence that a writer uses to prove the
main idea. These details can include facts, statistics, quotations, or anecdotes.

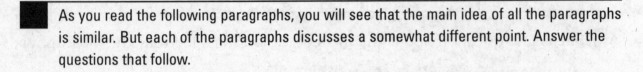 As you read the following paragraphs, you will see that the main idea of all the paragraphs
is similar. But each of the paragraphs discusses a somewhat different point. Answer the
questions that follow.

A. The act of laughing is actually good exercise. In an average laugh, the
heart, lungs, and other organs get a brief workout. Laughing can clear up
the respiratory system and speed up heart rate. If the laugh is especially
strong, it loosens muscles in the face, arms, and legs.

1. Underline the sentence that directly states the main idea made about
laughter in paragraph A.

B. But laughter is more than exercise. Some scientists believe that laughter
causes the body to produce a group of hormones. These hormones may
then release natural painkillers that can reduce suffering from arthritis,
allergies, or other ailments. According to this theory, laughter might
actually trigger relief from pain.

2. Underline the main idea in paragraph B.

C. In 1964, Norman Cousins, editor of *Saturday Review* magazine, was
diagnosed with a life-threatening disease. But instead of dying, Cousins
applied a laugh-yourself-to-health approach. Acting against medical
opinion, he booked a hotel room and read humorous books and watched
funny movies. Regular belly laughter, he found, worked like medicine so
that he was able to enjoy two hours of painless sleep at a time. Within a
few years, he had recovered completely.

3. Underline the main idea for paragraph C.

Reading: Main Idea and Supporting Details

Assess

Read the passage, and then answer the questions that follow. Circle the letter of the best answer choice.

She liked to grocery shop. She loved it in the way some people love to drive long country roads, because doing it she could think and relax and wander. Her parents wrote up the list and handed it to her and off she went without complaint to perform what they regarded as a great sacrifice of her time and a sign that she was indeed a very nice girl. She had never told them how much she loved grocery shopping, only that she was "willing" to do it. She had an intuition which told her that her parents were not safe for sharing such strong, important facts about herself. Let them think they knew her.

Once inside the supermarket, her hands firmly around the handle of the cart, she would lapse into a kind of reverie and wheel toward the produce. Like a Tibetan monk in solitary meditation, she calmed to a point of deep, deep happiness; this feeling came to her, reliably, if strangely, only in the supermarket.

—"Checkouts, Fifteen" by Cynthia Rylant

1. Which sentence states the main idea of the passage?

   A. Let them think they knew her.

   B. She had never told them how much she loved grocery shopping, only that she was "willing" to do it.

   C. She liked to grocery shop.

   D. She had an intuition which told her that her parents were not safe for sharing such strong, important facts about herself.

2. Which of the following details supports the main idea?

   A. She held her hands firmly around the handle of the cart.

   B. Her parents wrote up the list and handed it to her.

   C. She would shop in the produce department first.

   D. She calmed to a point of deep happiness only in the supermarket.

3. Which statement is the best summary of the passage?

   A. A daughter has difficulty fitting in to her family.

   B. A young girl derives comfort from an ordinary chore.

   C. A young girl finds a substitute for long country drives.

   D. Parents share their daughter's innermost feelings.

Reading: Generate Relevant Questions

Practice

It is especially important to preview technical documents and articles before you begin reading them. Previewing helps you activate your prior knowledge about a topic, learn new terms, and **generate relevant questions** about your reading. When you ask questions, you read actively and monitor your comprehension.

Use a text's features to help you generate questions. Here are some things to think about as you preview:

Text Feature	Questions You Might Ask About the Topic
Heads	■ What is the article about? ■ What do I want to know about the topic?
Topic Sentences	■ What do they tell me about the topic? ■ What details would I like to know about the topic?
Key Terms	■ What are the important terms? ■ What do they tell me about the topic?
Photographs or Other Graphics	■ What do the graphics show me about the topic? ■ What questions do they raise in my mind?

Preview the article on the next page. Then, answer the questions that follow.

1. Write two facts you know about the topic.

_____

_____

2. Use the heads and topic sentences to write two questions you would like to answer about the topic.

_____

_____

3. Write two questions suggested by the key terms.

_____

_____

Reading: Generate Relevant Questions

Assess

Read the following technical article. Then, answer the questions that follow.

The Surface of the Sun

The Sun's surface, which can only be seen with equipment that can withstand enormous temperatures and blinding light, contains several features.

Sunspots

Some areas of the Sun are cooler than others. The gases in these cooler areas do not shine as brightly as the areas near them. As a result, the cooler areas appear dark. The dark, cooler areas on the Sun's surface are called sunspots.

Prominences

Streams of flaming gas shoot out from the Sun's surface. These streams, called *prominences*, can shoot many thousands of kilometers above the Sun's surface. They form huge arches as they fall back into the Sun.

Solar Flares

Energy can build up in the Sun's atmosphere, usually near a group of sunspots. If the energy is given off suddenly, a *solar flare* is formed. Solar flares send streams of electrically charged particles into space. Although they usually last less than an hour, solar flares release large amounts of energy.

1. Write answers to two of the questions you generated before you read the article.

_____

_____

2. Write two more questions you thought about while you were reading.

_____

_____

3. Where might you find this information?

_____

_____

Name _____ Date _____

Vocabulary: Word Roots *-viv-*, *-dur-*, *-temp-*, and *-nov-*

A **root** is the basic unit of meaning of a word. Knowing the meanings of word roots can help you figure out the meanings of many new words. Study these examples.

Examples:

Root	Meaning	Words with the Root
-viv-	to live	revival, survive, vivid, vivacious
-dur-	to last, hold out	duration, endurance, durable, during
-temp-	time	temporal, tempo, temporary, contemporary
-nov-	new, recent	novelty, novice, innovation, renovate

A Replace each underlined word or phrase with the most appropriate word from the chart above.

1. _____ I woke with my heart pounding after an extremely underline{realistic} nightmare.

2. _____ Customers chose the product more for its underline{newness} than for its quality.

3. _____ The band chose music with a quick underline{speed} for dancing.

4. _____ I chose a underline{sturdy} pair of boots that should last for several winters.

B Complete each sentence with a word from the chart above.

1. Taking aspirin gives me only _____ relief from my headaches.

2. For a long-distance runner, _____ is as important as speed.

3. Many early settlers in America did not _____ their first winter.

4. I'm still just a _____ on the guitar, but I'm learning quickly.

Vocabulary: Word Roots -viv-, -dur-, -temp-, and -nov-

Assess

A Circle T if the statement is true or F if the statement is false. Then, write a sentence to explain your answer.

1. T/F A <u>vivacious</u> person would probably be quiet and reserved at a party.

_____

2. T/F You would need to know a subject very well to make an <u>extemporaneous</u> speech about it.

_____

3. T/F An <u>innovative</u> solution to a problem is one that has stood the test of time.

_____

4. T/F Someone who is <u>obdurate</u> is easily swayed by other people's opinions.

_____

B Circle the root in each word, and think about its meaning. Then, write the word's meaning on the first line. Use a dictionary to check the meaning. Finally, use each word in a new sentence.

1. endure _____

_____

2. revive _____

_____

3. temper _____

_____

4. renovations _____

_____

5. contemporary _____

_____

Grammar: Direct and Indirect Objects

Practice

A **direct object** is a noun or a pronoun that *receives* the action of a verb. An **indirect object** appears with a direct object and names the person or thing that something is *given to* or *done for*.

                    IO   DO
Example: Dad lent Tom his watch.

A Underline the direct object in each of the following sentences.

1. The excited crowd cheered the performers.

2. The overturned truck blocked two lanes of the expressway.

3. The center fielder caught the pop-up.

4. Mrs. Stein grows the best watermelon in the county.

5. The lawyer for the defense presented his case.

6. Cynthia grows flowers in her garden every spring.

B Underline the indirect object in each of the following sentences.

1. Mrs. Shaw showed Nick the diagram.

2. Greg sent Rosie a silver ring.

3. The commander gave his troops a tough assignment.

4. The boss promised her employees a raise in pay.

5. The millionaire left his temple thousands of dollars.

6. The shipping room clerk gave him a bulky package.

Grammar: Direct and Indirect Objects

Assess

A Underline the direct object in each of the following sentences.

1. The ambulance took the injured woman to the hospital.

2. In 1845, Henry Thoreau built a small cabin at Walden Pond.

3. Somebody has damaged the canoe.

4. The senator changed her mind about the energy bill.

5. Tina wanted new skates for her birthday.

6. Harold brought an apple pie to the housewarming party.

7. Kimberly tutors her brother on weekends.

8. Make sure to lock your door.

B Decide whether the underlined word in each sentence is a direct object or an indirect object. Write *DO* (direct object) or *IO* (indirect object) on the line next to each sentence.

1. _____ Ralph bought <u>Jennifer</u> a sandwich.

2. _____ The children baked their <u>mother</u> a cake for Mother's Day.

3. _____ Lorraine showed the doorman her <u>identification</u>.

4. _____ The soldier often wrote his <u>wife</u> long letters.

5. _____ Mom and Dad bought Sylvia a <u>watch</u> for graduation.

6. _____ The travel agent showed the <u>family</u> vacation packages.

Name _____ Date _____

Linking verbs connect the subject with a word in the predicate. A **predicate nominative** is a noun or pronoun that follows a linking verb and renames or identifies the subject of the sentence. A **predicate adjective** is an adjective that follows a linking verb and describes the subject of the sentence. Common linking verbs include forms of the verb *be* (*am, is, are, was, were*), *appear, become, feel, look, seem, smell, taste.*

           S   LV   PN

Predicate nominative: <u>Loon Lake</u> **is** a great place for swimming.

           S   LV   PA

Predicate adjective: The <u>water</u> **appears** very calm today.

A   Each subject is underlined. Underline each predicate nominative or predicate adjective and write *PN* or *PA* to identify each one. Circle the linking verbs.

1. _____ The <u>beach</u> seems pretty empty this afternoon.

2. _____ <u>It</u> is a good day to be here.

3. _____ <u>Karen and Bob</u> are fun at the beach.

4. _____ The summer <u>sun</u> feels hot on my back.

5. _____ Right now <u>it</u> is time to go into the water.

6. _____ Those <u>swimmers</u> wearing goggles are Jay and Ari.

B   Complete each sentence with a predicate nominative *(PN)* or a predicate adjective *(PA)*, as indicated.

1. The shells on this beach are (PA) _____.

2. It is (PN) _____ that can hurt our feet.

3. The ice cream tastes (PA) _____.

4. After their long swim, Jessie and Jake appear (PA) _____.

5. Tomorrow will be (PN) _____.

Grammar: Predicate Nominative and Predicate Adjectives

Assess

A Underline each predicate nominative or predicate adjective and write PN or PA to identify each one. Circle the linking verbs.

Example: __PN__ Dogs(are)my favorite pets.

1. _____ Toby's dog, Dixie, seems excited.

2. _____ However, his cat, Coco is calm as always.

3. _____ Dixie is the playful pet.

4. _____ Coco appears cool.

5. _____ Toby feels happy about both of his pets.

6. _____ Toby, Dixie, and Coco are really all great friends.

B Complete each sentence with a predicate nominative *(PN)* or a predicate adjective *(PA)*, as indicated.

1. Charlie's new dog bed is (PA) _____.

2. However, his favorite place to sleep is still (PN) _____.

3. Chasing rabbits in the field, Charlie never seems (PA) _____.

4. His wagging tail tells us that the new treats taste (PA) _____.

5. Before Charlie, our only pet was (PN) _____.

C Use each predicate nominative or predicate adjective from the previous exercise in a new sentence.

1. _____

2. _____

3. _____

4. _____

5. _____

Name _____ Date _____

Grammar: Combine Choppy Sentences

Practice

Avoid choppy, disconnected sentences by combining two or more related ideas in a single sentence. There are several methods of sentence combining including compound verbs, compound objects, predicate nominative, and predicate adjective.

Examples:

Choppy: I *started* my car. I *drove* to the store.
Compound Verb: I *started* my car and *drove* to the store.

Choppy: Linda is *amusing*. She is *interesting*.
Compound Predicate Adjective: Linda is *amusing* and *interesting*.

Combine the sentences to form a single sentence. Write your new sentence on the lines.

1. Our family came from Ireland. We visited there last year.

_____

_____

2. We will send the boxes today. You should get them on Friday.

_____

_____

3. I have a new skateboard. I do not know how to ride it.

_____

_____

4. Kari called yesterday. Jamie did not call until today.

_____

_____

5. We went to Ronnee and Rick's wedding. We threw rice on them afterward.

_____

_____

Grammar: Combine Choppy Sentences

A Combine the sentences in each of the following items.

1. The crowd cheered the football team. They waved banners in the air.

_____

_____

2. The play was too long. It was boring.

_____

_____

3. Mr. Lennon is baking chocolate chip cookies. He is baking brownies.

_____

_____

B Combine the sentences in each of the following items.

1. Several of us wanted to see the new horror movie. It was sold out.

_____

_____

2. In London, tourists can see Big Ben. They can also see Buckingham Palace.

_____

_____

3. Joseph's new phone can play music. It can also take pictures.

_____

_____

4. My nephew bought a package of baseball cards. He bought a can of soda.

_____

_____

Reading Kit 119

Writing: Book Jacket Copy

Book jacket copy is information appearing on a book's cover about the subject of the book. Its purpose is to attract the reader's interest. For example, book jacket copy for a biography would include the following:

- It would give a brief overview of the subject's life and main achievements.
- It would include some interesting details about the person.
- It might use humor or colorful language to appeal to readers.

Read the following paragraph about astronaut Sally Ride. Then, answer the questions and complete the activities that follow.

Sally Ride had "the right stuff." On June 18, 1983, she flew into history as America's first woman in space, serving as flight engineer and mission specialist on the shuttle *Challenger*. This talented athlete and brilliant scientist was chosen for her historic mission from over 8,000 applicants. Later, she played a key role in NASA's investigations of the tragic *Challenger* and *Columbia* shuttle disasters. Dr. Ride currently teaches physics at the University of California in San Diego and directs research at the California Space Institute.

1. According to the book jacket copy, what was Sally Ride's main accomplishment?

_____

2. Why do you think the jacket copy mentions that she was chosen from over 8,000 applicants to be an astronaut?

_____

3. What other information about Sally Ride does the jacket copy include?

_____

4. Imagine that a friend or relative of yours is the subject of a biography. Write a one-paragraph book jacket blurb about that person.

_____

_____

_____

_____

Name _____ Date _____

Read the following information about Astronaut John Glenn. Then, complete the activities that follow.

John Glenn
—born in 1921 in Ohio

—served as a pilot in World War II and Korea, flying over 100 combat missions

—awarded the Distinguished Flying Cross six times

—set transcontinental speed record in 1957 of 3 hours, 23 minutes

—has over 9000 hours of flying time

—became a NASA Project Mercury Astronaut in 1957

—became the first American to orbit the earth in a spacecraft in February, 1962

—retired from the military after 23 years in 1965 with the rank of Colonel

—elected to the U.S. Senate from Ohio in 1974; retired in 1999

—returned to space at the age of 77 in 1998

—logged over 200 hours in space

1. Identify the single most important fact about this person. _____

_____

2. List three other facts that could be included in book jacket copy for a

biography of this person. _____

_____

3. List several nouns and adjectives that could be used to describe this person.

_____

4. Write the first three sentences for the book jacket copy for a biography about this person.

_____

_____

_____

Writing: Script

Practice

A **script** is text that is meant to be spoken by one or more people. A script often includes actions and visual elements, as well as spoken words. The script may be used for a live presentation or a film or recording.

Any script should include the following:

- a clear indication of **who** is to speak and **what** each person is supposed to say
- any **actions** or **visual elements** to be used, set off from the spoken parts
- a well-defined **purpose** and **audience**
- **language** that appeals to the audience and serves the writer's purpose

Read the following short script for a public service announcement. Then, answer the questions and complete the activities that follow.

[*Series of images of people reading on a bus, at a table in a restaurant, lying down in bed. While these images are shown, we hear the following:*]

VOICEOVER: Take time to read. Wherever you are. Dip into a good book. You never know where you'll end up.

[*Show film footage of pilot taking off in 1920s plane, then footage of an astronaut walking on the moon, as we hear:*]

VOICEOVER: Take time to read. Take a trip to everywhere.

1. What is the purpose of this script? _____

_____

2. Who is its audience? _____

3. What visual elements does the script include, and how do they serve its

purpose? _____

_____

4. Who would you imagine speaking the Voiceover lines? _____

5. Imagine that you have been given the job of creating a script to promote an activity at your school or other organization. Write the beginning of the

script. _____

_____

Writing: Script

Read the following short script for a public service announcement. Then, answer the questions and complete the activities that follow.

[We see a MAN climbing a tree, carrying a can of Yum-Yum cat food. He talks to someone above him whom we don't see.]

MAN: Misty, please come down. See, I got Yum-Yum food now. Your favorite! I got rid of the bad kitty food. Please come down! Please—

[We see a dozen cats at the bottom of the tree, yowling up at the MAN.]

MAN: Wow, I shoulda got more Yum-Yum.

[MAN looks down. We see a tiger among the other cats.]

MAN: Uh oh . . .

1. What is the purpose of this script? _____

_____

2. Who is its audience? _____

3. How do the spoken parts of the script relate to its purpose? _____

_____

_____

4. What visual elements does the script include, and how do they serve its purpose?

_____

_____

5. Imagine that you have been given the job of creating a script to advertise a local restaurant. Write the beginning of the script.

_____

_____

_____

_____

Writing: Business Letter

Practice

A **business letter** is a letter concerning a business or a professional matter. For example, you would write a business letter to report a problem with a purchase or to apply for a job. A business letter should include the following:

- **heading**—the writer's address and date
- **inside address**—address where the letter will be sent
- **greeting**—a salutation to the person receiving the letter, punctuated with a colon
- **body**—brief, clear presentation of the writer's purpose
- **closing**—appropriate farewell
- **signature**—signed name of the sender
- formal, polite **language**
- standard **formatting**—either **block style** (all parts of the letter lined up on the left margin) or **semiblock/modified block style** (heading, closing, and signature lined up on the right side of the page)

Label the parts of the business letter shown here.

                                    New Inventions, Inc.
                3. _____   416 Main Street
                                    Smalltown, CA 95030
                                    January 31, 2007

Tyler Randall
Amazing Things, Inc.   1. _____
614 Central Boulevard
Bigtown, NY 10101

Dear Ms. Randall: 4. _____

We would like to meet with you soon to discuss merging our two companies. What time would be convenient for you?

                2. _____   Sincerely,

                                    Rand Marshall
                                    President, New Inventions

5. What style of formatting does this letter use? _____

Writing: Business Letter

Assess

A Answer the questions that follow about the business letter shown here.

531 First Street **A**
Suburb, PA 16901
January 31, 2007

The Right Stuff **B**
72 West Street
Middle City, NM 95011

To Whom It May Concern: **C** _____

I am returning the widget that I received from you last week. When I opened the package, the product was dented. Could you please refund my payment of $24.67? Please send it to the above address. Thank you. **D**

Sincerely, **E**

Madison Bellton **F**

1. Which letter identifies the inside address? _____

2. Which letter identifies the closing? _____

3. What format does this letter follow? _____

4. What is the purpose of this business letter? _____

B Write a business letter to a store owner to complain about or praise an employee who served you at his or her store. Use your own address but invent an address for the store owner. Use the modified block style.

_____

_____

_____

_____

_____

Literary Analysis: Persuasive Essay

Practice

A persuasive essay is short nonfiction written to get people to take a particular side on an issue. To convince readers, writers do the following:

- **Making appeals to reason:** Persuasive writers use logical arguments to show why their ideas are good. They use fact, statistics, or other evidence.

  Position: Letting the town's movie theater close is a bad idea.

  Appeal to reason: 90% of the townspeople said that they went to Sid's Theater at least twice this summer. If the theater closes, most people in town will miss it.

- **Making appeals to emotion:** Persuasive writers try to stir up readers' feelings. They use charged language, or words that call up strong feelings.

  Appeal to emotion: It is a crime to rob our children of the chance to munch popcorn and watch movies in Sid's Theater!

For each question, circle the letter of the best answer.

1. Which of the following is an example of a persuasive essay?

   A. a newspaper article telling why readers should vote for Smith
   B. an article giving the facts of an event
   C. a book about politics
   D. a magazine article about people's feelings

2. Which of the following is an appeal to reason?

   A. I am shocked and disturbed by the mayor's plan for stray animals!
   B. Only someone who hated puppies and kittens would support this plan!
   C. According to experts, the plan will cost twice as much as the mayor says.
   D. If you love this fair city, then you will vote against the mayor's plan.

3. Which of the following is an appeal to emotion?

   A. Many experts think the mayor's plan will not work.
   B. I told my seven-year-old daughter about the plan, and she started to cry.
   C. A similar plan was tried in another town, and it did not work.
   D. Most townspeople said they would not support the plan.

Literary Analysis: Persuasive Essay

Assess

For each question, circle the letter of the best answer.

1. Which of the following is an appeal to reason?

    A. Aren't you fed up with all the trash lying around the park?

    B. Studies show that fewer people use the park if it is littered.

    C. People who litter are acting like five-year-old children.

    D. How would you feel if someone came over to your house and littered?

2. Which of the following is an appeal to emotion?

    A. There are garbage cans along every path in the park.

    B. Litter feeds pests and adds to our health problems.

    C. Show some pride in our town and do not litter.

    D. It costs the town extra money to pay for extra cleanup.

3. Read the statement below. Then, choose the sentence that best supports it.

    We should not allow skateboarding in front of the library.

    A. Many people prefer in-line skates to skateboards.

    B. None of my friends go skateboarding.

    C. Recently, there have been three skateboarding accidents by the library.

    D. The ramp in front of the library is a great spot for skateboarding.

4. Read the sentence. Then, choose the statement that it supports.

    In a survey, 80% of bus riders said their regular bus was late by half an hour at least once last week.

    A. The town should make bus shelters more comfortable.

    B. The town should buy faster buses.

    C. The town should improve bus service.

    D. The town should buy larger buses.

Literary Analysis: Persuasive Speech

Practice

A **persuasive speech** is a speech given to change people's minds or get them to take a particular side on an issue. To convince listeners, persuasive writers use rhetorical devices. **Rhetorical** [ruh TOR i kuhl] **devices** are patterns of words and ideas that make ideas sound strong. They include the following:

- **Parallelism:** Stating similar ideas in similar ways. *Example:* The more money you have, the more money you spend. The more you spend, the more you want.

- **Restatement:** Stating the same idea in different words. *Example:* The condition of the town dump is a sad comment on our town. It is a disgrace and a shame on all of us.

- **Repetition:** Using the same word, phrase, or idea over and over again. *Example:* Who elected the man who made that law? We the people. And who's going to get that man to change that law? We the people.

- **Analogy:** Explaining a complicated thing by comparing it to a simple one. *Example:* The mayor is making new rules to clear out traffic downtown on weekends. His idea is a little like keeping your kitchen clean by telling your family not to use it. Sure, the kitchen will always be clean—but where are people going to cook and eat?

In the selection, underline the example of parallelism once. Underline the example of restatement twice. Circle the two examples of repetition. Then, explain what two things are being compared in the analogy. Write your explanation on the lines.

Eating poorly is like pumping dirt into the gas tank of a car. A gas tank filled with mud is not going to carry you very far, and a body fueled with junk food is not going to serve you very well. The idea here is simple. People understand it easily. I would say the idea is hard to forget. That's just what people do, though, every day, as soon as they get to the store—they forget. They just plain forget.

Well, I'm here to help you remember. The next time you get to the store and all those bright candy wrappers start calling your name and you are about to forget all common sense, just stop and think: You might just as well be pumping dirt into your car. At least buy yourself a green vegetable or two and add some gasoline to that tank of yours!

Analogy: _____

_____

Name _____ Date _____

Literary Analysis: Persuasive Speech

A For each question, write your answer in the appropriate blank.

1. Name an issue that you would be interested in hearing or giving a

persuasive speech about. _____

2. What position might a speaker take on this issue? _____

B Write your answer to each question on the line next to it.

1. _____ Which rhetorical device appears in this paragraph:
repetition or parallelism?

   "We'll fix the problem next year" is not an acceptable answer to me. In
fact, I am not sure anyone thinks it is an acceptable answer. My neighbors do
not find it an acceptable answer. Last week, the mayor said it was not an
acceptable answer.

2. _____ Which device appears in this paragraph:
restatement or analogy?

   This part of town is a fine area with beautiful old houses. We cannot let
anyone build even one ugly new building here. New buildings are like weeds.
If you let even one weed grow in your garden today, then tomorrow ten new
weeds will spring up. If we let one person build here today, then next year
we'll have to let another, and then another.

3. _____ Which device appears in this paragraph:
analogy or parallelism?

   To live in hope is to live at your best. To live in fear is to live at your worst.
Hope keeps you ready to work hard, ready to wait long, ready to forgive
easily. Fear leaves you too distracted to work, too nervous to wait, too
miserable to forgive.

4. _____ Which device appears in this paragraph:
restatement or parallelism?

   Our plans to add space to the library have come to a dead end. If we
want to help the library, we have to make a new beginning. We need to start
over again.

Reading Kit 129

Literary Analysis: Humorous Essay

Practice

A **humorous essay** is a short piece of nonfiction that is meant to make you laugh. Humorous writing can use these figures of speech:

- **Hyperbole** [hy PUR buh lee] is intentional exaggeration. For instance, your older sister might take a long time getting ready in the morning. To use hyperbole, you could say, "When my sister first stepped into the bathroom this morning, there were two babies living in the house next door. By the time she was finished, the babies had grown up, moved out, and raised families of their own."

- **Understatement** is the opposite of hyperbole. If you talk about something as if it were much less than it is, you are using understatement. Imagine that your friend is making dinner. Suddenly, smoke is pouring through the house. Your friend rushes into the kitchen. He comes out with a plate holding all that is left of dinner—a shrunken, blackened chicken with curls of smoke rising from it. You are using understatement if you say, "That chicken looks a little overcooked."

For each paragraph, write *Hyperbole* if it uses hyperbole. Write *Understatement* if it contains understatement.

1. _____ As soon as Tom arrives, Sara's dog starts growling. As soon as Tom sits down, the dog starts barking savagely at him. When Tom gets up, the dog snaps at him, ripping the sleeve of his shirt. Tom says, "Gee, I'm not sure he likes me."

2. _____ Brittany has just finished her diet, and she decides to treat herself. She goes to a restaurant, where she orders ice cream. Brittany expects to be served a small scoop. When the ice cream arrives, though, she sees it is five scoops with a mound of whipped cream on top. "Who ordered Mt. Everest?" she says. "I thought I ordered something to eat, not something to sled down!"

Literary Analysis: Humorous Essay

Assess

A For each question, write your answer in the appropriate blank.

1. Name one kind of writing, movies, or television shows that you find funny.

_____

_____

2. Explain what you find funny in them. _____

_____

3. Do you think a humorous essay could use the same kind of humor? Explain. (Remember that a humorous essay is a short work of nonfiction)

_____

_____

_____

_____

B For each paragraph, write *Hyperbole* if it uses hyperbole. Write *Understatement* if it contains understatement.

1. _____ There were a few problems at Mrs. Smith's picnic. First, there were the ants that came and got in people's clothing. Then, a small storm started. It must have been some sort of tornado, because it blew away most of the food and one of the picnic tables. Mrs. Smith felt bad for her guests and sent flowers to everyone who ended up in the hospital. She hopes the picnic will be a little more relaxing next year.

2. _____ I was sitting in my room when I heard a huge noise. It sounded as if a herd of elephants was running through the living room. Then, I realized it was my brother and his noisy friends.

3. _____ When Rodney really gets behind his bat and hits the baseball, the ball travels far. You will not see that baseball again. I heard that in outer space, just past Pluto, scientists have found a mysterious small object. When scientists finally see this object up close, I know exactly what they'll find—an old baseball, hit out of the park by Rodney.

Name _____ Date _____

Reading: Analyze Persuasive Appeals

Persuasive appeals use logic or emotion to bring about a response to the writer's argument. Persuasive writing may use words with either a positive or negative appeal, depending on what emotional reaction the writer intends readers to have.

 In each of the following advertisements, underline the words and phrases intended to appeal to an emotional need or desire. As a clue, the need or desire is given in parentheses.

1. Do you wish you knew the secret of how celebrities always seem to have perfect, radiant skin? Now you too can have a squeaky-clean, fresh, and glowing complexion. Use new Fabu-Face beauty cleansing lotion! (desire to be attractive)

2. Tired of spending your weekends laboring in your yard? This summer, try the Turf-King—the Cadillac of power lawn mowers. You will ride in comfort so yard work seems like no work at all! (desire for easier way to do chores)

3. You will simply love new Stay Slim Ice Milk. It is rich and thick and creamy—just like real homemade ice cream. It comes in all of the delicious flavors you have come to love, including chocolate, strawberry, butter pecan, and vanilla bean. But it has only a few calories per serving! (desire to eat sweets and still be on a diet)

4. When you buy Excelvision, you get the finest quality and the highest standards in workmanship. With high-quality images and the best in surround-sound audio, no other entertainment system even comes close. It costs more, but you deserve it. (desire for luxury)

5. Because you are the direct, no-nonsense type, because you are honest with yourself, because you are a real individual—you use Loner, the honest aftershave. (desire for individuality)

Reading: Analyze Persuasive Appeals

Assess

The following paragraphs depend heavily on emotional language to make their point. For each paragraph, underline all words and phrases that convey positive or negative feelings or impressions. Then, write a sentence summarizing in plain language how the paragraph is trying to influence the reader.

1. Don't abuse your hair with harsh chemicals. Let nature's own remedies caress as they gently cleanse. Use Herbal Rain Shampoo.

_____

_____

_____

2. Jody Pugh has shamelessly sidestepped any reference to the real issues in this campaign. Instead, he has indulged in enough mud-slinging to delight a whole pen of hogs. Through cowardly suggestions, he has attacked his opponent's patriotism and humanitarian concern for the people of this state. I believe, however, that the voters are too intelligent to be taken in by Pugh's empty words and petty lies.

_____

_____

_____

3. The Rancher: This generous eight-ounce serving of our finest ground round is a hearty meal in itself. The Rancher's country flavor is sealed by grilling over smoked hickory chips and is complemented by Granny Jones's down-home sauce. Served with enough crisp golden fries and super slaw to satisfy the hungriest cowhand.

_____

_____

_____

Reading: Evaluate Credibility and Analyze Author's Intent

Practice

"Vote for me! I will make sure the school does not adopt a dress code."

"Come to the movies with me now. You can meet Jan and Mike later."

You probably hear persuasive arguments like this every day. How can you tell which arguments you should listen to? Here are some things to think about before you change your mind about something:

- What is the author saying? (What is the argument?)
- What are the author's opinions on the subject?
- How does the author prove his or her points? (What is the evidence?)
- How does the author try to appeal to your emotions or your judgment?
- Does the author try to prove other opinions are wrong?

Read the following sentences. Then, write what you think the author is saying and why.

1. "Horror movies are terrible—they all use the same characters and plots. I prefer mysteries."

_____

_____

2. "You did a great job on that report. You can do even better on your next report if you use a few more sources."

_____

_____

3. "Your sister wants to go to the playground. If you take her, you can stay out later on Friday."

_____

_____

Name _____ Date _____

Read the following document, thinking about the author's intent and the credibility of the argument. Then, answer the questions that follow.

The Truth About Designer Clothes

Are designer clothes worth the money? Some people think designer clothes show that they have lots of money to spend. They want to look like one of the elite, like someone you could see on TV. While it is true that some people are impressed with logos, are these people worth impressing?

This probably sounds like something your mom or dad might say, but think about it. Sure, it feels good to look good, but there are lots of clothes that can make you look great at half the price. What matters most is that your clothes are right for *you*, that they complement your figure, and that they show something about the person you really are.

Is it worthwhile spending your entire allowance on one shirt? Instead, you could spend half of your allowance on a really nice shirt and the other half on a meal and a movie. Plus, friends who are attracted to you because of what is on your pocket may not be interested in the *real you*—the person underneath the logo.

1. What is the author saying about designer clothes?

   _____

   _____

2. How does the author prove his or her points?

   _____

   _____

3. Do you agree or disagree with the author? Explain your answer.

   _____

   _____

Vocabulary: Word Roots -tail-, -sum-, -cred-, and -duc(t)-

Practice

A **root** is the basic unit of meaning of a word. Knowing the meanings of word roots can help you figure out the meanings of many new words. Study these examples.

Examples:

Root	Meaning	Words with the Root
-tail-	to cut	curtail, retail, details, tailor
-sum-	to take	presume, resume, assume
-cred-	to trust, to believe	creed, credit, incredible
-duc(t)-	to lead	induce, conduct, introduce

A   Circle the letter of the word that completes each sentence correctly.

1. The _____ moved through the train collecting our tickets.
   A. conductor   **B.** consumer   **C.** tailor

2. You should avoid making _____ when you don't know all the facts.
   A. assumptions   **B.** credentials   **C.** details

3. It was unfair of her to take all the _____ for the work we did together.
   A. credit   **B.** conduct   **C.** presumption

4. The _____ made the pants too long.
   A. conductor   **B.** consumer   **C.** tailor

B   Replace each underlined word or phrase with the most appropriate word from the chart above.

1. _____ I got an <u>unbelievable</u> deal on a used car.

2. _____ After a brief time-out, the players <u>continued</u> the game.

3. _____ I asked her to <u>present</u> me to her friend.

4. _____ Would you please fill me in on the <u>specifics</u> of your plan?

Vocabulary: Word Roots -tail-, -sum-, -cred-, and -duc(t)-

Assess

A Revise each sentence so that the underlined vocabulary word is used logically. Be sure not to change the vocabulary word.

1. He had seconds on dessert because he wanted to <u>reduce</u> his sugar intake.

_____

2. The room was <u>sumptuously</u> furnished with hard chairs and bare floors.

_____

3. The <u>retail</u> price of a product is generally less than what the seller paid for it.

_____

4. Our local government had to <u>curtail</u> its spending because it had plenty of money.

_____

5. The candidate was chosen for the job because she had poor <u>credentials</u>.

_____

B Circle the letter of the word that is closest in meaning to the underlined word or phrase.

1. I <u>ate</u> cereal and juice for breakfast.
   A. consumed   **B.** entailed   **C.** induced

2. The club is open to people of every race and <u>religious belief</u>.
   A. assumption   **B.** creed   **C.** retail

3. Starting a business often <u>involves</u> borrowing money.
   A. consumes   **B.** deduces   **C.** entails

4. I try to <u>behave</u> myself with dignity in business situations.
   A. conduct   **B.** curtail   **C.** presume

5. The atmosphere in the noisy cafeteria is not <u>suitable</u> to study.
   A. conducive   **B.** credible   **C.** presumptuous

6. The businessman <u>subtracted</u> all his business expenses when doing his taxes.
   A. assumed   **B.** deducted   **C.** discredited

Grammar: Adjectives

Practice

An **adjective** is a word used to give a noun or a pronoun a more specific meaning. Adjectives modify nouns and pronouns by telling *what kind, which one, how many,* or *how much.*

A Underline the adjectives in the following sentences. The number in parentheses tells how many adjectives are in the sentence.

1. The little girl was wearing a blue coat with red trim on the collar. (3)

2. The last French emperor was Napoleon III. (2)

3. Antique dolls form the central part of the collection of rare toys. (3)

4. I paid the fine of six dollars with a personal check. (2)

5. A quick look through the dictionary will reveal many strange words. (3)

6. Poor Joe has the best vocabulary and the worst diction in the class. (3)

7. A double wish was granted by the mysterious elf. (2)

8. In the winter you need a sturdy sled and nerves of steel to tackle the big hill in the local preserve. (3)

9. The prize for first place cannot be awarded until next year. (2)

10. High rates for insurance are a primary cost of upkeep on a car. (2)

B In these sentences, write each adjective and the noun it modifies.

Example: The lonely girl liked to sit near the three tall trees in the backyard.

Answer: lonely—girl; three—trees; tall—trees

1. The proud peacocks were walking back and forth in the back garden.

_____

2. There was little choice among the several inexperienced people who came.

_____

3. Is Montreal or Toronto the major Canadian city?

_____

138 Reading Kit

Grammar: Adjectives

Assess

A In the following sentences, underline the adjectives and circle the nouns they modify. The number in parentheses tells how many adjectives are in each sentence.

Example: Dave's pal got an urgent telegram from his parents. (3)

Answer: Dave's—(pal); urgent—(telegram); his—(parents)

1. The restless crowd milled around until the second race. (2)

2. The wet chipmunk scurried into a tiny hole in the old stone wall. (4)

3. Two feeble old hounds lay near the ramshackle house. (4)

4. That orange tie doesn't go well with this blue suit. (4)

5. The thirsty athlete asked for a tall, cold glass of tart lemonade. (4)

6. During the airplane show, one young pilot performed several risky stunts with his old biplane. (7)

B Underline the adjectives in the following sentences. There are thirty adjectives in all.

1. Our town is building a fabulous new recreation center.

2. Small, snappish dogs can often outbark large ones.

3. Tim's left ankle twisted when he slid into third base.

4. The strong east wind rolled huge waves against the rocky shore of the lake.

5. The Coliseum is an impressive ruin of ancient Rome.

6. The lecture hall was lit by four gold sconces on one wall and three large chandeliers that hung from the ceiling.

7. Jeffrey's old hat and coat lay in a dusty corner.

8. The painters of the Italian Renaissance achieved splendid effects in their magnificent wall paintings.

Grammar: Adverbs

Adverbs are words that modify verbs, adjectives, and other adverbs. They answer the questions *Where? When? In what way?* and *To what extent?* about the words they modify.

> **Modifying a Verb:** The children *ate* their food *quickly*.
> (The adverb *quickly* modifies the verb *ate*.)
>
> **Modifying an Adjective:** The book was *rather* disappointing.
> (The adverb *rather* modifies the adjective *disappointing*.)

A   Underline the adverbs in each of the following sentences.

1. The tennis player swung forcefully at the ball.

2. Jared frequently attends concerts at the theater.

3. Lindsay's instructor showed her how to dance gracefully.

4. Do not leave your backpack there.

5. I answered three questions on the test incorrectly.

6. They did not fully believe my statement.

7. The small animals scurried quickly into the underbrush.

8. Sarah angrily protested the unfair treatment.

B   Underline each adverb and circle each word it modifies. The number in parentheses tells how many adverbs are in each sentence.

1. The host greeted his guests warmly and graciously. (2)

2. The injured player waited patiently as the trainer carefully bandaged his arm. (2)

3. The monster glared threateningly at our hero, growled angrily, and then sprang forward. (4)

4. I will never believe him again. (2)

Grammar: Adverbs

Assess

A Underline each adverb and circle each word it modifies.

1. Slowly and silently the cat crept into the house.

2. The band members noisily stomped onto the stage.

3. Virgil rose early and exercised halfheartedly for ten minutes.

4. She reluctantly admitted the rumors were true.

5. The gymnast leaped up and deftly executed a series of handsprings.

6. The crowd greeted the basketball team uproariously.

7. A great bolt of lightning flashed crazily across the sky.

8. Sometimes Susan really means what she says.

9. Mrs. Stein answered calmly, but her hands were moving nervously.

10. Doug and Chris hardly speak to each other.

B Fill in the blank in each of the following sentences with an adverb that modifies the verb.

1. Ed honked the car horn _____.

2. People in the office _____ meet their deadlines.

3. The photography exhibit had been organized _____.

4. My grandmother _____ plays chess in the park.

5. Mildred arrived _____ for her first day of work.

Grammar: Parallelism

Practice

Parallelism is the use of similar grammatical forms or patterns to express similar ideas. Parallel constructions place equal ideas in words, phrases, or clauses of similar types. Nonparallel constructions present equal ideas in an unnecessary mix of grammatical forms, producing awkward, distracting shifts for readers.

> **Nonparallel:** The Hollywood celebrity was *charming, witty,* and a *beauty.*
> **Parallel:** The Hollywood celebrity was *charming, witty,* and *beautiful.*

Rewrite each sentence, changing nonparallel forms into parallel grammatical forms. If a sentence is correct, write **Correct.**

Example: Scott's new car is flashy, showy, and costs a lot.

Answer: Scott's new car is flashy, showy, and costly.

1. Kurt Vonnegut's short stories have suspense, style, and insight.

_____

2. We will discuss Sandy's proposal and considering alternate plans.

_____

3. Many gases are invisible, colorless, and you can't taste them.

_____

4. The birds were turning their heads and extending their tail feathers.

_____

5. A good cook must master the techniques of roasting, frying, and baking.

_____

6. Her aim was teaching college English or to become a journalist.

_____

7. Eduardo's speech was tiresome, inaccurate, and it annoyed a lot of people.

_____

Grammar: Parallelism

Circle the letter of the *nonparallel* item in each group.

Example: The governor of the state wishes

    A. to lower taxes,
    B. to improve education, and
    C. would increase the number of state holidays.

1. With the money she had saved by working, Jennifer wanted

    A. to buy a set of encyclopedias,
    B. for enrolling in a course at the local art school, and
    C. to help pay for her recent dental expenses.

2. By the middle of the movie, I was able to figure out

    A. why the hero was involved with the children,
    B. who he really was, and
    C. his purpose in buying an old, condemned apartment house.

3. Every player can help lead the team to victory by

    A. practicing hard,
    B. studying the plays, and
    C. if he concentrates on the signals.

4. Mary's opinion about her supervisor is that he is

    A. a grouch,
    B. boring, and
    C. sarcastic.

5. Douglas wants a course that will help him become a better mechanic

    A. by helping him learn about foreign cars,
    B. to teach him about rebuilding engines,
    C. and by giving him practice with brake work.

6. Her aims were

    A. to study,
    B. to travel,
    C. and someday have a family.

Spelling: Tools for Checking Spelling

Practice

Computers have features called **spell-checkers** that can help you check a word's spelling. Unfortunately, spell-checkers will not notice a spelling error if the word you incorrectly typed is another word, correctly spelled. Also, a spell-checker may not always tell you if you capitalize a word incorrectly or misspell a name or an unusual word.

A **dictionary** can also help you check a word's spelling. Try to find the word by looking up different possible spellings of its opening sounds. For example, if you were not sure how to spell *metaphor,* you might look under *metaf, metaph,* or *metiph.* Keep in mind that dictionaries do not have separate entries for plurals or past-tense verbs formed in the regular way. Dictionaries usually list additional grammatical forms at the ends of entries.

Look over the words below. Notice the words with similar spellings and pronunciations. Think about how you would use a dictionary if you wanted to check the correct spelling of each. What possible spellings might you check?

eliminate	once	waist	February	colleagues
illuminate	ounce	waste	literally	colleges

A Each item lists four possible spellings that you might check if you were trying to find the correct spelling of a word in a dictionary. Circle the correct spelling that you would find.

1. aliminate   alliminate   eliminate   elliminate

2. colleagues   collegues   choleagues   chollegues

3. ilumanate   illumanate   iluminate   illuminate

4. aunce   aunse   ounce   ounse

5. litarally   littarally   literally   litterally

B For each sentence, underline the incorrect spelling that a spell-checker probably would not find. Then, write the correct spelling on the line before the sentence.

1. _____ She wants to eliminate waist from government spending.

2. _____ Fool me ounce, shame on you; fool me twice, shame on me.

3. _____ Did you mean that literal or metaphorically?

4. _____ He invited three business colleges to a small dinner.

Name _____ Date _____

Spelling: Tools for Checking Spelling

A Each item lists four possible spellings that you might check if you were trying to find the correct spelling of a word in a dictionary. Circle the correct spelling that you would find.

1. alumanate   alluminate   ilumanate   illuminate

2. eliminate   eliminnate   iliminate   illiminnate

3. coleagues   colleagues   koleagues   kolleagues

4. literally   literully   litirully   litrally

5. ounce   ounsce   ownse   ownce

B For each sentence, underline the incorrect spelling that a spell-checker probably would not find. Then, write the correct spelling on the line before the sentence. If the sentence has no errors, write correct.

1. _____ Ounce upon a time there was a mean dragon.

2. _____ My mother and her mother are colleague at work.

3. _____ My birthday is in February.

4. _____ Can this lamp eliminate the whole room, or will it leave
the corners dark?

5. _____ By dieting, she reduced the size of her waste by
two inches.

C In this paragraph, underline the three misspelled words that a spell-checker probably would not find. Write the correct spellings on the lines after the paragraph.

The company had a meeting in February. Several colleagues discussed ways to reduce spending. They decided to illuminate some of the business trips they took each year. They also decided not waist so much money on entertaining. Ounce they made these decisions, they ended the meeting and went back to work.

1. _____   2. _____   3. _____

Writing: Abstract

An **abstract** of a work is a type of summary. Readers check abstracts to see if an article or essay interests them or meets their research needs. An abstract should include the following:

- the main point of the original piece of writing
- a brief overview of the supporting details
- information helpful to someone who has not read the original

Read the following abstract. Then, answer the questions and complete the activities.

> Bill Cosby's "Go Deep to the Sewer" is an autobiographical essay that tells about his days playing football and stickball in the streets of Philadelphia. He and his friends had no fields to play on, only the streets. Cosby shows how resourceful and imaginative these boys were, turning parked cars and manhole covers into bases, end zones, or foul lines. He also shows how much the boys loved their games, playing even when it was too dark to see the football or when the car whose fender had been first base drove away.

1. According to the abstract, what is the main point of the original piece?

_____

2. What supporting information does the original writing include, as described in the abstract?

_____

3. If you were doing research about the history of football, does the article abstracted here seem relevant to your topic? Why or why not?

_____

_____

_____

4. List two questions you would have in mind about the article, based on the information in this abstract.

_____

_____

Writing: Abstract

Assess

A Read this brief article. Then, answer the questions and complete the activities that follow.

Lizards and snakes are both reptiles. Unlike their fellow reptiles, turtles and crocodilians, lizards and snakes are covered with small, overlapping scales, or hardened bits of skin. Many lizards and snakes are long and slender, with narrow heads. If asked, most people would say that the difference between a lizard and a snake lies in how each gets around. Lizards have legs, most people would point out, but snakes do not. You may be surprised to learn that the truth is slightly more complicated.

Snakes and lizards come from a common ancestor. Millions of years ago, part of the family lost its legs and became snakes. A few lizards, though, are also legless. These include the worm lizards of Australia and the glass snakes of Europe and America. Unlike snakes, these lizards still have bones where their legs would grow. From the outside, though, they look like snakes.

Chances are, if you see a legless reptile slithering away through the weeds on its belly, you are safe in assuming that you have just seen a snake. For a scientist, though, there are other differences that you can only see up close. Most lizards have eyelids, for example. Snakes have a kind of eyelid, but it is transparent and permanently covers their eyes. They cannot blink. Both lizards and snakes have ears, but snakes do not have openings for their ears on the outside of their heads. Most lizards do.

To tell whether a critter is a lizard or a snake, you need to check three characteristics: legs, eyelids, and ear openings. Even if the reptile has no legs, you should call it a lizard if it blinks its eyelids or has holes for its ears.

1. Write the main topic or idea of this article.

_____

_____

2. Give two examples of supporting information in this article.

_____

_____

3. List three topics for which this article might be a useful source.

_____

_____

4. On a separate sheet of paper, write a brief abstract of this article. Make sure to include only important details to help researchers figure out if they should use the article.

Writing: Proposal

A **proposal** is a type of writing that describes a possible action and tells why it should be taken. Businesspeople write proposals suggesting new products and new ways to sell them. All walks of professional life involve situations in which people propose ideas for others to act on. A proposal should include the following:

- a purpose: persuading a specific audience to follow a particular action
- a description of the action to be taken and a plan to accomplish it
- the benefits of that action

Read the following proposal. Then, answer the questions and complete the activities.

Together, the Photography, Journalism, and Art Clubs of Lincoln High School propose that the school hold an annual Art Fair. The purpose of this fair would be to display the visual and literary creations of students at Lincoln. Paintings, drawings, photographs, sculptures, stories, essays, and poems would be displayed. The fair could be set up in the Multi-Purpose Room, during a week sometime after January 1. Our members would contribute works for display and encourage other students to contribute. We would also do the setup and cleanup. Like the annual Science Fair, the Art Fair would encourage creative activity by students at Lincoln and give the Lincoln parents a chance to see how much creativity there is in our school.

1. What action is being proposed, and how will it be accomplished?

_____

_____

2. What are the benefits of the proposed action? _____

_____

_____

3. Who is the likely audience of the proposal? _____

_____

Writing: Proposal

A Read the following proposal. Then, answer the questions and complete the activities that follow.

The Adams Park Neighborhood Association proposes to the City Council that a major effort be made to clean up Adams Park. We are hoping to work in cooperation with the Council. In the last six years, the park has fallen into bad shape because of harsh weather and lack of money to pay for cleanup. What was once an attractive park has become ugly. The Neighborhood Association suggests the following actions: 1. removing debris; 2. adding new trash containers; 3. replacing cracked pavements on the paths; 4. replacing dead or dying trees and bushes with new plantings; 5. planting grass in the east meadow; and repairing the park's restrooms. The Neighborhood Association is offering the City $5000 and 500 hours of volunteer work toward reclaiming the park. We estimate that the cost will come to about $20,000.

1. What action is being proposed, and how will it be accomplished?

_____

_____

2. What are the benefits of the proposed action? _____

_____

3. Who is the audience of the proposal? _____

B Write a proposal to a local business to help sponsor a team or club of yours.

_____

_____

_____

_____

_____

_____

_____

Writing: Editorial

An **editorial** is a brief persuasive essay that presents and defends an opinion. Many editorials treat issues that affect the public. Most newspapers include pages with several editorials, written by their editors, along with other opinion pieces by independent writers. A editorial should include the following:

- a clear **thesis statement,** which presents an opinion about an issue
- **evidence** supporting that opinion
- **arguments** that anticipate and answer readers' objections
- **persuasive language** that adds force to your arguments

A Answer the questions and complete the activities that follow.

1. _____ Which of the following represents an opinion that could be a thesis statement for an editorial?

   A. Reality TV shows are much less expensive to make than television dramas or sitcoms.
   B. Reality TV may be less costly to produce, but it is junk and should not take the place of quality programs.

2. _____ Which of the following represents an opinion that could be a thesis statement for an editorial?

   A. Voting by computer will change the way our votes are counted.
   B. Voting by computer has many risks and not enough safeguards.

3. _____ Which of the following could serve as supporting evidence in an editorial arguing against voting by computer?

   A. Computers might be subject to hacking.
   B. Computers require experts to program them.

B Write a sentence expressing a clear opinion, suitable for an editorial, on the following subject, along with one supporting item.

year-round school: _____

_____

Writing: Editorial

Circle one of the following topics for an editorial. Then, complete the activities that follow.

changing the driving age	a current fad or style in clothing or entertainment
making the school year longer or shorter	requiring everyone to do service, either in the military or as a worker in the community
buying hybrid cars (cars that run on electricity to save gas)	using cell phones in public

1. Write a thesis statement expressing an opinion about your topic. _____

_____

_____

2. List one piece of evidence to support your opinion. _____

_____

_____

3. List one possible objection to or argument against your opinion. _____

_____

_____

4. List an argument to answer the objection in item 3. _____

_____

_____

Literary Analysis: Figurative Language

Practice

Figurative language is language that is used imaginatively rather than literally. Figurative language includes one or more figures of speech, literary devices that make unexpected comparisons or change the usual meaning of words. Some types of figures of speech include the following.

> **Simile:** a comparison of two unlike things using *like, as, than,* or *resembles*
>
> **Metaphor:** a comparison of one thing as if it were another
>
> **Personification:** giving human characteristics to a nonhuman subject

A Read each of the following sentences. If the sentence uses any figurative language, write *F* on the line. If the sentence uses only literal language, write *L* on the blank.

1. _____ Jack's hair and beard are bright blond.

2. _____ When he heard the scream, claws of fear tore at his scalp.

3. _____ The giraffe nibbled at the leaves on the tree.

4. _____ Dead on her feet, Marla collapsed onto the worn bus seat, glad her 24-hour shift was finally over.

5. _____ The tornado played with the car, picking it up in its jaws, then dropping it.

6. _____ The shark's fin cut the water like a razor slashing silk.

B Each of the following sentences uses a figurative comparison. Read the sentence and then circle the letter of the two things being compared.

1. The skin on the farmer's face was as wrinkled, weathered, and worn as the leather on a horse's harness.

   A. farmer—face   **B.** farmer—leather   **C.** skin—leather

2. Juana's dark eyes swam like fish behind her tinted glasses.

   A. eyes—glasses   **B.** eyes—fish   **C.** fish—glasses

Literary Analysis: Figurative Language

Assess

A Read each of the following sentences. If the sentence uses any figurative language, write *F* on the line. If the sentence uses only literal language, write *L* on the blank.

1. _____ Janice tiptoed through the house, trying not to wake the peacefully sleeping baby.

2. _____ Nicholas believes that it is unhealthy to be as thin as a pancake.

3. _____ The busy storekeeper growled at us like an old grizzly bear.

4. _____ The speaker rumbled and roared, burying his audience in an avalanche of words.

5. _____ A light breeze blew through the garden, and the fresh scent of flowers drifted into the house.

B Each of the following sentences has a figurative comparison. Underline the two things being compared. Then, on the blank, write a point of similarity between the two.

1. The snow and ice storm made the city look as if it were part of the Ice Age.

_____

2. My brother is a great cook; if he fried a hot dog, he could probably make it taste like charcoal-broiled steak.

_____

3. Uncle Tyrone's snores sound so much like a chainsaw they could probably cut wood.

_____

4. It was really quite small, but to a three-year-old girl, the park was an enormous, limitless forest.

_____

5. The old deserted movie theater was so musty and foul that it was the same as a sealed tomb opened for the first time in a thousand years.

_____

Literary Analysis: Sound Devices

Practice

Poets use **sound devices** to make sound effects with words. Sound devices help create the musical feeling of a poem. Study these sound devices:

Alliteration	repeated consonant sounds at beginnings of words *The breeze blew briskly.*
Consonance	repeated consonant sounds at ends of words *On the top of the step, he will tip his cap.*
Assonance	repeated vowel sounds *They roam the lonesome roads and never go home.*
Onomatopoeia	sounds that imitate meanings *With a pop and a hiss, the can burst open.*

A Circle the letter of the correct answer to each question.

1. Which of the following pairs of words is an example of alliteration?

   A. claws and paws   **B.** head and heart   **C.** ram and jam

2. Which of the following pairs of words is an example of onomatopoeia?

   A. gurgle and babble   **B.** flow and flower   **C.** serve and protect

3. Which of the following pairs of words is an example of assonance?

   A. deep and dark   **B.** smile and bright   **C.** sale and buy

4. Which of the following pairs of words is an example of consonance?

   A. drag and drop   **B.** crash and burn   **C.** pick and pack

B Read these lines from "Jabberwocky." Then, circle the letter of the correct answer.

   "Beware the Jabberwock, my son!
   The jaws that bite, the claws that catch!"

1. The sounds of the words *that* and *bite* are an example of

   A. alliteration   **B.** consonance   **C.** assonance

2. The sounds of the words *claws* and *catch* are an example of

   A. alliteration   **B.** assonance   **C.** onomatopoeia

Literary Analysis: Sound Devices

Assess

A Circle the letter of the sentence in each pair that is an example of each sound device.

1. Alliteration

  A. The statue looked across the empty field.

  B. The statue stared across the empty field.

2. Consonance

  A. It was only a hop, a skip, and a jump away.

  B. It was only a short distance away.

3. Assonance

  A. We saw the eagle rise high into the violet clouds.

  B. We saw the eagle soar high into the purple clouds.

4. Onomatopoeia

  A. We heard the sound of the bell.

  B. We heard the clang of the bell.

B For each sound device below, write one pair of words that is an example of the sound device.

1. onomatopoeia _____

2. assonance _____

3. consonance _____

4. alliteration _____

Literary Analysis: Imagery

Practice

Imagery is language that appeals to one or more of the senses—sight, hearing, touch, taste, and smell. Images create mental pictures for readers.

Read the following paragraphs. Then, fill in the blanks with the appropriate word from the box. To use the words correctly in the paragraph, you have to imagine that you are at the scene and that all of your senses are reacting to what is happening.

Zeppelins were a form of air transportation from 1914 to 1937. Zeppelins were huge, hydrogen-filled airships somewhat similar in appearance to the modern-day blimp. The most famous of these Zeppelins was the *Hindenburg*, which burst into flames after completing its first Atlantic crossing, killing over 30 of its passengers.

Suppose you had witnessed a disaster like a Zeppelin on fire. What physical sensations would you have experienced as you watched the flames? Imagine that you are writing an account of your experience in the paragraph below. Fill in the blanks with the words that follow the paragraph.

I looked up at the _____ sky. A _____ object

_____ overhead. Suddenly there was a _____

explosion. The airship burst into _____ flames, and

_____ smoke rose high into the air. Bits of _____

material were _____ from the aircraft. The strong

_____ of burning carried for miles, and the heat was

_____.

floated	red and yellow	blazing	flung	cloudy
deafening	torpedo-shaped	odor	billowing	intense

Literary Analysis: Imagery

Assess

As you read the following paragraph, try to imagine yourself as one of the people in the scene. Think about similar experiences that you have had in extremely cold weather or in this kind of setting. Then, answer the questions that follow.

The two young skaters were anxious to replace their shoes with the skates that would take them gliding in wide circles across the ice. As they walked out of the forest to the lake, JoBeth and William could feel the air bite on their cheeks above their scarves. They had already passed the familiar neighborhood houses, each made cozy and warm with its burning fireplace. Several ice fisherman had staked out their posts at the end of the lake. Each sat, hunched over and unmoving on a tree stump, a small stool, or an old crate, next to the holes they had cut in the ice and waiting for the pull of a hungry fish.

1. Would you see paved streets and highways?

_____

2. What kind of noises would you hear?

_____

3. What might you smell?

_____

4. How would the air feel?

_____

5. What kind of clothing would be worn in this climate?

_____

To imagine this scene, you have to react to what is written and add to or extend that imagery with sensations from your own experience.

Extending imagery as you read helps you understand more about what you are reading. Be sure to add only those sights, sounds, smells, tastes, and physical feelings that logically could be present.

Reading: Read Fluently

Reading fluently is reading smoothly and continuously. Reading fluently includes understanding what you read and enjoying the art and skill of the writer. Here are two tips for reading fluently.

- **Read in sentences.** To figure out where to pause or stop, pay attention to the punctuation, not the ends of lines.

- **Use your senses.** To understand the meaning of what you read, pay attention to words that appeal to sight, hearing, smell, taste, and touch.

A Read the following lines from "I Wandered Lonely as a Cloud." Circle the letter of the correct answer to each question.

> I wandered lonely as a cloud
> That floats on high o'er vales and hills,
> When all at once I saw a crowd,
> A host, of golden daffodils;
> 5 Beside the lake, beneath the trees,
> Fluttering and dancing in the breeze.

1. In order to read fluently, what would you do at the end of line 1?

   A. stop   **B.** pause   **C.** continue without stop or pause

2. In order to read fluently, what would you do at the end of line 2?

   A. stop   **B.** pause   **C.** continue without stop or pause

3. In order to read fluently, what would you do at the end of line 6?

   A. stop   **B.** pause   **C.** continue without stop or pause

---

B Circle the letter of the sense to which each of the following lines appeals.

1. "I saw a crowd, / A host, of golden daffodils;"

   A. sight   **B.** hearing   **C.** smell   **D.** taste   **E.** touch

2. "He clasps the crag with crooked hands;"

   A. sight   **B.** hearing   **C.** smell   **D.** taste   **E.** touch

Reading: Read Fluently

A Read the following lines from "Rocking" by Gabriela Mistral. Circle the letter of the correct answer to each question.

> The wind wandering by night
> Rocks the wheat.
> Hearing the loving wind,
> I rock my son.

1. In order to read fluently, after which line would you pause?

   A. line 1   **B.** line 2   **C.** line 3

2. In order to read fluently, after which line would you continue without stop or pause?

   A. line 1   **B.** line 3   **C.** line 4

3. In order to read fluently, after which lines would you stop?

   A. lines 1 and 2   **B.** lines 2 and 4   **C.** lines 3 and 4

B Circle the letter of the sense to which each of the following phrases appeals.

1. "the sparkling waves"

   A. sight   **B.** hearing   **C.** smell   **D.** taste   **E.** touch

2. "the tune without the words"

   A. sight   **B.** hearing   **C.** smell   **D.** taste   **E.** touch

Reading: Follow Technical Directions and Use Technology

Practice

You probably use technology every day. You wake to a clock radio, send e-mail, and listen to your iPod. You may learn how to use these devices by watching others, but you probably have to read directions to find out about new features. To do this, you need to **follow technical directions** to **use technology**. Here are some things to do before you read technical directions:

■ Scan the document to look for unfamiliar terms.

■ When you find a new term, look for a definition nearby or in a glossary.

■ Look at the graphics for clues about what you will learn.

■ If a procedure has steps, read all of the steps first. Then, do them one at a time.

Read the following technical directions. Then, answer the questions that follow.

Troubleshooting Your Cordless Phone

Please try these steps before calling tech support.

Problem	Solutions
CHARGE/IN USE LED does not light when handset is returned to base	1. Check that HANDSET is fully connected to BASE.
	2. Check that AC ADAPTER is plugged into both BASE *and* OUTLET.
	3. Check that charging contracts on HANDSET *and* BASE are clean.

1. What kind of technology is being discussed? _____

2. Define two technical terms in these directions. _____

_____

3. Why do you think the author uses uppercase letters in the directions?

_____

_____

Reading: Follow Technical Directions and Use Technology

Assess

A Read the following news article. Then, answer the questions that follow.

Wii Helps Patients Heal

Nintendo Wii, the gaming system, is finding its way into the most unusual places. Recently, therapists began using Wii Sports in rehabilitation facilities to get injured people to move again. Patients with movement and balance problems are using it to stimulate their muscles and restore their coordination. Virtual tennis and baseball help patients practice eye-hand coordination and track movement.

Seniors in nursing homes are also using Wii Sports for safe and stimulating exercise. They are playing virtual golf without leaving their recreation room. They are even racing cars. These games challenge their coordination and stimulate conversation and friendly competition.

In addition, injured soldiers are using Wii to regain their strength. The system allows soldiers to avoid boredom caused by repetitive stretching and lifting exercises. The graphics are stimulating because they change constantly and they simulate real-life activities.

1. What kind of technology is being discussed in the article?

_____

2. In what three ways is this technology being used today?

_____

_____

_____

3. Define three technical terms in these directions.

_____

_____

_____

_____

Vocabulary: Word roots *-fer-* and *-vert-* and prefixes *-ana-* and *mono-*

Practice

A **root** is the basic unit of meaning of a word. A **prefix** is one or more syllables added to the beginning of a word or word root to form a new word with a different meaning. Study these examples.

Examples:

Root or Prefix	Meaning	Words with the Root
-fer- [root]	to bring, to carry	transferred, conference, fertile
-vert- [root]	turn	convert, reverted, vertical
ana- [prefix]	up, back, against	analysis, anagram, anatomy
mono- [prefix]	one	monologue, monotonous, monorail

A Replace the underlined word in each sentence with a word from the chart above containing the root *-fer-* or *-vert-*.

1. _____ I <u>switched</u> to a different train halfway through my journey.

2. _____ I had to <u>change</u> feet to meters to solve the math problem.

3. _____ After his term as mayor expired, he <u>returned</u> to his previous rank of councilman.

4. _____ Several business leaders gathered for the <u>meeting</u>.

B Complete each sentence with a word from the chart above.

1. Alone on the stage, the actor delivered a lengthy

2. The medical student studied the structure of the body in class.

3. The town built a new   train to help people get around.

4. I've worked out a detailed   of the problem.

Vocabulary: Word roots *-fer-* and *-vert-* and prefixes *-ana-* and *mono-*

Assess

A Circle the letter of the word that is closest in meaning to the underlined word or phrase.

1. The scientists <u>investigated</u> the specimen.

　A. analyzed　　　　　**B.** diverted　　　　　**C.** transferred

2. The <u>ruler</u> held absolute power over the country.

　A. convert　　　　　**B.** monarch　　　　　**C.** referee

3. I decided to <u>put off</u> my college search until my senior year.

　A. defer　　　　　　**B.** infer　　　　　　**C.** prefer

4. The author draws a <u>comparison</u> between her main character and his home country.

　A. analogy　　　　　**B.** monopoly　　　　**C.** preference

5. I <u>turned over</u> the cup to show that I did not want any coffee.

　A. analyzed　　　　　**B.** inferred　　　　　**C.** inverted

6. The settlers <u>redirected</u> a nearby stream to water their fields.

　A. deferred　　　　　**B.** diverted　　　　　**C.** monopolized

B Revise each sentence so that the underlined vocabulary word is used logically. Be sure not to change the vocabulary word.

1. The <u>extrovert</u> was very shy around new people.

_____

2. The <u>monotonous</u> melody was very interesting to listen to.

_____

3. I never eat carrots because I <u>prefer</u> them to other vegetables.

_____

4. She decided to see a <u>psychoanalyst</u> about her back pain.

_____

5. The <u>fertile</u> land produced no crops at all.

_____

Grammar: Prepositions and Objects of Prepositions

Practice

A **preposition** is a word that relates a noun or pronoun to another word in the sentence. Although most prepositions, such as *at, by, in,* and *with,* are single words, some prepositions, such as *because of and in addition to,* are compound. The **object of the preposition** is the noun or pronoun at the end of a prepositional phrase.

> She quickly jumped *across the creek.*

The preposition *across* relates the object of the preposition, *creek,* to the verb *jumped.*

Underline each preposition and circle its object. The number in parentheses tells you how many phrases to look for.

Example: The mouse hid underneath the cabinet.

1. Go to the store and get milk for breakfast. (2)

2. When you buy the ice cream, get the flavor of the month and the usual chocolate. (1)

3. The children are sitting on the floor in the library waiting for the librarian to tell them a story. (3)

4. The man in the wheelchair rolled smoothly up the ramp and into the theater for his daughter's performance. (4)

5. The work on our patio will not be finished until Tuesday of the week after next. (4)

6. One box near the door belongs to a friend of mine named Hector Ruiz. (3)

7. At the end of the third quarter, our team was winning by three points. (3)

8. Look under the bed, in the hamper, or in the dryer for your lost sock. (4)

9. The corn mixture is in the cabinet above the stove. (2)

10. During the rainstorm, we stayed in the house, near the warm fire. (3)

Grammar: Prepositions and Objects of Prepositions

Assess

A Each of the following sentences contains a prepositional phrase. Write the preposition in the first column. Then, write the object of the preposition in the second column.

Preposition	Object	
1. _____	_____	The plane flew over the Grand Canyon.
2. _____	_____	We will meet after lunch.
3. _____	_____	The train moved toward its destination.
4. _____	_____	The ring fell down the drain.
5. _____	_____	Sal flattened the paper between two books.

B Underline each preposition and circle its object.

1. Shana and Yvette went to the mall with Shana's mother to shop for a new dress for the big dance.

2. While they were there, they ran into their friends Hannah and Janine in Robbins Department Store.

3. All of the girls were having trouble finding dresses they wanted to buy.

4. "If I find a dress I like, may I buy new shoes to go with it?" Shana asked her mother with pleading eyes.

5. "We will see," answered her mother with a deep sigh.

6. Finally, Yvette said to Shana, "You look wonderful in that black-and-white dress with the buttons down the front."

7. They paid for the dress and went up the escalator into the next department to look for the shoes.

8. Shana tried on many pairs of shoes and finally found a pair that was perfect with the dress.

Grammar: Prepositional Phrases

Practice

A **prepositional phrase** is a group of words beginning with a preposition and ending with a noun or pronoun. Prepositional phrases may function as adjectives or adverbs.

> Adjective phrase: The candidate *with the blonde hair* is my sister.
>
> Adverb phrase: The candidate answered the question *with skill.*

Underline the prepositional phrases, both adjective and adverb, in each of the following sentences. The number in parentheses tells how many prepositional phrases are in the sentence.

1. In this city we often encounter people with crazy ideas about life. (3)

2. At the end of the Civil War, large sections of the South had been devastated by the Union armies. (4)

3. Men and women with great manual dexterity are often successful in sports or in the arts. (3)

4. In the evening a warm wind came up from the southwest. (2)

5. Some of the most unusual animals in the world are found in the Galápagos Islands off the coast of Ecuador. (5)

6. The sales representative from the Incanta Manufacturing Company will be here within an hour. (2)

7. The vendor strolled among the people near the bandstand. (2)

8. Fortunately, the lion turned toward his keeper instead of the child. (2)

9. In the 1800s a man with a team of horses could plow only two acres of land in a day. (5)

10. Today a farmer can plow 120 acres in the same period of time. (2)

Grammar: Prepositional Phrases

Assess

Write the prepositional phrases on the line provided and tell whether each phrase is an adjective (**ADJ**) or adverb (**ADV**) prepositional phrase.

Example: My neighbor across the hall knocked on my door.

Answers: across the hall—ADJ; on my door—ADV

1. One of Mrs. Payne's stallions galloped across a busy road.

   _____

2. Ian spent the Word War II years between 1943 and 1945 behind enemy lines.

   _____

3. Lafayette was a French general who participated in the Revolutionary War.

   _____

4. Sherry raised the expensive marble statue right before my unbelieving eyes.

   _____

5. The woman was walking with a limp.

   _____

6. I looked over the ridge and saw the smoke from the cabin in the valley.

   _____

7. Ted fell behind the others and ran more and more slowly with every lap.

   _____

8. Joe heard a fearful noise in the attic.

   _____

9. "You must stay in bed all day!" she said.

   _____

10. The child stood beside the puddle briefly and then jumped across it.

   _____

Grammar: Vary Sentences With Phrases

Practice

A **preposition** relates a noun or pronoun to another word in the sentence. The noun or pronoun that follows the preposition is the **object of the preposition.** A **prepositional phrase** includes the preposition, the object, and all the words that come between them. In the example, the prepositional phrase is underlined.

| PREP. | OBJ. OF PREP. |

Prepositional phrase: We met Tony (outside) the Chinese restaurant.

Here are some common prepositions.

   Common prepositions: about, across, after, around, at, behind, down, for, from, in, near, of, on, outside, over, to, through, with, without
   Compound prepositions: in front of, instead of, next to, on top of

A Underline the prepositional phrase in each sentence. Then, write P above the preposition and OP above the object of the preposition.

1. I couldn't believe what I read in the newspaper yesterday.

2. There was an article about a 700-pound pumpkin!

3. It had won first prize at the County Fair.

4. When I stood next to it, I saw how enormous it was.

B Add a prepositional phrase to beginning of each sentence. Use the preposition indicated.

Example: A dog was barking. (Behind) <u>Behind my house</u>, a dog was barking.

1. Some birds fly south. (In) _____

_____

2. Three geese were honking loudly. (Across) _____

_____

3. The rooster crowed. (On top of) _____

_____

Name _____ Date _____

Grammar: Vary Sentences With Phrases

Assess

A Underline the prepositional phrase or phrases in each sentence. Then, write *P* above each preposition and *OP* above each object of the preposition. Two of the sentences have more than one prepositional phrase.

                       P   OP   P   OP

Example: The tornado came <u>from the west</u> and swept <u>through our town</u>.

1. The powerful wind pulled trees up by their roots.

2. Within 15 minutes, houses all around our town had been damaged.

3. We heard the constant sirens of fire trucks.

4. Near the garage, there were fallen branches and broken glass.

5. We will be talking about this tornado for a long time!

B Following the instructions, add a prepositional phrase to the *beginning* of each sentence or to the *end*. Use the preposition indicated.

Examples: The lights blazed. (In—*beginning*). In the arena, the lights blazed.

The lights blazed. (in—*end*). The lights blazed in the arena.

1. The band received an award. (For—*beginning*)

_____

2. The audience greeted them. (with—*end*)

_____

3. Later, the fans rushed. (toward—*end*).

_____

4. The limo was waiting. (In front of—*beginning*)

_____

Writing: Description of a Scene

Practice

A **description of a scene** creates a picture of a place in words. It allows your readers to see something in their minds' eye that you have seen in real life. Good descriptive writing also shares the writer's feelings about what is being described. A description of a scene should include the following:

- **vivid sensory details**—details that help readers imagine the sights, sounds, and smells of the scene, along with any other sensations like taste or touch

- a **main impression** of the scene—a single clear feeling or idea about the scene that your readers will remember when they think about the scene

- a clear **organization**—a logical order that you follow, which will help readers make sense of the details

---

A Identify the sense that each of the following words calls up.

1. _____ shrieking   4. _____ glittering

2. _____ perfumed   5. _____ smooth

3. _____ hushed   6. _____ bitter

B Read the following list of items and list a sensory detail or main impression for each, according to the directions.

1. rosebush (*sensory detail*): _____

2. campfire (*main impression*): _____

3. busy restaurant (*main impression*): _____

4. bus station (*sensory detail*): _____

C Choose a scene that you see every day; think of the scene at a particular time of day and during a particular type of weather. List several sensory details and one main impression that you would use to describe the scene.

_____

_____

_____

Name _____ Date _____

Writing: Description of a Scene

Circle one of the following scenes to describe. Then, complete the activities that follow.

school cafeteria at lunchtime   a community swimming pool in summer

the interior of an airplane   a Fourth of July parade

a snowstorm   a kindergarten

1. Write four sensory details that could describe your scene. _____

_____

2. List one main impression that would suit your scene. _____

_____

_____

3. List how the details of your scene could be organized in a description (for example, if you were describing a room, from ceiling to floor). _____

_____

4. Write a paragraph describing your scene, using the details, main impression, and organization you decided on above.

_____

_____

_____

_____

_____

_____

_____

_____

© Pearson Education, Inc. All rights reserved.

Reading Kit **171**

Writing: Editorial

An **editorial** is a brief persuasive essay that presents and defends an opinion. Editorials usually present views on issues of public interest. An editorial should include the following:

- a clear **thesis statement,** which presents an opinion about an issue
- **evidence** (such as facts, statistics, quotations, examples, and logical reasoning) supporting that opinion
- **arguments** that anticipate and answer readers' reasonable objections
- **persuasive language** that adds force to your opinion without being antagonistic

A Answer the questions about an editorial favoring building a new library.

1. _____ Which of the following is a *fact* supporting building a new library?

   A. Our library has suffered flood damage, and some areas are beyond repair.
   B. Our library is dark and old, and it is not a pleasant place to visit.

2. _____ Which statement might raise a *reasonable objection* to a new library?

   A. We don't need libraries anymore, since everyone can do research on the Internet.
   B. Building a new library would take funds away from other city projects.

3. How would you answer that reasonable objection? _____

   _____

4. _____ Which statement uses language that is more persuasive?

   A. Anyone who opposes the idea of building a new library is stupid and narrow-minded.
   B. A new library would be an asset to our city, enhancing our cultural opportunities.

B On a separate paper, write a short editorial expressing and supporting an opinion about one of the following subjects OR a subject of your own choosing.

   universal military service   school dress codes   banning junk food at schools

Writing: Editorial

Assess

Circle one of the following topics for an editorial. Then, complete the activities that follow.

an issue in your school or community   a health or public safety problem
a famous person to praise or criticize   a TV show to praise or criticize
a trend to praise or criticize   a popular fad

1. Write a thesis statement expressing an opinion about your topic. _____
_____

2. List one piece of evidence to support your opinion. _____
_____
_____

3. List one reasonable objection to your opinion. _____
_____
_____

4. List an argument to answer the objection in item 3. _____
_____
_____

Writing: Descriptive Essay

Practice

A **descriptive essay** creates a picture in words of a person, place, or thing. When you write a descriptive essay, you share a vivid experience. You make your readers see what you saw, hear what you heard, feel what you felt. A descriptive essay should include the following:

- **vivid sensory details**—details that help readers imagine the sights, sounds, and smells of the scene, along with any other sensations like taste or touch

- a **main impression** of the scene—a single clear feeling or idea about the scene that your readers will remember when they think about the scene

- a clear **organization**—a logical order that you follow, which will help readers make sense of the details

A Read the following list of items and list a sensory detail or main impression for each, according to the directions.

1. rainy day (*sensory detail*): _____

2. athlete (*main impression*): _____

3. forest (*main impression*): _____

B The sentences in this descriptive paragraph about a beach are not in logical order. Figure out the best order for them. Then, write the numbers of the sentences in that order, and circle the number of the sentence that expresses the overall impression, which should be the last sentence in the new arrangement.

   (1) Far out on the water, a boat flashed its sails in the sunlight. (2) The smell of suntan lotion perfumed the air above the sunbathers' blankets and chairs. (3) At the water's edge, a group of squealing children dug a complicated system of tunnels in the sand. (4) Gulls soared in the distance over the waves, swooping down for an occasional fish and barking their strange cries. (5) This was summer at the beach—pure joy and warmth that seemed to stretch to the ends of the earth and to last forever. (6) The waves whooshed in and out, sweeping boogie-board riders to the wet sand.

_____

_____

Writing: Descriptive Essay

Assess

Circle one of the following subjects to describe or choose a subject of your own. Then, complete the activities that follow.

a child	an automobile	an office building	a storm
a performer	your house	a summer night	a painting

1. Write four sensory details that could describe your subject. _____

_____

_____

2. List one main impression that sums up your subject. _____

_____

3. List how the details of your subject could be organized in a description (for example, if you were describing a room, from ceiling to floor). _____

_____

_____

4. Write a paragraph describing your subject, using the details, main impression, and organization you decided on above.

_____

_____

_____

_____

_____

_____

_____

_____

_____

Literary Analysis: Narrative Poetry

Practice

Narrative poetry is verse that tells a story. A narrative poem usually includes the following elements:

- a **plot**, or series of connected events
- a **setting**, or a specific time and place where the events of the story occur
- **characters**, or people, animals, or objects that participate in the action of the story

These are the same elements often found in a short story or a novel. In addition, a narrative poem may create a **mood**, or general feeling, such as joy, gloom, or suspense.

A In the following lines from "Casey at the Bat" by Ernest L. Thayer, some words are underlined. Circle the letter of the element of narrative poetry that is shown by the underlined words.

1. "The score stood two to four, with but <u>an inning left to play</u>"

   A. plot   **B.** setting   **C.** character   **D.** mood

2. "<u>With that hope</u> which springs eternal within the human breast"

   A. plot   **B.** setting   **C.** character   **D.** mood

3. "For <u>Casey, mighty Casey</u>, was advancing to the bat"

   A. plot   **B.** setting   **C.** character   **D.** mood

4. "But there is no joy in <u>Mudville</u>: Mighty Casey has struck out"

   A. plot   **B.** setting   **C.** character   **D.** mood

B Identify the mood or feeling of each of the following lines from "Casey at the Bat."

1. "It looked extremely rocky for the Mudville nine that day"

   A. happy   **B.** quiet   **C.** anxious   **D.** angry

2. "Then from the gladdened multitude went up a joyous yell—"

   A. hopeful   **B.** tragic   **C.** terrified   **D.** curious

3. "They saw his face grow stern and cold, they saw his muscles strain"

   A. bored   **B.** sad   **C.** mysterious   **D.** intense

Literary Analysis: Narrative Poetry

Assess

A Read the following lines from the narrative poem "Paul Revere's Ride" by Henry Wadsworth Longfellow. Then, answer the questions.

> Listen, my children, and you shall hear
> Of the midnight ride of Paul Revere,
> On the eighteenth of April, in Seventy-five;
> Hardly a man is now alive
> 5 Who remembers that famous day and year.
> He said to his friend, "If the British march
> By land or sea from the town tonight,
> Hang a lantern aloft in the belfry arch
> Of the North Church tower as a signal light,—
> 10 One, if by land, and two, if by sea;
> And I on the opposite shore will be,
> Ready to ride and spread the alarm
> Through every Middlesex village and farm,
> For the country folk to be up and to arm."

1. Write the line that names the main character of the narrative poem.

_____

2. Write the date and the place that tell the setting of the narrative poem.

_____

3. Based on these lines, what is the plot of the narrative poem?

_____

B Describe in your own words the mood or feeling of these lines of "Paul Revere's Ride."

_____

_____

_____

_____

Name _____ Date _____

Literary Analysis: Rhyme

Practice

Rhyme is the repetition of sounds at the ends of words. Study the four most common types of rhyme.

Exact rhyme: use of words that end with exactly the same sound	—here I opened wide the <u>door</u>— Darkness there, and nothing <u>more</u>.
Slant rhyme: use of words that end with similar sounds	She looks across the fields and <u>gazes</u> At waves and waves and waves of <u>daisies</u>.
End rhyme: rhyming of words at the ends of lines	Listen, my children, and you shall <u>hear</u> Of the midnight ride of Paul <u>Revere</u> On the eighteenth of April, in Seventy-<u>five</u>; Hardly a man is now <u>alive</u> Who remembers that famous day and <u>year</u>.
Internal rhyme: rhyming of words within the same line	The <u>jaws</u> that bite, the <u>claws</u> that catch

A **rhyme scheme** is a regular pattern of end rhymes. A rhyme scheme assigns a letter to each rhyme. In the box above, the end rhymes are *hear/Revere/five/alive/year*. The rhyme scheme of those lines is *aabba*.

Read "The Eagle," by Alfred, Lord Tennyson. Then, answer the questions.

> He clasps the crag with crooked hands
> Close to the sun in lonely lands,
> Ring'd with the azure world, he stands.
> The wrinkled sea beneath him crawls;
> 5 He watches from his mountain walls,
> And like a thunderbolt he falls.

1. Write the words that are **exact rhymes.** _____

2. Write the words that are **end rhymes.** _____

3. Write the **rhyme scheme** of "The Eagle." _____

Name _____ Date _____

Read the following lines of "To My Sister" by William Wordsworth. Then, answer the questions.

> It is the first mild day of March:
> Each minute sweeter than before,
> The redbreast sings from the tall larch
> That stands beside our door.
>
> 5   There is a blessing in the air,
> Which seems a sense of joy to yield
> To the bare trees, and mountains bare,
> And grass in the green field.

1. Write the words in the poem that are **end rhymes.** _____

_____

2. Write the words in the poem that are **exact rhymes.** _____

_____

3. Does the poem use any **slant rhymes**? If so, what are they? _____

_____

4. Does the poem use any **internal rhymes**? If so, what are they? _____

_____

5. What is the **rhyme scheme** of these lines of the poem? _____

_____

Literary Analysis: Lyric Poetry

Practice

Lyric poetry is poetry that expresses the personal thoughts and feelings of a speaker. Lyric poetry has a musical quality and uses vivid images. It conveys an emotion or mood, and it is usually short.

Study these three forms of lyric poetry.

sonnet	a fourteen-line poem often in iambic pentameter. A Shakespearean sonnet has three quatrains and one rhymed couplet (4 + 4 + 4 + 2)
haiku	three lines of five, seven, and five syllables. This Japanese form often uses nature imagery to convey strong emotion.
free verse	a poem without a regular pattern of rhythm or rhyme. Free verse often uses many sound and rhythmic devices.

A Read the final couplet of Edna St. Vincent Millay's sonnet "Night is my sister, and how deep in love." Then, write words from the lines that show why it is lyric poetry.

No one but Night, with tears on her dark face,
Watches beside me in this dark place.

1. Personal thoughts and feelings _____

2. Musical quality _____

3. Vivid image _____

4. Emotion or mood _____

B Read the following haiku. Then, answer the questions.

Behind the old house
Friendly crickets sing all night:
"Welcome" and "Goodbye."

1. How many syllables are there in line 1? _____

2. How many syllables are there in line 2? _____

3. How many syllables are there in line 3? _____

4. What nature image does the poem use? _____

Literary Analysis: Lyric Poetry

Assess

A Read the last six lines of Edna St. Vincent Millay's sonnet "Once more into my arid days like dew." Then, write words from the lines that show why it is lyric poetry.

> And once again, and wiser in no wise,
> I chase your colored phantom on the air,
> And sob and curse and fall and weep and rise
> And stumble pitifully on to where,
> Miserable and lost, with stinging eyes,
> Once more I clasp,—and there is nothing there.

1. Personal thoughts and feelings _____

2. Musical quality _____

3. Vivid image _____

4. Emotion or mood _____

B Read the lines from "I Hear America Singing" by Walt Whitman. Then, give examples from the poem that show why it is free verse.

> Each singing what belongs to him or her and to none else,
> The day what belongs to the day—at night the party of young fellows, robust, friendly,
> Singing with open mouths their strong melodious songs.

1. No regular rhythm: Count the number of syllables in each line and tell

whether any have the same number of syllables. _____

_____

2. No regular rhyme _____

_____

3. Sound devices, or repeated sounds in nearby words _____

_____

Reading: Paraphrase

Practice

Paraphrasing is using your own words to tell what someone else has written or said. When you paraphrase a poem, you express the main ideas of the poem in a simpler way. To paraphrase a long sentence, first break it down into smaller ideas.

- Begin by identifying subjects and verbs. A **subject** is a word in a sentence that tells who performs an action or who is being described. A **verb** is a word that tells what action the subject does. Words such as *is* and *are* are also verbs. They link a subject to its description.
- If a sentence has more than one subject or more than one verb, write separate sentences that each have one subject and one verb.
- If a sentence has colons, semicolons, or dashes, write separate sentences by replacing those punctuation marks with periods.

In the following example, the subjects are underlined once and verbs are underlined twice:

Lines from Poem: The <u>moon</u> <u>was shining</u> sulkily, / Because <u>she</u> <u>thought</u> the sun / had got no business to be there / After the day was done—
—from "The Walrus and the Carpenter" by Lewis Carroll

Broken Down: The moon was shining sulkily. She thought the sun had got no business to be there after the day was done.

A Read these lines from "Adventures of Isabel" by Ogden Nash. Then, answer the questions that follow.

> Isabel met an enormous bear,
>
> Isabel, Isabel didn't care;
>
> The bear was hungry, the bear was ravenous,
>
> The bear's big mouth was cruel and cavernous.

1. What are the two verbs in the first two lines of the poem?

_____

2. Rewrite the first two lines of the poem as two separate sentences.

_____

B On a separate sheet of paper, paraphrase the poem in activity A, telling what it means in your own words.

Name _____ Date _____

A Read these lines about the Wright brothers, inventors of the airplane, from "Wilbur Wright and Orville Wright" by Rosemary and Steven Vincent Benét. Then, answer the questions that follow.

> And so they built a glider, first,
> And then they built another.
> —There never were two brothers more
> Devoted to each other.
> 5 They ran a dusty little shop
> For bicycle-repairing,
> And bought each other soda-pop,
> And praised each other's daring.

1. What are the two subjects and the two verbs that are repeated in lines 1 and 2? (Remember, a subject tells who did something or tells who is being described. A verb tells what action was done or links a subject to its description.)

   Subject 1: _____ **Subject 2:** _____

   Verb 1: _____ **Verb 2:** _____

2. Rewrite the first two lines of the poem as two separate sentences.

   _____

3. What is the verb in line 5? _____

4. What is the verb in line 7? _____

5. What is the verb in line 8? _____

6. Rewrite lines 5 through 8 as three separate sentences.

   _____

   _____

B On a separate sheet of paper, paraphrase the poem in activity A, telling what it means in your own words.

Reading: Paraphrase a Text and Find the Main Idea

Practice

Informational texts are often filled with new ideas and terms. When you read such texts, it is helpful to preview the text to **find the main idea.** It is also helpful to **paraphrase the text** after reading, restating the main ideas in your own words. This last step ensures that you will remember what you have read. Here are some things to do to help you find a text's main idea and paraphrase its meaning:

- Before reading, preview the text. Look at the heads, topic sentences, and graphics for clues to the main idea.

- As you read, take a few notes about the text's important points.

- After you read, paraphrase the text, putting the main ideas into your own words.

Preview the following informational text and answer the first question. Then, read the text and answer the second question.

1. What information did you find about the text's main idea when you previewed?

_____

_____

Dominance Behavior Among Dogs

Domestic dogs exhibit many of the same behaviors as dogs in the wild, so it is vital for the dog trainer to understand the behavior of the species. Dogs in the wild live in packs, and their relationship to one another is understood by all of the pack members. The alpha dog is the pack leader, and he determines who eats first, among other things. He also nips or growls at dogs that misbehave or challenge his dominance.

2. Paraphrase the text, putting its main points into your own words.

_____

_____

Reading: Paraphrase a Text and Find the Main Idea

Assess

Before you read, preview the case study below and answer the prereading question. Then, read the article and answer the postreading question.

1. What do the headlines tell you about the case study's main idea?

_____

Case Study: Careers in Dog Training

Want to combine your love of dogs with your career?

Dogs are more popular today than ever before. People are busier today than ever before. Busy people often think a dog will be "no trouble," but there is more to owning a dog than petting it and taking it for an occasional run. In short, the need for dog trainers has never been greater.

What It Takes: Preparation

Dog trainers need to learn about dog behavior, about what dogs need, and about how they behave in the wild. Understanding the true nature of dogs helps trainers adapt their methods to the needs of each dog.

Prospective dog trainers also need to work with professionals to learn the "tricks of the trade." They must learn how to assess dog-owner relationships, find solutions to problem behavior, and be firm with both dogs and owners.

Getting a Job

New trainers should start with puppies, progressing to problem dogs once they gain experience and confidence. Great skill is required, for example, to retrain dogs that bite.

Rewards

The rewards of professional dog training are great, but so are the heartaches. New trainers must avoid becoming emotionally involved with their clients so they can approach problems clearly. However, nothing beats the happy wags and warmth of a successful dog-owner relationship.

2. Paraphrase the case study's main points.

_____

Vocabulary: Prefixes *pre-* and *im-* and suffixes -ment and -ion

Practice

A **prefix** is added to the beginning of a word or word root to change its meaning. The prefix *pre-* means "before." The prefix *im-* is used in many words to mean "not."

> pre + view = preview: "to look something over ahead of time"
>
> im + pure = impure: "not pure, unwholesome"

A **suffix** is added to the end of a word to change its meaning or part of speech. The suffix *-ment* refers to the act of doing something or the resulting state of being. The suffix *-ion* also refers to an act or condition. These two suffixes are often used to change verbs to nouns.

> excite + ment = excitement: "the state of being excited"
>
> create + ion = creation: "the act of creating"

A   Add *pre-* or *im-* to each underlined word to form a new word that fits the meaning of the sentence.

1. _____ I don't remember that event because it <u>dated</u> my birth.

2. _____ Sometimes all his childish pranks seem a little <u>mature</u>.

3. _____ My gratitude for all you've done is simply <u>measurable</u>.

B   Circle the letter of the correct answer to each question.

1. What happens when a person is put into <u>confinement</u>?

   A. that person is at liberty   **B.** that person is held captive

2. How would you describe a feeling of <u>contentment</u>?

   A. being satisfied with what you have   **B.** wishing for more than you have

3. What does it mean if you have a <u>decision</u> to make

   A. you have a choice about what to do   **B.** there is only one thing you can do

Vocabulary: Prefixes *pre-* and *im-* and Suffixes *-ment* and *-ion*

Assess

A   Revise each sentence so that the underlined vocabulary word is used logically. Be sure not to change the vocabulary word.

1. She stumbled through her class presentation because she was well <u>prepared</u>.

_____

2. His neighbors all praised him for his <u>immoral</u> behavior.

_____

3. I need this done <u>immediately</u>, so please take your time.

_____

4. The <u>preface</u> to a book is found at the end.

_____

B   Choose the correct word to complete each sentence. Write the word on the line.

1. amused   amusement

At the circus, some clowns performed for our _____.

We were all very _____ by their tricks.

2. reflected   reflection

The peaceful waters of the lake _____ the surrounding mountains.

We gazed at their _____ in the water.

3. complete   completion

I am determined to see this project through to _____.

I will not rest until all the work is _____.

4. puzzling   puzzlement

We all found his odd behavior very _____.

Everyone there was watching him with _____.

Grammar: Appositive Phrases

Practice

An **appositive phrase** is a noun or pronoun with modifiers that adds information to the noun or pronoun it is placed next to. Appositive phrases that contain modifiers are set off with commas. Using appositives is a good way to make your writing more concise.

Less Concise: Monica Gonzales' painting was an oil and batik. The painting greatly impressed Vincent Goff.

Appositive: Monica Gonzales' painting, *an oil and batik*, greatly impressed Vincent Goff.

A Underline the appositive phrases in the following sentences.

1. A kayak, a lightweight streamlined canoe, is easy to handle.

2. Farmingdale's, a new department store, has everything one could want.

3. Patrick, the temporary bookkeeper, is staying late this evening.

4. I want you to meet Roger Kraft, the student I am tutoring.

5. St. Patrick, the patron saint of Ireland, was born in Britain around A.D. 389.

B Combine the sentences using appositive phrases.

1. This novel is from the north branch of the library. The library is the building on Central Street.

_____

_____

2. Jamestown was founded in 1607. It was the first permanent English settlement in the New World.

_____

_____

3. The harpsichord is the predecessor of the piano. It is a stringed musical instrument.

_____

Grammar: Appositive Phrases

Assess

A Underline the appositive phrases in the following sentences.

1. The cardinal, the state bird of North Carolina, has a distinct, red plumage.

2. Cheryl, my best friend since second grade, has a black belt in karate.

3. The aurora borealis, sometimes called the northern lights, appears at night in northern latitudes.

4. Soy milk, a derivative of soybeans, is a good alternative for people who cannot drink dairy products.

5. The Code of Hammurabi, the earliest surviving system of civil laws, was written about 1800 B.C.

B Combine the sentences using appositive phrases.

1. Keisha Lewis is the new girl in our class. Next Friday Bill has a date with her.

_____

_____

2. Mrs. Franks teaches sculpture three evenings a week. She is a close friend of Mom's.

_____

_____

3. Hogans always face east. They are traditional dwellings of the Navajos.

_____

_____

4. Burke Hollow is my favorite Vermont village. It is especially pretty this time of year.

_____

_____

Grammar: Infinitives and Infinitive Phrases

Practice

An **infinitive** is a verb form preceded by the word *to* that acts as a noun, an adjective, or an adverb. An **infinitive phrase** is an infinitive with its modifiers or complements. Like infinitives, infinitive phrases can function as nouns, adjectives, or adverbs.

> Infinitive: <u>To disagree</u> would have been foolhardy.
>
> Infinitive Phrase: <u>To find a good mechanic</u> is no easy task.

A   Underline the infinitives or infinitive phrases in each sentence.

1. Frank wants to wait here for Mary.

2. Bonnie really wanted to win.

3. Above all, we wanted to be sure of his loyalty.

4. To accept stolen goods is a criminal offense.

5. Nick wanted to get seats near the stage.

6. Kiyo's decision was to stay on the team for one more year.

B   Underline the infinitive in each sentence. Then, write the part of speech it is used as on each line to the right.

1. Lawrence is the opponent to beat. _____

2. Where is a good place to eat? _____

3. The computer program is easy to learn. _____

4. Joe would be happy to help you. _____

5. The music began to play. _____

Grammar: Infinitives and Infinitive Phrases

Assess

A   Underline the infinitives or infinitive phrases in each sentence.

1. To plan a successful vacation takes a good deal of thought.

2. Cindy is only pretending to be ill.

3. Their responsibility is to recommend new products.

4. To fish for trout on a lazy day in summer is bliss.

5. We expect to live in this community for another five years.

6. To argue with Neil is to ask for trouble.

7. The management decided to open a new office in Boise.

8. People came from afar to see the memorial.

9. Politicians like to hear from the voters.

10. The ambition of everyone is to play in the finals.

B   Use each of the following infinitive phrases to write an original sentence.

1. to help others

_____

2. to travel across Africa

_____

3. to finish the job

_____

4. to relax in the pool

_____

5. to set the table

_____

Grammar: Common Usage Problems

Practice

Among and ***between:*** ***Among*** always implies three or more people or things. ***Between*** is generally used with only two people or things.

> Among: We shared the pizza <u>among</u> the four of us.

> Between: <u>Between</u> you and me, this pizza needs more cheese.

Like and ***as*** or ***as if:*** Do not use ***like*** when you should use ***as*** or ***as if.*** ***Like*** is a preposition that means "similar to." ***As*** and ***as if*** are conjunctions—words that begin clauses. Every clause has a subject and a verb. In the examples, the clauses are in bold type.

> Like: Frank's pizza tastes just <u>like</u> Mario's pizza.

>   Subj.   Verb
> As: Frank makes it just <u>as</u> **his grandfather did in Italy.**

>   Subj.   Verb
> As if: Mario is beginning to act <u>as if</u> **he finally has some competition.**

A   Complete each sentence correctly by inserting *between* or *among.*

1. Jo and her sisters were deciding _____ eating at home or going out.

2. They talked _____ themselves and ended up going out for pizza.

3. It was hard to decide _____ mushrooms, peppers, and sausage for the topping.

4. Jo and Bec had just enough money _____ them to pay the check.

B   Complete each sentence by correctly inserting *like, as,* or *as if.*

1. It looks _____ a new restaurant is opening on the corner.

2. I wonder if it will offer take-out _____ the old restaurant did.

3. Paul always says that there's nothing _____ home-cooking.

4. Andy acts _____ he could not survive without restaurants!

Grammar: Common Usage Problems

Assess

Circle the letter of the best answer.

1. In which item is *between* used correctly?

   A. Kansas is located between the Midwestern states.
   B. Between Ohio and Tennessee, you will find Kentucky.
   C. Michigan is located between three of the Great Lakes.

2. In which item is *among* used correctly?

   A. Among the two pine trees grows an apple tree.
   B. Many other trees grow among the house and the lake.
   C. Among the oak, the maple, and the spruce, which is tallest?

3. In which item is *like* used correctly?

   A. The apples finally looked like they were ripe.
   B. The farmer tested one; it tasted sweet like honey.
   C. Like he had expected, it was time to start harvesting.

4. Why is *as* used correctly in the following sentence?

   > As everyone knows, we elect a president every four years.

   A. It begins a clause.
   B. It is part of a prepositional phrase.
   C. It can be used in place of *like*.

5. Why is *as if* used correctly in the following sentence?

   > Unfortunately, it seems as if most of the voters stayed home.

   A. It begins a clause.
   B. It is part of a prepositional phrase.
   C. It can be used in place of *like*.

Spelling: Words with Affixes

Practice

Affixes are word parts that are attached to words to change their meaning or part of speech. Affixes attached to the ends of words are called **suffixes.** When you attach a suffix, the original word often has a small change in spelling.

Rules

Words ending in silent -e Drop the *e.*	wis<u>e</u> + -dom = **wis<u>d</u>om**
Words ending in consonant + y Change *y* to *i.*	accompan<u>y</u> + -ment = **accompan<u>i</u>ment**

Special Problems

A final letter may change.	consum<u>e</u> + -tion = **consum<u>p</u>tion** preten<u>d</u> + -ious = **preten<u>t</u>ious**
A final syllable may change.	ecsta<u>sy</u> + -ic = **ecsta<u>t</u>ic** gener<u>ous</u> + -ity = **gener<u>os</u>ity** maint<u>ain</u> + -ance = **maint<u>e</u>nance** procl<u>aim</u> + -ation = **procl<u>a</u>mation**
A final syllable may be dropped.	spontane<u>ous</u> + -ity = **spontane<u>i</u>ty**

In some cases, the original word stays the same, even when you think it might not:

pronounce + -able = pronounceable

For each item, join the suffix to the word in parentheses. Write the new word in the blank to complete the sentence.

1. (spontaneous + -ity) Joel rehearses all his remarks and never shows

_____ .

2. (pretend + -ious) Janine is _____ and acts as if she is better than others.

3. (ecstasy + -ic) Keishon was _____ when she received a nearly perfect report card.

Name _____ Date _____

Spelling: Words with Affixes

A For each item, add the suffix to the word to form a new word. Write the new word on the line provided.

1. ecstasy + -ic = _____

2. maintain + -ance = _____

3. spontaneous + -ity = _____

4. pretend + -ious = _____

5. wise + -dom = _____

B For each item, join the suffix to the word in parentheses. Write the word in the blank to complete the sentence.

1. (pronounce + -able) Is that word _____, or is it hard to say?

2. (accompany + -ment) She sang the song with piano _____.

3. (generous + -ity) Because of her _____, the hospital will have a new wing.

4. (proclaim + -tion) The king issued a _____ that banned loud music.

C Complete this paragraph by combining each numbered word and suffix into a new word. Write the new word on the line after the parentheses. Be sure to spell it correctly.

Yesterday the queen issued a (1 proclaim + -tion) _____.

She said that everyone must cut down on fuel (2 consume + -tion)

_____. Drivers can no longer travel alone but instead must

have an (3 accompany + -ment) _____ of passengers. Cars

need good (4 maintain + -ance) _____ so that they do not

waste fuel. People who care about the environment are (5 ecstasy + -ic)

_____ about the queen's new rules.

Writing: Description of a Movie Scene

Practice

A **description of a scene in a movie** is a picture in words that guides filmmakers when they make a movie. The screenwriter begins each scene with a few sentences about how the scene should look. A description of a scene in a movie should include the following:

- **concrete setting information and details:** when and where the scene takes place; what the weather and landscape or buildings look like if the scene is outdoors; what a room looks like, if the scene is indoors; anything that the audience is meant to see

- **descriptions of the characters:** information about the identity, appearance, and clothing of the people in the scene, as well as instructions about where they are at the beginning of the scene

- **instructions for the camera's movement:** A movie scene involves camera movement. For instance, the camera may begin with a **long shot** very far out from the scene or a **medium shot** creating an overview of the scene and then move in for a **close-up.** The camera may also **pan** from one side, giving a sweeping view of the scene.

Imagine that you are going to film an outdoor scene from your own life. Complete the following items.

1. Setting information:

   A. season _____   **B.** time of day _____

2. Outdoor location details:

   A. landscape/building details _____

   B. weather _____

3. Character information:

   A. identification of characters _____

   _____

   B. age, clothing, appearance of each: _____

   _____

   C. where each is at start of scene: _____

   _____

4. Camera instructions: _____

   _____

Writing: Description of a Movie Scene

Assess

A Circle one of the following subjects for a movie scene or choose a subject of your own. Then, complete the activities that follow.

the opening scene of a story, novel, or play you have read
a historical event
a moment in the life of someone you know
an especially enjoyable time in your family
a typical beginning of the school day at your school
a dream

1. Setting information (time, place, interior or exterior): _____

_____

_____

2. Location details: _____

_____

3. Character information (identification, age, clothing, appearance of each

character + where each is in the scene): _____

_____

_____

_____

4. Camera instructions: _____

B Write a paragraph describing the scene you planned above.

_____

_____

_____

_____

_____

Writing: Poem

Practice

A **poem** is a concentrated type of writing ideal for expressing strong emotion or imaginative description. Poems can cover many subjects and can express deep feelings, tell funny stories, and paint vivid pictures. They vary greatly in style, from traditional rhyming verse to modern free-form poems. The following features are in many poems:

- **definite form**—lines with clear beginnings and endings; often grouped in **stanzas**

- **rhythm**—pattern of stressed/unstressed syllables ("Quoth the Raven, Nevermore!")

- **rhyme**—words that echo each others' sounds (*beat* and *street*)

- **imagery**—words that refer to strong sensory experiences ("a shrieking wind")

- **figures of speech**—words that make imaginative connections, such as **similes,** which use the words *like* and *as* to compare unlike things ("The porcupine was as fat as a beachball"); **metaphors,** which say that one thing is another thing ("My heart was a bonfire"); **personification,** which gives human qualities to objects and animals ("The moon smiled down on our camp").

A Follow the instructions to complete each of the following items.

1. Two words that rhyme with *soar.* _____

2. A word or phrase that rhymes and has the same rhythm as "What a treat!"

_____

3. Two sense images for summer. _____

4. One figure of speech that compares something to a soldier. _____

_____

B On a separate sheet of paper, write a poem about an object you use all the time. Your poem may (but does not have to) rhyme and should include several images. It may (but does not have to) use figurative language.

Writing: Poem

A Follow the instructions to complete each of the following items.

1. Two sense images for the emotion of *joy:* _____

_____

2. Two figures of speech for the idea of *memory:* _____

_____

B Follow the instructions to write several short poems.

1. Describe an object in a poem of three lines. Line 1 has three syllables, line 2 has six syllables, and line 3 has eight syllables.

_____

_____

_____

2. Write a six-line poem in which something that is not human speaks. At least four of the lines should begin with the word *I.*

_____

_____

_____

_____

_____

_____

C On a separate sheet of paper, write a poem that tells a story, either true or fictional. Your poem may rhyme, but it does not have to.

Writing: Response to Literature

Practice

When you write a **response to literature,** you explain some aspect of a literary work and give your reaction to it. You should include the following:

- **thesis statement**—a short expression of your overall response to the work
- **a definite focus** either on a single aspect of the work (for example, the setting of a story) or an overall interpretation and evaluation of the work
- **specific evidence** from the work (often in the form of quotations) to develop and support your opinions

Here is an example of an introduction to a response to literature:

(**Thesis statement:**) <u>Carl Sandburg's poems are original and easy to understand. For these reasons, his poems are memorable.</u>
(**Focus:**) His <u>imagery</u> in particular is fresh and sticks with the reader.
(**Evidence:**) Most readers remember this image from his poem "Fog": <u>"The fog comes / on little cat feet."</u>

A Follow the instructions to complete each question.

1. Imagine that you read a short story called "The Breaks" that you really like. You loved the characters, and you want to read more stories about the main character, Nick. Write a thesis statement for the response to this story.

_____

_____

2. What focus should your response to the story about Nick have?

_____

B Match each thesis statement on the left with the lines from "The Rider," a poem by Naomi Shihab Nye, that best support it on the right.

1. _____ Nye's images are colorful and unusual.

2. _____ Nye uses simple, ordinary words.

A. "A boy told me / if he rollerskated fast enough / his loneliness couldn't catch up to him"

B. "while you float free into a cloud of sudden azaleas, luminous pink petals . . . "

Writing: Response to Literature

Assess

A Read the following haiku by Matsuo Bashō, translated by Daniel C. Buchanan. Then, answer each of the questions.

> Temple bells die out.
> The fragrant blossoms remain.
> A perfect evening!

1. If you were writing a response to this poem focusing on its imagery, or the word-pictures it presents, what words would you quote?

   _____

   _____

2. If your written response to this poem were to focus on the poem's emotion,

   what would your thesis statement be? _____

   _____

3. This poem is a haiku, which means that its first line has five syllables, its second line has seven syllables, and its third line has five syllables. Haiku usually present a single, strong image from nature that invites readers to imagine and think. If your written response were to focus on the appeal of this particular form of poetry, what would your thesis statement be?

   _____

   _____

B Write a paragraph responding to Bashō's poem.

_____

_____

_____

_____

_____

_____

_____

_____

Literary Analysis: Dialogue and Stage Directions

Practice

Dialogue is the conversation of characters in a play or short story. The dialogue advances the action of the plot and also shows the personality traits of the speakers. In a play, dialogue generally follows the name of the speaker and is not enclosed by quotation marks.

> DAVID. My sister is captain of her tennis team. Maybe she could teach you.
>
> SALLY. That would be awesome! Do you think she really would?

Stage directions are notes in the text of a play that describe how the work should be performed, or staged. Stage directions may describe one or more of the following: scenes, lighting, sound effects, and the appearance and physical actions of the characters.

> Scene i. The school cafeteria. It is lunchtime. The doors burst open.
>
> [*Enter Peter and Lateesha. They walk quickly to the far table.*]

A For each line of dialogue, write the name of the speaker. Then, explain what the line adds to your understanding of the events or the characters.

> JEN. Uncle, do you know why Rohan seems so sad?
>
> MONTY. I don't know the reason, and I can't persuade him to tell me.
>
> JEN. But have you really questioned him at all?
>
> MONTY. Yes, I have, and so have some other friends.

1. **Speaker** _____ **What I Learned** _____

2. **Speaker** _____ **What I Learned** _____

3. **Speaker** _____ **What I Learned** _____

4. **Speaker** _____ **What I Learned** _____

B You are writing a play about a high school student. In the opening scene, it is early morning in the kitchen. Write some stage directions to set the scene and tell how the character looks and moves.

_____

_____

_____

Literary Analysis: Dialogue and Stage Directions

Assess

A For each line of dialogue, write the name of the speaker. Then, explain what the line adds to your understanding of the events or the characters.

> CAL. The ship has arrived, bringing the prince and his new wife!
>
> LUCIA. Will they reside in the palace or at the country estate?
>
> CAL . I have heard tell that the princess is happiest in the city.
>
> LUCIA . Then, surely they will stay here, and we can expect many lively entertainments.

1. Speaker _____ **What I Learned** _____

2. Speaker _____ **What I Learned** _____

3. Speaker _____ **What I Learned** _____

4. Speaker _____ **What I Learned** _____

B For each item, write **D** if it is a line of dialogue or **SD** if it is a stage direction.

1. _____ The ship is here! The ship is here!

2. _____ [*Cal enters excitedly and runs up to Lucia*]

3. _____ [*People are beginning to line the dock. There is noise in the distance.*]

4. _____ If we don't hurry, we will miss getting a place at the front of the crowd.

5. _____ [*From the rear, the royal guards enter with trumpets blaring.*]

Literary Analysis: Blank Verse

Practice

Blank verse is unrhymed poetry with a regular meter, or pattern of beats. A line of blank verse follows these rules:

- It has five pairs of syllables called *feet*. Each foot is an iamb. An **iamb** consists of one unstressed syllable followed by a stressed syllable. In these examples, the stressed syllables are in capital letters with stress marks above them.

       /   /   /   /   /
     OcTOber WAS a MONTH of WIND and RAIN.

- Together the five iambic feet in the line of blank verse are called **iambic pentameter.** Notice in the preceding example that each of the five stressed syllables follows an unstressed syllable.

Shakespeare often uses prose and verse to show the social rank of the characters. Aristocratic or high-born characters usually speak in blank verse. Minor, low-born, or comic characters do not speak in verse. They speak in prose.

A In each of the following lines of blank verse, use stress marks (**/**) to indicate the stressed syllables. The first item has been done for you.

         /   /   /   /   /
1. And stay, good nurse, behind the abbey wall

2. When you are young, your life is full of fun.

3. The clock struck nine when I did send the nurse.

4. She rests at ease beneath some shady tree.

B Circle *H* if the speaker is "high-born" or *L* if "low-born." Explain your answer.

   As I told you, my young lady bid me inquire you out. What she bid me say, I will keep to myself; but first let me tell ye, if ye should lead her in a fool's paradise, it were a very gross kind of behavior, as they say.

H / L _____

_____

_____

Literary Analysis: Blank Verse

Assess

A Circle the correct answer to each question.

1. Which of the following is an element of blank verse?

   A. rhyming lines in iambic pentameter
   B. lines in iambic pentameter that do not rhyme
   C. lines that do not rhyme and have no particular meter

2. Which of the following lines is written in iambic pentameter?

   A. That beautiful, quiet woman, your old friend . . .
   B. The highwayman came riding, up to the old inn door.
   C. I'll tell thee as we pass, but this I pray . . .

3. In what way does Shakespeare often show the difference between high-born and low-born characters?

   A. High-born characters speak in blank verse, whereas the low-born speak in prose.
   B. High-born characters speak in rhyme, whereas the low-born speak without rhyme.
   C. Low-born characters speak in blank verse, whereas the high-born speak in prose.

B Insert stress lines above the stressed syllables in these lines of iambic pentameter. The first one has been done for you.

     /   /   /   /   /
1. We sat together at one summer's end.

2. More lovely are you than a velvet rose.

3. We met, we wooed, and made exchange of vow.

C Read each passage. Decide whether the speaker is an aristocrat or a commoner. In the space provided, write **H** for "high-born" or **L** for "low-born."

1. ____ The clock struck nine when I did send the nurse;
   In half an hour she promised to return.
   Perchance she cannot meet him. That's not so.

2. ____ Help me into some house, Benvolio, or I shall faint. A plague on both your houses! They have made worm's meat of me.

Literary Analysis: Dramatic Speeches

Practice

Plays often include these types of **dramatic speeches:**

- **Soliloquy:** a long speech in which a character—usually alone onstage—expresses his or her true thoughts or feelings. Soliloquies are unheard by other characters.

- **Aside:** a character revealing his or her true thoughts or feelings in a brief remark that is unheard by other characters

- **Monologue:** a long speech by one person. Unlike a soliloquy, a monologue is addressed to one or more other characters.

A Circle the letter of the type of dramatic speech described in each item.

1. Romeo gives a long speech to the Friar, pouring out his feelings for Juliet.

   A. monologue   **B.** soliloquy   **C.** aside

2. After her mother exits, and she is alone, Juliet gives a long speech expressing her worries about taking a sleeping potion that will make her appear dead.

   A. monologue   **B.** soliloquy   **C.** aside

B Read the following summaries of characters' speeches. Then, in the space provided, identify the type of dramatic speech the summary refers to: *soliloquy, aside,* or *monologue.*

1. _____ Tyrone's father asks him how the fight between Tyrone's hockey team and their opponents started at the game last night. Tyrone gives an angry and emotional speech, telling in detail how name-calling from both sides led to a general free-for-all.

2. _____ In a mystery drama, Glen, alone on stage, tries to deal with a difficult problem. In a speech, he describes hearing his sister and her husband planning a crime. Glen knows he should call in the police, but he expresses fears about hurting his family's good name and seeing his dear sister and brother-in-law go to prison.

3. _____ In a comedy about a family on camping trip, the father leads the others into a dark forest and loses his way. One of the children looks at the audience and says, "Uh oh, here we go again!"

Literary Analysis: Dramatic Speeches

Assess

A Circle the correct answer to each question.

1. Which of the following describes an aside?

   A. a character expressing his or her true thoughts or feelings in a short remark that is not heard by other characters
   B. a long speech by a character alone onstage, expressing thoughts and feelings
   C. a long speech given by one person and addressed to other characters

2. Which of the following describes a monologue?

   A. a character expressing his or her true thoughts or feelings in a short remark that is not heard by other characters
   B. a long speech by a character alone on stage, expressing thoughts and feelings
   C. a long speech given by one person and addressed to other characters

3. Which of the following describes a soliloquy?

   A. a character expressing his or her true thoughts or feelings in a short remark that is not heard by other characters
   B. a long speech by a character alone on stage, expressing thoughts and feelings
   C. a long speech given by one person and addressed to other characters

B Read the following summaries of characters' speeches in *Romeo and Juliet.* Then, in the space provided, identify the type of dramatic speech the summary refers to: *soliloquy, aside,* or *monologue.*

1. _____ Romeo has threatened to stab himself. In a long speech, Friar Lawrence criticizes Romeo and advises him to count his blessings.

2. _____ Juliet has told the Nurse she is on her way to Friar Lawrence to make her confession. After the Nurse leaves, Juliet, alone on the stage, pours out her feelings of dislike for the Nurse.

3. _____ Lady Capulet refers to Romeo as a villain. Without Lady Capulet hearing her, Juliet says that he may be a villain but no other man makes her heart ache so.

Literary Analysis: Dramatic Irony

Dramatic irony is a contradiction between what a character thinks and says and what you know to be true. For instance, in Act III of *Romeo and Juliet*, Capulet plans Juliet's wedding to Paris. He does not know what you know: Juliet is already married to Romeo.

Dramatic irony involves you emotionally in the story. It produces suspense, or a feeling of tension. You wonder when the character will find out what you already know.

A Write *DI* for each item that describes a case of dramatic irony. Write *NDI* for each item that does not contain dramatic irony.

1. _____ In a play, the character Kayla is searching for her long-lost brother. She asks for help from George. The two have a few adventures as they search. At the end of the play, they find a box of old papers and photographs. Examining these papers and photographs, they realize that George is Kayla's lost brother.

2. _____ In a play, John is the king's favorite son. When John is alone, the audience sees him put on a mask and ride in disguise to another kingdom nearby. There, he steals horses and destroys crops. The next day, people from the nearby kingdom complain to the king. The king tells them that he will find whoever is responsible and put him in jail forever. He does not realize he is talking about his own favorite son.

B For the following example of dramatic irony, explain the difference between what a character thinks or knows about the situation and what you know.

In a play, Sally and Linda are sisters. Troops invade their city, and Sally falls injured on the street. As the audience watches, an old woman opens her door and pulls Sally inside. Later, Linda comes looking for Sally. She stops at the old woman's house. She is about to knock. Just then, a friend runs up to her and says, "I think we may have found Sally at the hospital!" Linda leaves without knocking on the old woman's door.

What I Know _____

What the Character Knows or Thinks _____

Literary Analysis: Dramatic Irony

Assess

A Circle the correct answer to each question.

1. Which is the best definition of dramatic irony?

   A. an emotional story filled with suspense

   B. when the audience knows something that a character does not

   C. drama written to point out problems in society

   D. drama in which the main character suffers

2. What is one likely effect of dramatic irony?

   A. a feeling of suspense or tension

   B. an unhappy ending

   C. a case of mistaken identity

   D. a happy ending

B Write *DI* for each item that describes a case of dramatic irony. Write *NDI* for each item that does not contain dramatic irony.

1. _____ In a play, a husband and wife discuss owning a pet. The wife leaves. When the husband is alone onstage, he tells the audience that he will surprise his wife by buying her a dog. After he goes offstage, his wife comes onstage and says that she will surprise her husband by buying him a cat.

2. _____ In a play, Karl works late every night on his novel. Then, he falls in love with Carol. Carol does not like his novel or the fact that he writes. Karl decides he will no longer write. He sends his novel to a publisher and forgets all about it. He tries to convince Carol to marry him, but she refuses. Finally, Carol breaks up with him. Karl is very unhappy. That same day, he gets a letter telling him that his novel is being published.

C In the following example of dramatic irony, explain the difference between what a character thinks or knows about the situation and what you know.

In a play, Princess Karen decides to trade places with her maid, Terry. Terry will pretend to be the princess, and Karen will pretend to be the maid. The two travel to a foreign city. There, the prince falls in love with Karen. Karen is still pretending to be a maid, so the prince is worried. His father will not allow him to marry a maid, only a princess.

What I Know _____

What the Character Knows or Thinks _____

Literary Analysis: Tragedy and Motive

A **tragedy** is a drama in which the main character meets with disaster. The tragic hero's downfall is usually the result of one of the following:

- *fate,* or the idea of a preplanned, unavoidable destiny
- a serious character flaw
- some combination of both

Motive is an important element in a tragic hero's character. A character's motive is the reason for his or her thoughts or actions and usually leads to his or her downfall. Although tragedies are sad, they can also be uplifting. They show the greatness of the human spirit when faced with challenges.

A Read each plot description. On the line provided, write **T** if you think the action described is a tragedy. Write **NT** if you think it is not a tragedy.

1. _____ Abby pays to have her inkjet printer repaired; however, when she gets it back, it still does not work.

2. _____ Mr. Loman, once a top sales representative, quits his job when a younger man threatens his position. Because his pride has been hurt, Mr. Loman withdraws from his life and finally dies of misery.

3. _____ A king, while crossing a river, ignores his men's warnings and is swept away and drowned.

4. _____ Maria prepared a special dinner for her parents' anniversary. While carrying the main course to the dining room, the platter falls to the floor.

B On the line provided, list three words or phrases from this Prologue to *Romeo and Juliet* that hint that the play is a tragedy.

> From forth the fatal loins of these two foes
> > A pair of star-crossed[1] lovers take their life;
> Whose misadventured piteous overthrows[2]
> > Doth with their death bury their parents' strife.

[1] **star-crossed:** ill-fated by the unfavorable positions of the stars.

[2] **Whose . . . overthrows:** whose unfortunate, sorrowful destruction.

Literary Analysis: Tragedy and Motive

Assess

Read the following story. Then, answer the questions that follow.

Isabella met Javier when she was five and he was seven. Even at such a young age, Isabella knew that their meeting was fate and that someday they would marry. Blinded by her love for Javier, Isabella never thought about a future without him. For fifteen years, Isabella kept her love for Javier a secret. When war broke out in the eastern part of the country, Javier, like many other young men, decided to go off and fight. On the eve of his departure, Javier declared his love to Isabella and asked her to marry him. Overjoyed, she quickly agreed and demanded that they marry that very same day. Javier, however wanted to wait until he returned from the war. Six months passed without a word from Javier, and Isabella was consumed with worry. Then, on the anniversary of the day they first met, Isabella received word that Javier was killed in battle. Isabella was inconsolable and vowed to never marry. She died all alone at the age of eighty-seven, still wearing the ring her love had given her.

1. Would this story be considered a tragedy? Explain.

_____

_____

_____

2. What words or phrases in the passage are characteristic of tragedies?

_____

_____

3. What possible motives does Isabella have for wanting to marry Javier the same day he asks her?

_____

_____

4. Does Isabella have a tragic flaw? Explain.

_____

_____

_____

Literary Analysis: Archetypal Theme

Practice

An **archetype** is a character, plot, image, or setting that appears in literature from around the world and throughout history. One reason that archetypes are so widespread is that they relate to general truths about life. Archetypes are also said to reflect the workings of the human mind.

Common archetypes include the following:

- **Characters:** the hero, the outcast, the evil stepmother, the wise prophet or sage
- **Plot types:** the quest or search, the task, the journey, the birth of the hero, the triumph of good over evil
- **Symbols:** water as a symbol for life; a rose as a symbol for love; fire as a symbol for power

A **theme** is the central idea, message, or insight of a literary work. **Archetypal themes** are those that develop or explore fundamental ideas. One example of an archetypal theme is ill-fated love, which appears in folklore, mythology, and literature from all over the world.

In the spaces provided, put a check mark to identify the items that are archetypal themes. If an item is not an archetypal theme, leave the space blank.

_____ **1.** the conflict of good vs. evil

_____ **2.** a king's wise adviser

_____ **3.** the birth and recognition of a hero

_____ **4.** a young person's journey of discovery

_____ **5.** a flame symbolizing remembrance

_____ **6.** a child's first bike ride

_____ **7.** an evening news broadcast

_____ **8.** planting a garden

_____ **9.** a young person's quest for identity

_____ **10.** the marriage of young lovers

Literary Analysis: Archetypal Theme

Assess

A   In the spaces provided, give one example of an archetype for each category shown.

1. Character _____

2. Plot Type _____

3. Symbol _____

4. Theme _____

B   In the spaces provided, put a check mark to identify the items that qualify as archetypal themes. If an item does not qualify, leave the space blank.

_____ **1.** coming of age

_____ **2.** the victory of good over evil

_____ **3.** a child's visit to the circus

_____ **4.** disguise in a party costume

_____ **5.** a hero's quest

_____ **6.** broadcast of a football game on TV

_____ **7.** humanity vs. nature

_____ **8.** a rose as a symbol of love

_____ **9.** publication of a popular new novel

_____**10.** fathers and sons

Reading: Summarize

Practice

Summarizing is briefly stating in your own words the main points in a piece of writing. Pausing to summarize what you have read helps you to check your understanding before you read further. A good summary is much shorter than the original. It includes only the main idea and the most important details.

Read the example. Then, circle the letter of the best answer for each question.

Original

The freshman class at Springfield High School held a fundraiser last Saturday, November 19. The fundraiser was held in the Springfield High gym. The weather was nice and sunny, and the event was a sell-out, with ticket sales and donations totaling $495. The money will go toward the annual freshman picnic, which will be held on May 19. The most exciting part of the evening was a performance by the band Spring Break. This talented foursome consists of Ray Lopez on rhythm guitar and vocals, Ben Bradley on lead guitar, Kira Sax on bass and vocals, and Terrence Owens on drums.

Summary

Saturday's fundraiser at Springfield High School raised $495 for the annual freshman picnic. A performance by the band Spring Break was a highlight of the sold-out benefit.

1. What is the main idea of the original example?

   A. The picnic is on May 19.

   B. The freshman class held a fundraiser.

   C. Spring Break performed.

   D. Terrence Owens plays the drums.

2. Which of these sentences gives the most important information?

   A. The weather was nice and sunny. . . .

   B. The fundraiser was held in the Springfield High gym.

   C. The event was a sell-out, with ticket sales and donations totaling $495.

   D. This talented foursome consists of Ray Bradley on lead guitar. . . .

3. What word could be deleted from the summary without taking away important information?

   A. fundraiser

   B. annual

   C. freshman

   D. sold-out

4. Why is the date of the freshman picnic not included in the summary?

   A. Everyone already knows it.

   B. The report is on the band.

   C. It is the main idea of the paragraph.

   D. It is not a main idea.

Reading: Summarize

A   Read the following passage. Then, answer the question and complete the activities that follow.

Our bodies are adapted to Earth's gravity. Our muscles are strong in order to overcome gravity as we walk and run. Our inner ears use gravity to keep us upright. And because gravity wants to pull all our blood down into our legs, our hearts are designed to pump hard to get blood up to our brains.

In space, the much weaker gravity makes the human body change in many unexpected ways. In microgravity, your blood is rerouted, flowing from the legs, which become thin and sticklike, to the head, which swells up. The extra liquid in your head makes you feel like you're hanging upside down or have a stuffed-up nose.

—from "Life Without Gravity" by Robert Zimmerman

1. What is the main idea of the passage? _____

_____

2. Name two details that support the main idea. _____

_____

3. Write a brief summary of the passage on the lines provided. _____

_____

_____

_____

_____

_____

_____

_____

_____

_____

Reading: Analyze Text Information

Texts about the same topic can contain very different information. Someone writing about music, for example, could write about how music is composed, why people make music, or a favorite kind of music. It is important, then, to **analyze text information** to determine a text's main idea and the author's purpose. Here are some things to look for when you analyze text information:

■ What does the author want you to understand? (main idea)

■ How does the author support the main idea? (supporting details)

■ Is the author trying to describe or explain something, to persuade readers to take a position, or to tell a story? (author's purpose)

Read the following excerpt. Then, answer the questions that follow.

Visit Mexico!

Mexico has beaches, mountains, history, culture, and so much more! It is a foreign country on our own doorstep, filled with charm and excitement.

Mexico City, the capital of Mexico, is a special treat. It is the oldest city in North America. Built more than 450 years ago by the Aztecs, visitors can still see ancient pyramids in a bustling, modern city.

1. What is the main idea of this brochure?

_____

2. What details support the main idea?

_____

_____

3. What is the author's purpose? Explain your answer.

_____

_____

Reading: Analyze Text Information

Assess

Read this excerpt from an atlas entry. Then, answer the questions that follow.

Mexico

Quick Facts

Capital: Mexico City
Major Language: Spanish
Population: 109,000

Location

Mexico forms a link between the United States, to its north, and Central America, to its south. The Pacific Ocean borders Mexico on the west, while the Gulf of Mexico and the Caribbean Sea form its eastern border.

Place

Mexico is a narrow country with large mountain ranges near its East and West coasts. Because it lies on several of Earth's tectonic plates, Mexico has many volcanoes and has been rocked by major earthquakes.

Region

Mexico's terrain is so varied that it has several climate zones. The south has a tropical climate, while the north is more temperate. The north also has many dry areas, while the south has a higher annual rainfall. In addition, the climate in the mountains varies by altitude, with the lowest temperatures in the highest mountains and the highest temperatures near the coasts.

1. What is the main idea of this atlas entry?

_____

2. What details support the main idea?

_____

3. What is the author's purpose? Explain your answer.

_____

4. What might you expect to see in the rest of this entry?

_____

Vocabulary: Word roots -loque- and prefixes trans-, pro-, en-, and ambi-

Practice

A **root** is the basic unit of meaning of a word. A **prefix** is one or more syllables added to the beginning of a word or word root to form a new word with a different meaning. Study these examples.

Example:

Root or Prefix	Meaning	Words with the Root
-loque- [root]	talk, speak, say	eloquent, loquacious
trans- [prefix]	across, over, through	transport, transition
pro- [prefix]	forward	proceed, proposal
en- [prefix]	in, into, within	engraved, entreaty
ambi- [prefix]	both	ambiguous, ambidextrous

A   Circle the letter of the correct answer to each question.

1. When would an actor deliver a <u>soliloquy</u>?

   A. in a scene with other characters
   B. while alone on stage

2. What does it mean to say that a material is <u>translucent</u>?

   A. the material blocks out light
   B. light can pass through the material

3. If you are <u>ambivalent</u> about a decision, how do you feel?

   A. you are drawn toward more than one possible choice
   B. you feel convinced that a single choice is the right one

4. What does it mean if someone has <u>entrusted</u> you with a duty?

   A. that person expects you to carry out the duty
   B. that person does not believe that you will carry out the duty

5. When would the <u>prologue</u> to a play be presented?

   A. at the beginning of the play
   B. at the end of the play

Vocabulary: Word roots *-loque-* and prefixes *trans-, pro-, en-,* and *ambi-*

Assess

A Write the word from the list that best fits the meaning of each sentence.

ambitious   entangled   propelled   loquacious   transmit

1. She was so _____ that it took her ten minutes to finish a sentence.

2. I used a fax machine to _____ the photos to all my relatives.

3. The motion of the oars _____ the boat through the water.

4. Unfortunately, one of the oars became _____ in some weeds and got stuck.

5. The _____ teenager was determined to found a successful business before he was thirty years old.

B Revise each sentence so that the underlined vocabulary word is used logically. Be sure not to change the vocabulary word.

1. I was certain of his intentions because he answered all my questions <u>ambiguously</u>.

_____

2. The audience was very bored by the politician's <u>eloquent</u> speech.

_____

3. The teacher said to <u>proceed</u> with our experiment, so we waited for further instructions.

_____

4. I was <u>enraged</u> by her kind remarks about my family.

_____

5. The vegetables were all home-grown, so we had to pay to <u>transport</u> them to our house.

_____

Grammar: Participles and Participial Phrases

Practice

A **participle** is a verb form that is used as an adjective. **Present participles** end in *-ing*. The **past participles** of regular verbs end in *-ed*.

A **participial phrase** is a group of words that functions as an adjective in the sentence and contains a participle.

> Present Participle: the *pounding* noise
>
> Past Participle: *troubled* child
>
> Participial Phrase: *Feeling restless*, I took a walk around the harbor.

For each sentence, underline the participles or participial phrases it contains. Then, circle the noun each participle or participial phrase modifies.

Example: Has anyone kept a record of all the (money) spent on this project?

1. Dressed in his old uniform, Dad participated in the Memorial Day parade.

2. Working hard for six months, Gladys saved enough money for a Caribbean cruise.

3. Hank is sitting beside the man reading a newspaper.

4. Any car parked illegally in an alley will be towed immediately.

5. Yesterday the whole family attended the concert held at Stanley Park.

6. Gasping for breath, the swimmer was pulled from the churning water.

7. At the end of the month, any toys left in the playroom will be given to charity.

8. Did he get all of those weary cattle driven safely to the range?

9. The approaching storm caught us by surprise as it raced over the bluffs to our left.

10. The letter announcing my prize in the contest arrived today.

Name _____ Date _____

For each sentence, change the italicized words into a participle modifying the noun at the beginning of the phrase. Write your new phrase on the line provided.

Example: How could the birds stay on the branches *that were blowing*?
Answer: blowing branches

1. The lion *that was roaring* scared him.

_____

2. The pipe *that had broken* leaked water.

_____

3. Adam will not wear a shirt *that is torn*.

_____

4. She claimed she had a parrot *that talked*.

_____

5. A person *who is depressed* is not much fun.

_____

6. The condor *that was soaring through the air* excited the crowd.

_____

7. It is an idea *that makes someone excited*.

_____

8. We saw a movie *that depressed everyone*.

_____

9. Children *who were crying* were there.

_____

10. I love to view the stars *that are shining*.

_____

Grammar: Gerunds and Gerund Phrases

Practice

A **gerund** is a form of a verb that acts as a noun. It can function as a subject, an object, a predicate noun, or the object of a preposition. A **gerund phrase** is a gerund and its modifiers. A gerund phrase also acts as a noun.

Subject: *Swimming* is fun.

Direct Object: Don dislikes *arguing*.

Predicate Noun: His hobby is *gardening*.

Object of the Preposition: Those shoes are perfect for *jogging*.

Underline the gerund or gerund phrase in each sentence.

1. Is there a reward for returning your ring?

2. Jousting in tournaments was once popular in Europe.

3. We reward our employees by giving them bonuses.

4. Hunting on these premises is not allowed.

5. I hate raking leaves in the fall.

6. Decorating our new apartment has been expensive.

7. The people stopped listening to the announcer.

8. Bill improved his grade by studying.

9. Donnie's biggest fear was opening the cellar door.

10. Hearing people shout in study hall annoys me.

Grammar: Gerunds and Gerund Phrases

Assess

Underline the gerund or gerund phrase in each sentence. Then, tell whether it is used as a subject, direct object, predicate noun, or object of a preposition.

Example: Peter and Nancy have always hated washing dishes.
Answer: washing dishes—direct object

1. Her main objective in life is becoming a successful writer.

   _____

2. I resented paying ten dollars for a second-hand sweater.

   _____

3. Do not punish Stan for forgetting his homework.

   _____

4. Linda cannot stand waiting for anyone.

   _____

5. Rita's big mistake was quitting her job.

   _____

6. Tina's favorite pastime is sitting around the snack shop.

   _____

7. Frightening the neighbors was not their intention.

   _____

8. Ask Coach Nelson about postponing the tournament.

   _____

9. By leaving early, we avoided the rush-hour traffic.

   _____

10. My brother's summer project is painting the dock.

    _____

Grammar: Combine Sentences With Phrases

Practice

To avoid a series of too many simple sentences, combine some sentences by converting the idea in one sentence into a modifying phrase in another sentence. Sentences can be combined by using appositive phrases or verbal phrases. When adding a modifying phrase to a sentence, place the phrase close to the word it modifies to avoid confusion.

A Combine each pair of sentences into one sentence by using a modifying phrase.

Example: Lawrence is an expert fisherman. He has won many fishing contests.
Answer: Lawrence, an expert fisherman, has won many fishing contests.

1. The breeze was coming in from the north. It cooled the sweltering island.

_____

2. Robert Frost wrote "Birches." He was a New England poet.

_____

3. Ted refused to put up the tent. He was worried about spraining his back.

_____

4. The council will meet in Frankfort. Frankfort is the capital of Kentucky.

_____

B Underline the misplaced modifier in each sentence.

1. Lazar likes the picture of the ferryboat that you sent him.

2. She needs someone to do the work badly.

3. The mangy yellow dog followed the car with a stubby tail.

4. After they had been sharpened, the students distributed the pencils.

5. The visitors usually ride the mules staying at the lodge.

6. The angry lion growled a warning at the hunter with bared teeth.

Grammar: Combine Sentences With Phrases

A Combine each pair of sentences into one sentence by using a modifying phrase.

1. Sarah was blinking continuously. She said she had something in her eye.

_____

2. Al was sipping a glass of tea. He daydreamed peacefully.

_____

3. Mr. Taylor is my neighbor. He is a famous civil rights lawyer.

_____

4. Bonnie waited around until five o'clock. She was hoping to get a chance to speak to Mrs. Gleason.

_____

5. Earthquakes and volcanic eruptions can cause tsunamis. Tsunamis are large, rapidly moving waves.

_____

B Rewrite each sentence, correcting its misplaced modifier.

1. Burnt to a cinder, I could not eat the marshmallow.

_____

2. The actor saddled his horse in faded blue jeans.

_____

3. The pears were eaten by the children that had been left on the kitchen table.

_____

4. The woman informed the police that the thief had escaped by phone.

_____

Writing: Letter to an Advice Columnist

Practice

People sometimes write **letters to advice columnists** to ask for help with solving personal problems. They ask columnists to make suggestions to help them decide what to do. Advice columnists usually print readers' letters in a newspaper or other publication and then respond by giving their ideas about what the readers might do to improve their situations. Typical topics for letters to advice columnists include difficult relationships, family troubles, and conflicts at work.

When you write a letter to an advice columnist, you should

- introduce or describe yourself (you do not have to use your real name);
- explain your problem clearly and briefly; and
- ask for advice.

Read the following letter to an advice columnist. Then, answer the questions and complete the activities that follow.

Dear Annie,

I am a sixteen-year-old boy. I got my first after-school job this year. I found out today that a coworker has been saying things about me that are not true. He told others at work, including our boss, that I am rude to customers and that I am lazy. I am actually very polite to customers and work very hard. The boss is never around, so she probably believes my coworker. What should I do?

Signed, John M.

1. Who is John? What kind of person is he? _____

_____

_____

2. What is the problem John is trying to solve? _____

_____

_____

3. What advice might the columnist give to John? _____

_____

_____

Writing: Letter to an Advice Columnist

Assess

A Choose a problem to write about in a letter to an advice columnist. You may write as yourself or make up a problem that someone like you might have. Then, answer the questions and complete the activities that follow.

1. What problem will you write about? _____

2. How will you organize your letter? _____

_____

_____

_____

3. Write your letter on the lines below.

_____

_____

_____

_____

_____

_____

_____

_____

_____

_____

_____

B On a separate sheet of paper, write a possible response from an advice columnist.

Writing: Parody

Parody is writing that imitates and makes fun of another piece of writing. Here are a few ways you can create a parody.

- parodying **style**—the way a writer uses words. To make fun of a serious style, you could use that style to describe silly events.

- parodying **characters, ideas, and events**—You might parody Romeo and Juliet by changing one or two facts about them. For example, you might describe them as 40-year-olds, not teenagers. You might parody ideas and events by having Juliet reject Romeo instead of returning his love.

Here is an example that parodies both Shakespeare's style and his characters.

> Hark! What baseball through yonder window breaks? / It is that punk, Romeo—he never could throw straight!

Read the following passage. Then, complete the activities.

"Oh, darling!" said Bruno. "My love for you is far, far deeper than the ocean. Has anyone ever found the bottom of the ocean? My love is far, far wider than the Grand Canyon. Has anyone ever jumped across the Grand Canyon?"

"Oh, Bruno," said Marta. "You are so romantic! I could listen to you forever!"

"And I could speak to you forever, Marta my dearest," said Bruno. "But come, I have a table waiting for us at the best restaurant in town. Shall we?" He helped Marta into her fur coat and led her to his sports car.

1. Describe these elements in the passage. Give an example for each.

   A. how Bruno speaks to Marta

   _____

   B. the way Bruno and Marta act with each other

   _____

2. Write a few sentences of a parody of this passage. In your parody, imitate and make fun of at least two of the elements listed above.

   _____

   _____

   _____

Writing: Parody

Read the following passage. Then, complete the activities.

"Engage engines!" barked Commander Linda Spackle, captain of the Starship *Excel*.

"Engines engaged!" yelled Officer Yurt from her station.

"Our mission is to prevent the Zone from taking over that star cluster," said Commander Spackle, pointing at the glowing screen. "We have no time for chatter! Everyone to work!"

Suddenly, the starship was rocked by an explosion. Alarms began to go off.

"Commander, we've been hit by a pulse bomb," yelled Officer Smith.

"The work of the Zone, I am sure!" muttered Commander Spackle, grinding her teeth. She brought her right fist down on her left palm. "We have no choice. Activate the Draconic Shield."

"But Commander," gasped Officer Yurt. "Use of the Draconic Shield within 50 parsecs of a star colony is a clear violation of—"

"When I need advice about the law, I'll call a lawyer," said Commander Spackle, her voice dripping with sarcasm. "When I need to protect my ship, I'll use any means I have. Now, move!" She shouted the last words.

"Aye, aye, Commander," said Officer Yurt, giving a salute.

1. Describe these elements of the passage. Give an example for each.

A. the way Commander Linda Spackle speaks and gestures

_____

B. how the commander acts with Officer Yurt and the rest of the crew

_____

C. the type of problems the commander faces

_____

D. the type of weapons and ships used in the story

_____

2. On a separate sheet of paper, write a brief parody of this passage. In your parody, tell what happens next in the story. Make fun of at least three of the elements listed above.

Writing: Editorial

An **editorial** is an article in a newspaper or other publication that gives an editor's opinion on an issue of concern. Editors often share their opinions about politics, social problems, current events, and more.

In an editorial, the writer should

- explain the issue or event being discussed;
- clearly state an opinion;
- support the opinion with facts and examples.

Read the following editorial from a school newspaper. Then, answer the questions that follow.

Recently, there was a near-tragedy in the school's parking lot. A reckless driver was in too much of a hurry to leave the campus at lunchtime and almost mowed down an innocent student who was walking to his car. I am as concerned as anyone else about this frightening incident. However, I do not agree with the principal's suggestion to close the campus. He does not want to allow students to leave the school for lunch anymore. I do not think this is the best way to make our parking lot safer.

1. What is the issue or event being discussed in this editorial? _____

_____

2. What is the writer's opinion on the issue? _____

_____

3. What is missing from this editorial? _____

_____

4. What are some reasons that the writer might have given to support his or

her opinion? _____

_____

_____

_____

_____

Writing: Editorial

Imagine that you are the editor of the school's newspaper. Identify a current event or issue about which you have an opinion. Complete the activities that follow.

1. Identify a current event or issue about which you have a strong opinion.

_____

2. State your opinion about this topic or issue. _____

_____

3. List three facts, examples, or reasons that support your opinion. _____

_____

_____

_____

4. Write the first paragraph or two of your editorial on the following lines.

_____

_____

_____

_____

_____

_____

_____

_____

_____

_____

Writing: Abstract

An **abstract** is a short summary of a longer piece of writing. Abstracts help readers decide if they want to read the longer works. To write an abstract, follow these steps.

- Write a topic sentence that briefly states the main idea of the longer work.
- Pick out two to five important details that directly support the main idea.
- Write a concluding sentence that summarizes the author's point.

A Complete the activities to help you prepare to write an abstract. You may choose any story, play, or novel you have read so far this year. Or, you may choose instead to write an abstract of a television show or movie you have seen recently.

1. **Title of work** _____

2. **Main idea** _____

3. **Important details** _____

_____

_____

_____

_____

_____

4. **Concluding sentence** _____

_____

B On the lines below, write a one-paragraph abstract of the work you chose.

_____

_____

_____

_____

Writing: Abstract

Assess

Read the following article. Then, write an abstract on the lines.

Shakespeare's Globe Theater

Most of Shakespeare's plays were performed in his company's Globe theater. The Globe was a public theater. Public theaters were built around roofless courtyards without artificial light. Performances, therefore, were given only during daylight hours. Surrounding the courtyard were three levels of galleries with benches on which wealthier playgoers sat. Less wealthy spectators, called groundlings, stood and watched a play from the courtyard, which was called the pit.

No one is certain exactly what the Globe looked like, though Shakespeare tells us it was round or octagonal. It was open to the sky and held between 2,500 and 3,000 people. The stage was a platform that extended into the pit. Actors entered and left the stage from doors located behind the platform. The second-level gallery right above the stage was used as an upper stage for scenes such as the balcony scene in *Romeo and Juliet*.

There was no scenery in the theaters of Shakespeare's day. As a result, one scene could follow quickly after another. However, the actors wore elaborate Elizabethan clothing. Audiences usually enjoyed every minute of the resulting fast-paced and colorful productions.

Abstract

_____

_____

_____

_____

_____

_____

_____

_____

_____

Writing: Persuasive Letter

Practice

A **persuasive letter** is meant to convince readers to agree with the writer's point of view or to take some action. A persuasive letter usually includes these features.

- An explanation of the issue or situation that calls for actions or opinions
- A thesis statement (sentence that states the writer's position or point of view)
- Supporting facts and ideas that help convince readers to agree or take action
- A strong conclusion

Read the following persuasive letter. Then, answer the questions that follow.

Dear Mom and Dad,

   I would like you to extend my curfew. I believe I am old enough now to stay out later, particularly on the weekends. Since I turned sixteen, I have been very responsible. I have followed your rules, and I believe I have shown you that you can trust me. Well, there was that one time that I went to the movies without permission. I am always careful, and I am a good driver. I have a great group of friends who also have curfews.

                                                    Sincerely,

                                                    Christina

1. What is Christina trying to convince her parents to think or do? _____

_____

2. Which of the following is missing from Christina's persuasive letter?

   A. identification of her intended audience
   B. a clear statement of what she wants her parents to think or do
   C. support for her argument
   D. a concluding sentence

3. Which sentence could Christina remove to make her arguments stronger?

   A. I would like you to extend my curfew.
   B. Since I turned sixteen, I have been very responsible.
   C. I have followed your rules, and I believe I have shown you that you can trust me.
   D. Well, there was that one time that I went to the movies without permission.

234 Reading Kit

Writing: Persuasive Letter

Assess

Circle one of the following topics. Fill in a specific choice if necessary. Then, complete the activities that follow.

School dress code

Lowering the voting age

Music piracy (downloading songs illegally)

A political candidate: _____

A current event or issue: _____

The best author of all time: _____

1. Identify your audience. _____

2. Write a thesis statement (topic sentence) that clearly identifies what you want your readers to do or agree with.

   _____

   _____

3. List three supporting facts, examples, or emotional appeals you can use to convince readers to agree with you or to take action.

   _____

   _____

4. Write the first paragraph or two of your persuasive letter on the following lines.

   _____

   _____

   _____

   _____

   _____

   _____

   _____

Writing: How-to Essay

A **how-to essay** provides step-by-step instructions that tell readers how to accomplish a specific task. How-to essays should feature the following elements.

- specific factual information presented logically and accurately
- step-by-step directions for each stage in the process
- examples and definitions that demonstrate key concepts
- instructions that anticipate readers' questions

Read the following how-to essay. Then, answer the questions and complete the activities that follow.

This amazing card trick will astound your friends. Before you do the trick, look at the bottom card in the deck and remember it. Ask a friend to pick a card, look at it, and put it on top of the deck. Then, have your friend cut the deck. Turn the cards over one at a time. Watch for the card that was on the bottom of the deck. When you come to it, the next card will be the one your friend picked, but don't say a word. Just remember it and keep turning. When all the cards have been turned over, say that you can't seem to find your friend's card. Ask him to shuffle the deck and say you'll try once more. After the cards have been shuffled, turn them over one at a time until you come to your friend's card. Pick it up and hand it to him.

1. What does this essay tell readers how to do? _____

_____

2. Transitional words and phrases (such as *first*, *next*, or *after that*) help readers follow step-by-step instructions. List three transitional words and phrases from the how-to essay above.

_____

_____

3. The conclusion of this how-to essay is weak. It simply ends with the final instruction. Write a strong concluding sentence that could be added to the end of this essay.

_____

_____

_____

Writing: How-to Essay

Assess

Circle one of the following topics. Then, answer the questions and complete the activities that follow.

how to make a hamburger   how to set up a tent

how to bag groceries   how to wash a car

how to paddle a canoe   how to become physically fit

1. On the lines below, list all the materials, tools, and information your readers will need to accomplish the activity you plan to describe.

_____

_____

_____

_____

2. List the five main steps a person would have to complete to accomplish the task. Write them in the order they should occur.

_____

_____

_____

_____

3. What problems might your readers have while trying to accomplish the activity? How might they solve each problem?

_____

_____

_____

_____

Literary Analysis: Comedy

Practice

A **comedy** is a funny play, movie, or other dramatic work. Comedies have happy endings. They are written to make people laugh. Here are some elements used in comedy.

- **comic situations**—funny situations involving tricks played on characters, misunderstandings, and mistakes about who somebody is. For example, characters might play a prank on Joe, an ordinary worker, by telling him he is the king. When he says he is not the king, they tell him that a long illness has made him forget who he is. They call him "Your Majesty" and give him anything he wants.
- **dramatic irony**—a situation where the audience knows something that a character does not.
- **funny names**
- **witty dialogue**—conversations, speeches, or remarks that are funny. Witty dialogue includes the clever insults traded by two characters. It includes one character's wisecracks.

For each summary, circle the elements of comedy that appear in it. You may circle more than one element. Then, underline one example in the summary of each element you have circled.

1. Sara tells Jane about her plan to trick Bob. Bob is hiding in the closet and hears every word. Later, he goes along with the trick. Sara thinks she is fooling him, but the audience knows better.

Element: comic situation / dramatic irony / funny names / witty dialogue

2. **Professor Humphrey Wheezer:** Lance Dashboard, you are a dense ox.

   Lance Dashboard: Ten socks? Where?

   Professor Humphrey Wheezer: I said, you are a dense ox.

   Lance Dashboard: Professor, I don't see even one sock. Are you feeling OK?

Element: comic situation / dramatic irony / funny names / witty dialogue

3. Ashley and Sara are mad at each other, so they are not speaking. By accident, they take the same elevator. The elevator breaks down, and the two are stuck together for an hour.

Element: comic situation / dramatic irony / funny names / witty dialogue

Literary Analysis: Comedy

Assess

A Circle the correct answer to each question.

1. Which is the best definition of a comic situation?

    A. when the audience knows something that a character does not

    B. a serious situation that occurs because of a prank

    C. a case of mistaken identity or of a character who does not know enough

    D. a funny situation involving a prank or a misunderstanding

2. Which is the best definition of dramatic irony?

    A. when the audience knows something that a character does not

    B. a funny situation involving a prank, a misunderstanding, or mistaken identities

    C. a serious situation that occurs because of a prank or a misunderstanding

    D. a case of mistaken identity or of a prank

B For each summary, circle the elements of comedy that appear in it. You may circle more than one. Then, underline an example of each element you circled.

1. Sam's roommate Jeff has invited his cousin to stay with them. Their apartment is small, so Sam is not looking forward to the visit. Later, Sam meets Sally. He complains about Jeff's cousin to her. Neither Sam nor the audience know that Sally IS Jeff's cousin.

Element: comic situation / dramatic irony / funny names / witty dialogue

2. **Dr. Prod:** Let me take your pulse.

    Harry Clunker: You're already taking my money. Sure, take my pulse, too.

    Dr. Prod: Hmmm. Normal. OK, I need your pressure, too.

    Harry Clunker: Doctor, pressure like mine you don't need.

Element: comic situation / dramatic irony / funny names / witty dialogue

Literary Analysis: Satire

Practice

Satire is writing that makes fun of something. Writers write satire to make people laugh. Some also hope to change the way people act. Writers of satire use these devices:

- **exaggeration**—making something look bigger, more extreme, or more important than it actually is. Writers use exaggeration to make people laugh. They also use exaggeration to make people's faults and society's problems more obvious.

- **sarcasm** or **irony**—language that means the opposite of what it says. For example, a writer may mention the "wonderful complexity" of a plan that is so complicated that no one can understand it.

Read each item. Write *Satire* if it is a satire. Write *No satire* if it is not. If it is a satire, write who or what it is making fun of. Then, circle one example of irony in the item and underline one example of exaggeration.

1. _____ Many Americans are concerned about keeping fit. More and more of them get their exercise by jogging. Sporting goods stores now sell a variety of equipment for joggers. For example, specially designed exercise shoes are very popular. Some of these running shoes have special bouncy material in the soles. Track suits with strips of reflective cloth are also in demand. These suits ensure that the jogger will be seen by drivers, even when it is dark out. Joggers spend millions of dollars every year to ensure that they have the latest and best equipment.

Target of satire: _____

2. _____ Another victim of the jogging craze has been reported. Yesterday, Ms. Irene Phelps, 72 years old, laced up her brand-new pair of Atomic sneakers and prepared for her morning run. Ms. Phelps apparently did not realize that these sneakers now come equipped with a "rocket-assist" feature. After running a few feet at her usual speed, Ms. Phelps accidentally triggered the sneakers' ignition system and was immediately launched over a fence and across her neighbor's yard. Fortunately, Ms. Phelps was wearing her Atomic jogging suit at the time. This suit is designed to protect its wearer from rain, snow, radioactivity, and on-coming trucks, so Ms. Phelps was barely scratched.

Target of satire: _____

Literary Analysis: Satire

A For each question, circle the letter of the best answer.

1. What is the main purpose of satire?

    A. to make fun of the foolishness of a person or society

    B. to inform people of the facts

    C. to help people understand themselves better

    D. to persuade people to buy a product

2. Which of the following is the best definition of *irony*?

    A. words that mean what they say

    B. words that mean the opposite of what they say

    C. words used to criticize society

    D. words used to make fun of a person's foolishness

B Read each item. Write *Satire* if it is a satire. Write *No satire* if it is not. If it is a satire, write who or what it is making fun of. Then, circle one example of irony in the item and underline one example of exaggeration.

1. _____ Computers keep getting smaller and more powerful. The first computers filled entire rooms. Then came desktop computers, which fit in a box the size of small television set. More recently, we have seen computers that fit in the palm of a person's hand. Because of the shrinking size of computers, people can now use their cell phones to take pictures, send e-mail, or to surf the Internet. Soon, people will run every part of their lives from a small handheld computer.

Target of satire: _____

2. _____ Computers keep getting smaller and more powerful. My new computer can send e-mail and record phone calls at the same time. Because the computer is about the size of a thumbtack, though, it is easy to hit a wrong key. The other morning at around 5 A.M., I hit a wrong key and turned on all the television sets in my neighborhood. When the police came, the computer took several great pictures of them. Unfortunately, it must have fallen out of my pocket in the back of the squad car. I don't know how I'll live without it.

Target of satire: _____

Reading: Draw Conclusions

Practice

A **conclusion** is a logical opinion or idea you reach by pulling together several facts or details. To draw conclusions about a written work, look for important details or clues. Then use your own prior knowledge and experience to fill in the gaps as you piece together all the information.

Read the example. Then, circle the letter of the best answer for each question.

"OK," said Ben. "I bought the balloons. Is there anything else you want me to do?"

"Yes," said Tanya. "Can you give me a ride to the bakery? I don't want to walk home carrying that big cake."

"Let's wait until Mom leaves to pick up Ana at school," said Ben. "I don't want her to suspect anything."

1. What do you think Ben and Tanya are doing?

    A. learning how to bake a cake
    B. planning to take their mother to the circus
    C. playing a trick on their mother
    D. planning a surprise party for their mother

2. Who do you think is older, Ben or Tanya? _____

3. Why do you think so? _____

4. What conclusion can you draw about Ana?

    A. She is Ben and Tanya's sister.
    B. She loves cake.
    C. She is a stranger.
    D. She cannot keep a secret.

Reading: Draw Conclusions

Assess

Read the following passage. Then, answer the questions that follow.

The view from Tyson's Peak this morning was amazing. We could see all the way to the mainland. The boats below us looked like children's toys bobbing in a bathtub. Brook Hollow Road was a twisting snake, winding its way through the tiny village. The striking view, the warm sunlight, and the refreshing breeze made us agree that we had never visited a more wonderful place. We are already planning to return next summer.

1. Based on details in this passage, where is Tyson's Peak probably located? Put a check mark next to your answer.

 _____ **A.** on an island

 _____ **B.** in a city

 _____ **C.** on the prairie

 _____ **D.** in the desert

2. What are two details that helped you draw this conclusion?

 _____

 _____

3. How does the writer feel about the setting described in this passage?

 _____

4. Which of the following conclusions does *not* seem correct, based on the passage? Put a check mark next to your answer.

 _____ **A.** The writer is on vacation.

 _____ **B.** The writer is alone.

 _____ **C.** The writer is having a good time.

 _____ **D.** The writer is not afraid of heights.

5. What details in the passage helped you answer question 4?

 _____

 _____

Reading: Evaluate the Author's Credibility

Practice

Credible means "able to be believed or trusted." When you **evaluate the author's credibility,** you judge whether he or she is knowledgeable and fair—whether what he or she writes can be believed or trusted.

■ **Knowledge** Imagine that you read a report on science by a fifth-grade student. You will probably decide that this writer is not as credible as an experienced scientist.

■ **Fairness** A **biased** writer is one who has formed opinions before looking at the evidence.

A credible author has a good knowledge of his or her subject. A credible author avoids bias and presents a balanced view. To evaluate an author's credibility, ask yourself: How much does the writer probably know about the subject? Does the writer show bias, or does the writer give strong support for his or her opinions?

A   Read each item. Write *Knowledgeable* if the writer described is probably knowledgeable about his or her topic. Write *Lacks Knowledge* if not.

1. _____ Al Cherry reviews art for a large newspaper. He has written art reviews for twenty years. He studied art at college and in graduate school. He teaches art history classes at the local college.

2. _____ Alexandra Thomas reviews art for a newspaper that is given away free in local supermarkets. Alexandra works at the bank. In college, she studied business. She writes reviews for the paper as a favor to her cousin, who owns the paper.

B   Read each item. Write *Biased* if the item describes a likely case of bias. Write *Unbiased* if it does not.

1. _____ George Jones, a movie reviewer, is a good friend of Jack Smith, a director. He writes a review of Jack's latest mystery movie. In the review, he says the movie is "full of suspense." Most viewers agree, though, that the movie is boring.

2. _____ Ned Farmer, a book reviewer, knows the writer Ashley Miller personally. Ned does not like her at all. Ned writes a review of Ashley's new book. In his review, Ned lists three good points about the book. He also lists two important flaws. He gives examples to support each of his judgments.

Reading: Evaluate the Author's Credibility

Assess

A For each question, circle the letter of the best answer.

1. What does it mean to say an author has *credibility?*

A. The author writes well.

B. The author's writing may be believed.

C. The author is paid well.

D. The author knows what is popular.

2. Which is the best definition of *bias?*

A. a good assumption

B. an opinion formed before looking at the evidence

C. a logical argument

D. a lengthy quotation presented to support an opinion

B Read each item. Write *Knowledgeable* if the writer described is probably knowledgeable about his or her topic. Write *Lacks Knowledge* if not.

1. _____ Bret Landers used to work as a guide for people on fishing and hunting trips. He has won a number of fishing trophies and has invented a special fishing lure of his own. He writes reviews of books on fishing for a sports magazine.

2. _____ Last month, Chad Holmes started surfing. So far, he loves the sport. He got excited when he heard that there was a new book on the topic. He bought a copy and read most of it. Then, he posted his review of the book on his Web site.

C Write *Biased* if the item describes a likely case of bias. Write *Unbiased* if it does not.

1. _____ Susan Green, a book reviewer, writes a review of Sam Black's new history book. In her review, she says that Sam's book is "full of mistakes." However, she does not give any examples of these mistakes.

2. _____ Abby Lock, a book reviewer, is a big supporter of the mayor and his ideas. Samantha Ward, a reporter, is a strong critic of the mayor. Samantha writes a book about ways to make the city better. Abby writes a negative review of the book. In her review, she writes that "Ward thinks our city is a terrible place to live." In fact, the book says, "Life in our city could be improved," not that it is a terrible place to live.

Vocabulary: Word root -nym-

Practice

A **root** is the basic unit of meaning of a word. Knowing the meanings of word roots can help you figure out the meanings of many new words. The Latin word root -*nym*- or -*nom*- means "name." This root appears in the word *acronym*, which refers to a word formed by putting together the first letters of several other words. This word also contains the prefix *acro*-, meaning "high," because when the individual words are listed vertically, the acronym appears reading down, as in the following example:

> North
> Atlantic
> Treaty
> Organization

A Think about whether each sentence below makes sense, given the meaning of the underlined word. Circle "Y" if it makes sense and "N" if it does not. Then explain your answer. If the sentence does not make sense, write a new sentence using the word correctly.

1. I usually carry bills several different <u>denominations</u> in my wallet, including at least one twenty and at least two singles.

_____

_____

2. Y/N The students used <u>synonyms</u> to solve the math problem.

_____

_____

3. Y/N The term koala bear is actually a <u>misnomer</u> because koalas are not related to bears.

_____

_____

4. Y/N We <u>nominated</u> her to head the environmental committee because she had no experience in that field.

_____

_____

Vocabulary: Word root -nym-

A Replace the underlined word or phrase in each sentence with a word containing the root -nym- or -nom-. Choose the words from the following list.

> anonymous
> antonyms
> nomenclature
> nominal
> nominees

1. The words *easy* and *difficult* are _____.

2. Each of the _____ at the award ceremony hoped to be the winner.

3. The Latin _____ for different species is used mostly by biologists.

4. I could not figure out who had sent me the _____ letter.

5. We were disappointed with her performance on the committee because she paid only _____ attention to her duties.

B Now take each of the words from the list above and use it in a new sentence that shows the word's meaning.

1. anonymous: _____

_____

2. antonym: _____

_____

3. nomenclature: _____

_____

4. nominal: _____

_____

5. nominee: _____

_____

Name _____ Date _____

A clause, a group of words that contains a subject and a verb, can be a **main** (independent) **clause** or a **subordinate** (dependent) **clause.** If the group of words is complete and makes sense by itself, it is a main clause. If the group of words needs additional information to make sense, it is a subordinate clause.

Main clause:	Rudy stayed home
Subordinate clause:	because he did not feel well.

A Identify each underlined clause as main or subordinate. Write *M* for main or *S* for subordinate.

1. _____ <u>I sat on the bench for three quarters</u> because I had been injured.

2. _____ I get motion sickness <u>whenever I ride in a vehicle</u>.

3. _____ <u>Because it was so heavy</u>, Carlo could not lift the cage himself.

4. _____ <u>The workers were exhausted</u> after cutting down trees all day.

5. _____ After the mills closed, <u>many people left Lawrence to find work elsewhere</u>.

6. _____ <u>If you want to become a doctor</u>, you will have to study for many years.

7. _____ <u>Ben will baby-sit the twins tomorrow</u>, although they often misbehave.

B Complete the following sentences, adding at least one subordinate clause.

1. Patrice found the perfect costume

_____

2. We tried to eat with chopsticks

_____

3. The tomatoes were ripe

_____

Grammar: Main and Subordinate Clauses

Assess

A In each of the following sentences, underline the main clause and circle the subordinate clause.

1. When Allison called me on the phone, I was not at home.

2. Grandpa led an active life until he hurt his hip while skiing.

3. People should turn off their cell phones when they go to the movies.

4. If you are careful, you can make a beautiful vase on the potter's wheel.

5. Alfred cannot go to the movies unless he does his work first.

B Write whether the following items are main or subordinate clauses. If a clause is main, rewrite it and add a subordinate clause to make a complete sentence. If a clause is subordinate, rewrite it with the correct capitalization and punctuation.

Example: since I was bored
Answer: subordinate; Since I was bored, I went to a movie.

1. a show always entertains

_____

2. because a friend recommended it

_____

3. though the show was great

_____

4. I kept quiet

_____

5. if it was a sad scene

_____

Grammar: Adverb Clauses

Practice

A **clause** is a group of words containing a subject and a verb. A **subordinate clause** is one that contains a subject and a verb but does not express a complete thought. It is often introduced by a **subordinating conjunction.** Here are some common subordinating conjunctions:

> after although because before if unless when whenever

An **adverb clause** is a subordinate clause that is used as an adverb. In a sentence, it modifies a verb, an adjective, or another adverb. To vary your writing, you can combine two sentences by turning one of them into an adverb clause. Notice that when an adverb clause comes at the beginning of a sentence, it is followed by a comma.

> **Two sentences:** The concert ended. Then, we stopped for pizza.
> **Combined:** <u>After</u> the concert ended, we stopped for pizza.
> └──── adverb clause ────┘

A   Underline the each adverb clause, and circle the subordinating conjunction.

1. When the weather is hot, we turn on the air conditioner.

2. I will not put down this book until I have finished it.

3. The parade will begin at 10:30 unless it rains.

B   Combine each pair of sentences, using the subordinating conjunction indicated.

1. The bus arrives. The campers will wait in the gym. (until)

_____

2. There is a long period without rain. Many plants will not survive. (if)

_____

3. Miami is a large city. Los Angeles is even larger. (although)

_____

4. Mr. Jackson got a new job. The Jackson's moved to Charlotte. (because)

_____

Grammar: Adverb Clauses

Assess

A Circle the letter of the correct answer.

1. What is the adverb clause in this sentence?

   Before the campaign ends, the candidates will meet in three debates.

   A. Before the campaign ends

   B. the candidates will meet

   C. the candidates will meet in three debates

   D. in three debates

2. What is the subordinating conjunction in this sentence?

   Rachel Beck would certainly win if the election were held today.

   A. certainly

   B. if

   C. would

   D. today

B Underline the each adverb clause and circle the subordinating conjunction.

1. Until the prices go down, we will not buy that new laptop computer.

2. The contest will begin precisely at 3:00 unless there is a rain delay.

3. After the icebreakers open the channel, the ships can pass through.

4. The journalist double-checked the facts before he sent in his report.

C Combine each pair of sentences, using the subordinating conjunction indicated.

1. He has soccer practice. Steve goes to the library after school. (unless)

   _____

2. A fox lives in the woods nearby. The farmer rarely sees it. (although)

   _____

3. Many good-hearted people volunteer. Disasters occur. (when)

   _____

4. The price of gas has risen. Airfares have also risen. (because)

   _____

Spelling: Using Silent e

Practice

To spell words with silent *e* correctly, it will help if you know why the silent *e* is used. Study this list of reasons that silent *e* is most often used.

- To turn a short vowel into a long vowel (a vowel that says its name): *rem̲ote, revis̲e*
- To turn a hard *c* or *g* into a soft *c* or *g*: *resour̲ce, college*
- To avoid ending a word in *v* or *u*, which is rare in English: *alternativ̲e, involv̲e*
- To avoid a syllable with no vowel: *rectangle* (not *rectangl*)
- To avoid being confused with a plural: *dense* (not *dens*), *tense* (not *tens*)

When you add an ending to a word that ends in silent *e*, you should usually drop the *e* if the ending begins with a vowel but keep the *e* if the ending begins with a consonant.

involve + ing = involving   involve + -ment = involvement

A For each item, add the ending to the word to form a new word. Write the new word on the line provided.

1. alternative + -ly = _____   **3.** involve + -ing = _____

2. revise + -ion = _____   **4.** dense + -ity = _____

B For each word in capital letters, underline the other word that uses silent *e* for the same reason. Then, explain the reason for the silent *e*. An example is done for you.

Example: DANCE: line   <u>rage</u>   believe

Reason: <u>To turn a hard *c* or *g* into a soft *c* or *g*</u>

1. RESOURCE: alternative   college   dense

Reason: _____

2. CREDIBLE: revise   resource   rectangle

Reason: _____

3. REMOTE: revise   involve   college

Reason: _____

Spelling: Using Silent e

Assess

A For each item, add the ending to the word to form a new word. Write the new word on the line provided.

1. resource + -ful = _____   **3.** involve + -ment = _____

2. revise + -ing = _____   **4.** dense + -ly = _____

B For each word in capital letters, underline the other word that uses silent *e* for the same reason. Then, explain the reason for the silent *e*. An example is done for you.

Example: CONVINCE: behave   mine   <u>age</u>

Reason: <u>To turn a hard *c* or *g* into a soft *c* or *g*</u>

1. COLLEGE: dense   resource   alternative

Reason: _____

2. RECTANGLE: credible   revise   remote

Reason: _____

3. REVISE: involve   remote   dense

Reason: _____

4. DENSE: credible   tense   resource

Reason: _____

C Underline the three misspelled words in the paragraph. Give the correct spellings of the words you underlined.

  Andrea and Joe were going to get married, but now they are reviseing their plans. They are putting off the wedding until Andrea finishes colleg. She wants to finish so that she can get a better job. She also does not want to end her involvment in school sports.

1. _____   **2.** _____   **3.** _____

Writing: Play

A **play** is a story told mostly through dialogue and characters' actions. The writer of a play identifies each speaker, writes the lines each character will speak, and describes actions the characters will perform.

Some plays include **dramatic irony.** Dramatic irony comes from a situation in which the audience knows something the characters do not. For example, a professional tennis player brags to his fans that he has never been defeated, but the audience knows that he is about to lose a big match to a rookie player.

Read the following brief scene from a play. Then, answer the questions that follow.

NARRATOR. That night, Alicia had no idea she was about to win the lottery. Nor did she know the troubles it would bring.

ALICIA. Mom, if I won the lottery, I'd never be sad again. I would buy the family a huge house and anything any of us wanted. I'd give all my friends cars for Christmas. I'd give money to the poor, and I'd put my sisters and myself through college. It would be so great!

MOM. [rolling her eyes] That would be great! Too bad it will never happen. Stop living in a fantasy world, Alicia, and come help me make dinner.

1. How does the reader know who is speaking? _____

_____

2. How does the audience know what is about to happen to Alicia? _____

_____

3. How do you know that neither Alicia nor her mother know that Alicia is

going to win the lottery? _____

_____

4. What is the dramatic irony in this scene? _____

_____

_____

Writing: Play

A Explain why the following scene would be an example of dramatic irony.

A football player runs to the goal. The sun briefly blinds him as he believes he crosses the goal line. He spikes the ball and begins a victory dance while the spectators groan. He has stopped two feet from the goal line. Players from the opposing team tackle him, and his team loses the game.

_____

_____

B Read this description of a scene. Then, rewrite the scene as lines from a play.

Katie meets Steve, a new boy in her school. Trying to amuse Steve, Katie makes fun of a popular rock star. The audience knows that the rock star is Steve's aunt. Steve thinks that Katie will be very embarrassed when she finds out, so he asks Katie what she would do if she found out that he was related to the rock star. Katie does not believe him and laughs.

_____

_____

_____

_____

_____

_____

_____

_____

_____

_____

Writing: Research Report

Practice

A **research report** presents and interprets information gathered through the deep study of a subject. Here are the steps for completing a research report.

- choose your topic
- narrow your topic by writing a question that guides your research
- gather information through research
- write a thesis statement (a topic sentence that clearly states what you intend to prove in your report)
- write a rough draft
- elaborate and revise
- proofread your work for correct grammar, spelling, and punctuation
- write a final draft
- include a bibliography or works-cited list that provides a complete listing of research sources formatted in an approved style

Use the information above to help you answer the following questions.

1. What should you do right after you choose a topic for your research report?

_____

2. What is a thesis statement? Why is a thesis statement important in a research report?

_____

_____

3. Why is a bibliography or a works-cited list important?

_____

_____

4. What steps must take place after you write your rough draft and before you can write your final draft?

_____

_____

Writing: Research Report

Complete the activities that follow.

1. Imagine that you will be writing a research report for your social studies class. Brainstorm four possible topics for your report and circle the one you would choose.

   _____

   _____

2. Write a guiding question that would help you narrow your topic and focus your research.

   _____

   _____

3. Write a thesis statement that establishes what you would try to prove in your report.

   _____

   _____

4. List the steps you would take to complete the rest of your report.

   _____

   _____

   _____

5. What kinds of sources would you use to help you conduct your research on this topic?

   _____

   _____

6. How would you give proper credit to your sources in your report?

   _____

Literary Analysis: Epic Hero

Practice

An **epic** is a long poem that tells the story of important events in the history or folklore of a nation or culture. An **epic hero** is the larger-than-life main character. For example, Odysseus is the epic hero in the *Odyssey*. His larger-than-life characteristics include his great strength, his incredible aim with a bow-and-arrow, and his cleverness.

Epic heroes usually have the qualities that are valued by the society they belong to. The ancient Greeks valued skill with the bow and cleverness, so their hero Odysseus has those qualities.

For each question, circle the letter of the best answer.

1. Which of the following is the best description of an epic?

   A. a short story about the heroes of a nation or culture

   B. a nonfiction book about the heroes of a nation or culture

   C. a brief article about the heroes of a nation or culture

   D. a long poem telling stories about the heroes of a nation or culture

2. An epic hero is a larger-than-life character. Which of the following is the best example of an epic hero?

   A. a man who is tall

   B. a man who wins a race

   C. a man who has the strength of fifty men

   D. a man who steals a lot of money

3. An epic hero often does adventurous deeds or acts. Which of the following is the best example of an epic hero's adventurous deed?

   A. a battle in which the hero kills a dreaded monster

   B. a meeting in which the hero stands up for the rights of his friends

   C. a social event in which the hero meets new friends

   D. a lazy boat ride on a summer afternoon

4. An epic hero usually has the characteristics that are valued by a society. Suppose that a society valued honesty above all else. Which of the following would you expect to be true of that society's epic hero?

   A. He is always kind and generous.

   B. He always tells the truth.

   C. He solves problems cleverly.

   D. He always wins his battles and defeats his enemies.

Literary Analysis: Epic Hero

Assess

For each question, circle the letter of the best answer.

1. Which of the following is the best description of an epic hero?

   A. a clever adventurer described in an epic

   B. a larger-than-life character who is the main character of an epic

   C. a wise ruler described in an epic

   D. a cultural leader described in an epic

2. Which of the following statements is ALWAYS true about an epic?

   A. It is written in Greek or Latin.

   B. It is valued by all societies.

   C. It is a long narrative poem.

   D. It celebrates battle victories.

3. Which of the following statements is ALWAYS true about an epic hero?

   A. The hero is very smart.

   B. The hero does great acts, such as killing monsters.

   C. The hero fights anyone he meets.

   D. The hero travels throughout the world, spreading peace.

4. An epic hero demonstrates traits that are valued by a society. Suppose that a society valued cleverness above all else. Which of the following is the BEST example of a trait of that society's epic hero?

   A. He always tells the truth.

   B. He gives all his riches to the poor.

   C. He always finds ways to solve problems.

   D. He is always brave during battles.

Literary Analysis: Epic Simile

Practice

An epic is a long poem about the history of a nation or culture. A simile uses the words *like* or *as* to compare. An **epic simile** is simile that describes the second thing in great detail.

Ordinary Simile: Kathy chased Ron, but Ron ran as fast as a rabbit.
Epic Simile: Ron ran like a rabbit startled by a hunter. The hunter takes aim quickly, but the rabbit is faster than the hunter's eye. With its heart beating fast, the rabbit dives into the bushes. Its tail vanishes last, a quick flash of white in the green leaves. So ran Ron, and he quickly vanished.

Epic similes add color and interesting detail to an epic. They reveal much about the time and the culture in which the epic takes place.

For each question, circle the letter of the best answer.

1. How is an epic simile different from a normal simile?

 A. An epic simile usually contains such words as *like* or *as*.

 B. An epic simile describes an aspect of a hero.

 C. An epic simile is longer and much more involved.

 D. An epic simile compares fewer things.

2. Which of the following is the best example of an epic simile?

 A. His home was a castle on steep cliff.

 B. His home was like a castle, a mighty fort, safe from all storms, a fine and grand place to eat and rest.

 C. His home seemed as big as a castle.

 D. His home was big, made of stone, with green shutters and a huge iron gate, and it was set far back from the road.

3. What does this epic simile tell you about the culture?

 Like a farmer sowing seeds, the mighty hero sent his enemies running. The farmer flings a handful to the left, a handful to the right. So the hero moved through the battlefield, dealing blows to the left and to the right. His enemies scattered like seeds in the wind.

 A. Some people of the culture lived in big cities.

 B. Some people of the culture used farm machinery.

 C. Some people of the culture were simple farmers.

 D. Some people of the culture made their living by fishing.

Literary Analysis: Epic Simile

Assess

For each question, circle the letter of the best answer.

1. What is the best definition of an epic simile?

A. a long comparison of a human and a god

B. a long comparison filled with detailed descriptions

C. a long comparison in which animals are given human traits and voices

D. a long comparison of epic heroes

2. How is an ordinary simile different from an epic simile?

A. Ordinary similes do not usually contain *like* or *as*.

B. Ordinary similes are not metaphors.

C. Ordinary similes appear only in narrative poems from early cultures.

D. Ordinary similes are brief comparisons using simple images.

3. Which of the following is the best example of an epic simile?

A. All men marvel at a mighty flash of lightning, which is gone the moment it is seen. So ran his horse, like lightning in the mountains.

B. The horse was as fast as lightning.

C. The horse was shiny, velvety black, with a streaming tail and a graceful gait that made everyone turn for an appreciative stare.

D. To its owner, the horse was a treasure more valuable than gold.

4. What does this epic simile tell you about the culture where the epic takes place?

The warriors crept toward the ships quietly, like a wolf on the hunt. In his hunger, the wolf whines a little when he catches a scent. Yet he holds back his bark, for fear of frightening off his victim.

A. The people of this culture lived where there are wolves.

B. The people of this culture worshiped wolves.

C. The people of this culture enjoyed hunting.

D. The people of this culture kept wolves as pets.

Literary Analysis: Contemporary Interpretations of Classical Works

Practice

A **contemporary interpretation of a classical work** is a modern piece of writing based on an ancient story. In the new version, the modern author makes an **allusion,** or reference, to a character, place, or other aspect from the ancient story.

Read the following summaries. Then, answer the questions that follow.

The Ancient Tale of Harrodophius and Ralphokeus

Harrodophius was a great ruler of the land of Kreti. He was proud of his strength and said he would give his kingdom to anyone who could beat him at wrestling. The god Craya heard his boast and thought his pride was not fit for a mere mortal. The god sent Ralphokeus, a poor wrestler from the town of Grati to challenge Harrodophius. The two wrestled, and Ralphokeus won. Harrodophius gave up his crown to him, but Ralphokeus was generous. From that day on, Ralphokeus ruled all summer, and Harrodophius ruled all winter.

The Story of Harry Whatafuss and Ralph Okeedokee

Harry was a successful car dealer in the town of Creditcard. He bragged that no one would ever sell as many cars as he did. Then, a car dealer named Ralph moved into town. Harry offered free balloons for the customers' kids, but Ralph offered free movie tickets. More customers bought cars from Ralph, and Harry's business started to fail. Ralph generously offered to become partners with Harry.

1. What do Harrodophius and Harry Whatafuss have in common?

   A. Both are characters in an ancient work.

   B. Both are successful car dealers.

   C. Both face challenges by a strong opponent.

   D. Both must give up a kingdom.

2. The town of Creditcard is an allusion to which detail in the original work?

   A. the town of Grati

   B. the land of Kreti

   C. the god Craya

   D. the wrestling match

3. How is the modern version different from the original?

   A. The challenge involves business rather than warfare.

   B. The challenge involves warfare rather than business.

   C. It introduces a god named Craya, who did not appear in the original.

   D. It involves a challenge to a boastful character.

Literary Analysis: Contemporary Interpretations of Classical Works

Assess

Read the following summaries. Then, answer the questions that follow.

The Ancient Tale of Natalious and Brendavia

Natalious was the fastest runner in Athens. People said that the god Mercury had put invisible wings on her sandals. Natalious thought that no one would ever beat her in a race, so she didn't bother to train. She lounged in the marketplace all day, snacking on figs. At the Olympic Games, Natalious proudly took her starting position for the race. But the god Mercury punished her. He sent a runner Brendavia to compete with her. He really did give Brendavia invisible wings on her sandals, and she won the race.

The Story of Natalie and Brenda

Natalie was the fastest runner in Avondale. She was so fast that everyone thought that she had some form of secret training equipment. Natalie was very confident, and as the city track meet approached, she slacked off on her training. She watched a lot of television and ate a lot of junk food. At the track meet, she saw a runner named Brenda, a newcomer to Avondale. Brenda had trained well, and was a great runner. She easily won the race.

1. ____ What do Natalious and Natalie have in common?

   A. They lounge around the marketplace instead of training for the race.

   B. They are both punished by a god.

   C. They are both fast runners who do not bother to train for a big race.

   D. They both train hard.

2. ____ The "secret training equipment" mentioned in the modern version is an allusion to what in the original?

   A. mysterious herbs

   B. Brenda's running shoes

   C. the winged sandals

   D. figs

3. ____ How is the modern version different from the original?

   A. The challenge involves a tennis game rather than a race.

   B. The challenge involves a city track meet rather than the Olympic Games.

   C. It introduces the god named Mercury, who did not appear in the original.

   D. It mentions that Natalie snacks on figs.

Reading: Analyze Cultural and Historical Context

Practice

The **cultural and historical context** of a story, poem, or other work of literature is the specific time and place where it was written. To understand the work, you may need to understand its context:

> **Example:** In a story written in the nineteenth century, Fred moves West. He worries about his family in Kentucky. He waits for months for a letter from them.
>
> **What Context Explains:** Why didn't Fred just call his family?
>
> **Context:** In the nineteenth century, there were no telephones or e-mail providers. There were no airplanes or cars. The only way to communicate across a long distance was through the mail, which could take a long time.

The context of a work includes beliefs and customs as well as specific events.

> **Example:** In a letter written in the sixteenth century, a woman writes that her husband went walking at night and so fell sick.
>
> **Context:** In the sixteenth century, people believed that the air at night was filled with unhealthy vapors or clouds.

For each question, circle the letter of the best answer.

1. Imagine that you read these sentences in a diary written by a woman in colonial America.

   > My brother John is going to a fine school, Harvard College. How I wish I could go there and study all those wonderful books! I am a young woman, though. Everyone knows that women do not study at college. It is not proper.

   Judging from the letter, what did people of the writer's time believe about women?

   A. Women should study hard.

   B. Women were not meant to be educated.

   C. Women were equal to men.

   D. Women should go to the same schools as men.

2. Which best describes the historical context of the letter?

   A. In colonial times, people believed in the value of education.

   B. In modern times, people believe in the value of education.

   C. In colonial times, people did not believe in equality for women.

   D. In modern times, people believe in equality for women.

Reading: Analyze Cultural and Historical Context

Assess

A Circle the likeliest description of the cultural and historical context of the work.

1. The Blackfoot Indians tell the myth of a boy who brought the first horses to people. The boy went on a quest. With the help of one spirit, he was able to get the horses from the spirit who owned them.

   A. The Blackfeet believe that important parts of their lives, such as horses, come from spirits.
   B. The Blackfeet do not know very much about breeding or riding horses.

2. In 1950, Ray Bradbury published a short story called "There Will Come Soft Rains." The story tells of a time in the future when atomic bombs have wiped out entire cities.

   A. The United States used the first atomic bombs against Japan in 1945. People of the day were frightened that such powerful atomic weapons might destroy humanity.
   B. Another country, the Soviet Union, had tested its own atomic bomb in 1949. As a result, people knew that they were safe from atomic bombs.

3. In a Hindu story from India, King Sibi wounds himself to protect the life of a dove and to keep a promise. The god Indra praises the king's goodness and heals him.

   A. Hindus believe that doves were sent by the gods to punish people.
   B. Hindus believe that all life is sacred.

B Read about the work of literature. Write a brief description of the cultural and historical context of the work. Then, explain what the context helps you understand.

In a story about King Arthur and his knights, a giant green knight comes to Arthur's castle. He challenges the knights to fight him. No one speaks up at first. Gawain is very concerned. He thinks that if no one fights the knight, then the world will think King Arthur's knights are cowards. He tells the giant knight he will fight him, with the king's permission.

Context _____

What the context helps me understand _____

_____

Reading: Identify Characteristics of Various Types of Texts

Practice

You probably read magazines, newspapers, and other texts to find out about new movies, music, and sports. As you read, you **identify the characteristics of various types of texts** by thinking about the main points and the purpose of each one. Then, you evaluate what you read against what you know about the topic. Finally, you decide what *you* think.

You probably complete all of these steps without thinking that you are following a process. Here are some questions to ask yourself as you read real-life texts:

- What are the major points?
- What facts does the author use to support these points?
- What opinions does he or she present?
- What is the purpose of the text?

Read the following commentary. Then, answer the questions that follow.

Super Heroes

I have a secret: I love superheroes. I love to see the "good" guys and girls come to the rescue. It could be Superman throwing off his glasses, Spiderman throwing webs out of his fingers, or Wonder Woman flashing her indestructible bracelets. Whoever it is, I want to see seemingly normal, everyday people burst the bonds of daily drudgery and reveal their inner hero. I love their optimism, their fearlessness in the face of evil, and their willingness to risk everything to keep the world safe. So, yes, I am probably too old for them, but superheroes are not only for children. The world would be dull indeed without them.

1. What is the main idea of the commentary?

   _____

   _____

2. Why does the author feel this way?

   _____

   _____

3. What is the purpose of the commentary?

   _____

   _____

Reading: Identify Characteristics of Various Types of Texts

Assess

Read the following article about different movie versions of Superman. Then, answer the questions that follow.

Superman Takes to the Skies—Again and Again

What is it about Superman that makes every generation see him as a hero? Created in 1932 by Jerry Siegel and Joe Shuster, Superman first appeared in a comic book in 1938. Since then, he has appeared in countless comic strips, radio serials, TV series, and movies. In fact, Superman is credited with starting the superhero trend.

The story of Superman began when he was born on the planet Krypton. Soon after, he was adopted by an Earth family. He did not develop his supernatural abilities until he reached his teens, but by that time, his Earth parents had given him a strong moral sense. Once he realized the extent of his powers, Superman decided to use them to benefit humans.

Perhaps the attraction is that any nerdy, fumbling teen could be a superhero. Or perhaps the attraction is that anyone around you might save you from danger. Whatever his attraction, it is clear that Superman has touched the imaginations of generations of people around the world.

1. What is the main idea of the article?

_____

_____

2. What facts does the author use to support this idea?

_____

_____

3. What is the purpose of the article?

_____

_____

4. What is the difference between the text on the opposite page and the one this page?

_____

_____

Vocabulary: Prefixes *be-* and *dis-*

Practice

A **prefix** is added to the beginning of a word or word root to change its meaning. The prefix *be-* can mean "around," "to make," or "covered with." Take a look at these examples:

> be- + little = belittle: "to make something seem small; to mock"
> be- + grime + -ed = begrimed: "covered with grime, dirty"

The prefix *dis-* means "away," "apart," or "not," as in the following examples:

> dis- + close = disclose: "to reveal, to make known"
> dis + satisfied = dissatisfied: "not satisfied

A For each definition listed, write a word that combines the underlined word with the prefix *be-* or *dis-* to form a new word that matches the definition. Then use the new word in a sentence.

1. _____ a lack of <u>respect</u>

_____

2. _____ to make a <u>friend</u> of someone

_____

3. _____ to set off the <u>charge</u> in a firearm

_____

4. _____ for a ship, to get stuck in <u>calm</u> waters

_____

5. _____ to cover with <u>dew</u> or a similar liquid

_____

6. _____ poorly <u>organized</u>

_____

Vocabulary: Suffixes *-ory* and *-ist*

Assess

A Write the word from the list that best fits the meaning of each sentence.

| bedraggled | bereaved | betrothal |
| dismissed | disposal | dispensed |

1. The teacher _____ the class ten minutes early.

2. At one time, couples would formally announce their _____ a year before their wedding.

3. After the funeral, dozens of well-wishers sent cards to the _____ widow.

4. The pharmacist _____ drugs to the patients.

5. As cities grow, the _____ of waste becomes a bigger concern.

6. She came in from the rain looking wet and _____.

B Add *be-* or *dis-* to each underlined word to form a new word that fits the meaning of the sentence.

1. _____ Though she said she was sorry, her sneering face <u>lied</u> her words.

2. _____ After the ship pulled up at the dock, the passengers <u>embarked</u>.

3. _____ He fell from the ladder and <u>located</u> his shoulder.

4. _____ My overalls became <u>sprinkled</u> with paint as we worked.

5. _____ He appeared <u>mused</u> by his friend's long, strange story.

6. _____ I used a stick to <u>lodge</u> the stone from the hole.

Grammar: Simple and Compound Sentences

Practice

A **simple sentence** contains a subject and a predicate and expresses a single idea. The predicate contains the verb and tells what the subject is or does. A simple sentence may contain a compound subject and a compound verb. In the examples, the subjects are underlined once, and the predicates twice.

> Simple sentence: Lissa plays soccer.
> With compound subject: Lissa and Spencer play soccer.
> With compound verb: Spencer plays and eats at school.

A **compound sentence** contains two or more simple sentences joined by a comma and a coordinating conjunction (**and, but, or, nor, so, for**).

> Lissa plays soccer, and Spencer also plays soccer.
> Lissa and Spencer play soccer, but Kerrie and Sam play tennis.

A   Underline each simple sentence in the following compound sentences. Then, circle the coordinating conjunction.

1. "The Gift of the Magi" has a surprise ending, and "The Necklace" also has one.

2. Poetry is often beautiful, but sometimes it is difficult to understand.

3. You can explain the directions, or you could draw me a map.

4. Pears and apples are good, but I prefer peaches and plums.

B   Combine each pair of sentences into a compound sentence, using the coordinating conjunction indicated. Remember to use a comma before the conjunction.

1. Enjoy watching the animals. Do not feed them. (but)

_____

2. Carl and Jane work hard all week. They relax on the weekend. (and)

_____

3. The trains have stopped running. We will take a bus. (so)

_____

Grammar: Simple and Compound Sentences

A Underline each simple sentence in the following compound sentences. Then, circle the coordinating conjunction.

Example: <u>Firefighters take great risks,</u> (and) <u>they are always on call.</u>

1. On Saturday we will have a party, and we will invite the whole neighborhood.

2. David and Daniel are twins, but they don't look anything alike.

3. You can watch the news on television, or you can read it on the Internet.

4. Jay's family rents DVDs online, so they don't have to go to the video store.

B Combine each pair of sentences into a compound sentence, using the coordinating conjunction indicated. Remember to use a comma before the conjunction.

1. Read the poem out loud. You will really appreciate the images. (and)

_____

2. Do come again. It is always a pleasure to see you. (for)

_____

3. Turn down the air conditioner. We will all freeze! (or)

_____

C Write a compound sentence using the coordinating conjunction indicated.

1. Birds and hamsters make good pets. (but)

_____

2. You may sell tickets at the door. (or)

_____

3. Please remember to turn off your cell phone. (so)

_____

Grammar: Complex and Compound-Complex Sentences

Practice

A **complex sentence** consists of an independent clause and one or more subordinate clauses. An **independent clause** contains a subject and a verb and can stand alone as a complete idea. A **subordinate clause** contains a subject and a verb, but it cannot stand alone as a complete idea. Some words that introduce subordinate clauses include *before, after, if, when, because, which, that,* and *who.* In the example, the subjects are underlined once, and the verbs twice, and the subordinate clause is in bold type.

We supported the Lions, **who were** in second place.

A **compound-complex sentence** consists of two or more independent clauses and one or more subordinate clauses. The independent clauses are joined by a word such as *and, but,* or *or.*

The Cougars were favored, *but* we supported the Lions, **who were** in second place.

A Write *C* for each complex sentence and *C-C* for each compound-complex sentence. Circle the words that connect or introduce the clauses.

1. _____ When Lori got home, she checked her e-mail.

2. _____ She deleted the junk mail, which annoyed her, and then she read the messages from her friends.

3. _____ Because she was hungry, she went to the kitchen to find a snack.

4. _____ Lori discovered the cookies that her mother had made, and she sat down to eat them with a glass of milk.

5. _____ Before she had taken even her first bite, the phone rang.

B Using the underlined word, add a subordinate clause to each compound sentence.

1. Chris will shop, and I will cook <u>if</u> _____.

2. Mike likes poetry, but Kayla likes stories, <u>which</u> _____.

3. <u>After</u> _____, I will play a video game, or I will watch TV.

Name _____ Date _____

Grammar: Complex and Compound-Complex Sentences

Assess

A Write *C* for each complex sentence and *C-C* for each compound-complex sentence. Circle the words that connect or introduce the clauses.

1. _____ When we arrived at the gate, James was nowhere to be seen.

2. _____ The game had started, and we needed James because he had the tickets.

3. _____ Mari, who had a cell phone, called James, but he didn't answer.

4. _____ Before she could try again, James showed up with a sorry look on his face.

5. _____ He told us that he had misplaced the tickets, but he finally found them in his backpack.

6. _____ When we got to our seats, we saw the first goal scored.

7. _____ Next time, I will hold the tickets, or we will make sure that James doesn't lose them.

B Using the underlined word, add a subordinate clause to each independent clause to form a complex sentence.

1. We will move the party from the deck into the house <u>if</u> _____.

2. I listen to rock, but Matt prefers reggae, <u>which</u> _____.

3. The grass has turned brown <u>because</u> _____.

C Using the underlined word, add an independent clause to each complex sentence to form a compound-complex sentence.

1. When fall comes in the North, the leaves turn red, <u>and</u> _____.

2. I tried on the new jacket that Aunt Edna gave me, <u>but</u> _____.

3. After we have lunch, Dad will rake the leaves, <u>or</u> _____.

Grammar: Fragments and Run-ons

Practice

A **sentence fragment** is a group of words that does not express a complete thought but is punctuated as if it were a sentence. To correct a fragment, make sure that the group of words has a subject and a verb and that it makes sense by itself.

Sentence Fragment: About a trip to the Grand Canyon.
Complete sentence: <u>Alex</u> <u>dreamed</u> about a trip to the Grand Canyon.

Run-on sentences include sentences that are joined without any punctuation and those joined by only a comma (called comma splices). To correct a run-on, write two separate sentences or add a conjunction, such as *and, but, so,* or *or.*

Run-on: The pigeons stay all winter they don't migrate south.
Corrected: The pigeons stay all winter. They don't migrate south.
Comma splice: The car wouldn't start, we had to take the bus.
Corrected: The car wouldn't start, **so** we had to take the bus.

A   For each item, write *F* if it is a fragment or *S* if it is a sentence.

1. _____ Whenever we attend the St. Patrick's Day parade.

2. _____ Crowds on the parade route waving and clapping.

3. _____ Bands play.

B   Rewrite each fragment, turning it into a complete sentence.

1. The new store on the corner. _____

2. By the time the show ended. _____

3. The toad hopping in the grass. _____

C   Correct each run-on sentence or comma splice.

1. The rain has stopped, the trees are still wet.

_____

2. We painted the walls blue we painted the ceiling white.

_____

Grammar: Fragments and Run-ons

Assess

A For each item, write *F* if it is a sentence fragment or *S* if it is a sentence.

1. ____ Getting cable TV.

2. ____ One hundred and fifty channels available.

3. ____ The History Channel is Taylor's favorite.

B Rewrite each sentence fragment, turning it into a complete sentence. If an item is not a fragment, write *correct*.

1. Staying up past 11:00 P.M. to watch the talk shows.

_____

2. Watches football on the weekend.

_____

3. North Carolina won.

_____

4. Hockey playoffs tomorrow at 4:00 P.M.

_____

C Correct each run-on sentence and comma splice.

1. Our friends came over some brought refreshments.

_____

2. Amy made the popcorn, Manuel poured the drinks.

_____

3. I started the movie everyone kept talking.

_____

Writing: Everyday Epic

An **epic** is a long narrative poem about a larger-than-life hero. An everyday epic does not have to be a poem, but it should include these features:

- It focuses on a person from everyday life who has heroic qualities.
- It describes the subject's achievements and qualities such as bravery, a sense of adventure, or the ability to meet tough challenges.
- It tells why the writer admires the subject.

Read the following paragraph. Answer the questions and complete the activities that follow.

> My cousin Reno is the bravest person I know. He has to be brave to do his job. No, Reno is not a fireman or a policeman. He is a high-rise window washer in New York City. His "office" is a small scaffold dozens of stories in the air. Reno is not only brave. He is also modest. Once I asked him how he keeps from being afraid. "It's easy," he said. "I don't look down!"

1. According to the writer, why is Reno heroic? _____

2. What are two words the writer uses to describe Reno?

   _____

   _____

3. For each item below, explain why the person could be considered a hero.

   A. a short boy on the school basketball team

   _____

   _____

   B. a student who has moved to the United States from another country

   _____

   _____

   C. a person who is training to run her first marathon

   _____

   _____

Writing: Everyday Epic

Assess

A Complete the sentences that follow.

1. _____ is an everyday hero in my life.

2. This person is heroic because _____

_____

_____

3. Three words that describe the person's heroic qualities are _____

_____

4. This person inspires me because _____

_____

_____

B Write a one-paragraph everyday epic about the person on the following lines.

_____

_____

_____

_____

_____

_____

_____

_____

_____

_____

_____

_____

_____

Writing: Biography

Practice

A **biography** is a work of nonfiction in which the writer tells about another person's life. An interesting biography includes these features:

- It presents facts and details about the subject.
- It describes important events in the subject's life.
- It brings the subject to life for readers.

Read the following paragraph. Then, complete the activities that follow.

Ali Mitchell has always had rhythm. As a toddler, he banged his spoon against his cereal bowl with a regular beat. As a child, he tapped his fingers on the table in time to any song that was playing on the radio. His parents bought him his first drum set when he was six. He began taking drum lessons, and formed his first band when he was in seventh grade. The music teacher at his school saw that Ali had a special talent. The teacher introduced Ali to a local jazz musician. Now Ali plays in a band with musicians who are more than twice his age.

1. List three facts about Ali that you learned from this paragraph.

_____

_____

_____

2. Name one important event in Ali's life.

_____

_____

3. Circle the letter of the detail that might be included in a biography about Ali Mitchell. Then, on the lines provided, explain why the other details do not belong in Ali's biography.

A. a description of the sounds made by different types of drums
B. a quote from Ali that explains how he feels about drumming
C. a comparison of jazz music and rock and roll

_____

_____

_____

Name _____ Date _____

Writing: Biography

Choose one of the following people as the subject for a biography you will write. Put a check mark next to your choice. Then, complete the activities that follow.

☐ a friend   ☐ a sports figure
☐ a relative   ☐ an actor
☐ a person from history   ☐ other

1. Write the person's name.

_____

2. List three facts about the person.

_____

_____

_____

3. Name one important event in the person's life.

_____

_____

4. Write the first paragraph of your biography on the following lines.

_____

_____

_____

_____

_____

_____

_____

_____

_____

Writing: Timed Essay

A **timed essay** is a written response to a prompt or question given to you by your teacher. The essay must be completed within a specific—and brief—time period. Use these steps to help you write your timed essays:

- **Choose your topic**—Choose the topic you know best.

- **Make a Quick Outline**—A *thesis statement* explains the main point of your essay. State your thesis in the *introduction*. Present at least two main ideas that support your thesis in the *body*.

- **Fill in the Details**—Using your outline, draft your response by including facts, examples, and quotations that support your ideas.

- **Revise**—Make sure all of your details support your thesis.

A Read each of the following timed essay topics. Then, put a checkmark next to the topic that you would use for your timed writing prompt.

☐ Choose an invention that has significantly influenced modern society. Discuss the advantages and disadvantages.
☐ Describe a place you go to relax and explain why and how this place is relaxing.
☐ Describe an important lesson you have learned while in school.

B Complete each of the instructions.

1. Using the topic you chose, write your thesis statement on the lines.

_____

_____

2. Write two main points that support your thesis statement.

_____

_____

3. For each main point you listed in item 2, list two facts, examples, or quotations that support your ideas.

A. _____

_____

B. _____

_____

Writing: Timed Essay

A Read each of the timed essay topics. Then, put a checkmark next to the topic that you will use for your timed writing prompt.

☐ Explain why you would or would not want to live in a large city.
☐ Name someone you consider to be a modern hero or heroine and explain why.
☐ Do you think that sports help develop good character? Discuss.

B Complete each of the instructions.

1. Using the topic you chose, write your thesis statement on the lines provided.

_____

_____

2. On the lines below, write two main points that support your thesis statement.

_____

_____

3. For each main point you listed in item 2, list two facts, examples, or quotations that support your ideas.

_____

_____

_____

_____

4. Draft the opening paragraph of your essay.

_____

_____

_____

_____

_____

Literary Analysis: Protagonist and Antagonist

Practice

The **protagonist** is the main character in a work of literature. The protagonist is the character readers learn most about and care most about. The protagonist is often a good person. However, he or she may have serious flaws.

Often, the protagonist has an **antagonist**—a character or force that opposes the protagonist. The antagonist is usually another character, but it can also be a force, such as a tornado or poverty. The protagonist must struggle against, or fight, the antagonist.

Read the following story. Then, answer the questions that follow.

Jack liked Kayla, but he was nervous about talking with her. One day, he was walking up the school steps when she walked by, wheeling her bicycle. He complimented her on the model. She told him how much she loved to bike. Before Jack knew what he was saying, he asked her to go biking with him next weekend. Amazingly, she said yes. Just then, Al came up the steps.

"Talking about biking?" said Al. "What a coincidence. Kayla, you know I've been meaning to show you some tricks for off-road biking. Why don't I join you this weekend?" He turned to Jack. "You do have a mountain bike, right?"

Jack saw right away that Al was trying to impress Kayla and to embarrass him. "Of course," said Jack. Unfortunately, Jack did not own a mountain bike. He owned a beat-up old ten-speed. That night, he asked his father if he could get one. The answer was no. What was Jack going to do?

1. Who is the protagonist?

   A. Jack's father   **C.** Al
   B. Jack   **D.** Kayla

2. Who or what is the antagonist?

   A. the bicycle   **C.** Jack
   B. Jack's father   **D.** Al

3. Which statement is always true about the protagonist in a story?

   A. He or she is often a force of nature.
   B. He or she must always fight or struggle against another character.
   C. He or she is always a good person.
   D. He or she is the main character.

Literary Analysis: Protagonist and Antagonist

Assess

Read the following story. Then, answer the questions that follow.

Jane and Pat were best friends. For months, they had planned a summer party together. Then, Pat won a scholarship to a summer tennis camp in a nearby town. She would be back in time for the party, but she would be gone for about four weeks.

Jane spent most of the time reading and swimming in the pool at the city center. She was lonely, and missed Pat very much. Finally, the day arrived for Pat to come home. Jane called her and left a message on the answering machine, welcoming her home. Pat never called back. Jane began to worry. Finally, she called Pat again. This time Pat answered the phone.

"Pat! Are you OK? I've been so worried!" said Jane.

"Hi, Jane," Pat answered. "Can I call you back? Sandy, a girl I met at tennis camp is here, and we're kind of busy."

"OK, but we need to talk about our party."

"Oh, Jane, that party is little kid stuff. I was hoping you had forgotten about it."

1. Who is the protagonist?

    A. Jane   **C.** tennis camp

    B. Pat   **D.** Sandy

2. Who or what is the antagonist?

    A. Pat   **C.** tennis camp

    B. Sandy   **D.** Jane

3. Which statement is always true about story characters?

    A. The reader learns more about the antagonist than about the protagonist.

    B. The antagonist is always a bad person, and the protagonist is always a good person.

    C. The reader learns more about the protagonist than about other characters.

    D. The protagonist is usually a force of nature.

Literary Analysis: Author's Purpose and Philosophical Assumptions

Practice

An **author's purpose** is his or her main reason for writing. Writers may write to entertain readers, as in a story. They may write to inform them, giving readers facts on a topic. They may also write to persuade readers to believe something or to take a particular action.

An author's work will often express his or her **philosophical assumptions,** or basic beliefs. For example, an author might write a story about a man who is punished for dishonesty. The author is expressing this basic belief: "It is important to be honest at all times."

Read the following story. Then, answer the questions that follow.

At the age of 50, Eleanor Mayhew was definitely a no-nonsense kind of person. All her neighbors thought she was boring. She didn't believe in fancy cars or television comedies. And she absolutely *hated* those newspapers that are often displayed at the supermarket checkout aisle, the kind with headlines about some movie star being kidnapped by aliens. "Rubbish!" she would mutter as she paid for her no-nonsense beans and fresh tomatoes. Everyone was shocked when they found out that Eleanor was once a famous rock star. That certainly taught a lesson to people who said she was boring!

1. What is the best definition for the term *philosophical assumption?*

   A. the author's purpose for writing   **C.** the author's bibliography
   B. the author's basic beliefs   **D.** the author's protagonist

2. Which of these statements best summarizes the philosophical assumption of the author of this story?

   A. Eleanor Mayhew was a really boring person.
   B. Most supermarket tabloid newspapers are trashy.
   C. People are usually right when they form opinions of others.
   D. People are not always what they seem to be.

3. Which of the following best describes this author's purpose for writing?

   A. to persuade readers to adopt a no-nonsense attitude
   B. to inform readers about the tall tales in supermarket tabloids
   C. to entertain the reader with an interesting character
   D. to convey a mood of suspense and danger

Name _____ Date _____

Read the following story. Then, answer the questions that follow.

Going to the baseball game with Uncle Frank was the biggest thrill of my whole summer. The Astros were doing really well, and people were talking about their World Series chances. I brought my glove just in case a foul ball came my way. In the row in front of me, two older kids sat, laughing and talking throughout most of the game. I heard one of them call the other one Pete. A few times, I heard them make fun of me. Once, I heard Pete say, "Look at the girl with the fielder's glove. What could SHE ever catch, except a cold?"

In the bottom of the eighth inning, Lance Berkman came up to bat. He hit a line drive right toward me. I was so excited that I dropped my glove. It landed on Pete's head. He spilled ice-cold soda all over his pants. Then, Uncle Frank caught Berkman's foul. When the kids looked back, I said, "Yes, he caught it, but it looks like Pete might catch a bad cold." They laughed really hard. It felt good.

1. Which of these statements best summarizes the basic beliefs of the author of this story?

   A. It's almost impossible to catch a foul ball at baseball games.

   B. People shouldn't make fun of others.

   C. People shouldn't drink ice-cold sodas at baseball games.

   D. Foul balls can be dangerous to people sitting in the stands at a baseball game.

2. Which of the following phrases means about the same as *basic beliefs*?

   A. the author's antagonist

   B. the author's purpose for writing

   C. the author's psychological problems

   D. the author's philosophical assumptions

3. Which of the following best describes this author's purpose for writing?

   A. to persuade readers to attend baseball games

   B. to find a lesson in a memorable personal experience

   C. to inform the reader about the rules of baseball

   D. to convey a serious or somber mood

Literary Analysis: Tall Tale and Myth

Practice

A **tall tale** is an American folk story that contains some or all of the following: humor, a larger-than-life hero, amazing deeds that are hard to believe, and hyperbole (exaggeration).

Many ancient cultures had stories called **myths.** Some myths told about the actions of gods. Others told how certain traditions, such as festivals, started, or why natural things, such as thunder and lightning, happen. Others told of heroic humans. **Mythic heroes** often have a god or goddess as a parent, gain special knowledge or gifts, and face tasks that seem impossible.

A   For each item, list all of the characteristics of a tall tale that it shows.

1. A great storm was stirring. It lifted up half of the state of Kansas and set it down in Missouri. Then, just to be fair, it lifted half of Missouri and set it down in Kansas.

   _____

2. When Big Bill heard the storm was coming, he decided it was about time to clean his house. He took out his biggest rope, twirled it three times around his head, and roped in the storm. He pulled that storm all the way across Nebraska and set it loose in his home.

   _____

   _____

B   For each item, list all of the characteristics of a myth or of a mythic hero that appear in it.

1. Apollo was the Greek god of music and light. He killed the monster Python, a giant snake. In honor of this victory, Apollo started the Pythian Games, a sports event that was held every four years.

   _____

2. The hero Hercules was a son of the Greek god Zeus and a mortal woman. Because of a crime he committed, Hercules had to perform twelve Labors. The Labors included battling fire-breathing monsters and moving rivers. Hercules was incredibly strong, though, and he had the help of the gods. He completed all twelve Labors.

   _____

Literary Analysis: Tall Tale and Myth

Assess

A For each item, circle each characteristic of a tall tale that it clearly shows. You may need to circle more than one characteristic.

1. When Paul Bunyan was growing up, he used to eat forty bowls of oatmeal in the morning. Then, after this snack, he would have breakfast.

   humor   larger-than-life hero   amazing deeds   hyperbole

2. In Paul's logging camp, the tables were so long that the men serving food wore roller skates. They had to move fast, otherwise the food would get cold before they reached the other end of the table.

   humor   larger-than-life hero   amazing deeds   hyperbole

3. Paul's blue ox, Babe, was so big that it took a crow a whole day to fly from of one of Babe's horns to the other.

   humor   larger-than-life hero   amazing deeds   hyperbole

B For each item, circle each characteristic of a myth or of a mythic hero that it most clearly illustrates. You may need to circle more than one characteristic.

1. An Ashanti myth of Africa tells that, in the beginning of things, the sky-god Nyame kept all stories for himself. Anansi the spider wished to have the knowledge in these stories, so he made an agreement with Nyame. If Anansi could capture four hard-to-catch creatures, Nyame would give him the stories. Anansi succeeded, and that is why people tell stories today.

   actions of a god   why life is the way it is   why a natural event occurs

2. The Hopi Indians tell that once Coyote went hunting with Eagle. The Coyote said the hunting was poor because there was not enough light. Then, they found a spirit village. In the village were two boxes that controlled light. Coyote and Eagle stole the boxes. Eagle let Coyote carry them, but only if he promised not to open them. Coyote was too curious. He opened them, and the Sun and the Moon escaped. The world grew dark and cold, and that is why there is winter.

   actions of a god   why life is the way it is   why a natural event occurs

Reading: Compare and Contrast

Practice

When you **compare and contrast** two people or things, you tell about the similarities and differences between them. When you compare and contrast two characters, you look for similarities and differences in these categories:

- **characters' appearance and personal qualities**—what each character is like. For example, one character might be weak, while the other is strong.

- **characters' background**—what each character's past life has been like. For example, one character might come from a rich family, while the other comes from a poor family.

- **characters' actions**—what each character does. For example, one character might go to college, while the other goes to work.

- **characters' motives**—the reasons the character has for doing things. For example, one character might want to get a lot of money. The other character might want to help others.

- **characters' fate**—what happens to each character. For example, one character might end up winning, while the other character loses.

Read each item about Sally and Beth. Then, explain what similarity or difference between them is shown in the item. Finally, circle the category of the similarity or difference you wrote about.

1. **Sally:** grew up with Beth in a wealthy family
   Beth: grew up with Sally in a wealthy family

_____

appearance/personality   background   actions/feelings   motives   fate

2. **Sally:** invents a medicine to cure a deadly disease
   Beth: steals the formula for the medicine so that she can make money

_____

appearance/personality   background   actions/feelings   motives   fate

3. **Sally:** wins a prize for her invention
   Beth: goes to jail

_____

appearance/personality   background   actions/feelings   motives   fate

Reading: Compare and Contrast

A Read each item about Richard and Ralph. Then, explain what similarity or difference between them is shown in the item. Finally, circle the category of the similarity or difference you wrote about.

1. Richard: is friendly and outgoing
   Ralph: is shy but smart

_____

appearance/personality background actions/feelings motives fate

2. Richard: wants to be popular at school
   Ralph: wants to win a prize at the Science Fair

_____

appearance/personality background actions/feelings motives fate

3. Richard: goes along with the popular kids when they make fun of Ralph
   Ralph: stands up for himself and tells them they are being rude

_____

appearance/personality background actions/feelings motives fate

4. Richard: apologizes to Ralph for making fun of him
   Ralph: accepts Richard's apology

_____

appearance/personality background actions/feelings motives fate

5. Richard: is happy when he forms his own small group of friends and no longer worries about being popular
   Ralph: is happy when he wins first prize at the Science Fair

_____

appearance/personality background actions/feelings motives fate

B On a separate sheet of paper, write a paragraph in which you compare Richard and Ralph. Conclude your paragraph with a sentence or two answering this question: What lesson does the comparison of these characters teach?

Reading: Analyze Primary Sources

Practice

Today, you can find information in many locations, including books, magazines, and the Internet. Some information will be from primary sources and some from secondary sources. Each type of source offers different kinds of information and different perspectives. Here is a summary of what primary and secondary sources offer.

Type of Source	Features
Primary Source	• firsthand evidence of historical events • created at the time of the event, often by people who witnessed the event • may offer personal insight into the event • examples: letters, newspapers, maps, diaries, photographs
Secondary Source	• created with primary sources and/or other secondary sources • created after the event took place • may be more objective than a primary source • examples: textbooks, encyclopedias, art created after the event

Here are some questions to ask when you **analyze primary sources:**

- Who created the primary source?
- When was the source created?
- Why was the source created?
- Is the source reliable?

For each primary source below, write two questions you might ask as you analyzed the source to determine if it is reliable.

1. a photograph _____

_____

2. a newspaper article _____

_____

3. an eyewitness description of an event _____

_____

Reading: Analyze Primary Sources

Assess

Read the two primary source excerpts below, both from autobiographies. Then, answer the questions that follow.

from Fighting the Flying Circus
by Captain Eddie Rickenbacker

Hastily getting out of doors, I looked over the dark sky, wondering as I did so how many of our boys it would claim before this day's work was done! For we had an important part to play in this day's operations. Headquarters had sent us order to attack all the enemy observation balloons until infantry's operations were completed…. The safety of thousands of our attacking soldiers depended upon our success….

1. What is the topic of this excerpt? _____

_____

2. Why do you think the author wrote it? _____

_____

from The Way to Rainy Mountain
by N. Scott Momaday

My grandmother had a reverence for the sun, a holy regard that now is all but gone out of mankind. There was a wariness in her, and an ancient awe. She was a Christian in her later years, but she had come a long way about, and she never forgot her birthright. As a child she had been to the Sun Dances…. She was about seven when the last Kiowa Sun Dance was held in 1887 on the Washita River above Rainy Mountain Creek. The buffalo were gone….

3. What is the topic of this excerpt? _____

_____

4. Why do you think the author wrote it? _____

_____

5. What information do these two primary sources offer that might not be

available in a secondary source? _____

_____

Name _____ Date _____

Vocabulary: Word roots -min-, -spect-, -merg-, and -fer-

Practice

A **root** is the basic unit of meaning of a word. A **prefix** is one or more syllables added to the beginning of a word or word root to form a new word with a different meaning. Study these examples.

Examples:

Root or Prefix	Meaning	Words with the Root
-min-	small, little, less	minority, diminished, minute
-spect-	see, look, examine	inspected, prospect, spectators
-merg-	dip, plunge	emerge, submerge, emergency
-fer-	to carry, to produce	transfer, referral, fertile

A Replace each underlined word or phrase with the most appropriate word from the chart above.

1. _____ My appetite gradually <u>lessened</u> as I ate.

2. _____ In the spring, the butterfly <u>came out</u> from its cocoon.

3. _____ The settlers chose a <u>productive</u> region for their new village.

4. _____ I carefully <u>examined</u> the package before signing for it.

B Complete each sentence with a word from the chart above.

1. After the next election, power will _____ to the new president.

2. During the hurricane, the governor declared a state of _____.

3. The resolution failed because only a _____ of the voters supported it.

4. The boat race attracted a large crowd of _____.

Vocabulary: Word roots -min-, -spect-, -merg-, and -fer-

Assess

A Revise each sentence so that the underlined vocabulary word is used logically. Be sure not to change the vocabulary word.

1. The cars on the road <u>merged</u> from one lane to two.

_____

2. I took a <u>ferry</u> to get from one side of the street to the other.

_____

3. I thought the complicated task could be carried out with <u>minimal</u> effort.

_____

4. If he weren't so <u>introspective</u>, maybe he'd sometimes think before speaking.

_____

B Circle the root in each word, and think about its meaning. Then, write the word's meaning on the first line. Use a dictionary to check the meaning. Finally, use each word in a new sentence.

1. prospect _____

_____

2. submerge _____

_____

3. minutia _____

_____

4. confer _____

_____

Grammar: Commas

Practice

Use **commas** to indicate a short pause in your writing. Use this guide:

Use commas to separate	Use commas to set off
• two independent clauses in a compound sentence when used with a conjunction: They laughed, <u>and</u> they cried.	• an introductory word, phrase, or clause: At the yard sale, we bought a tent.
• three or more words, phrases, clauses in a series: The dog ran <u>down the path,</u> <u>across the field,</u> <u>and into the</u> <u>woods.</u>	• parenthetical or nonessential expressions: Ari, who is older, is an inch shorter than Ken.
• parts of dates, places, or certain titles: We flew to <u>Ames,</u> <u>Iowa,</u> <u>on</u> May <u>2,</u> <u>2006.</u>	• direct quotations: The coach said, "Take a break."

Referring to the rules, insert commas where needed in the following sentences.

1. The ocean is calm in summer rough in winter and beautiful all year.

2. The lobster boats will return soon so we are watching for them.

3. Portland Maine has many great seafood restaurants.

4. We visited cousins in New Orleans on February 12 2005.

5. The island which is in the middle of the lake has a sandy beach.

6. Kyle said "Let's row the canoe over tomorrow for a swim."

7. They decided to invite Luis who is Juan's younger brother.

8. In addition they decided to pack a lunch to take with them.

9. When he heard about the plans Juan shouted "I'm ready!"

Grammar: Commas

A Insert commas where needed in the following sentences. Put a *C* next to any sentences that do not need commas.

1. Gregory wants eggs for breakfast soup for lunch and spaghetti for dinner.

2. Kate also likes eggs for breakfast but she wants a sandwich for lunch.

3. On Monday October 8 the new cafeteria opened.

4. The cafeteria begins serving lunch at 11:30 and closes at 2:00.

5. Kate loves the sandwiches but Gregory does not like the soup.

B Insert commas where needed in the following sentences. Put a *C* next to any sentences that do not need commas.

1. The gray fox which is a member of the dog family can climb trees.

2. Although mostly active at night this fox sometimes hunts during the day.

3. John who was riding his bike on a desert path spotted a gray fox.

4. He said "I thought there was a coyote in front of me."

5. "I was surprised that it turned out to be a gray fox looking for food."

C Rewrite this paragraph, inserting commas where needed.

On July 4 we are having a barbecue. Jane will bring hot dogs salad and corn. Becca will supply napkins cups and plates. Pam said "I will make brownies which are my specialty." As always Ty will bring the charcoal and do the grilling.

_____

_____

_____

_____

Grammar: Colons, Semicolons, Ellipsis Points

Practice

A **colon** (:) is used mainly to list items after an independent clause. A **semicolon** (;) is used to join independent clauses that are closely related or to separate items in a series that already contain several commas. **Ellipsis points** (. . .) usually indicate (1) words that have been left out of a quotation, (2) a series that continues beyond the items mentioned, or (3) action occurring or time passing in a narrative.

> Colon: Jason likes three kinds of movies: action, adventure, and sci-fi.
> Semicolon: Renee surfs; Paco swims; Rob water skis.
> Ellipsis points: You know, you'll need paper, pencils . . . the usual.
> "I will be a star," she thought, "someday . . . "

A For each item, insert a colon and complete the sentence. For item 4, write an original sentence using a colon.

1. I want to visit these three cities _____.

2. Here are two rules for bicycle safety _____.

3. Pack these things for the hike _____.

4. _____

B For each item, insert semicolons where needed.

1. Caroline wants to visit Ashville Tim wants to visit Nashville.

2. We were in Oxford, Ohio, on May 2 Kent, Ohio, on May 4 and Lima, Ohio, on May 8.

3. Cleveland is on Lake Erie Chicago is on Lake Michigan Toronto is on Lake Ontario.

C For each item, insert ellipsis points where needed.

1. Cal wondered what would summer be like without Nina around?

2. The mayor said, "We will clean up the waterfront we will fix the streets."

3. The beach was as we had expected: crowds heat greasy fries

Name _____ Date _____

Grammar: Colons, Semicolons, Ellipsis Points

Assess

A For each item, insert a colon and complete the sentence. For items 4 and 5, write original sentences, correctly using a colon.

1. This cell phone comes in three colors _____.

2. I'll give you one reason to see the movie _____.

3. We have band practice three days a week _____.

4. _____

5. _____

B For each item, insert semicolons where needed. For items 4 and 5, write original sentences, correctly using semicolons.

1. Nadia sings soprano Lucy sings alto.

2. The band included Sami, who played bass Lynn, who played guitar and Jared, who played drums.

3. The first show was at 7:00 P.M. the second show was at 9:00 P.M. the third show was at 11:00 P.M.

4. _____

5. _____

C For each item, insert ellipsis points where needed.

1. Jessie thought she had done the right thing but she couldn't be sure

2. For sure, there would be cake and ice cream and favors and

3. Lincoln's speech begins, "Four score and seven years ago"

4. Donald wondered what that ticking sound could be

5. "You you can't blame me," he stammered.

Grammar: Sentence Structure and Length

To give your writing interest, **vary the structure and length of your sentences.** Here are several ways to vary the structure:

Begin with an adverb clause: <u>When weather permitted,</u> they rode their bikes.
Begin with a subject complement: <u>Beautiful</u> was the day when they started out.
Begin with a direct object: <u>The best</u> they saved for last.
Reverse the subject and verb: So sweetly <u>sang</u> <u>the birds</u>.

To vary the length of your sentences, combine short sentences into a long sentence or break up a long sentence into two short sentences, as in this example:

The festival began at 10:00 A.M., but we went at 4:00 P.M., when the crowds were smaller, and we could see the performers more easily.
The festival began at 10:00 A.M., but we went at 4:00 P.M. By then, the crowds were smaller, and we could see the performers more easily.

A Rewrite each sentence, putting the underlined words at the beginning. Remember to insert a comma after an adverb clause.

1. The divers saw colorful fish <u>wherever they looked.</u>

_____

2. They were <u>surprised</u> to find an old sea chest.

_____

3. They would divide <u>the treasure</u> among themselves.

_____

B Break up this long sentence into short sentences.

When the discovery of the treasure made the evening news, suddenly the divers became famous, and some people even declared that they were the rightful owners of the treasure.

_____

_____

_____

Grammar: Sentence Structure and Length

A Rewrite each sentence, putting the underlined words at the beginning. (Change the order of other words as needed to make sure the sentence still makes sense.) Remember to insert a comma after an adverb clause.

1. Ann gave <u>the nuts</u> to her brother.

   _____

2. She saved <u>the chocolates</u> for herself.

   _____

3. The caramel-filled were <u>the most delicious,</u> and she ate them first.

   _____

4. Ann would be happy <u>if the whole box were filled with caramel-filled chocolates.</u>

   _____

5. Ann's brother had finished the nuts <u>before the evening was over.</u>

   _____

B Combine the short sentences into one long sentence, and break up the long sentence into short sentences.

1. Volcanoes erupt. Lava streams down the mountainside. Nearby residents flee.

   _____

2. When we went to Italy, we visited the ruins of the ancient city of Pompeii, which was destroyed during an eruption of the volcano Mount Vesuvius in A.D. 79, although the molten lava preserved many of the buildings.

   _____

   _____

   _____

Spelling: Spelling on College Entrance Exams

Practice

Spelling is sometimes tested on college entrance exams. Follow these guidelines:

- When adding a prefix to the beginning of a word, do not drop any letters:

  ac- + claim = <u>ac</u>claim   mis- + shapen = mi<u>ss</u>hapen

- When adding an ending that begins with a vowel to a word that ends in silent *e*, drop the *e* unless the word ends in *ce* or *ge*.

  prece<u>de</u> + -<u>ing</u> = prece<u>ding</u>   *but*   coura<u>ge</u> + -ous = coura<u>ge</u>ous

- When adding an ending that begins with a vowel to a word that ends in a single vowel + a single consonant, double the consonant only if the stress stays on the last syllable.

  occ<u>ur</u> + -ed = occu<u>rr</u>ed   occ<u>ur</u> + -<u>ence</u> = occu<u>rr</u>ence
  pref<u>er</u> + -<u>ing</u> = prefe<u>rr</u>ing   *but*   pref<u>er</u> + -<u>ence</u> = pref<u>er</u>ence

- Be careful spelling words that sound alike or nearly alike, such as *adapt* ("to change") and *adopt* ("to take on") or *parenthesis* (singular) and *parentheses* (plural).

  The book was <u>adapted</u> as a movie. (not <u>adopted</u>)
  Put the answer in <u>parentheses</u>. (not <u>parenthesis</u>)

- Use memory tricks to help you spell words that give you trouble. In this example, the three *O*'s at the beginning will help you remember to spell *sophomore* with three *o*'s.

  <u>O, O, O,</u> I love being a s<u>o</u>ph<u>o</u>m<u>o</u>re.

A   For each item, add the ending to the word to form a new word.

1. mis- + shapen = _____   **3.** courage + -ous = _____

2. precede + -ing = _____   **4.** occur + -ed = _____

B   On the line before each sentence, write *correct* if the underlined word is spelled correctly. If it is not, write the correct spelling of the underlined word.

1. _____ You can <u>adapt</u> this office computer for home use.

2. _____ I am a <u>sophamore</u> at George Washington High School.

3. _____ The author won <u>aclaim</u> for her first novel.

4. _____ Put the word in <u>parenthesis</u> instead of using commas.

Name _____ Date _____

Spelling: Spelling on College Entrance Exams

Assess

A For each item, add the ending to the word to form a new word. Write the new word on the line provided.

1. ac- + count = _____

2. occur + -ence = _____

3. prefer + -ed = _____

4. precede + -ing = _____

5. courage + -ous = _____

B On the line before each sentence, write *correct* if the underlined word is spelled correctly. If it is not, write the correct spelling of the underlined word.

1. _____ We can fly or drive but our <u>preferrence</u> is to go by train.

2. _____ A <u>sophomore</u> year comes before a junior year.

3. _____ Strange events were <u>occuring</u> every day.

4. _____ The <u>mishapen</u> leaf cast an odd shadow.

5. _____ You can use a pair of <u>parenthesis</u> or a pair of brackets.

C Underline the correct word from the choice in parentheses.

1. _____ It is often hard to (adapt, adopt) to change.

2. _____ We used to ignore lateness, but now we will (adapt, adopt) a new policy.

3. _____ You forgot a closing (parenthesis, parentheses) before the period.

Writing: Journal Entries

Practice

A **journal** is a written record of events that includes the writer's thoughts and feelings. A person might write journal entries every day or from time to time. A journal entry usually includes these features:

- It is written from the first-person point of view. The writer uses the pronoun *I*.

- It presents events in the order in which they happen.

- It tells what the writer thinks and feels about the events he or she describes.

- It may include the date, the time, or even the place.

Read the following paragraph. Then, complete the activities that follow.

October 18

I'm really disappointed! Mr. Ortiz finally announced the roles for the Drama Club production. I was positive I'd get a lead part, but somehow I ended up in the chorus. I have a small solo at the end of the first act, but I really wanted a bigger part. The one good thing is that Karina is in the chorus, too. At least I'll get to hang out with my best friend at play practice.

1. What event does the author describe?

_____

2. How does the author feel about what happened?

_____

3. List two recent events that you could write about in a journal entry.

_____

_____

4. What is your main thought or strongest feeling about each event?

_____

_____

_____

_____

Name _____ Date _____

Writing: Journal Entries

A Choose an event from your own life to write about in a series of journal entries. Then, complete the activities that follow.

1. What event will you write about? _____

2. Put details of the event in time order. On line 1, write what happened first. On line 2, write what happened next. On line 3, write what happened last.

   1. _____

   2. _____

   3. _____

3. Write your journal entries on the lines below.

_____

_____

_____

_____

B Choose a character from a book or story you have read recently. Write three journal entries from that character's point of view that describes an important event.

1. Write the character's name. _____

2. Write your journal entry on the following lines. Make sure to use the pronoun *I*.

_____

_____

_____

_____

_____

_____

Writing: Letter

A **letter** is a written form of communication from one person or group to another. It is written in a standard format that includes a heading, greeting, body, closing, and signature. There are two main types of letters:

- A *friendly letter* is written to someone with whom the writer wants to communicate in a personal, friendly way.

- A *business letter* is written for a formal purpose. A letter to a company requesting product information is an example of a business letter.

You can write a friendly letter to someone you do not know or do not know well. However, the less well you know the person, the more respectful and formal your style needs to be.

A Read the example. Then, complete the activities that follow.

[HEADING] 327 Winding Way
Louisville, KY

[GREETING] October 14

Hi Jess,   [BODY]

  I got your package today, and I'm so excited! I can't believe you burned all those CDs for me! I've been listening to them all day. They're all so good, I can't decide which one I like best.

  Mom says we can come out to visit you again in the spring. I can't wait! I'm saving my money so we can go to the mall and the movies like last time.

Love,   [CLOSING]
Asha   [SIGNATURE]

1. Is this an example of a friendly letter or a business letter? _____

2. Check the item that is *not* an example of a friendly letter.

   A. letter to a pen pal in another country

   B. letter to a company asking for a replacement part for a camera

   C. letter to former neighbor asking about her life in a new town

3. List three people to whom you might send a friendly letter.

   _____

4. List two topics you might discuss in a letter to a person on your list.

   _____

Name _____ Date _____

Writing: Letter

Assess

Complete the activities.

1. Name a person to whom you might send a letter.

_____

2. List two or three topics you might discuss in a letter to that person.

_____

_____

3. Fill in the lines below to draft your letter. If you are writing a business letter, use a polite, formal style. If you are writing a friendly letter, you can use a more relaxed style.

[HEADING]

_____

_____

_____

[GREETING]

_____

[BODY]

_____

_____

_____

_____

_____

_____

[CLOSING]

_____

[SIGNATURE]

_____

Writing: Comparison-and-Contrast Essay

A **comparison-and-contrast essay** discusses the similarities and differences between two or more subjects. A strong comparison-and-contrast essay should include these elements:

- a topic involving two or more subjects that are alike and different
- accurate facts and details about each subject
- a presentation of each subject using **subject-by-subject** or **point-by-point** organization. A subject-by-subject organization presents all the details about one subject, then all the details about the next subject. A point-by-point organization discusses one aspect of both subjects, then another aspect of both subjects, and so on.

A Read the example. Then, complete the activity and answer the questions that follow.

Cats do not mind being left alone during the day. In fact, cats are so independent, they may not even come when you call them.
Dogs, on the other hand, need companionship. They like to play with their owners and can be trained to come, fetch, and beg.

1. Put a check mark next to the type of organization used in this example.

☐ subject-by-subject   ☐ point-by-point

2. What are the two points of comparison in the example?

_____

_____

3. What could be a third point of comparison between cats and dogs?

_____

4. Write a paragraph in which you compare two animals. Use at least two points of comparison.

_____

_____

_____

_____

Name _____ Date _____

Writing: Comparison-and-Contrast Essay

Assess

Circle one of the following topics. Then, complete the activities that follow.

two characters in a movie you have seen   two people you know
two sports or activities   two seasons or times of day
two places you have visited   other: _____

1. Write your specific topic on the line.

_____

2. List facts and details about each subject.

_____   _____

_____   _____

_____   _____

_____   _____

3. List three similarities and/or differences that you will write about.

_____

_____

_____

4. Choose an organization—either subject-by-subject or point-by-point—for your essay.

_____

5. Write the first paragraph of your comparison-and-contrast essay on the following lines.

_____

_____

_____

_____

_____

Literature-Based Strategies

Predictogram Relating Words

About the Strategy

Predictograms ask students to use what they know about words and phrases from a selection to make predictions about its content and structure. Prediction activities involve students in the text, engage their attention, and give them a stake in the outcome of a story.

A sample predictogram is provided using the story "Seventh Grade."

Predictogram Relating Words

(Title) _Seventh Grade_ **2**

Look at the words below. Draw lines between any items you think might be connected. Explain your connection on the line you draw. You might choose several connections with some words and none with others.

1 embarrassed

rosebushes of shame

a new year, new experiences

confusing, like the inside of a watch

Victor (the main character)

bouquets of love

bluff

3

impress

Victor is trying to impress someone.

with greater conviction

Step 1

Choose nine words, phrases, or quotations from the selection that will help students predict what a story will be about.

Step 2

Encourage students to use the title as they make their predictions.

Step 3

Remind students to think about what they already know about the words and phrases.

Skills and Strategies: *predict outcomes, activate prior knowledge, draw conclusions*

Idea Exchange

Keep in Mind

• Choose appropriate words, phrases, quotations, and topical cues, such as titles or key words, to help students make associations.

• Model one prediction before individuals begin.

• Be sure students return to their predictograms after reading to confirm their predictions.

All Together Now

You might use the relating words predictogram to begin a class discussion. Students could state their predictions rather than writing them down.

Predictogram Relating Words

(Title) _____

Look at the words below. Draw lines between any items you think might be connected. Explain your connection on the line you draw. You might choose several connections with some words and none with others.

Predictogram Literary Features

About the Strategy

Predictograms ask students to use what they know about words and phrases from a selection to make predictions about its content and structure. Prediction activities involve students in the text, engage their attention, and give them a stake in the outcome of a story.

The following model is based on "All Summer in a Day."

Predictogram Literary Features

(Title) __All Summer in a Day__ **2**

Look at the selection title above and this list of words and phrases to write sentences that predict who and what this story might be about.

1

teacher	silence was so immense	jungle
solemn and pale	remembered a warmness	Margot
muffled cries	turning their faces up	Venus
9 years old	rocket men and women	a closet
then looked away	raining for seven years	soon
It's stopping.	very frail	running

Characters: _____

Setting: _____

3

Problem: _____

Events: _____

Outcome: _____

Mystery Words or Phrases: _____

Step 1

Choose five to ten words or phrases from the selection that will help students predict what the story will be about.

Step 2

Encourage students to use the title as they make their predictions.

Step 3

Remind students to think about what they already know about the words and phrases.

Skills and Strategies: *predict outcomes, activate prior knowledge, draw conclusions*

Idea Exchange

Keep in Mind
• Choose appropriate words, phrases, and topical cues, such as titles or key words, to help students make associations.
• Model one prediction before individuals begin.
• Be sure students return to their predictograms after reading to confirm their predictions.

Solo Exploration
Encourage students to use this predictogram to plan their own writing. They can collect their ideas in the box and sort them according to literary feature as a prewriting strategy. **(writing)**

Predictogram Literary Features

(Title) _____

Look at the selection title above and this list of words and phrases to write sentences that predict who and what this story might be about.

```
┌─────────────────────────────────────────┐
│                                         │
│                                         │
│                                         │
│                                         │
│                                         │
│                                         │
│                                         │
└─────────────────────────────────────────┘
```

Characters: _____

_____

Setting: _____

_____

Problem: _____

_____

Events: _____

_____

_____

Outcome: _____

_____

Mystery Words or Phrases: _____

_____

Predictogram Asking Questions

About the Strategy

Predictograms ask students to use what they know about words and phrases from a selection to make predictions about its content and structure. Prediction activities involve students in the text, engage their attention, and give them a stake in the outcome of a story.

Look at the following example.

An asking questions predictogram works well with any fictional piece in which the words and phrases selected suggest questions to the reader.

Predictogram Asking Questions

(Title) __A Ribbon for Baldy__ **2**

Look at the title of the selection above and the words or phrases below. Can you think of any questions to ask about this selection?

1

project	Why is a project important in this story?
posture	
Little Baldy	
cone-shaped	
broom-sedge	
fire	
corn row	
corkscrew	

Choose one of your questions and write a paragraph answering it.

3

Question: _____

Answer: _____
_____
_____
_____
_____
_____
_____

Step 1

Choose eight words or phrases from the selection that will help students write questions to predict what a story will be about.

Step 2

Encourage students to use the title as they make their predictions.

Step 3

Remind students to think about what they already know about the words and phrases as they answer the question.

Skills and Strategies: *predict outcomes, activate prior knowledge, draw conclusions*

Idea Exchange

Keep in Mind

• Choose appropriate words, phrases, and topical cues, such as titles or key words, to help students write their questions.

• Model one prediction before individuals begin.

• Be sure students return to their predictograms after reading to confirm their predictions.

Buddywork

Suggest to students that they use the glossary at the end of a chapter in their social studies book to create an asking questions predictogram. They can use their predictograms to help them set purposes for reading the chapter. **(cross-curricular connection)**

Predictogram Asking Questions

(Title) _____

Look at the title of the selection above and the words or phrases below. Can you think of any questions to ask about this selection?

Choose one of your questions and write a paragraph answering it.

Question: _____

_____

Answer: _____

_____

_____

_____

_____

_____

Predictogram Using Quotations

About the Strategy

Predictograms ask students to use what they know about words and phrases from a selection to make predictions about its content and structure. Prediction activities involve students in the text, engage their attention, and give them a stake in the outcome of a story.

Look at the following example.

A using quotations predictogram works well with any fictional piece in which characters can be identified by their words.

Predictogram Using Quotations

(Title) Becky and the Wheels-and-Brake Boys

Look at the title above and the descriptions of each character below. Can you predict who might have said each of the following? Write the quotation next to the character who might have said it.

1

"D'you think you're a boy?"

"I can't get rid of it, mam.

"What am I going to do?"

Character	Quotation
Becky: a young girl who wants a bike	**3**
Mum: Becky's mother	

2

Now write a paragraph about one of the characters using the quotations above.

_____

_____

_____

_____

Step 1
Choose three to ten quotations from the selection that will help students predict what a story will be about.

Step 2
Choose two main characters and write a brief description of each.

Step 3
Ask students to match the quotations with the characters who might say them.

Skills and Strategies: *predict outcomes, activate prior knowledge, draw conclusions*

Idea Exchange

Keep in Mind
• Choose identifying quotations and topical cues, such as titles or key words, to help students make associations.
• Model one prediction before individuals begin.
• Be sure students return to their predictograms after reading to confirm their predictions.

All Together Now
Students could take turns reading the quotations with differing inflections. The class could predict how each sentence might be said in the context of the story. While reading they can check their predictions.

Predictogram Using Quotations

(Title) _____

Look at the title above and the descriptions of each character below. Can you predict who might have said each of the following? Write the quotation next to the character who might have said it.

Character	Quotation

Now write a paragraph about one of the characters using the quotations above.

_____

_____

_____

_____

K-W-L Chart

About the Strategy

K-W-L is a strategy for reading expository text that helps students use their prior knowledge to generate interest in a selection. K-W-L also helps students set purposes for reading by encouraging them to express their curiosity for the topic they will be reading about. K-W-L encourages group members to share and discuss what they know, what they want to know, and what they learn about a topic.

List selections for which you would like to use a K-W-L chart.

Step ❶

Students brainstorm what they know or think they know about the topic.

Step ❷

Students list questions they hope to have answered as they read.

Step ❸

Students list what they learn as they read.

K-W-L Chart

Topic: Abraham Lincoln

What We **K**now	What We **W**ant to Know	What We **L**earned
Lincoln was president of the United States.	What was Lincoln's childhood like?	Lincoln was born in a log cabin and was poor as a child.
Lincoln grew up poor.	How was Lincoln educated?	Lincoln went to school when he could and read everything he could find.
	What kind of person was Lincoln?	Lincoln was a good wrestler and runner and loved to tell jokes and stories.
❶	❷	❸

Skills and Strategies: *activate prior knowledge, generate questions, set purpose, summarize facts*

Idea Exchange

Keep in Mind

• If students are unsure of a fact they listed in column one, they can turn it into a question in column two.

• Encourage students to find out the answers to any unanswered questions.

Solo Exploration

Students can use a K-W-L chart to set purposes for reading a daily newspaper. Before reading, students should think about what they know (e.g., the weather forecast from listening to the radio) and what they want to know. **(cross-curricular connection)**

K-W-L Chart

Topic: _____

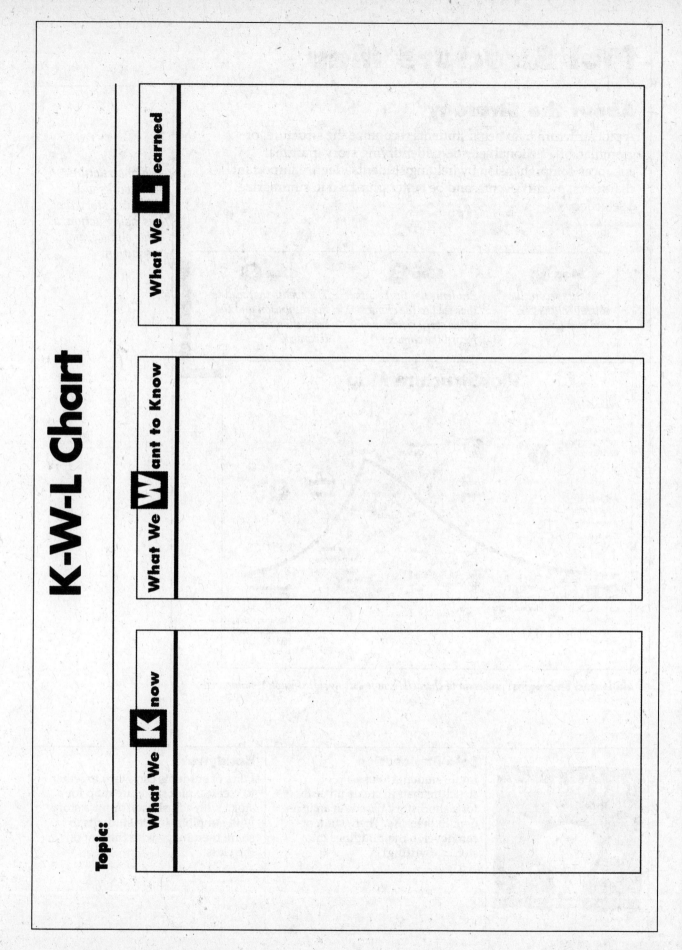

What We **K**now	What We **W**ant to Know	What We **L**earned

Plot Structure Map

About the Strategy

A plot structure map helps students recognize the structure, or grammar, of a fictional selection. Identifying story grammar enhances comprehension by helping students identify important characters, predict events, and be better prepared to summarize a selection.

A plot structure map works well with any story that has rising action, a clear climax, and a resolution.

Step 1
Students record the setting, characters, and problem.

Step 2
Students list the events that lead to the climax of the story before they record the climax.

Step 3
The events that lead to the resolution and the resolution itself are recorded.

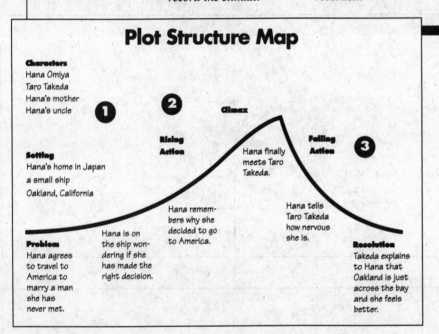

Plot Structure Map

Characters
Hana Omiya
Taro Takeda
Hana's mother
Hana's uncle

Setting
Hana's home in Japan
a small ship
Oakland, California

Problem
Hana agrees to travel to America to marry a man she has never met.

1

Hana is on the ship wondering if she has made the right decision.

Rising Action

2

Hana remembers why she decided to go to America.

Climax

Hana finally meets Taro Takeda.

Falling Action

3

Hana tells Taro Takeda how nervous she is.

Resolution
Takeda explains to Hana that Oakland is just across the bay and she feels better.

Skills and Strategies: *understand characters, note setting, identify plot, summarize*

Idea Exchange

Solo Exploration
Invite students to use a plot structure map to create an outline for a short story based on an incident in their life. Then, students can develop their outlines into stories. **(writing)**

Buddywork
Pairs of students can work together to create a plot structure map for a story with a flashback or for a story with subplots. Invite students to share their maps with the rest of the class.

Plot Structure Map

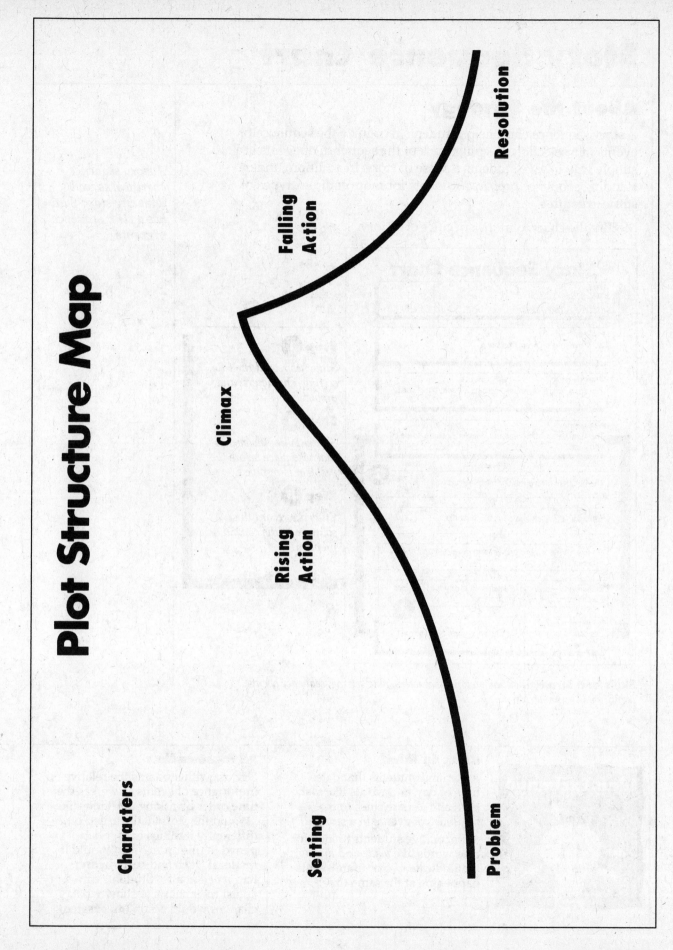

Characters

Setting

Rising Action

Climax

Falling Action

Problem

Resolution

Story Sequence Chart

About the Strategy

A story sequence chart helps students recognize the sequence of events in a selection. Keeping track of the sequence of events is a simple way to give students a sense of story. In addition, understanding sequence prepares students for more complex types of story structures.

Modify the chart to fit the specifics of a story.

A story sequence chart works well with any story that has a clear sequence of events.

Story Sequence Chart

1 **Title:**
Zlateh the Goat

Setting:
a village and the road to town

Characters:
Aaron, a boy; Reuven, his father; Zlateh, their goat

Problem:
The family needs money and Reuven decides to sell the goat.

Events **2**

The butcher offers money for the goat.

Aaron and Zlateh leave for the butcher.

On their way, a huge snowstorm develops and they get lost.

Zlateh and Aaron take shelter in a haystack, where Zlateh provides warmth and milk. **3**

Solution:
The family is grateful to Zlateh and decides never to sell the goat.

Step 1

Students record the title, setting, characters, and problem.

Step 2

Students list the events that take place before the problem is resolved.

Step 3

Students record the solution to the central problem.

Skills and Strategies: *understand characters, note setting, sequence events, identify plot, summarize*

Idea Exchange

Keep in Mind

• Remind students that dates, time of day, and words like *first*, *next*, and *last* are clues to the sequence of events in a story.

• Encourage students to look for clue words like *while* and *during* that indicate two or more events happening at the same time.

All Together Now

Discuss with students the relative importance of events as well as the time order by asking questions like "Would the story have turned out differently if things hadn't happened in this order?" or "Would it matter if 'such and such' hadn't happened at all?" Students can adjust their charts to show what changes would occur. **(discussion)**

Story Sequence Chart

Title:

Setting:

Characters:

Problem:

Events

Solution:

Story Triangle

About the Strategy

A story triangle is a creative way to think about and summarize a story. Like a traditional story map, the story triangle helps students recognize story elements. However, a story triangle allows students to respond personally to a story since students must describe rather than just list characters, events, and problems.

The following model is based on the story "Seventh Grade."

Story triangles work well with all types of fiction, including realistic and historical fiction.

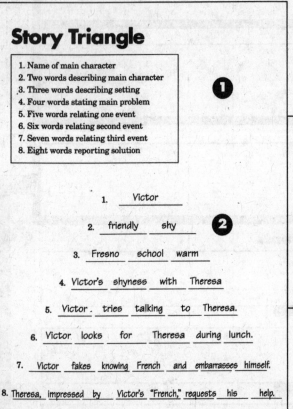

Story Triangle

1. Name of main character
2. Two words describing main character
3. Three words describing setting
4. Four words stating main problem
5. Five words relating one event
6. Six words relating second event
7. Seven words relating third event
8. Eight words reporting solution

①

1. _____ Victor _____

2. _friendly_   _shy_   **②**

3. _Fresno_   _school_   _warm_

4. _Victor's_ _shyness_ _with_ _Theresa_

5. _Victor_ _tries_ _talking_ _to_ _Theresa._

6. _Victor_ _looks_ _for_ _Theresa_ _during_ _lunch._

7. _Victor_ _fakes_ _knowing_ _French_ _and_ _embarrasses_ _himself._

8. _Theresa,_ _impressed_ _by_ _Victor's "French,"_ _requests_ _his_ _help._

Step ①

Students follow the directions at the top of the page to fill in the story triangle.

Step ②

Encourage students to be creative as they choose words, phrases, and sentences.

Skills and Strategies: *understand characters, note setting, identify plot, summarize*

Idea Exchange

Keep in Mind

• If students get stuck in the middle, encourage them to start with the last line and work backward.

• When using a story triangle with another story, be sure to change the guidelines to match the story.

Solo Exploration

After students complete their story triangles, they can circle any vague words they used. Encourage students to choose synonyms that are more interesting and specific to replace the vague words.

Story Triangle

1. Name of main character
2. Two words describing main character
3. Three words describing setting
4. Four words stating main problem
5. Five words relating one event
6. Six words relating second event
7. Seven words relating third event
8. Eight words reporting solution

1. _____

2. _____ _____

3. _____ _____ _____

4. _____ _____ _____ _____

5. _____ _____ _____ _____ _____

6. _____ _____ _____ _____ _____ _____

7. _____ _____ _____ _____ _____ _____ _____

8. _____ _____ _____ _____ _____ _____ _____ _____

Story-Within-a-Story Map

About the Strategy

A story-within-a-story map helps students identify the plot events of this complex text structure. Keeping track of plot events enhances comprehension by helping students recognize the change in narrative that is part of this structure.

Story-within-a-story maps work well with fiction in which the plot includes a story within the story.

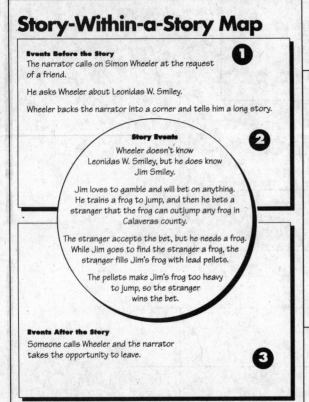

Story-Within-a-Story Map

Events Before the Story ❶
The narrator calls on Simon Wheeler at the request of a friend.

He asks Wheeler about Leonidas W. Smiley.

Wheeler backs the narrator into a corner and tells him a long story.

Story Events ❷
Wheeler doesn't know Leonidas W. Smiley, but he does know Jim Smiley.

Jim loves to gamble and will bet on anything. He trains a frog to jump, and then he bets a stranger that the frog can outjump any frog in Calaveras county.

The stranger accepts the bet, but he needs a frog. While Jim goes to find the stranger a frog, the stranger fills Jim's frog with lead pellets.

The pellets make Jim's frog too heavy to jump, so the stranger wins the bet.

Events After the Story
Someone calls Wheeler and the narrator takes the opportunity to leave. ❸

Step ❶

At the top, students write the plot events that take place before the story is told.

Step ❷

In the inner circle, students list the plot events of the story.

Step ❸

At the bottom, students write the events that happen after the story is told.

Skills and Strategies: *use story elements, use text structure/genre, sequence*

Idea Exchange

Keep in Mind

If students are having difficulty recognizing this text structure, have them reread to look for the point in the story when the narrative shifts.

Solo Exploration

Suggest that students do a story-comparison map for the story and the story within the story to look for similarities and differences between them.

Story-Within-a-Story Map

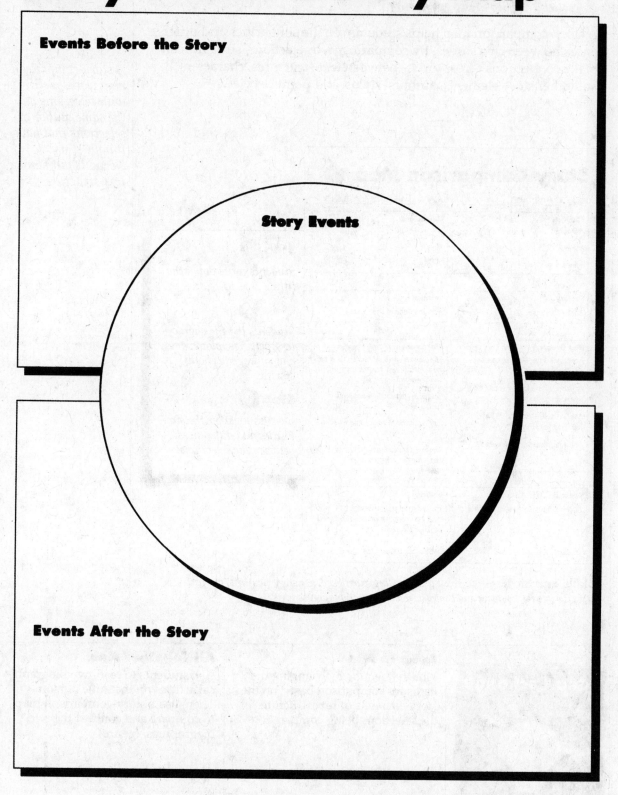

Events Before the Story

Story Events

Events After the Story

Story-Comparison Map

About the Strategy

A story-comparison map helps students see the similarities and differences between two stories. By comparing two selections, students can make connections across texts—between text structures, characters and other story elements, authors' styles, and points of view.

A story-comparison map works well with selections by the same author or selections that have unique story elements but similar text structures.

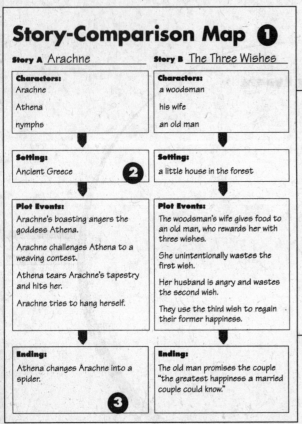

Story-Comparison Map 1

Story A Arachne

Story B The Three Wishes

Characters:
Arachne
Athena
nymphs

Characters:
a woodsman
his wife
an old man

Setting:
Ancient Greece

Setting:
a little house in the forest

Plot Events:
Arachne's boasting angers the goddess Athena.

Arachne challenges Athena to a weaving contest.

Athena tears Arachne's tapestry and hits her.

Arachne tries to hang herself.

Plot Events:
The woodsman's wife gives food to an old man, who rewards her with three wishes.

She unintentionally wastes the first wish.

Her husband is angry and wastes the second wish.

They use the third wish to regain their former happiness.

Ending:
Athena changes Arachne into a spider.

Ending:
The old man promises the couple "the greatest happiness a married couple could know."

Step 1
Students write down the titles.

Step 2
Students list the characters, settings, plot events, and endings for both stories.

Step 3
Discuss together the similarities and differences between the selections.

Skills and Strategies: *recall prior reading experience, use story elements, use text structure/genre, compare and contrast, make connections across texts*

Idea Exchange

Keep in Mind
Modify the map by changing the items for comparison based on the story elements or text structures of the selections being compared.

All Together Now
Ask students to read two biographical articles on the same person. Then, use a story-comparison map to compare and contrast the two biographies. **(genre)**

Story-Comparison Map

Story A _____   Story B _____

Characters:

Characters:

Setting:

Setting:

Plot Events:

Plot Events:

Ending:

Ending:

Cause-Effect Frame

About the Strategy

A cause-effect frame helps students identify what happened and why it happened in both fictional and nonfictional texts. When students can see that there are causal relationships between events or ideas in text, they can make generalizations about other causal relationships in new texts and in life situations.

Cause-effect frames work well with any selection that has clear cause-and-effect relationships.

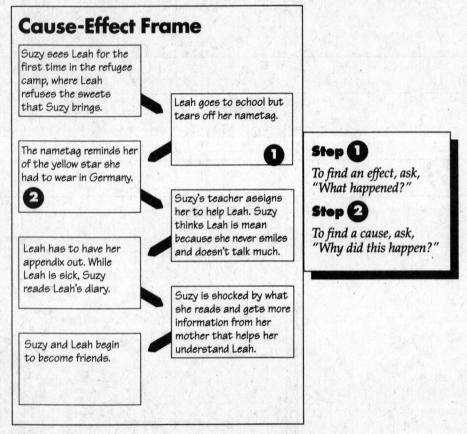

Cause-Effect Frame

Suzy sees Leah for the first time in the refugee camp, where Leah refuses the sweets that Suzy brings.

Leah goes to school but tears off her nametag.

1

The nametag reminds her of the yellow star she had to wear in Germany.

2

Suzy's teacher assigns her to help Leah. Suzy thinks Leah is mean because she never smiles and doesn't talk much.

Leah has to have her appendix out. While Leah is sick, Suzy reads Leah's diary.

Suzy is shocked by what she reads and gets more information from her mother that helps her understand Leah.

Suzy and Leah begin to become friends.

Step 1
To find an effect, ask, "What happened?"

Step 2
To find a cause, ask, "Why did this happen?"

Skills and Strategies: *summarize, sequence, cause-effect, make inferences*

Idea Exchange

Keep in Mind
• Suggest that students look for clue words, such as *since, as a result, consequently, therefore,* and *thus.*
• Remind students that some causes are not stated in the text. Students will have to figure out the cause by looking at what happened and asking themselves, "Why might this have happened?"

Solo Exploration
Help students see that they can use cause-effect frames as a way to organize their writing. Students can choose an important school issue and use a cause-effect frame to outline the main point. Ask students to place the outlines in their portfolios to use for future writing. **(portfolio)**

Cause-Effect Frame

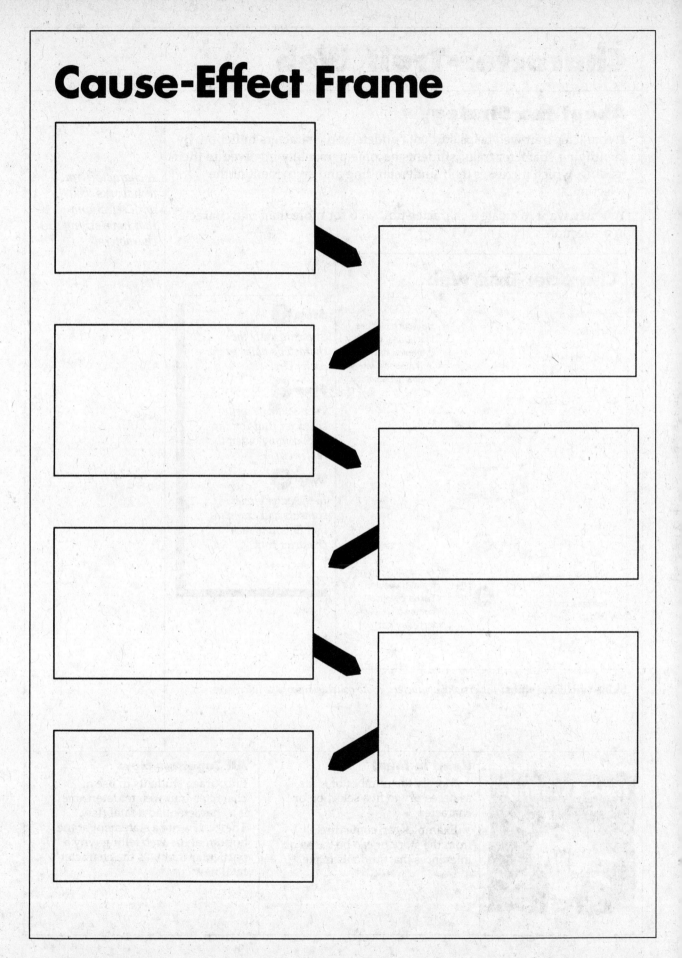

Character-Trait Web

About the Strategy

A character-trait web helps students understand characters in fiction. By identifying character traits, students become personally involved in their reading, which increases their understanding and enjoyment of the selection.

You may want to create a character-trait web for more than one character in a selection.

A character-trait web works well with selections that have strong characters.

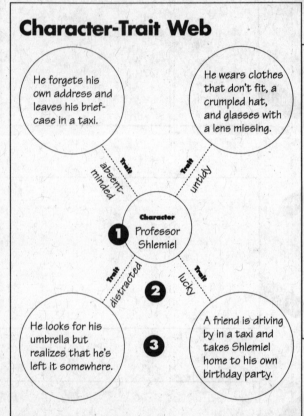

Character-Trait Web

He forgets his own address and leaves his brief-case in a taxi.

He wears clothes that don't fit, a crumpled hat, and glasses with a lens missing.

Trait absent-minded

Trait untidy

Character 1 Professor Shlemiel

Trait distracted 2

Trait lucky

He looks for his umbrella but realizes that he's left it somewhere. 3

A friend is driving by in a taxi and takes Shlemiel home to his own birthday party.

Step ❶

Students write the character's name in the center circle.

Step ❷

Then students write character traits on the lines coming out of the center circle.

Step ❸

In the outer circles, students add examples that illustrate each character trait.

Skills and Strategies: *understand characters, draw conclusions, make inferences*

Idea Exchange

Keep in Mind
- Modify the number of traits as necessary to fit a selection or character.
- Examples can come directly from the story or can be based on inferences that students make.

All Together Now

Encourage students to use a character-trait web to determine if a character had a fatal flaw. They can write a statement at the bottom of the web telling why a particular trait was the character's fatal flaw.

Character-Trait Web

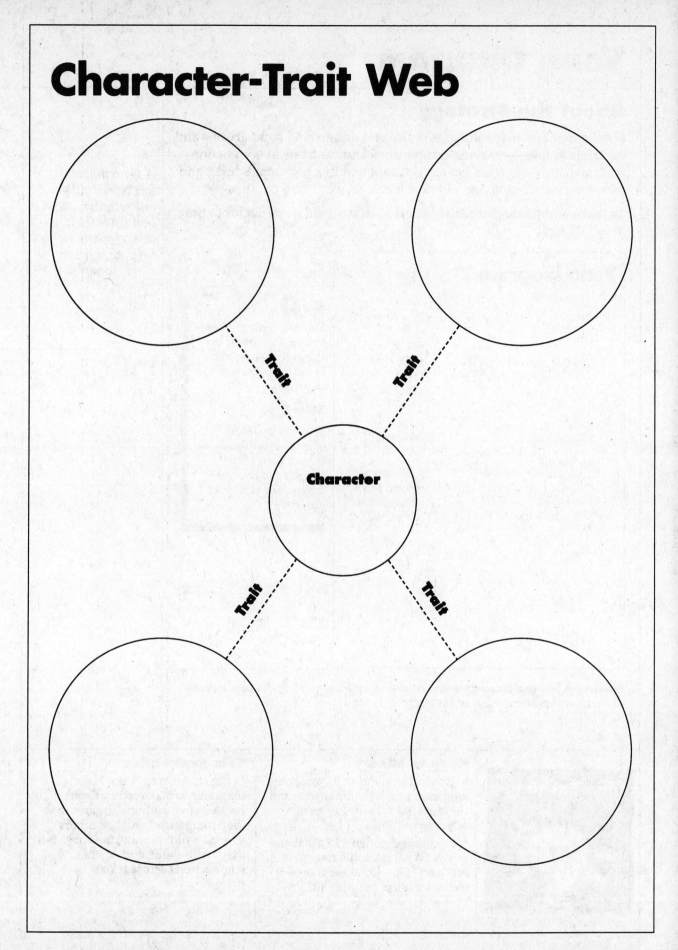

Venn Diagram

About the Strategy

A Venn diagram helps students notice and understand comparisons and contrasts in text. By making comparisons and contrasts in both fiction and nonfiction, students can clarify ideas within a text, across texts, and between prior knowledge and new ideas.

To make additional comparisons and contrasts, add more circles to the Venn diagram.

A Venn diagram works well with any selection that lends itself to a comparison between ideas or story elements.

Venn Diagram

Lion — **1** — Three bulls — **2**

tries to attack bulls

spreads evil reports

attacks the bulls

spend time in a pasture

protect one another at first

believe the evil reports and withdraw from one another

Step 1

Students write any similarities between the two things being compared in the intersection of the circles.

Step 2

Students write the differences between the two things being compared in the non-intersecting portion of each circle.

Skills and Strategies: *compare and contrast, summarize, use story elements, make connections across texts, use prior knowledge*

Idea Exchange

Keep in Mind

• Remind students to look for clue words that signal comparisons and contrasts, such as *like*, *different*, and *however*.

• Encourage students to ask themselves "What does this remind me of?" and "How are these things or characters alike or different?"

Solo Exploration

Invite students to create Venn diagrams to make comparisons between two authors. Suggest that they compare where the authors live, how old they are, the subjects they write about, and so on. **(connections across texts)**

Venn Diagram

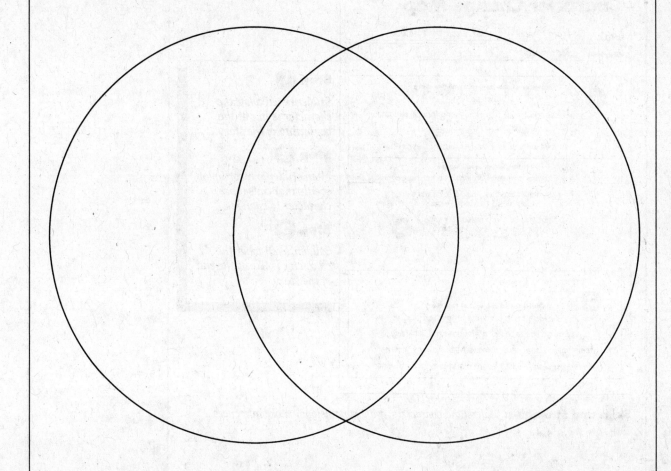

Character-Change Map

About the Strategy

A character-change map helps students understand characters in fiction. By analyzing a character over the course of a story, students can see how a character changes in response to plot events.

The following character-change map is modeled using an excerpt from *I Know Why the Caged Bird Sings*.

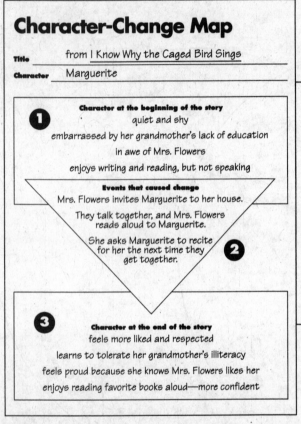

Character-Change Map

Title: from I Know Why the Caged Bird Sings

Character: Marguerite

1 Character at the beginning of the story
quiet and shy
embarrassed by her grandmother's lack of education
in awe of Mrs. Flowers
enjoys writing and reading, but not speaking

Events that caused change
Mrs. Flowers invites Marguerite to her house.

They talk together, and Mrs. Flowers reads aloud to Marguerite.

She asks Marguerite to recite for her the next time they get together.

2

3 Character at the end of the story
feels more liked and respected

learns to tolerate her grandmother's illiteracy

feels proud because she knows Mrs. Flowers likes her

enjoys reading favorite books aloud—more confident

Step ❶
Students tell what the character is like at the beginning of the story.

Step ❷
Then students record plot events that cause the character to change.

Step ❸
Students tell what the character is like at the end of the story.

A character-change map works well with selections that have dynamic characters.

Skills and Strategies: *understand characters, draw conclusions, make inferences*

Idea Exchange

Keep in Mind
You may want to ask students to map the changes in more than one character in a selection.

Solo Exploration
To help students see that cause-and-effect relationships are often a part of change, suggest that they create a cause-and-effect map for the changes a character goes through in a story.

Character-Change Map

Title _____

Character _____

Character at the beginning of the story

Events that caused change

Character at the end of the story

Details Web

About the Strategy

A details web helps students organize information in fictional or non-fictional text when many details are centered around one key or main idea. By completing the web, students see the relationship between the key or main idea and the details that support it.

A details web works well with informational selections.

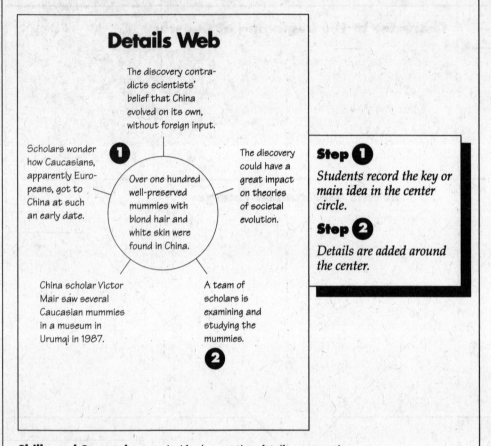

Details Web

The discovery contradicts scientists' belief that China evolved on its own, without foreign input.

1

Scholars wonder how Caucasians, apparently Europeans, got to China at such an early date.

Over one hundred well-preserved mummies with blond hair and white skin were found in China.

The discovery could have a great impact on theories of societal evolution.

China scholar Victor Mair saw several Caucasian mummies in a museum in Urumqi in 1987.

A team of scholars is examining and studying the mummies.

2

Step 1
Students record the key or main idea in the center circle.

Step 2
Details are added around the center.

Skills and Strategies: *main idea/supporting details, summarize*

Idea Exchange

Keep in Mind

- If there is more than one key or main idea in a selection, create a separate details web for each idea.
- Help students identify the main idea of a nonfictional selection by asking "What is the most important idea in the selection?"

Solo Exploration

Encourage students to create details webs to help organize their thoughts for a panel discussion or debate. Students can write the discussion/debate topic in the center of the web and brainstorm ideas in support or opposition. **(discussion)**

Details Web

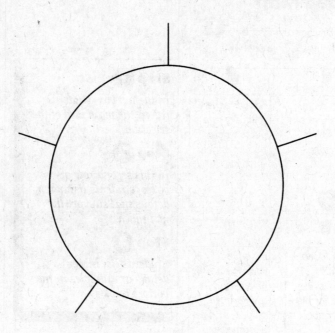

Main Idea Map

About the Strategy

A main idea map helps students recognize the main idea of a nonfictional selection and distinguish between the main idea and supporting details. Students determine the relative importance of what they read by organizing and reorganizing information from the text.

Main idea maps work well with any nonfictional selection that is organized around one main idea supported by major and minor details.

Main Idea Map

Libraries stimulate and nurture free thought. **1**

| Anaya says that worlds wait in every book. | Anaya says a library is a place where love begins. | Anaya says a library is a place where people should gather. |

2

| As a child, he uses his library card as a ticket to magical worlds that feed his imagination. | In high school, he writes poetic love notes for his classmates. | He sees libraries as havens, as gathering places, and as storehouses of knowledge. |

3

Step 1

In the top box, students record the main idea of the selection.

Step 2

In this second row of boxes, students list major details that support the main idea.

Step 3

Students list minor details or examples in the bottom row.

Skills and Strategies: *main idea/supporting details, summarize, analyze information*

Idea Exchange

Keep in Mind

• Encourage students to think about the most important idea in the selection to figure out the main idea.

• Remind students that the main idea is not always stated in the text. Sometimes students will have to state the main idea in their own words.

• Sometimes it's easier to see a main idea *after* listing the details.

Solo Exploration

Invite students to use the information in a main idea map to create a pie chart showing the importance of the details. Each detail becomes a slice of the pie, with more important details making up the larger slices. **(cross-curricular connection)**

Main Idea Map

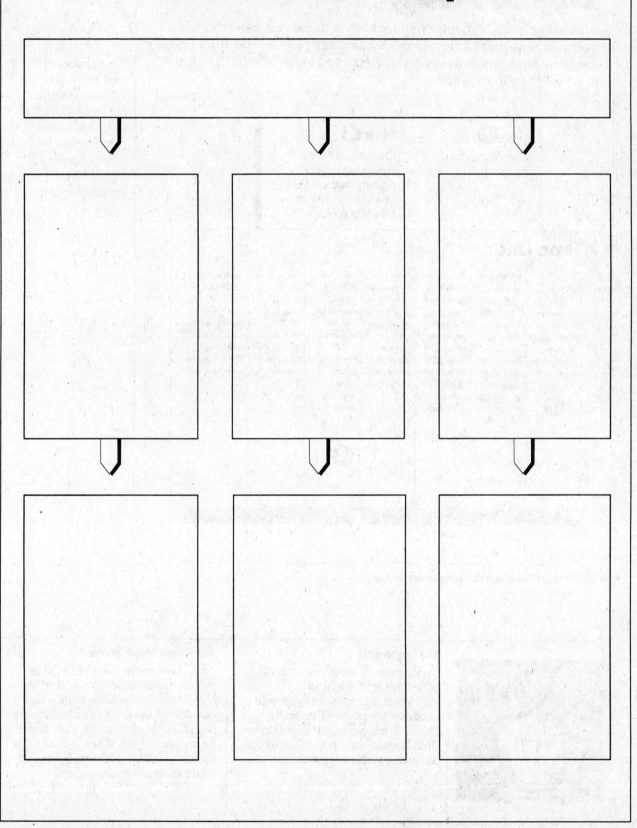

Time Line

About the Strategy

A time line helps students organize both fictional and nonfictional events in sequential order along a continuum. Not only do students see the events in order, but they are also exposed to the overall time frame in which the events occurred.

Time lines work well with any fictional or non-fictional selection in which understanding the order of events would help comprehension.

Step ❶

Students record the first event.

Step ❷

Students add the remaining events, placing them on the time line relative to the other events.

Time Line

After church, Pepys goes to a meeting to talk about ways to keep the plague from growing. ❶	Alderman Hooker tells the story of a man and his wife who took their last surviving child from an infected house in London.	Pepys mentions the good news that there has been a decrease of over five hundred in the number of new cases of the plague.	Pepys is very sad to hear of the people he knows who have lost someone to the plague or are sick themselves.	Jane, one of Pepys' maids, wakes him and his wife in the middle of the night to tell them about a great fire in the city. ❷	Pepys goes out to track the progress of the fire, then goes to Whitehall to make a report.	As the fire continues to burn, Pepys and his family are forced to pack up their belongings and evacuate their home.
Sept. 3, 1665		Sept. 14, 1665		Sept. 2, 1666		

Skills and Strategies: *summarize, sequence*

Idea Exchange

Buddywork

Invite pairs of students to create time lines into the future. They can list events that they imagine will occur before people live on the moon. Students might place their time lines in their portfolios to use for future writing. **(portfolio)**

All Together Now

As a class, make a list of the clue words in a selection organized by chronological, or time, order. You can add to the list as you read other selections organized by time order. Remind students to include clue words that indicate simultaneous order (*meanwhile, during*, etc.).

Time Line

Enumerative Text Frame

About the Strategy

An enumerative article states a main idea and lists examples to support the main idea. Students can use an enumerative text frame to help them recognize this type of expository text structure. Becoming aware of this and other expository text structures improves students' reading, particularly in the content areas.

An enumerative text frame works with selections that are organized according to this text structure.

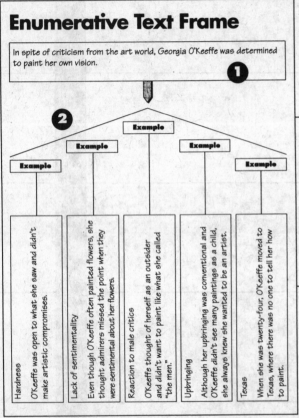

Enumerative Text Frame

In spite of criticism from the art world, Georgia O'Keeffe was determined to paint her own vision. **1**

2

Example
Example
Example
Example
Example

Hardness
O'Keeffe was open to what she saw and didn't make artistic compromises.

Lack of sentimentality
Even though O'Keeffe often painted flowers, she thought admirers missed the point when they were sentimental about her flowers.

Reaction to male critics
O'Keeffe thought of herself as an outsider and didn't want to paint like what she called "the men."

Upbringing
Although her upbringing was conventional and O'Keeffe didn't see many paintings as a child, she always knew she wanted to be an artist.

Texas
When she was twenty-four, O'Keeffe moved to Texas, where there was no one to tell her how to paint.

Step **1**
Students fill in the main idea at the top of the graphic organizer.

Step **2**
Students list examples that support the main idea.

Skills and Strategies: *main idea/supporting details, use text structure/genre, use text features, analyze information*

Keep in Mind

If students are having difficulty recognizing this text structure, suggest they look for clue words such as *first*, *next*, and *finally*.

Solo Exploration

Try using this graphic organizer to help students make predictions. After telling students the main idea of an enumerative article, suggest that they fill in examples they predict will be used to support the main idea. Remember to have students return to their predictions after reading.

Enumerative Text Frame

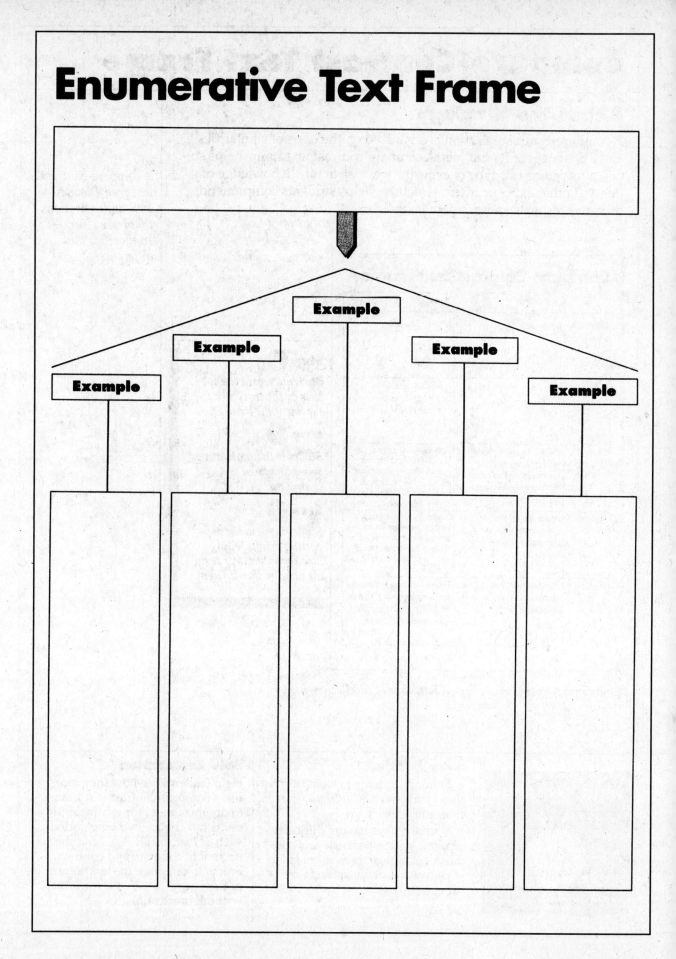

Compare-Contrast Text Frame

About the Strategy

A compare-contrast selection is organized on the basis of similarities and differences of its subjects. A compare-contrast text frame helps students recognize this type of expository text structure. Knowledge of this and other expository text structures helps students comprehend content-area texts and compare texts.

A compare-contrast text frame works well with selections that have clear similarities and differences.

Compare-Contrast Text Frame

	"A Problem" ❶	"Luck"
Main Character ❷	Sasha Uskov	Arthur Scoresby
Setting	The study of the Uskov home	A military academy and a battle in the Crimean War ❸
Conflict	Sasha has disgraced his family by getting into debt and cashing a false promissory note at the bank.	Scoresby is really a blundering soldier, but every military situation works in his favor and he becomes famous and highly decorated.
Denouement	After his family has forgiven him, Sasha demands money from his uncle.	Scoresby wins a great victory because he makes a mistake and moves his regiment left instead of right and forward instead of back.
Theme	Forgiveness does not always lead to responsibility.	Those who create heroes, like the clergyman, can be held responsible for the false heroes' actions.

Step ❶

Students record the subjects or the two texts at the top of the frame.

Step ❷

Students list the features being compared and contrasted.

Step ❸

Students fill in the supporting details telling how the subjects or texts are alike and/or different.

Skills and Strategies: *compare-contrast, draw conclusions, use text structure/genre, use text features*

Idea Exchange

Keep in Mind
• Remind students to look for clue words, such as *different from, alike,* and *resemble.*
• If students are having difficulty recognizing comparisons and contrasts, encourage them to consider what features of the subjects are being compared.

Solo Exploration
Help students see how they can use a compare-contrast text frame to organize ideas for writing. Students can choose two time periods such as the Middle Ages and the present to compare and contrast. Students can place the text frames in their portfolios to use for future writing. **(portfolio)**

Compare-Contrast Text Frame

Cause-Effect Frame Multiple Causes

About the Strategy

This type of cause-effect frame helps students identify what happened and multiple reasons why it happened in both fictional and nonfictional texts. When students can see that there are causal relationships between events or ideas in text, they can make generalizations about other causal relationships in new texts and in life situations.

This cause-effect frame works well with any selection that has clear cause-and-effect relationships with multiple causes.

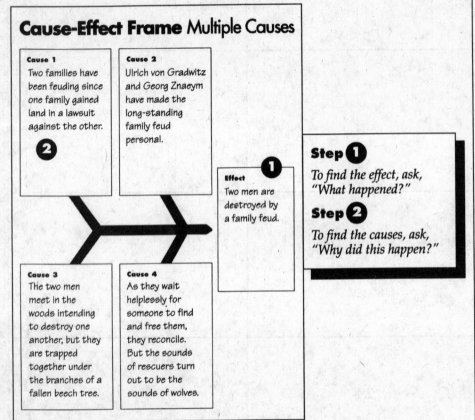

Cause-Effect Frame Multiple Causes

Cause 1
Two families have been feuding since one family gained land in a lawsuit against the other.

Cause 2
Ulrich von Gradwitz and Georg Znaeym have made the long-standing family feud personal.

Effect ❶
Two men are destroyed by a family feud.

Cause 3
The two men meet in the woods intending to destroy one another, but they are trapped together under the branches of a fallen beech tree.

Cause 4
As they wait helplessly for someone to find and free them, they reconcile. But the sounds of rescuers turn out to be the sounds of wolves.

Step ❶
To find the effect, ask, "What happened?"

Step ❷
To find the causes, ask, "Why did this happen?"

Skills and Strategies: *summarize, sequence, cause-effect, make inferences*

Idea Exchange

Keep in Mind
- If students have trouble identifying cause-and-effect relationships, suggest they look for clue words, such as *since, as a result, consequently, therefore,* and *thus.*
- Remind them that not all causes are stated directly in the text.

All Together Now
Try posing a question for students, such as "What would life be like if freedom of the press were not guaranteed under the First Amendment?" Ask students to suggest possible effects. **(cross-curricular connection)**

Cause-Effect Frame Multiple Causes

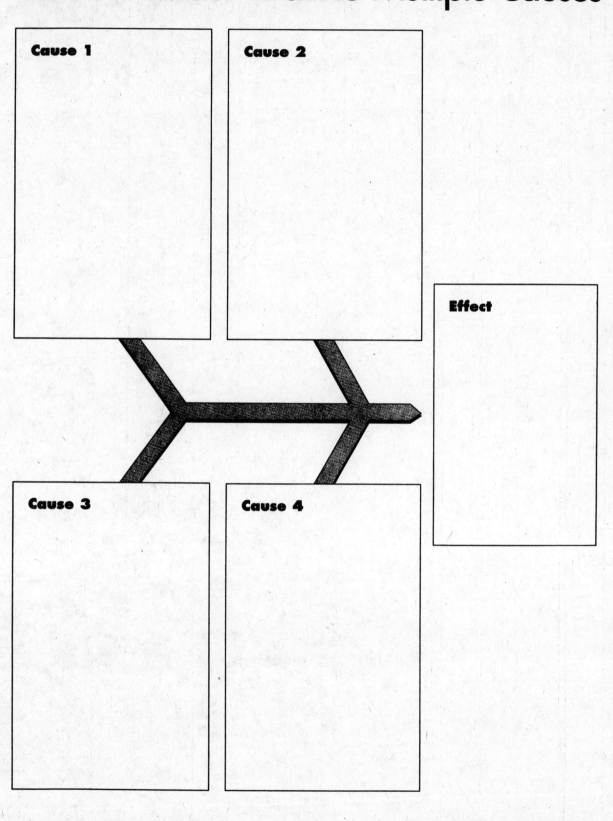

Cause 1

Cause 2

Effect

Cause 3

Cause 4

Classroom Management for Differentiated Instruction

The Challenge of Academic Text Reading

Most students enter classrooms woefully underprepared to independently navigate their reading assignments across the subject areas. While they may be able to tackle recreational reading of teen novels and magazines with relative ease, they often lack the academic language and strategic knowledge necessary for comprehending and studying concept and data rich texts. The challenging narrative and non-fiction selections students will be assigned in the course of an academic year are meant to be approached as learning tasks, not recreational activities. As such, these texts must be read multiple times with a clear learning purpose in mind.

Such an approach to reading is far from typical of adolescents engaging today's standards-driven Language Arts curricula. It is absolutely essential for teachers to assume an active instructional role, responsibly preparing students with the linguistic and strategic tools necessary for this potentially daunting task.

Strategies for Structuring Reading

The worksheets that follow offer strategies a teacher can draw on in taking this active role. The following worksheets give concrete formats for structuring students reading:

- Choral Reading
- Oral Cloze
- Silent Independent Rereading
- Structured Partner Reading

Sophisticated texts require rereading, and scaffolding the types of reading students do on each pass is essential to bringing them into a more sophisticated engagement with the text. Here is one recommended way of using these strategies to scaffold readings:

First Reading—Oral Cloze with broad task
Second Reading—Silent rereading with detailed task
Conclude—Class discussion/debriefing

Strategic Questioning

In traditional content-area reading instruction, the teacher assigns independent reading followed by an end-of-text question and answer session, in which the teacher and a handful of students dominate the discussion, leaving struggling readers disengaged and confused. Research suggests that struggling readers need explicit guidance in emulating the behaviors of competent readers.

This guidance must include breaking the reading into manageable chunks, approaching each section of text with a concrete question or purpose, and rereading sections for different levels of details. Teachers should pose increasingly complex questions while modeling a more active and strategic approach to reading.

The following worksheets give strategies to assist struggling readers in formulating appropriate reading questions and in connecting their guide questions to concrete tasks.

- Preparing-to-Read Questions
- Reading Guide Questions
- A Range of Appropriate Questions
- Question Frames

Choral Reading

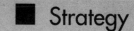

■ Strategy

A common primary-grade practice, choral reading can also work very well with older readers. Choral reading is effective because it requires that each student, regardless of level or proficiency in English, actively engage in attending to the text while it provides a nonthreatening atmosphere in which to practice. Many teachers find it helpful to use choral reading one row or group at a time. This modification tends to be less demanding and more manageable for diverse learners.

Tips to ensure success with choral reading:

- Request students to "Keep your voice with mine" to discourage them from racing ahead.
- Choose relatively short passages (e.g., 300–500 words).
- Follow with a silent rereading. Now that all students have basic access to the text, a second reading can elicit deeper understanding, supply an opportunity to apply previously taught strategies, answer inductive questions, and so on, while reinforcing the message that "constructing meaning is your job. I am here to help, not to do it for you."

Oral Cloze

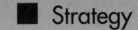
The oral cloze is a choral reading adaptation of a commonly used reading-comprehension assessment process, in which words are selectively deleted from a brief passage, and students are prompted to fill-in reasonable word choices. In the oral cloze, the teacher reads aloud while students follow along silently. The teacher occasionally omits selected words, which the students chime in and read aloud together. The oral cloze is useful in guiding students in an initial read of a difficult passage, thereby insuring that struggling readers will have access to the text. Often during teacher read-alouds, students listen passively, read ahead, or remain off-task. This strategy keeps students on their "reading toes" by giving them a concrete job while allowing teachers to check participation.

Tips to ensure success with cloze reading:

- To begin, demonstrate the oral cloze by contrasting it with a traditional read-aloud. Read a few sentences aloud without assigning students a role or task. Clarify the importance of being an active, thoughtful reader when the goal is accountable reading to learn, often with an assessment (e.g., quiz or paper). Explain that you will be reading aloud, and their job is to follow along, reading at the same pace and chorally chiming in when a word is occasionally omitted. Then reread the same sentences leaving out 2–3 words so that students see the contrast and grasp their active role.

- Choose to leave out meaningful words (e.g., nouns, verbs, adjectives) that most students can easily pronounce (prepositions and other connecting words do not work well).

- Take care to not distract students by leaving out too many words, not more than one per sentence (e.g., in a 50-word paragraph, delete 2–3 words).

- Pick words that come at a natural pause.

- Pick words (if any) that you have pretaught, providing students with a meaningful context for the new word.

- Provide students with an additional concrete active-reading task or question directing their attention to the content of the passage. On the first read, this task should be fairly broad and easy (e.g., Circle two adjectives describing how the character felt).

- In a mixed-ability class with many struggling readers, consider guiding students' reading with two rounds of the oral cloze before assigning a silent reading task. On the second reading, omit different words and pick up the pace a bit while providing an additional focus question or task.

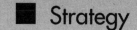

■ **Strategy**

After facilitating students in their first reading of a challenging passage using the oral cloze, prepare them for an active independent rereading of the passage.

The essential element here, as with both choral and cloze reading, is to make sure the students have a job, a task during reading that increases their attentiveness, cognitive focus, and accountability. Rereading silently to answer a question previously posed to the class as a whole efficiently meets this goal. Teachers may pose useful questions that the class reads silently to answer. Over time, students are taught to construct a range of questions themselves before such class reading (moving from literal to inferential).

After each section is read, engage students in a brief discussion to clarify questions and vocabulary and to ensure common understanding of essential big ideas in the text. You may choose to guide students in mapping or note-taking from the text at this point as well.

Tips to Get the Most From Structured Silent Rereading

- Chunk the text into 1–4 paragraph sections within which students silently reread and actively identify information necessary to respond to the teacher's focus question.

- Request that anyone who finishes before you convene the discussion go back and reread the section to look for additional details in the text.

- The first few times, model how one thinks while reading to find answers to a question. Think aloud to give students a "window" on this sophisticated cognitive task.

- Encourage students to discuss their thinking, as well as their answers, during whole-class discussion. For example, focus on such issues as *"How did you know?"* or *"Why did you think that?"*

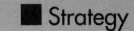

Research has consistently pointed to partner reading as a potent strategy to increase the amount of actual reading students engage in, while providing access for all students to key ideas in the text. Partner reading is an excellent way to ensure that all students are actively engaged in the text and accountable for doing their jobs.

Tips to get the most from structured partner reading:

- Rank-order students by overall literacy and proficiency in English. In a group of 30 students, for example, students #1 and #15 are the first readers and #16 and #30 are the first coaches.
- Ensure that activities are fully reciprocal—students should spend equal time in the roles of reader and coach.
- Provide specific directions and demonstrate the roles of reader and coach (e.g., "First reader: Whisper-read the first paragraph, coaches follow along, fix mistakes, and ask the comprehension questions.").

The Reader

The reader reads a paragraph or a page or reads for a given amount of time. Touching under the words may be helpful if the students have extremely limited literacy.

The Coach

The coach encourages and supports the reader.

1. If the reader asks for a word, the coach will say the word.

2. If the reader makes a mistake, the coach will correct the error using the following steps:

   a. Point to the word and say, *"Can you figure out this word?"*
   b. If the reader cannot figure out the word in five seconds, say *"This word is __."*
   c. Have the reader repeat the word and then reread the sentence.

   Why reread the entire sentence?

   - Improve comprehension.
   - Practice the word again—read it fluently in context.
   - Hold students accountable for reading more carefully.

After students have mastered the basic sequence, add various comprehension strategies, such as retelling main ideas after each page or section.

Summarize/paraphrase. State the main idea in ten words or less. (Using only ten words prompts students to use their own words.)

Predict and monitor. Reader predicts what will happen next, reads a paragraph/section and then determines if the prediction was accurate, revises as needed, summarizes, and predicts again, continuing for a set amount of time.

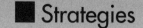

Provide focused questions to guide students before reading.

If students have background knowledge regarding the subject, it is very helpful to pose a few open-ended questions to elicit a lively brainstorming session prior to reading. Cueing students to examine any related visual support, as well as the title, can assist students in focusing their thinking more productively.

> What are the possible effects of eating too much junk food?
> Take a look at this school lunch menu in the photograph and identify with
> your partner two healthy and two unhealthy foods.

Instructional Tip: Guide students to share answers with a teacher-selected partner; take care to designate roles (1s and 2s) to insure ALL are active participants.

When students lack critical background knowledge related to a topic, brainstorming alone is often insufficient. Students will benefit from carefully formulated questions before and during each reading segment to focus their attention on the most important information. Without a concrete purpose when tackling each segment of a text, less proficient readers are apt to get mired in confusing details and distracted by unfamiliar yet non-essential vocabulary. Thus, it is essential to provide students a very specific question to guide their initial reading.

> What are the three most important reasons cited by the author in favor of
> recycling? How can recycling actually save money?

Provide questions during the reading process.

It is critical that teachers guide less proficient students in reading each segment of text at least twice, providing a clear task each time. Posing a thoughtful question before students read challenging text will help them understand the active and focused approach necessary for reading to learn. Global questions are most appropriate for initial reading, followed by questions that require more careful analysis and attention to detail in subsequent reading.

> 1st **read:** What is this section in our article on teen health mainly about?
> **Task:** Identify a word or phrase that names our topic (e.g., *teen diet*).
>
> 2nd **read:** Why is the author so concerned about adolescent diet?
> **Task:** Identify two reasons stated by the author.
>
> 3rd **read:** Since the snack foods provided at school are a major cause of poor
> adolescent health, why do you think schools continue to sell them?
> **Task:** Write down a specific reason you think schools still make candy, sodas,
> and chips so easily available in vending machines.

Instructional Tip: Complement the guide question with a concrete task to increase student accountability and increase focus and attention.

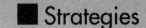
There are common text elements that teachers can utilize to frame reading guide questions and model an alert and strategic reading process for students.

Use headings and topic sentences to generate reading guide questions.

Model for students how to turn a heading into a reading guide question for the initial reading of a passage. Be sure to prompt them to translate the question into a concrete task for which they will be held accountable in subsequent class discussion.

> **Subheading:** Recycling Saves Money
>
> **Guide question:** How does recycling save money?
>
> **Task:** "I need to identify two ways that recycling helps people save money."

Students need to approach each paragraph within a section of text with a clear sense of what they need to attend to in and extract from their reading. While a heading often provides the overall topic for a section of text, topic sentences provide a more specific focus for developing reading guide questions for discrete paragraphs.

> **Subheading:** Recycling Saves Money
>
> **Topic sentence, paragraph one:** "Because of the recent downturn in the auto industry, Smithville has come up with a creative recycling program to support their cash-strapped schools."
>
> **Guide Question:** What is Smithville's recycling program?
>
> **Task:** I need to identify the key features of Smithville's recycling program.

Helping struggling students develop genuine competence in formulating and applying reading guide questions is rather labor intensive. Students who are accustomed to approach all forms of reading material in a generic, unfocused manner will require considerable hand-holding through a gradual release process that moves systematically from "I'll do it" (teacher modeling) to "We'll do it" (unified class with teacher guidance) to "You'll do it" (partner practice) to "You do it on your own" (independent practice).

Provide questions after reading a passage.

After students have navigated a demanding text and achieved basic comprehension, they are well positioned to extend their thinking by responding to higher-order questions requiring greater reflection and application. These questions are the interesting and provocative ones that teachers long to pose but that fall flat unless students have been prepared.

> How could we set up a viable recycling program in our school community?
>
> If you had two minutes to address the school board, what are the three best arguments you would provide to support the development of a district wide recycling program?

A Range of Appropriate Questions

Begin with "on the surface" questions.

Why? Struggling readers must be able to identify the most essential information in the reading *before* they are guided in grappling with more abstract analysis/interpretation. Otherwise, many students will not have the cognitive tools to benefit from the discussion.

What? Ask questions that require literal, factual recall and text-based answers that students can point to, underline, or circle.

> What is an endangered species? What are two examples of endangered species mentioned in this article? How are environmentalists working with oil companies to protect the red-tailed hawk?

Include "under the surface" questions.

Why? To comprehend challenging reading material, students must go beyond the factual basics of the text. Getting the gist certainly is no small feat for many struggling readers. However, it is important to help less proficient students acquire a more in-depth understanding and the strategic know-how required for mature comprehension.

What? Ask questions that require students to make inferences from or to analyze and synthesize text-based information, as well as to make inferences connecting new ideas from the text with prior knowledge.

> Why has it been difficult for environmentalist and oil companies to work together in protecting the red-tailed hawk? What environmental factors are placing some animal species in danger in your community?

Teach students the questions for reading to learn.

Why? Less proficient readers have often spent their early literacy development with relatively undemanding stories. In the classroom, they have largely responded to the "who, where, and when" questions appropriate for stories, leaving them ill equipped to reply to the "why, how, and what" demands of information text comprehension.

What? Teachers need to teach specific tasks involved in responding to questions associated with informational texts. Students need to understand that when asked a "why question" (e.g., Why have many schools outlawed soft drink sales?), they need to read, looking for specific reasons. It is not enough simply to model the questions; students must understand what prompted you to ask that specific question and the kind of information the question suggests.

> Why? = For what reasons? What are the reasons?
> How? = What was the process? What was the sequence?
> What? = Definition (What is _____?)
> What? + signal word   What are the <u>benefits</u> of _____?
>   What was the <u>reaction</u> to _____?

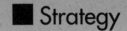

Teaching students how to generate their own questions is an important comprehension-enhancing element of structured silent reading. Underprepared readers are often overly dependent on teachers and have not learned to self-question as they read. According to the research of Taffy Raphael,[1] students who understand how questions are written are more capable of analyzing and answering them than students who lack this understanding. One useful model, derived from Bloom's *Taxonomy*,[2] was developed by Stiggins[3] using Question Frames for different levels of questions to provide initial support for students during self-questioning:

Recall (Literal) ("I can put my finger on the answer in the text.")
  What is the name of _____?
  Define _____.
  Identify the _____.
  Who did _____?
Analysis (Inferential) ("I combine my knowledge with the author's information to understand.")
  What is the main idea?
  The most important part of _____ is _____ because _____.
  The essential parts are _____.
Compare/Contrast ("I analyze similarities and differences.")
  Compare the motives of _____ to those of _____.
  What are the most important differences/similarities between _____ and _____?
Prediction ("I predict based on the evidence so far.")
  What do you think will happen in the next _____?
  Predict what you think _____ will do. Why?
  What would happen if _____?
Evaluation ("I make and defend judgments.")
  What is your opinion of _____?
  What is the best solution to the problem of _____?
  Defend why _____ is a better solution than _____.

Question Frames are helpful when teaching diverse learners to ask questions beyond simple recall/literal questions. Teacher modeling and well-supported initial practice are key to assisting all students in generating different types of questions.

---

1. Raphael, T. "Teaching Learners About Sources of Information for Answering Questions." *Journal of Reading* (1984), vol. 28(4), 303–311.
2. Bloom, B. *Taxonomy of Educational Objectives*. New York: Longmans, Green, 1956.
3. Stiggins, R. "Improving Assessment Where It Means the Most: In the Classroom." *Educational Leadership* (1985), 43, 69–74.

Vocabulary

To succeed in narrowing the language divide, a school-wide comprehensive academic vocabulary program must include the following four components:

1. **Fluent, wide reading.** Vocabulary for academic purposes grows as a consequence of independent reading of a variety of texts (in particular, informational texts) and increasing reading volume.

2. **Direct scaffolded teaching of critical words.** Students learn new words via various explicit, teacher-directed instructional strategies.

3. **Teaching word-learning strategies.** When taught the tools to exploit context, analyze prefixes, and various other strategies, students can independently learn new word meanings while reading independently.

4. **Daily participation in structured, accountable contexts for daily speaking and writing.** Academic language develops when students are engaged in rigorous and meaningful application of newly acquired vocabulary and syntax in structured speaking and writing tasks.

The following group of worksheets, marked with the triangle icon, provide concrete strategies for addressing many of these objectives for vocabulary development:

- Preteaching Vocabulary: Convey Meaning
- Preteaching Vocabulary: Check Understanding
- Vocabulary Development
- Choosing Vocabulary Words
- Possible Sentences
- Word Analysis/Teaching Word Parts
- Assessing Vocabulary Mastery

Concept development goes hand in hand with vocabulary enrichment. The following worksheets, also labeled with the triangle icon, provide strategies for concept development:

- List-Group-Label
- Concept Mapping/Clarifying Routine
- Using Concept Maps

The remaining worksheets in Part 3, marked with the circle icon, offer strategies for structuring academic discussion and writing.

Preteaching Vocabulary: Convey Meaning

- If your goal is simply to familiarize students with a word to help them recognize and comprehend it in a reading, follow steps 1–4.

  1. Pronounce the word (and give the part of speech).

  This article focuses on an *ecstatic* moment in a high school student's life.

  2. Ask students to all repeat the word.

  Say the word *ecstatic* after me. (ec stat' ic)

  3. Provide an accessible synonym and/or a brief explanation.

  Ecstatic means "extremely happy."

  4. Rephrase the simple definition/explanation, asking students to complete the statement by substituting aloud the new word.

  If you are extremely happy about something, you are _____ (students say *ecstatic*).

- If your goal is to familiarize students with a word that is central to comprehending the reading and that you also want them to learn, continue with step 5, then check for understanding.

  5. Provide a visual "nonlinguistic representation" of the word (if possible) and/or an illustrative "showing" sentence.

  Showing image: a picture of a man happily in love.
  Showing sentence: Julio was *ecstatic* when Melissa agreed to marry him.

Have students fill out a vocabulary worksheet as you preteach the words; doing so involves them more directly and provides them with a focused word list for later study and practice.

Sample Vocabulary Note-Taking

Term	Synonym	Definition/Example	Image
ecstatic, *adj.*	extremely happy	feeling very happy, excited, or joyful *Julio was <u>ecstatic</u> when Melissa agreed to marry him.*	
distraught, *adj.*	extremely worried and upset	feeling very worried, unhappy, or <u>distressed</u> *Mark was <u>distraught</u> to learn that the camp bus had left without him.*	

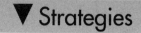
1. Focused Questions

Ask focused questions to see if students seem to grasp the word's meaning (as opposed to questions such as *Any questions? Do you understand?* or *Is that clear?*). Questions may be initially directed to the unified group for a thumbs-up or thumbs-down response; to teams using Numbered Heads; or to pairs using Think-Pair-Share, followed by questions to individuals.

> - Would you be ecstatic if you won the lottery?
> - Would you be ecstatic if you were assigned a 20-page report to complete over the Spring break?
> - Would you be ecstatic if you won two front-row tickets to a concert given by your favorite band?
> - Would you be ecstatic if your mother bought your favorite brand of breakfast cereal?

2. Images

If the word is crucial (for the lesson and their academic vocabulary tool kit), consider asking students to generate their own relevant images or examples.

> - Turn to your partner and ask what has happened recently that made him/her ecstatic. Or ask what would make him/her ecstatic. Be prepared to share one example with the class.
> - What other images might we associate with *ecstatic?* Think of one or two, turn to your partner and discuss, and then be prepared to share one of your images with the class.

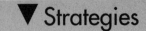

▼ Strategies

Words that are new to students but that represent familiar concepts can be addressed using a number of relatively quick instructional tactics. Many of these (e.g., synonyms, antonyms, examples) are optimal for prereading and oral reading, which call for more expedient approaches.

Brief Strategies for Vocabulary Development (Stahl[4])

- **Teach synonyms.** Provide a synonym that students know (e.g., link *stringent* to the known word *strict*).

- **Teach antonyms.** Not all words have antonyms, but for those that do, thinking about their opposites requires students to evaluate the critical attributes of the words in question.

- **Paraphrase definitions.** Requiring students to use their own words increases connection-making and provides the teacher with useful informal assessment—"Do they really get it?"

- **Provide examples.** The more personalized the example, the better. An example for the new word *egregious* might be *Ms. Kinsella's 110-page reading assignment was egregious indeed!*

- **Provide nonexamples.** Similar to using antonyms, providing nonexamples requires students to evaluate a word's attributes. Invite students to explain why it is not an example.

- **Ask for sentences that "show you know."** Students construct novel sentences confirming their understanding of a new word, using more than one new word per sentence to show that connections can also be useful.

- **Teach word sorting.** Provide a list of vocabulary words from a reading selection and have students sort them into various categories (e.g., parts of speech, branches of government). Students can re-sort words into "guess my sort" using categories of their own choosing.

---

4. Stahl, S. A. *Vocabulary Development.* Cambridge, MA: Brookline Books, 1999.

Restrict your selections to approximately six to eight words that are critical to comprehending the reading passage/segment you intend to cover in one lesson (e.g., one Science chapter section; a three-page passage from a six-page short story.)

- Choose **"big idea"** words that name or relate to the central concepts addressed in the passage (in subject areas outside of English Language Arts, these central lesson terms are typically highlighted by the publisher).

- Choose high-use, widely applicable **"academic tool kit"** words that student are likely to encounter in diverse materials across subject areas and grade levels (e.g., *aspect, compare, similar, subsequently*).

- Choose high-use **"disciplinary tool kit"** words for your subject area that you consider vital for students to master at this age and proficiency level (e.g., *metaphor, policy, economic, application, species*).

- Choose **"polysemous"** (multiple meaning) words that have a new academic meaning in a reading in addition to a more general, familiar meaning (e.g., "wave of immigrants" in U.S. History vs. a greeting or an ocean wave).

- Identify additional academic words, not included in the reading selection, that students will need to know in order to engage in **academic discourse** about the central characters, issues, and themes (especially for literary selections).

- Be careful not to overload students with low-frequency words that they are unlikely to encounter in many academic reading contexts, especially words that are not essential to comprehend the gist of the text.

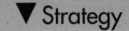
▼ Strategy

   Possible Sentences (Moore and Moore[6]) is a relatively simple strategy for teaching word meanings and generating considerable class discussion.

1. The teacher chooses six to eight words from the text that may pose difficulty for students. These words are usually key concepts in the text.

2. Next, the teacher chooses four to six words that students are more likely to know something about.

3. The list of ten to twelve words is put on the chalkboard or overhead projector. The teacher provides brief definitions as needed.

4. Students are challenged to devise sentences that contain two or more words from the list.

5. All sentences that students come up with, both accurate and inaccurate, are listed and discussed.

6. Students now read the selection.

7. After reading, revisit the Possible Sentences and discuss whether they could be true based on the passage or how they could be modified to be true.

   Stahl[7] reported that Possible Sentences significantly improved both students' overall recall of word meanings and their comprehension of text containing those words. Interestingly, this was true when compared with a control group and when compared with Semantic Mapping.

---

6. Moore, P. W., and S. A. Moore. "Possible Sentences." In E. K. Dishner, T. W. Bean, J. E. Readence, and P. W. Moore (eds.). *Reading in the Content Areas: Improving Classroom Instruction*, 2nd ed. Dubuque, IA: Kendall/Hunt, 1986, pp. 174–179.
7. Stahl, op. cit.

▼ Strategy

Word Analysis/Teaching Word Parts helps many underprepared readers who lack basic knowledge of word origins or etymology, such as Latin and Greek roots, as well as discrete understanding of how a prefix or suffix can alter the meaning of a word. Learning clusters of words that share a common origin can help students understand content-area texts and connect new words to those already known. For example, a secondary teacher (Allen[8]) reported reading about a character who suffered from amnesia. Teaching students that the prefix *a-* derives from Greek and means "not," while the base *-mne-* means "memory," reveals the meaning. After judicious teacher scaffolding, students were making connections to various words in which the prefix *a-* changed the meaning of a base word (e.g., *amoral, atypical*).

The charts below summarize some of the affixes worth considering, depending on your students' prior knowledge and English proficiency.

Prefix	Meaning	Percentage of All Prefixed Words	Example
un-	not; reversal of	26	uncover
re-	again, back, really	14	review
in-/im-	in, into, not	11	insert
dis-	away, apart, negative	7	discover
en-/em-	in; within; on	4	entail
mis-	wrong	3	mistaken
pre-	before	3	prevent
a-	not; in, on, without	1	atypical

Suffix	Meaning	Percentage of All Suffixed Words	Example
-s, -es	more than one; verb marker	31	characters, reads, reaches
-ed	in the past; quality, state	20	walked
-ing	when you do something; quality, state	14	walking
-ly	how something is	7	safely
-er, -or	one who, what, that, which	4	drummer
-tion, -sion	state, quality; act	4	action, mission
-able, -ible	able to be	2	disposable, reversible
-al, -ial	related to, like	1	final, partial

---

8. Allen, J. *Words, Words, Words: Teaching Vocabulary in Grades 4–12.* York, ME: Stenhouse, 1999.

Following are three meaningful and alternative assessment formats that require relatively little preparation time:

1. Select only four to six important words and embed each in an accessible and contextualized sentence followed by a semicolon. Ask students to add another sentence after the semicolon that clearly demonstrates their understanding of the underlined word as it is used in this context. This assessment format will discourage students from rote memorization and mere recycling of a sample sentence covered during a lesson.

   Example: Mr. Lamont had the most <u>eclectic</u> wardrobe of any teacher on the high-school staff.

2. Present four to six sentences, each containing an underlined word from the study list, and ask students to decide whether each word makes sense in this context. If yes, the student must justify why the sentence makes sense. If no, the student must explain why it is illogical and change the part of the sentence that doesn't make sense.

   Example: Mr. Lamont had the most <u>eclectic</u> wardrobe of any teacher on the high-school staff; rain or shine, he wore the same predictable brown loafers, a pair of black or brown pants, a white shirt, and a beige sweater vest.

3. Write a relatively brief passage (one detailed paragraph) that includes six to ten words from the study list. Then, delete these words and leave blanks for students to complete. This modified cloze assessment will force students to scrutinize the context and draw upon a deeper understanding of the words' meanings. Advise students to first read the entire passage and to then complete the blanks by drawing from their study list. As an incentive for students to prepare study cards or more detailed notes, they can be permitted to use these personal references during the quiz.

Because these qualitative and authentic assessments require more rigorous analysis and application than most objective test formats, it seems fair to allow students to first practice with the format as a class exercise and even complete occasional tests in a cooperative group.

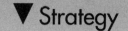

▼ Strategy

List-Group-Label (Taba[5]) is a form of structured brainstorming designed to help students identify what they know about a concept and the words related to the concept while provoking a degree of analysis and critical thinking. These are the directions to students:

1. Think of all the words related to _____. (a key "big idea" in the text)
2. Group the words listed by some shared characteristics or commonalities.
3. Decide on a label for each group.
4. Try to add words to the categories on the organized lists.

Working in small groups or pairs, each group shares with the class its method of categorization and the thinking behind its choices, while adding words from other class members. Teachers can extend this activity by having students convert their organized concepts into a Semantic Map that becomes a visual expression of their thinking.

List-Group-Label is an excellent prereading activity to build on prior knowledge, introduce critical concepts, and ensure attention during selection reading.

---

5. Taba, H. *Teacher's Handbook for Elementary Social Studies.* Reading, MA: Addison-Wesley, 1988.

Research by Frayer et al.[9] supports the strategy of teaching by Concept Mapping:

1. identifying the critical attributes of the word.
2. giving the category to which the word belongs.
3. discussing examples of the concept.
4. discussing nonexamples.

Others have had success extending this approach by guiding students through representation of the concept in a visual map or graphic organizer. The Clarifying Routine, designed and researched by Ellis,[10] is a particularly effective example:

1. Select a critical concept/word to teach. Enter it on a graphic clarifying map like the sample for *satire.*
2. List the clarifiers or critical attributes that explicate the concept.
3. List the core idea—a summary statement or brief definition.
4. Brainstorm for knowledge connections—personal links from students' world views/prior knowledge (encourage idiosyncratic/personal links).
5. Give an example of the concept; link to clarifiers: "Why is this an example of ———————?"
6. Give nonexamples. List nonexamples: "How do you know ——————— is not an example of ———————"
7. Construct a sentence that "shows you know."

Term: SATIRE		
Core Idea: Any Work That Uses Wit to Attack Foolishness		
Example • A story that exposes the acts of corrupt politicians by making fun of them **Nonexample** • A story that exposes the acts of corrupt politicians through factual reporting **Example sentence** • Charles Dickens used satire to expose the problems of common folks in England.	**Clarifiers** • can be oral or written • ridicule or expose vice in a clever way • can include irony, exaggeration, name-calling, understatement • are usually based on a real person or event	**Knowledge Connections** • Political cartoons on the editorial pages of our paper • Stories TV comics tell to make fun of the President—as on *Saturday Night Live* • My mom's humor at dinner time!

9. Frayer, D. A., W. C. Frederick, and H. J. Klausmeier. *A Schema for Testing the Level of Concept Mastery* (Technical Report No. 16). Madison, WI: University of Wisconsin Research and Development Center for Cognitive Learning, 1969.
10. Ellis, E. *The Clarifying Routine.* Lawrence, KS: Edge Enterprises, 1997.

Students benefit from graphic presentations of the connections between the ideas they are learning. Each Unit Resources booklet includes Concept Maps— graphic organizers that illustrate the logical relationship among the skills taught in a Part or a Unit. In Grades 6 through 10, the Concept Maps focus on the Literary Analysis, Reading Skill, and Academic Vocabulary skills in each Part. In Grades 11 and 12 and in *World Masterpieces*, each Map connects the Literary Analysis skills in a Unit to the trends and themes of the period covered.

Steps

1. Review the Concept Map and identify the skills you will cover.

2. Distribute copies of the Concept Map to students. Identify those skills and concepts you will teach and have students circle or otherwise note them. Elicit from students any prior knowledge they may have about the ideas you have introduced. In addition, you may wish to ask them about their own interests in connection with the ideas. In later classes, you can make connections to students' prior knowledge and interests as relevant.

3. Briefly note the connections between ideas on the Concept Map. For example, you might explain that the "Big Picture" or "Main Idea" in the Part is the short story. Using the Concept Map, explain that a plot is an important part of a short story.

4. Emphasize for students that the skills you have identified represent a goal for the class: Everyone will be working toward mastery of those skills.

5. In succeeding lessons, refer students to their Concept Maps at appropriate junctures. As you introduce a selection, review the relevant portion of the Concept Map with students so that they clearly grasp the goals you are setting.

6. As you conclude teaching the selection, review the Concept Map with students to see how the skills are connected with other concepts they have learned. Have students add the name of the selections they have completed to the appropriate blanks. Have students log the additional assignments they complete, such as Extension Activities, in the Learning Log on the chart.

7. As you conclude instruction for a Part or for a Unit, review with students the skills they have covered and the logical connections among the skills.

Grateful acknowledgment for the idea of the Concept Map is made to B. Keith Lenz and Donald D. Deshler, who develop the idea in their book *Teaching Content to All: Evidence-Based Inclusive Practices in Middle and Secondary Schools* (New York: Pearson Education, Inc., 2004).

- Students listen while the teacher poses a question or task.

- Students are given quiet time to consider what they know about the topic and record a number of possible responses. This may be a simple list of words and phrases or a focused quick-write. It is also helpful to provide students with a series of response prompts to complete prior to being asked to share aloud. In this way, less proficient academic language users will have a linguistic scaffold to bolster their linguistic output along with their confidence in sharing aloud.

   For example, if students are being asked to make predictions about what will happen in the next chapter of *The Joy Luck Club*, they might be provided with these sentence prompts to complete:

   I predict that Waverly's mother will be (disappointed in / proud of) her daughter's behavior because . . .

   Based on Waverly's relationship with her mother, I assume that her mother will react very (positively / negatively) because . . .

- The teacher whips around the class in a relatively fast-paced and structured manner (e.g., down rows, around tables), allowing as many students as possible to share an idea in 15 seconds or less.

- After several contributions, there tends to be some repetition. Students point out similarities in responses using appropriate language strategies (e.g., *My idea is similar to / related to . . .*), rather than simply stating that their ideas have already been mentioned. This fosters active listening and validation of ideas.

- The teacher can record these ideas for subsequent review or have students do a quick-write summarizing some of the more interesting contributions they heard during the discussion.

Numbered Heads and Think-Write-Share-Pair

Numbered Heads

- Students number off in teams, one through four.
- The teacher asks a series of questions, one at a time.
- Students discuss possible answers to each question for an established amount of time (about 30 seconds to 90 seconds, depending on the complexity of the task).
- The teacher calls a number (1–4), and all students with that number raise their hand, ready to respond.
- The teacher randomly calls on students with the specified number to answer on behalf of their team.
- Students are encouraged to acknowledge similarities and differences between their team's response and that of other teams (e.g., *We predicted a very different outcome. Our reaction was similar to that of Ana's group.*).
- The teacher continues posing questions and soliciting responses in this manner until the brainstorming or review session is finished.

Think-Write-Pair-Share

- Students listen while the teacher poses a question or a task.
- Students are given quiet time to first answer the question individually in writing.
- Students are then cued to pair with a neighbor to discuss their responses, noting similarities and differences. Students encourage their partners to clarify and justify responses using appropriate language strategies:

  How did you decide that?

  In other words, you think that . . .
- It is often helpful to structure the roles (first speaker, first listener) and designate the time frames:

  First speakers, you have 90 seconds to share your answers with your partner.
- After rehearsing responses with a partner, students are invited to share with the class.
- The teacher asks a series of questions, one at a time.
- Students discuss possible answers to each question for an established amount of time (about 30 seconds to 90 seconds, depending on the complexity of the task).

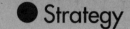

Students who bring special learning needs to the writing process are more likely to internalize the assignment expectations if the task is first clearly outlined on the board or in a handout. They must, in turn, hear the assignment described and, subsequently, have the opportunity to paraphrase what they understand the actual assignment expectations to be—ideally, orally to a partner and in writing to the teacher. If all students are then encouraged to turn in two clarification questions about the assignment, less proficient writers will have a safe and structured venue for monitoring their comprehension and articulating instructional needs. In so doing, passive or apprehensive students are more likely to vocalize any misunderstandings about the task in a timely and responsible manner, rather than realizing the night before the paper is due that they are unsure how to proceed.

Sample Description of a Writing Assignment

Writing Assignment Guidelines:
A Color That Has Special Significance

Write a detailed expository paragraph providing specific reasons that your chosen color has special meaning in your life. Your justification paragraph must include these qualities of effective expository writing:

- An appropriate title (e.g., *Jade Green: A Link to My Heritage*)
- A topic sentence that lets the reader know that you will be discussing the relevance of a particular color to specific aspects of your life
- Transition words that introduce each of your new points about your chosen color (e.g., *first of all, in addition, furthermore, moreover*)
- Specific reasons for selecting this color, including details and relevant commentary that help the reader easily understand the color's special significance
- A visible effort to include new vocabulary from this unit
- An effort to use subordinating conjunctions to join related ideas
- A concluding statement that thoughtfully wraps up your paragraph
- Proofreading goals for the final draft:
  - complete sentences (no fragments or run-on sentences)
  - correct verb tenses
  - correct spelling

Your first draft is due on _____. Please bring two copies of your draft for a peer-response session

---

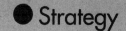

As demonstrated in your *Prentice Hall Literature* Teacher's Edition, one concrete way to structure linguistic equity and to scaffold the vocabulary demands of a challenging writing assignment is to provide students with an array of sentence starters, including practical vocabulary options relevant to the specific writing task and topic. Another equally important scaffold for students writing in a second language or second dialect is a word-form chart that highlights important forms of a base word germane to the assignment.

Following is a list of sentence starters and a relevant word-form chart for a writing assignment on a personally significant color.

Sentence Starters to Discuss a Color You Value

_____ is my favorite color because I associate it with _____. (my future career, my love of nature, my personality, my hobby)

This color reflects/represents/is associated with my interest in _____. (salsa dancing, R & B music, physical fitness, environmental protection)

This color symbolizes/is a symbol of _____. (my culture, my ethnicity)

I have included/selected/chosen the color _____ because _____.

The color _____ is meaningful/valuable/significant to me because _____.

I appreciate/value/like/am fond of the color _____ because/since _____.

Sample Word-Form Chart

Noun	Adjective	Verb	Adverb
symbol	symbolic	symbolize	symbolically
meaning	meaningful		meaningfully
value	valuable	value	valuably
relevance	relevant		relevantly
importance	important		importantly
relationship	related	relate	
association	associated	associate	
significance	significant	signify	significantly
preference	preferred; preferable	prefer	preferably
fondness	fond		fondly

Professional Development
Articles

The Literacy Challenge of Diverse Learners

Introduction

The number of children in the country who can be classified as diverse learners because of the special circumstances they bring to public education is growing at a pace that currently outstrips educators' abilities to keep up. Unless significant educational changes are made in response to the dramatic changes occurring in classrooms throughout the country, including the development and utilization of instructional strategies that address the needs of diverse learners, the number of children who "fall through the cracks" in public education will continue to rise.[1]

The 2000 census confirmed what demographers had been documenting for the previous decade: America is more diverse than ever. Certainly, the diversity of our population is a significant asset to our nation in many ways; however, it also places considerable stress on our educational system to effectively accommodate the range of learning needs found in students today. A typical high-school classroom includes students who are diverse in terms of their experiential, linguistic, cultural, socioeconomic, and psychological backgrounds. The range of student needs, interests, motivation, and skill levels often presents heightened challenges to both curriculum and instruction. It should be clearly acknowledged that the individual needs of some students require additional specialized support in basic reading skills, English language development, study skills, and behavioral/emotional/social domains. However, the goal of a comprehensive Language Arts program remains the provision of "universal access" for all students to an intellectually rich and challenging language arts curriculum and instruction, in addition to whatever specialized intervention may be required.

Universal access exists when teachers provide curriculum and instruction in ways that allow all learners in the classroom to participate and to achieve the instructional and behavioral goals of general education, as well as of the core curriculum. Teachers will succeed in providing universal access if they teach in heterogeneous, inclusive classrooms and consistently

---

1. Kame'enui, Edward, and Douglas Carnine. *Effective Teaching Strategies That Accommodate Diverse Learners.* Upper Saddle River, NJ: Prentice Hall, 1998.

and systematically integrate instructional strategies that are responsive to the needs of typical learners, gifted learners, less proficient readers, English language learners, and students who are eligible for and receiving special education services.

Although each student population represented in the classroom may require specific interventions and supports, these learner populations also share many common characteristics, such as the need to build on prior knowledge, the need for systematic vocabulary development, and the need for systematic instruction in strategic reading approaches, to name a few key curricular and instructional areas. Through identification of these shared needs and the implementation of teaching and learning strategies responsive to these needs, the general education teacher, with the support of specialists and other staff, can make significant inroads in designing inclusive lessons that are responsive to the learning and behavioral needs of all learners.

This book provides numerous suggestions to assist teachers in designing English Language Arts lessons that strive for universal access. The suggestions focus specifically on the instructional needs of students who are less proficient readers, students who are English language learners, and students with identified special education needs. The next section describes the reading process and what it takes to be a proficient reader. The remaining sections explore the specific needs of the three focus student populations: English language learners, less proficient readers, and students with special education needs.

It may be helpful to read the chapters in the order in which they are presented, moving from general considerations to suggestions that address the specific needs of these three student groups. You may also find it helpful to begin with those chapters that address your greatest area of need or interest.

The information is these chapters is designed to provide concrete and easily implemented instructional suggestions for responding meaningfully to the diverse learning needs of high-school students in the Language Arts.

A clear consensus has emerged in the field of reading education supporting the notion that reading is a complex process of constructing meaning from text. Successful readers must bring an array of interrelated skills, knowledge, and strategies together in order to understand written English. Skillful readers are able to decode the words accurately and fluently, connect their meanings to prior knowledge, and continually monitor their emerging understanding as they read. In other words, successful readers are active, thoughtful, and strategic learners able to make meaning from what they are reading.

Factors That Affect Reading Success

Successful reading is largely determined by the elaborate interaction of four factors: learner characteristics, skill and instructional variables, demands of the text, and nature of the classroom environment. To better understand these elements, we will examine each in turn, as well as the way they interact to affect successful reading.

Learner Characteristics

Each learner brings unique characteristics to the learning experience. For example, students who are less proficient readers may experience attention and memory issues that make reading especially challenging. English language learners may be highly capable students who, because of limited vocabulary or experiences in their new country, lack the schema for understanding the ideas encountered in text. Students with disabilities may experience cognitive, behavioral/social, and/or physical challenges that make the development of reading skill more challenging.

Skill and Instructional Factors

Reading success is largely determined by the particular skills an individual reader brings to the reading act. For example, the ability to fluently and accurately decode the words in a given reading selection is a necessary but not sufficient condition for successful reading. In addition, the ability to activate and build prior knowledge along with the related ability to connect what one is reading to existing knowledge are essential for proficient comprehension. Moreover, comprehension is significantly determined by a student's level of English acquisition, vocabulary, and skillful use of various reading comprehension strategies such as summarization or self-questioning.

An essential personal aspect of successful reading is the extent to which a reader is actively engaged in the reading, has a clear purpose for reading, and is interested in the content being explored. Skillful readers have learned helpful mental habits such as perseverance, managing and directing attention, being aware of and monitoring their thoughts and feelings as they read. Skilled readers are active participants in the reading act—reading is not a spectator sport.

Instructional interventions provided in the classroom play a significant role in students' development of these skills. Explicit, systematic instruction in decoding and fluency, the incorporation of activities that build and enhance prior knowledge, the provision of explicit vocabulary instruction, and the direct teaching, modeling, and practicing of comprehension strategies will lead to students' skill development and their enhanced engagement and interest in the complexities of the reading act.

Text-Based Factors

It is immediately apparent that the types of texts encountered by students vary widely and create different levels of challenge for different readers. Just as the make and model distinguish one automobile from another, text-based factors differentiate one text from another. While some of these factors may be largely cosmetic in nature, others, such as sentence length, novel vocabulary, density of the concepts, or clarity of the organizational pattern, can have a significant influence on reader comprehension. For example, the presence of well-designed reader aids, including pictures, charts, graphs, and focus questions, can provide additional support to naive readers.

Perhaps the most fundamental distinction in text-based factors affecting reading success is that of narrative (story) reading vs. expository (informational) reading. Expository texts are generally written to inform or persuade the reader using very different organizational patterns from those typically utilized in narratives. For example, information in content-area reading, such as in science and social studies, is often arranged according to structures such as chronological sequence, comparison and contrast, cause and effect, main idea and supporting details, and so forth. Many students are quite comfortable reading stories but find themselves ill equipped to deal with the demands of informational content-area texts.

Classroom Environment

The classroom environment affects everything and everyone within it, including the nature of the reading/literacy program. Specifically, the classroom environment can be viewed as composed of both physical and social-psychological dimensions.

Research suggests that students learn best in a friendly, respectful setting where

- they feel a sense of safety/order and are comfortable taking risks.
- they understand the purpose of and value the tasks at hand.
- they have high expectations/goals for learning.
- they feel accepted by their teacher and peers.

These general factors are of particular import when thinking about what accounts for successful reading. Students will often have significant gaps in their skill, knowledge, proficiency in English, and be self-conscious concerning their lagging literacy.

It is important to be respectful and truthful with students about what it will take to significantly improve their abilities in the Language Arts: It takes PRACTICE, and lots of it. Literacy cannot be "done to" students—it is a collaborative enterprise that is "done with" students. To be sure, teachers provide excellent direct instruction, guided practice, specific feedback, coaching, and more, yet students must understand their roles as active self-directed learners. The intentional design of a caring yet "on purpose" classroom climate creates the condition within which the hard work of improving literacy can take place.

Summary

Understanding that successful reading comprises a complex interaction of factors—learner, skills and instruction, text, and environment—provides a template for thinking about how classrooms can provide universal access to a rich core curriculum for the diverse range of learners in today's high-school classrooms. Secondary students need a balanced Language Arts program based on their individual needs. All students require a firm foundation in fluent/automatic decoding, broad background knowledge of various subjects, ever-expanding vocabularies, all coupled with an array of comprehension strategies to fit the purpose for reading as well as the type of text being read.

In the following section, we examine strategies for developing lesson plans that support diverse learners in meeting rigorous grade-level standards in the Language Arts.

The number of immigrant, migrant, and refugee students in the United States who have little knowledge of the English language is growing exponentially. In fact, students who are learning English as an additional language are the fastest-growing segment of the school-age population. While the number of English language learners (ELLs) nationwide has skyrocketed, their academic achievement trails behind that of their native English-speaking peers. National studies of English language learners have shown that they are likely to come from disadvantaged socioeconomic backgrounds, attend low-income schools, and have parents with limited English proficiency. These students are also judged by their teachers to have weaker academic abilities, receive lower grades, and score well below their classmates on standardized tests of mathematics and reading.[1] Moreover, in a large-scale California study, secondary schools reported that even long-term resident ELLs entered high school with only fourth to sixth grade academic competencies.[2]

Differential Preparation for Second-Language Schooling

Secondary-school curricula are based on assumptions about basic reading and writing skills and elementary subject matter foundations. However, the growing population of secondary English language learners is tremendously diverse, particularly with regard to their educational backgrounds. These students enter U.S. schools with varying degrees of curricular preparation and a vast range of language proficiencies, in English and their native language. At times, it may seem that the one thing these diverse students have in common is the need to accelerate their English language and literacy acquisition in order to participate more fully in their secondary schooling.

Although some have parents with impressive levels of formal education and professional job experiences, many come from less privileged families, challenged by limited functional literacy even in their native language. Newcomers from war-torn regions and rural areas of developing countries are apt to arrive severely under-schooled, with fragmented native language literacy training and weak subject matter foundations.

---

1. Moss, M., and M. Puma. *Prospects: The Congressionally Mandated Study of Educational Growth and Opportunity.* Washington, DC: U.S. Department of Education, 1995.
2. Minicucci, C., and L. Olsen. "Programs for Secondary Limited English Proficiency Students: A California Study." *Focus,* Vol. 5. Washington, DC: National Clearinghouse for Bilingual Education, 1992.

These youths predictably require compassion, considerable time, and patient modeling simply to adjust to basic school routines and expectations before they can ever begin to concentrate on phonemic awareness lessons, let alone literary analysis.

On the other hand, more fortunate immigrant youths have benefited from rigorous and sustained elementary schooling in their native country and make the transition to American classrooms more effortlessly. Literate in their home language, these second-language learners have already internalized critical scripts for schooling and often function above equivalent grade levels in math or science. However, these traditionally educated newcomers still face a daunting transition to daily instruction in a language they have only begun to study, along with curriculum content, teaching practices, and skills that may not have been emphasized in their native schooling.

Our secondary schools also serve increasing numbers of students who have been raised and educated entirely in the United States but who speak a language other than English at home. These continuing English language learners were either born in the United States or arrived here as very small children. Many of these long-term U.S. residents are not literate in their home language and remain struggling English readers well into the upper grades and beyond. They may demonstrate a comfortable handle on the social domain of both languages but flounder with grade-level reading and writing tasks.

In summary, with regard to prior schooling, secondary English language learners tend to fall into one of three general and frequently overlapping categories:

1. Recent adolescent immigrants who have received continuous native language schooling prior to immigration to the United States and are prepared with relatively strong academic and study skills to apply to new subject matter

2. Language minority students continuing into secondary schools from U.S. elementary schools with insufficient English fluency and literacy to compete in challenging academic areas

3. Immigrant, refugee, and migrant students with sporadic or no prior schooling who consequently enter lacking basic literacy and elementary curricular foundations.

Second-Language Literacy Development

Statistics on the academic achievement of English language learners demonstrate a dire need for informed attention devoted to literacy, the cornerstone of all academic abilities.

Nonetheless, given the extreme variability in these students' educational histories, they must be offered different pathways to eventual academic success. One approach to literacy instruction will not fit all English language learners. However, the instructional practices outlined in this chapter and throughout this manual should greatly assist them in participating more fully in a heterogeneous secondary Language Arts classroom.

Those with significant gaps in their elementary educational backgrounds will require a thoughtful and sustained literacy intervention program, complemented by a substantive and protracted English language development program. Their acute and compelling academic needs cannot be accommodated solely within the confines of the general education Language Arts classroom, an after-school tutorial, or a reading intervention program.

Similarly, literate and academically prepared newcomers will still need a viable English language development program to enable them to transfer the knowledge and skills they acquired in their native language schooling to the curricula they are studying in the United States. Literate adolescents who are virtual beginners in English will also benefit from a separate reading support class, to help them readily acquire the basic phonology, morphology, and syntax of English and to more efficiently transfer the reading skills they have already mastered in their native language. Students who can already read relatively fluently in their first language will make an easier transition to English decoding than bilingual classmates who are nonreaders. These literate second-language learners will therefore need to move more rapidly than struggling ELL readers, from initial skill-building lessons that focus on decoding, word recognition, and pronunciation to explicit instruction in comprehension strategies such as prediction, questioning, and summarizing that will help them deal more productively with the reading demands of content-area classrooms.

Reading in a Second Language

Research findings suggest that reading processes in a second language are not significantly different from those in a first language.[3] For example, both rely on the reader's background knowledge regarding the topic and text structure to construct meaning, and both make use of cueing systems (graphic,

---

3. Grabe, W. "Current Developments in Second Language Reading." *TESOL Quarterly* (1991), 25, 375–406.

syntactic, phonological, semantic) to allow the reader to predict and confirm meaning.

While literacy processes in first and second languages may be quite similar, two crucial areas of difference must be addressed. First, initial reading and writing in English will be slower and more painstaking for second-language learners because of their lack of overall fluency. The second-language learner is often in the process of acquiring basic oral language while simultaneously developing literacy skills in English. Limited proficiency in a second language can cause a proficient reader in the native language to revert to poor reading strategies, such as reading word by word. Also, some students may not even have the native language literacy skills to transfer concepts about print and strategies to the second language.

Secondly, ELL students are likely to have less prior knowledge and relevant vocabulary to process new information while reading academic English assignments. Furthermore, readers' background knowledge is often culture-bound and may not match the content needed for a given reading text. ELL students with a limited range of personal and educational experiences on a reading topic will therefore have little to draw upon to construct meaning from a selection even if they are able to accurately decode.

Academic Language Development

Many adolescent ELL students come to school with sufficient social language for everyday classroom interactions yet are severely lacking in the academic English foundations to tackle a poem or follow the instructions on a standardized test. This is because academic vocabulary is primarily developed through school-based reading and repeated exposure during content-based classroom activities.

The average native English-speaking student enters elementary school with an internalized understanding of the syntax and phonology of English, plus a working vocabulary of several thousand words. This vocabulary base is enhanced each year through new school experiences and reinforced in home and community settings. In striking contrast, the language minority student enters U.S. schooling with a tenuous grasp of the phonology and syntax of the English language, a scant working English vocabulary, and rare opportunities for practice and expansion of this knowledge outside the classroom. As a consequence, they must develop content-specific language and literacy skills along with conceptual foundations, all the while competing with native English-speaking classmates who may also be challenged by grade-level Language Arts curricula, but who at least operate from a relatively firm foundation in basic academic English and years of exposure to high-frequency social English vocabulary.

Implications for English Language Arts Instruction

A number of implications for instruction can be drawn from these descriptions of the academic language and literacy challenges of ELL students. Novice English readers will require extensive and dynamic instructional "front-loading" in order to effectively grapple with challenging literacy tasks. Teachers all too often concentrate their energies on the damage-control phase, when it becomes clear that students either failed to comprehend or felt too overwhelmed to even try to tackle a reading task. Explaining critical concepts and language after the fact does little to engender reader confidence or competence for the next task. The students may walk away with a better grasp of the plot development in *The Joy Luck Club* but have no sense of how to proceed with the next chapter. Instead, conscientious literacy mentors essentially "teach the text backwards" by devoting far more instructional time to the preparation and guidance phases of lessons. Since a second-language reader may be approaching an assignment with impoverished background knowledge and weak English vocabulary, it makes sense to concentrate on classroom activities that build strong conceptual and linguistic foundations, guide them into the text organization, model appropriate comprehension strategies, and provide a clear purpose for reading. This responsible preparation will in turn help to create the kind of nurturing affective and cognitive arena that communicates high expectations for their literacy development and encourages them to persist and take risks.

Instructional Considerations When Preparing Lessons to Support English Language Learners

All of the instructional practices detailed in Part 3 of this booklet will support ELL students in making strides in their second-language literacy development and in becoming vibrant members of the classroom community of learners. Following are some additional reminders of ways in which you can support ELL students at various stages of your lesson planning to deal more productively with the reading and writing demands of English Language Arts curricula.

Phase 1: Preteach

- Pull out a manageable number of key concepts.

- Identify vocabulary most critical to talking and learning about the central concepts. Don't attempt to cover all of the vocabulary words you anticipate they will not know. Do more than provide synonyms and definitions. Introduce the essential words in more meaningful contexts, through simple sentences drawing on familiar issues, people, scenarios, and vocabulary. Guide students in articulating the meanings of essential terms through these familiar contexts and hold them responsible for writing the definitions in their own words.

- Present key words when they occur within the context of the reading selection or activity. Make the words as concrete as possible by linking each to an object, photo, drawing, or movement.

- Post the new essential vocabulary in a prominent place in the classroom to create a word bank of organized lesson terminology.

- Examine your lesson to see what types of language functions students will need to participate in various activities. For example, if they are being asked to make predictions about upcoming paragraph content in an essay based on transition words (e.g., *therefore, in addition, consequently*), students will need to be taught some basic sentence patterns and verbs to express opinions (e.g., "I predict that . . ."; "Based on this transition word, I conclude that . . ."). If being asked to agree or disagree with the arguments in a persuasive article, students will need to learn some sentence patterns and verbs to convey agreement or disagreement (e.g., "I don't agree with the author's argument that adolescents don't have a work ethic because . . .").

- Engage students in prereading activities that spark their curiosity and involve them in all four language modes.

- Assess students' prior knowledge related to key concepts through participation structures and collaborative group discussions with realia (e.g., photographs, objects) serving as a visual trigger.

- Utilize realia and visuals needed to make the concepts less abstract.

- Use multimedia presentations such as CD-ROM and videos to

familiarize students with the plot, characters, and themes of a narrative text prior to reading, but don't use it as a replacement for reading.

- Provide a written and oral synopsis of the key content prior to actually asking students to read a selection if the sentence structures and vocabulary are particularly demanding.

- Use graphic organizers and semantic maps to help students grasp the central content in an accessible manner prior to reading.

- Lead a quick text prereading, or "text tour," focusing student attention on illustrations; chapter title and subtopics; boldface words; summary sections; and connection of chapter to theme, previous chapters, activities, and concepts.

- When possible, build in opportunities for "narrow reading," allowing students to read more than one selection on the same topic, to build concept and vocabulary recognition that will support their reading more fluently and confidently.

Phase 2: Teach

- Clearly establish a reading purpose for students prior to assigning a manageable amount of text.

- Describe and model strategies for navigating different kinds of text. Provide a convincing rationale for each new strategy and regularly review both the purpose and process.

- Familiarize students with a manageable tool kit of reading comprehension and study strategies and continue practicing these selective strategies. In this way, students end the school year with a viable approach unattainable through sporadic practice with a confusing array of new reading behaviors.

- Introduce a new strategy using a text that isn't too difficult in order to build credibility for the strategy and ensure student success. Otherwise, if a selection is too difficult and the strategy fails to deliver for students, they will have little faith in experimenting with the new strategy on future texts.

- Whenever possible, get students physically involved with the page, using highlighters, self-sticking notes, and a small piece of cardboard or heavy construction paper to focus and guide their reading from one paragraph or column to the next.

- Alternate between teacher-facilitated and student-dominated reading activities.

- Do "think-aloud" reading to model your cognitive and metacognitive strategies and thought processes.

- Assign brief amounts of text at a time and alternate between oral, paired, and silent reading.

- Guide students through the process of reading and comprehending a passage by reading aloud to them and assisting them in identifying the text organization and establishing a clear reading purpose.

- Allow students to read a passage while listening to an audiotape recorded by a classmate, cross-age tutor, or parent volunteer.

- Have students engage in "repeated readings" of the same brief passage to build word recognition, fluency, and reading rate.

- Provide some form of study guide in order to focus their reading on the critical content and prevent them from getting bogged down with nonessential details and unfamiliar vocabulary. A partially completed outline or graphic organizer is more task based and manageable than a list of questions to answer, which often results in simple scanning for content without really reading and comprehending material.

- Demonstrate your note-taking process and provide models of effective study notes for students to emulate.

Phase 3: Assess

- Prepare both text-based and experientially based questions, which lead students from simply getting the gist of a selection to establishing a personal connection to the lesson content.

- Build in task-based and authentic assessment during every lesson to ensure that ELL students are actually developing greater proficiency with new content and strategies. Quick writes, drawings, oral and written summaries, and collaborative tasks are generally more productive indicators of lesson comprehension than a closing question/answer session.

- Provide safe opportunities for students to alert you to any learning challenges they are experiencing. Have them submit anonymous written questions (formulated either independently or with a partner) about confusing lesson content and process, and then follow up on these points of confusion at the end of class or in the subsequent class session.

- Ask students to end the class session by writing 3–5 outcome statements about their experience in the day's lesson, expressing both new understandings and needs for clarification.

- Make sure that assessment mirrors the lesson objectives. For example, if you are teaching students how to preread expository text, it isn't relevant to assess using comprehension questions. A more authentic assessment of their ability to apply this strategy would be to provide them with a photocopy of an expository selection and ask them to highlight and label the parts one would read during the actual prereading process. It would be relevant, however, to ask them to identify two reasons for engaging in a text prereading before tackling the entire selection.

- Build in opportunities for students to demonstrate their understandings of texts that draw upon different language and literacy skills: formal and informal writing assignments, posters, small-group tasks, oral presentations, and so on.

- Don't assign ELLs tasks that require little or no reading or lesson comprehension. For example, don't allow them to simply draw a picture while other students are writing a paragraph. Instead, make sure that you have adequately scaffolded the task and equipped them with a writing frame and model to guide them through the process. While one might argue that this is multimodal and tapping into multiple intelligences, it is actually conveying expectations for their development of academic competence in English.

- Make sure that students understand your assessment criteria in advance. Whenever possible, provide models of student work for them to emulate, along with a nonmodel that fails to meet the specified assessment criteria. Do not provide exemplars that are clearly outside their developmental range. While this may be an enriching reading task, it will not serve as a viable model. Save student work that can later serve as a model for ELLs with different levels of academic preparation.

- Develop accessible and relevant rubrics for various tasks and products that are customized to the task rather than generic assessment tools. Introduce a rubric in tandem with exemplars of successful and less productive work to help them internalize the assessment criteria. Guide students in identifying the ways in which sample work does or does not meet established grading criteria.

Phase 4: Extend

- Consider ways in which students can transfer knowledge and skills gleaned from one assignment/lesson to a subsequent lesson.

- Build in opportunities for students to read a more detailed or challenging selection on the same topic in order to allow them to apply familiar concepts and vocabulary and stretch their literacy muscles.

- Recycle pre- and postreading tasks regularly, so students can become more familiar with the task process and improve their performance. If they are assailed with curricular novelty, ELLs never have the opportunity to refine their skills and demonstrate improved competence. For example, if you ask them to identify a personality trait of an essential character in a story and then support this observation with relevant details in an expository paragraph, it would make sense to have them shortly afterwards write an identical paragraph about another character.

- Discuss with students ways in which they can apply new vocabulary and language strategies outside the classroom.

- Praise students' efforts to experiment with new language in class, both in writing and in speaking.

- Demonstrate the applicability of new reading and writing strategies to real-world literacy tasks. Bring in potentially more engaging reading selections that will pique their interest and provide a more compelling rationale for applying a new strategic repertoire. Design periodic writing tasks for an authentic audience other than the teacher: another class, fellow classmates, and so on.

Characteristics of Less Proficient Learners

Every high-school classroom has a number of less proficient students, individuals who begin the year one, two, or more years below grade level yet who do not qualify for special education services and may not be English language learners. It is important to keep in mind that most accommodations made for English learners and special needs students will be helpful for all kinds of diverse learners, including less proficient learners. However, it is worthwhile to briefly examine some of the learner characteristics of less proficient students in comparison with their average achieving peers. An appreciation of these distinctions will provide a useful foundation for understanding the importance of using the various "universal access" strategies described throughout this chapter and incorporated into the Prentice Hall Literature program.

Attention and Memory

Research suggests that underachieving students have difficulty in organizing and categorizing new information during instruction. Typically, less skillful students do not effectively order, classify, and arrange information in meaningful ways during learning, frequently leaving them confused and missing the "big picture." Long-term memory is often adversely affected due to the lack of meaningful connections established and difficulty with noticing how new information relates to prior knowledge. In addition, underprepared students frequently do not know how to focus their attention on the important aspects of a classroom presentation, demonstration, or reading selection. In either case, the intentional use of explicit strategies coupled with interactive review and extension activities can make a significant difference in providing poorly prepared students full access to the Language Arts curriculum.

Lesson Planning and Instructional Accommodations for Attention and Memory

Phase 1: Preteach

- Gain attention requesting a simple physical response (e.g., "Everyone, eyes on me please," "Touch number one," and so forth). Students need to show you they are ready.
- Keep the lesson pace moving along briskly—a "perky not pokey" pace is helpful.
- Clarify or introduce critical "big ideas" or conceptual anchors that the reading or lesson or activity is built around (e.g., an example, a metaphor, a demonstration).
- Use brief choral responses when the answer is short and identical (e.g. "Everyone, the answer to number one is _____.").
- Use brief partner responses when the answer is open-ended and longer (e.g., "Ones, tell twos the most important new information revealed in the last paragraph.").
- After students have had a chance to rehearse or practice with a partner, randomly call upon them to build prior knowledge or raise questions the text may answer.
- Use graphic organizers, charts, and concept maps to assist students with focusing on critical concepts as well as categorizing and organizing information to be studied/learned.

Phase 2: Teach

- Engage students in a "read/reflect/discuss/note" cycle of filling out the graphic organizers/concept maps collaboratively as you progress through the reading or lesson.
- Do a brief oral review using partners (e.g., think-write-pair-share) to ensure that all students are firm on the big ideas/critical concepts.
- Cue students to take special note of crucial information and explore why this information is so critical.
- Engage students in the active use or processing of the new information (e.g., paraphrase, give an example, write a response).
- Emphasize connections between new and known information.
- Connect new learning to student's personal experience (e.g., coach students to create analogies or metaphors using prior knowledge).

Phase 3: Assess

- Ask students to explain their graphic organizer/concept map to a partner. Monitor selected students and determine their level of understanding—reteach/provide additional examples as necessary.

- Provide students the opportunity to reorganize, prioritize, and otherwise reflect on the key aspects of the lesson.

- Systematically monitor retention of key information or "big ideas" over time using "quick writes" (brief written summaries to a prompt), random questioning, observing student interactions, written assignments, and so on. Reteach, provide additional examples, invite students to elaborate, and so on, as necessary.

Phase 4: Extend

- Have students design investigations or projects using the information in new ways.

- Design homework assignments that require students to go beyond the text to apply lessons learned to their lives or to other circumstances.

- Challenge students to organize information in novel ways, come up with different categories, and otherwise elaborate the information being studied.

- Draw explicit connections and prompt students to induce connections between information studied earlier in the term and new ideas encountered in the current reading selection.

Learning Strategies and Use

Perhaps the most ubiquitous characteristic of less proficient students is their lack of effective and efficient strategies for accomplishing various academic tasks, from writing a persuasive essay to taking notes during a lecture to responding to a piece of literature. Less skillful students tend to have a very limited repertoire of learning strategies and have little awareness of how to monitor the use of learning strategies during reading, writing, and other academic activities. In contrast, successful learners are active, "strategic," and flexible in their employment of appropriate learning strategies tailored to the demands of a particular academic task or assignment.

Kame'enui and Carnine[4] suggest three critical design principles teachers need to keep in mind when addressing the issue of learning strategies with underprepared or diverse learners.

---

4. Kame'enui, Edward and Douglas Carnine, op. cit.

1. Important learning strategies must be made overt, explicit, and conspicuous.

2. Strong verbal and visual support, or "scaffolding," should be provided to ensure that diverse learners understand when, where, and how to use the strategies.

3. Judicious review of new learning strategies is required to allow less prepared students enough practice to incorporate the new strategy into their learning routines.

It is important to note that differences between less proficient students and average achievers in their use of learning strategies is not based on organic or biological differences. In other words, it is their lack of experience and preparation that is the critical difference. Fortunately, less proficient learners are quite capable of acquiring effective learning strategies and significantly improving their academic performance when provided with direct instruction in the "what-why-how-when" of strategy use in a highly focused educational setting.

Lesson Planning and Instructional Accommodations for Learning Strategies

Phase 1: Preteach
- Clarify the rationale for learning the new strategy in terms, examples, and results the students value (e.g., "Where in school or life would it be useful to know how to write a persuasive essay?").
- Brainstorm for examples of successful strategy usage with interactive tactics such as "give one, get one" to involve all students (e.g., each student lists as many ideas as possible in 3–4 minutes and then has 3–5 minutes to compare with a peer and "give one" idea to them as well as "get one" from them to extend their brainstormed list).
- Provide personal examples of how you have used this strategy to your academic advantage.
- Directly teach any "pre-skills," or prerequisite skills, students need to perform the strategy.

Phase 2: Teach
Explicitly model the use of the strategy, including a significant focus on thinking aloud during the execution of each step in the strategy.

- Provide students with a brief summary of the strategy steps or an acronym to facilitate retention of the strategy.

  Example:

  POWER: Prepare, **O**rganize, **W**rite, **E**dit, **R**evise

  (Archer & Gleason 2000)

- Guide students in practicing the strategy using less demanding content that allows students to focus on the new strategy. Gradually transition to more difficult content.

- Break the strategy down into explicit steps, ensuring that students are able to perform each step and combine steps to use the whole strategy.

- Structure partner-mediated practice in which students take turns practicing the strategy and providing feedback to one another (e.g., taking turns reading a paragraph or page and paraphrasing the gist in 12 words or less).

Phase 3: Assess

- Monitor partners during strategy practice to observe competence, areas for review, and so forth.

- Randomly call on students to informally demonstrate their strategy knowledge.

- Include explicit use of strategies taught as part of the quiz, paper, report, project, and other formal assessments.

Phase 4: Extend

- Discuss with students where else in or out of school they could use the strategy.

- Provide extra credit or some other incentive to encourage the use of the strategy in other content area classes.

- After they have gained some degree of mastery, encourage students to modify and otherwise personalize the strategy to better fit their learning style or needs.

Vocabulary and Reading Fluency

Vocabulary differences between struggling and average students are apparent from the primary years in school and tend to get worse over time. It is not surprising that less prepared learners engage in far less reading in and out of school, resulting in substantially impoverished vocabularies.

In addition, their ability to read fluently and accurately is often diminished, further compounding the issue and rendering reading a frustrating and defeating experience.

There is no shortcut, or "quick fix," for vocabulary building, but teachers can make a tremendous difference by sustained attention to the following practices:

- Directly teaching key conceptual vocabulary using strategies that take students beyond simple memorization
- Teaching students how to learn words and concepts from context
- Encouraging wide reading in and out of school; students who have serious fluency problems (e.g., reading below 100 words per minute in grade-level text) will require sustained practice daily in repeated reading of instructional level/age-appropriate texts

Lesson Planning and Instructional Accommodations for Vocabulary and Fluency

Phase 1: Preteach

- Select conceptually rich, critical vocabulary for more detailed instruction before reading.
- Choose age- and level-appropriate passages for students to use repeated reading strategies (e.g., on prerecorded tapes, partner reading, choral reading with small groups).

Phase 2: Teach

- Directly teach the meanings of critical, conceptually rich vocabulary required for full understanding of the passage or lesson.
- Pick vocabulary strategies that take students beyond simple repetition of the definition to prompt active construction of new connections between the concept and their prior knowledge. Such strategies include
  —creating semantic maps showing how words are related
  —using the words in sentences that "show you know" the meaning
- Define the critical attributes of the concept in short bulleted phrases and create examples and nonexamples of the concept, prompting students to explain why the exemplar does or does not have the attributes of the concept under consideration (a graphic organizer showing the attributes and examples/nonexamples can be very useful).

- Engage students in word sorts: Provide 10–20 vocabulary words for students to place into preset categories (e.g., parts of speech, words descriptive of the character or not, and so on).
- Pair students at similar instructional levels for repeated reading practice; have the more proficient student read a paragraph or a page and then have the less proficient student reread the same section.
- Practice repeated reading of instructional-level passages of 150–200 words in length with prerecorded tapes, set goals, and individually graph and monitor fluency daily, finishing with a written retelling of the passage.
- Teach students important generative word roots (e.g., Latin and Greek) and common affixes. Practice sorting and combining to examine how they work (e.g., -spec-: spectrum, spectacle, inspection, speculation).
- Model and practice the use of context in predicting word meanings during reading, thinking aloud to demonstrate to students how textual cues direct your thinking.

Phase 3: Assess

- Randomly call on students to provide examples of the vocabulary word under examination.
- Monitor students during partner discussion of selected critical vocabulary words.
- Evaluate students during small-group discussion, written products, and so on.
- Directly monitor the fluency of selected students via one-minute timings. Note rate, accuracy, and expression.

Phase 4: Extend

- Encourage students to informally use recently taught vocabulary words in "show you know" sentences during classroom conversations, written products, and so on.
- Intentionally revisit newly acquired vocabulary during discussion, while thinking aloud during demonstrations, and so on.
- Encourage students to practice fluency building via repeated reading at home, appropriate CD-ROM technology, and cross-age tutoring of younger students, in which the target student must prepare a story to read fluently with his or her tutee.

Motivation and Academic Identity

Motivation is complex and difficult to define, but most experts agree that it is significantly related to how much success or failure one has experienced relative to the activity in question. Less proficient secondary students typically do not see themselves as capable of sustained reading, inquiry, or writing in a challenging academic setting. The old cliché "Nothing succeeds like success" is relevant to this discussion. To build motivation and encourage the development of a productive "academic identity," it is important to engage less proficient students in challenging lessons while simultaneously incorporating adequate support or instructional scaffolding to increase the likelihood students will experience success. In addition, helping students to explore their thinking as they read and write through structured dialogues and thinking aloud can be very helpful. Noted reading researcher David Pearson calls this process a "metacognitive conversation," allowing less proficient students to gain an understanding of how successful readers and writers think as they work. In a manner of speaking, teachers can provide less proficient students with an academic or cognitive role model. For example, modeling a simple self-monitoring strategy during writing such as "remember your audience" can assist students in keeping multiple perspectives in mind as they compose.

Lesson Planning and Instructional Accommodations for Motivation and Academic Identity

Motivation and academic identity do not lend themselves to the Preteach, Teach, Assess, and Extend lesson format. In a sense, motivation is more "caught than taught" and will be the result of successfully engaging students in the curriculum. However, there are a number of general strategies that are useful to consider including:

- **Self-selected reading** Allow less proficient students regular opportunities to read material they are interested in, at their instructional level.
- **Goal setting** Engage students in setting personal goals for various academic tasks, such as pages/chapters read per week, strategy usage, words read per minute during fluency practice, and so forth.

- **Metacognitive dialogues** Ask students to informally share their perceptions, approaches, and fears regarding various school-related challenges. Students and teachers then share their thoughts and feelings about how they used various strategies to become more successful.
- **Book clubs, book reviews, newsletter reviews, e-mail postings** These provide an audience for students' opinions about books they have read.
- **Partnerships** Have students build partnerships with peers and with younger students, community members, and business personnel.
- **Negotiated choices** As appropriate, involve students in negotiating alternative assignments, options, and novel ideas to reach common goals.
- **Model an "academic identity"** Invite teachers/students/other adults into the classroom to share how they developed as literate citizens.

Summary

Less proficient high-school students are underprepared for the academic challenges of a rigorous grade-level Language Arts program in a variety of ways. Many of their difficulties can be linked to difficulties with attention and memory, learning strategies, vocabulary and reading fluency, and motivation/academic identity. Secondary Language Arts teachers can have an extremely beneficial effect on the learning of less proficient students by the sustained focus on appropriate strategies for preteaching, teaching, assessment, and extension beyond the lesson.

Students with special education needs are a highly diverse student group. Although their learning needs vary greatly, a majority of children identified as special education students will experience mild to severe difficulties in becoming proficient and independent readers and writers. Through instruction that incorporates adaptations and modifications and is delivered in collaborative ways, students with disabilities can gain literacy skills and be active participants in general education Language Arts curricula and instruction.

Characteristics of Special Education Learners

Eligibility for Special Education

Federal law IDEA '97 (Individuals with Disabilities Education Act, P.L. 105–17) specifies the disabling conditions under which students are found eligible to receive special education services. These disabling conditions may be clustered into the two broad categories of high incidence and low incidence disabilities (see chart on the following pages for descriptions of disabling conditions). Each student with a disability may experience specific cognitive, communicative, behavioral/social/emotional, physical, and learning issues. Students may exhibit all, or some combination, of the characteristics listed for their particular disability and, in the case of some students, have more than one disability (e.g., a student identified as having a learning disability may also have a communicative disorder). Because of the heterogeneity of the special education student population, even within categories of disability, an Individualized Education Program (IEP) is created for each student found eligible to receive special education services.

Disabling Conditions

High Incidence Disabilities	Descriptors	Reading Instruction Consideration
• *Speech or Language Impairment*	• Speech disorders include difficulties in articulation, voice, and fluency. • Language impairments may include difficulties in phonology, morphology, syntax, semantics, and pragmatics.	• When possible, provide opportunities for intensive instruction in decoding and word-recognition skills (e.g., computer drill and practice programs; flash cards of frequently encountered words). • Provide time for students to read the text multiple times to gain fluency (e.g., repeated readings; paired reading). • Explicitly teach vocabulary and provide strategies for dealing with unknown words (e.g., teaching syllabification skills; teaching meaning of prefixes and suffixes). • Explicitly teach more complex language patterns (e.g., compound sentences) and literary elements (e.g., idioms; metaphors).
• *Learning Disabilities*	• Students exhibit average to above-average intelligence combined with uneven academic performance patterns (i.e., perform at an average to above-average level in some academic subjects, while experiencing significant difficulties in others). • Students experience processing difficulties (e.g., have difficulty taking in oral and print information and in expressing ideas orally and in writing). • Students may experience attention and social/behavioral challenges.	• Preteach "big ideas" and vocabulary. • Provide multiple opportunities for students to read text to gain fluency. • Explicitly teach vocabulary using activities that are multisensory and require active participation (e.g., acting out meanings of words; drawing images to represent word meanings; tape-recording words and word meanings; using computer software programs). • Explicitly teach comprehension strategies by modeling the steps, guiding the students through the steps, and monitoring for implementation (e.g., webbing and outlining; predicting; summarizing). • Provide multiple avenues for demonstrating comprehension of text (e.g., writing, drawing, speaking, acting out scenes).
• *Emotional Disturbance*	• Students experience difficulty learning that is not due to cognitive, sensory, or health factors. • Students may have difficulty forging and maintaining interpersonal relationships.	• Make students accountable during large-group, small-group, and paired reading (e.g., have them take notes and make and check predictions; ask questions of all group members, not just a spokesperson; have students complete individual quizzes to check for understanding).

continued

	• Students may display inappropriate behaviors or feelings under normal circumstances. • Students may experience feelings of unhappiness or depression. • Students may have physical symptoms or fears associated with personal or school problems.	• Explicitly teach skills for working in groups (e.g., how to ask questions; how to state an opinion; how to disagree with another person's ideas). • Provide structure and establish routines for reading activities and transitions (e.g., specify expectations during large-group reading; establish routines for how students are to complete comprehension activities). • Become familiar with the student's behavior plan and systematically implement it in the classroom (e.g., use the reinforcers and consequences identified in the plan to build consistency for the student).
• *Mental Retardation*	• Students will demonstrate subaverage (in students with mild/moderate mental retardation) to significantly subaverage (in students with severe mental retardation) intellectual functioning. • Students will demonstrate overall low performance in adaptive behavior domains (e.g., taking care of personal health needs).	• Preteach and reteach vocabulary and concepts as needed. • Make concepts concrete by linking concepts to the students' daily lives. • Explicitly model what is expected, and when able, provide examples of completed projects. • Provide multiple avenues for students to engage with text (e.g., books on tape, paired reading, passages in hypertext format). • Provide multiple exposures to the same text and its key vocabulary. • Provide multiple ways for students to demonstrate understanding of text.
• *Low Incidence Disabilities*	**Note:** Students with low incidence disabilities may have average to above-average intelligence or may experience cognitive impairments ranging from mild to severe.	**Note:** Students with low incidence disabilities may have average to above-average intelligence or may experience cognitive impairments ranging from mild to severe.
• *Deaf/Hard of Hearing*	• Students who are deaf or who have some degree of hearing loss	• Present ideas visually. • Capture key ideas from discussions in written form on the overhead or chalkboard. • Use FMI systems when available. • When orally reading text, reduce background noise as much as possible; when conducting small-group or paired reading activities, consider having the groups move to other rooms or spaces. • Work with the interpreter or special education staff to identify adaptations and modifications.

continued

• *Blind/Low Vision*	• Students who are blind or who have some vision	• Present ideas auditorially and through tactile modes to support student access. • Work with the special education teacher to secure large-print text, Braille text, books on tape, and AAC reading devices. • Work with the special education staff to identify specific adaptations and modifications.
• *Deaf/Blindness*	• Students who have concomitant hearing and visual impairments	• Work with the special education staff to identify specific adaptations and modifications. • Gain understanding and a level of comfort in using the AAC devices the student is using in the classroom.
• *Other Health Impaired*	• Students with health conditions that limit strength, vitality, or alertness (e.g., heart condition, sickle cell anemia, epilepsy, AIDS)	• Work with the special education staff to identify adaptations and modifications. • Gain understanding of the child's condition and day-to-day and emergency medical needs. • Develop plans for dealing with students' absences.
• *Orthopedic Disabilities*	• Students with physical disabilities (e.g., club-foot, bone tuberculosis, cerebral palsy)	• Work with the special education staff to identify specific adaptations and modifications. • Work with the special education staff to secure adapted materials and AAC devices, as appropriate (e.g., book holder; computer voice-recognition system that allows student to dictate written assignments). • Adapt routines and activities to take into consideration the student's physical needs (e.g., room arrangement that allows for mobility in a wheelchair; procedures for distributing and collecting materials; procedures for forming work groups.)
• *Autism*	• Students experience difficulty in verbal and nonverbal communication • Students experience difficulties in social interactions • Is commonly referred to as a "spectrum disorder" because of the heterogeneity of the group	• Work with the special education staff to identify specific adaptations and modifications. • Structure group and paired activities to take into consideration the child's needs; teach social skills and supports for working in small group and paired situations. • Connect concepts and vocabulary to the interests of the student. • Work with the special education staff to implement behavioral/social plans to provide consistency. • Establish and maintain routines to ensure predictability within the classroom.

continued

• *Traumatic Brain Injury*	• Students who experience an acquired injury to the brain • Injury results in total or partial functional disability or psychological impairment (e.g., cognition, language, memory, attention, reasoning)	• Work with the special education staff to identify specific adaptations and modifications. • Adapt routines and activities to take into consideration the student's physical needs (e.g., room arrangement that allows for mobility in a wheelchair). • Take into consideration student's language, memory, and attention skill needs when constructing class assignments and activities. • Preteach and reteach concepts and vocabulary as appropriate.

Individualized Education Plan

The IEP serves to guide general and special education teachers, related service providers, and parents in designing and delivering educational programs that maximize students' school participation and learning. The IEP includes goals, objectives, and benchmarks that outline what an individual student is expected to learn and achieve during the course of the academic year, as well as the types of services and special adaptations and modifications that are to be put into place to support the educational achievement of the student. For example, in the area of Language Arts instruction, a student's IEP may include the following goal and objectives:

Goal: Jamal will improve in reading comprehension skills as measured by the district-adopted standardized test.

Objective: Given narrative passages written at the seventh-grade level, Jamal will correctly write the name(s) of the main character(s) and outline, in writing, the main events of the passages in correct sequence for three out of four passages by December.

Objective: Given expository passages written at the seventh-grade level, Jamal will correctly write the main idea of the passages and at least three supporting details for three out of four passages by February.

The IEP goes on to identify specific services the student will need in order to achieve these goals and objectives. A range of services is available to students with disabilities through their IEP. Services fall along a continuum and include the option of students receiving instruction in general education classrooms with special education supports and participating in specialized instruction delivered by special education teachers in special education classrooms for one or more periods a day. The type of service delivery to be provided is determined individually for each student through the IEP meeting. The general education teacher, in partnership with the special education staff and the student's parents and, when appropriate, the student, determine the type of service delivery that is most appropriate for a student based on his or her learning needs.

Many students with disabilities are educated in general education classrooms alongside their general education peers. Service-delivery models that support student participation in general education classrooms go by various names, including mainstreaming, integration, and inclusion. All have the underlying same intent—to provide for the needs of students with disabilities in the least restrictive environment, alongside their general education peers.

In the case of Jamal, the service delivery option selected and specified in his IEP may look something like this:

> Student will participate in the general education Language Arts class and in one period of special education reading resource support each day. The special education teacher will team with the general education Language Arts teacher at least two days per week to provide instruction in the general education Language Arts class.

IEPs also specify the types of curricular, instructional, and behavioral adaptations and modifications that are to be put into place to support the student's achievement. For Jamal, the following adaptations and modifications may be specified in the IEP:

> The student will receive instruction in learning strategies to identify characters, story sequence, and main ideas and supporting details. The student will be provided a story map for identifying the main character(s) and for sequencing story events. The student will be provided a main idea/supporting details map when working with expository passages.

The IEP is a guide that details the types of goals, educational program, and adaptations and modifications a special education student is to receive. The IEP is developed by a team and is reviewed at least annually. General education teachers, special education professionals, administrators, parents, and students all have a voice in the development of the individual IEP.

Lesson Planning and Instructional Accommodations

When developing Language Arts lesson plans for inclusive classrooms of general and special education learners, teachers will want to consider the addition of teaching and learning strategies that will support universal access to the content. Teachers will need to be familiar with the unique learning needs and requirements of the students and their goals, objectives, and benchmarks and, through collaboration with other IEP team members, incorporate those needs and strategies into the classroom.

This process does not need to be as intimidating as it sounds because there are some common, relatively unintrusive teaching and learning strategies that can be implemented in the classroom to address students' specific needs, as well as support the learning of the other students present in the classroom. For example, students with disabilities can greatly benefit from activities that preteach and reteach concepts, that explicitly link lesson content with prior experience and knowledge, that directly teach the meaning of critical vocabulary words, and that explicitly model how tasks are to be completed. This is true for other learners as well, including less proficient readers and students who are English language learners. Lesson plans that include explicit instruction in behavioral and social expectations also help to ensure student participation and learning. Pacing is also an issue. Some students with disabilities will require a somewhat slower pace or an ongoing review of key concepts if they are to grasp key understandings and skills. Also, activities need to be considered in light of the students' disabilities. For example, will special materials be needed (such as materials with enlarged print for students with low vision or adapted manipulatives that can be used by a student with a physical disability)? If participating in student-mediated instruction (e.g., small-group learning), what type of preparation will students receive for participating in these activities? Will the activities provide necessary supports to ensure student participation (e.g., will directions be explicit and in writing as well as presented verbally)?

There are a number of other simple adaptations and modifications general education teachers can implement in the classroom to directly address the literacy learning needs of students with disabilities. In fact, in many cases, these adaptations and modifications will assist all learners in the classroom, including typically developing readers, English learners, and less proficient readers. A beginning list of suggestions for meaningfully including students with disabilities in the general education Language Arts curriculum is presented in the chart at the end of this section. Although presented in terms of disabling conditions, the suggestions apply across conditions.

It is also helpful to think of instructional considerations that specifically apply to the four phases of instruction: Preteach, Teach, Assess, and Extend. A beginning list of suggestions is provided below.

Phase 1: Preteach

- Identify the most critical and high-utility vocabulary words for comprehension of the passage. Provide explicit instruction in the meaning of these words that incorporates instruction in the understanding of prefixes, suffixes, word roots, synonyms, and antonyms.
- Provide an overview of key ideas and concepts presented in the text using study guides, outlines, or maps.
- Explicitly connect text content with the students' lives.
- Preteach key concepts.

Phase 2: Teach

- Present all ideas orally and visually and, when possible, incorporate tactile and kinesthetic experiences as well.
- Stop often to discuss key ideas and check for understanding.
- Limit the presentation of information or discussion of key topics to short periods of time (no more than ten minutes) to enhance attention.
- Require students to demonstrate that they are listening and following along (e.g., taking notes, running a finger along the text).
- Incorporate active reading strategies (e.g., choral reading, paired reading) to assist students in maintaining attention.
- Provide necessary adaptive materials as appropriate (e.g., enlarged print).
- Incorporate the same comprehension and learning strategies over extended periods to allow for mastery. This will provide students with multiple opportunities to practice a strategy and to become comfortable in its application. This will also prevent "strategy clutter," which can occur when a student has too many strategies to draw from and is not facile enough with any to allow for ease of use.

- Provide specific and step-by-step instructions. Model what the students are to do, step-by-step.

Phase 3: Assess

- Go beyond questioning techniques to assess students' understanding by having them write questions about what they have learned, identify those sections they find are unclear or confusing, or complete short writes of the key points.
- When having students work in groups or pairs, set up procedures that maintain individual student accountability (e.g., students each having to write, draw, or state a response).
- When appropriate, have students self-manage and chart their performance. Academic performance, homework and assignment completion, and behavior could be charted.

Phase 4: Extend

- Provide examples of completed projects.
- Allow students to work in pairs or small groups.
- Provide outlines of what is to be done, with suggested dates and timelines for project completion.

Collaboration as a Key to Student Achievement

One of the most critical things a general education teacher can do is to collaborate with the special education teachers and staff. Special education staff have extensive expertise in working with students with disabilities and are there to support each student with an IEP. These professionals are available as support systems for general education teachers and parents. The chart that follows presents a brief list of potential special educators that you may want to contact when working with students with disabilities in your general education classroom.

General education teachers can do a great deal to ensure that students with disabilities are meaningfully included in the life of the classroom. The attributes listed on the next page are important to all classrooms, but they play a key role in the creation of a classroom culture and climate that supports the participation and achievement of students with disabilities.

- Exploring differences and the importance of the acceptance of differences
- Setting clear expectations for all students that take into consideration students' learning styles and needs
- Providing students with reasonable choices
- Setting up instructional activities that foster the development of relationships between students and between students and teachers
- Demonstrating mutual respect, fairness, and trust

For example, in the case of Jamal, you could work with the special education teacher to identify those learning strategies you are already teaching in the classroom that will assist Jamal. You may want to invite the special education teacher into the classroom to provide instruction in other critical learning strategies that would assist all of your students in becoming better readers and writers, including Jamal. Because Jamal is receiving resource-room support one period per day, you may want to discuss with the special education teacher the type of instruction he is receiving during the support period and together work to develop a plan that links the curriculum of the two learning environments. You will most likely be involved in assessing whether Jamal is achieving his goals and objectives and in providing instruction to support their achievement.

Summary

Students with disabilities are a highly heterogeneous group of learners. Their cognitive and behavioral, social, and physical needs can present unique challenges in the classroom, but through careful and strategic planning and collaboration among professionals and parents, these students can be contributing and vital members of the classroom community, as well as readers and writers. It is the professionals' responsibility, in consultation with the parents, to ensure universal access to the curriculum for these students. Lesson planning and the inclusion of adaptations and modifications within lessons are beginning points for achieving the goal of universal access for students with disabilities.

Special Education Teachers and Service Providers

Support Provider	Roles	How They Can Support the General Education Teacher
Special Education Teacher • resource teacher • itinerant teacher • special-day class teacher • inclusion specialist	• Is intimately familiar with students' IEP goals, objectives/benchmarks, and the students' academic, communicative, and behavioral/emotional needs • Has expertise in how to adapt and modify curriculum and instruction to meaningfully include students with disabilities in general education classrooms and curriculum • Has expertise for providing remedial support and intensive intervention services for students with disabilities	• Can answer questions about students' learning needs • Can explain the students' IEP and what can be done in the general education class to support student achievement of IEP goals and objectives/benchmarks • Can help you develop ways to adapt and modify instruction that will help students learn • Can work with you in the classroom to support the students' participation and achievement
Para-professional	• May be assigned to "shadow" a student in the general education classroom • Can assist in adapting and modifying curriculum and instruction for the particular student(s) • May serve to monitor students' academic and behavioral/emotional needs and intervention plans • May assist students in meeting physical, mobility, and health needs	• Can assist you in addressing the student's needs (e.g., can provide a one-on-one explanation that you may not be able to furnish because of the other students in the classroom) • Can be responsible for adapting and modifying instructional activities and assignments, with guidance from you and the special education teachers • Can oversee the implementation of specialized intervention plans • Can be responsible for the student's physical, mobility, and health needs
Audiologist	• Expertise in measuring students' hearing levels and evaluating hearing loss	• Can give you suggestions for how to work with students who have partial or total hearing loss • Can give you suggestions for how to deal with a student who refuses to wear his or her hearing aids in class

Physical and Occupational Therapist	• Physical therapist generally focuses on gross motor development (e.g., walking, running) • Occupational therapist generally focuses on fine motor development (e.g., using writing tools)	• Can give you suggestions for how to modify requirements to take into consideration students' motor and physical needs
School or Educational Psychologist	• Expertise in educational testing administration and interpretation • May also have training in counseling and working with students in crisis situations	• Can help you understand testing results and may be able to come into the classroom to observe and give you suggestions for working with a particular student • Can help you work with a student who is in crisis (e.g., divorce, death)
Augmentative and Alternative Communicative Specialist	• Expertise in assessing students' AAC needs • Expertise in developing programs that assist students in using alternative means for communicating verbally and in writing (e.g., communication boards; using speech synthesizer software)	• Can explain to you how a student's AAC device works • Can give you suggestions for how to make adaptations and modifications that support the student's use of the AAC device in the classroom (e.g., physical arrangement of the learning environment; assignment adjustments)
Educational Therapist	• Expertise in assessment and remediation for students experiencing learning problems • May serve as a case manager and build communicative links between school, home, and related service providers	• Can give you suggestions for how to adapt instruction to meet the student's needs • Can give you suggestions for communicating with parents and for working with the special education staff

ANSWERS

Unit 1

Literary Analysis: Narrative Essay

Practice, p. 2

    1. C; 2. B; 3. C; 4. D

Assess, p. 3

    1. A; 2. B; 3. D; 4. A

Literary Analysis: Plot and Conflict

Practice, p. 4

A 1. A; 2. B; 3. D

B The conflict is between Julie and Debbie.

Assess, p. 5

A 1. A; 2. B; 3. C; 4. D

B 1. The conflict is between James and Sal.

    2. **Sample answer:** The conflict is between Isabel and the poison.

Literary Analysis: Point of View

Practice, p. 6

A 1. first-person 2. omniscient 3. limited

B 1. a narrator outside the story

    2. **Sample answer:** No, I did not learn as much about Dean's thoughts. The story gives Chris's exact thoughts, but it describes only how Dean acts.

    3. third-person limited

Assess, p. 7

A 1. First person; **Sample answer:** The narrator says *I*.

    2. Third person; **Sample answer:** The narrator is not one of the characters.

B 1. Marla's; 2. the spy's

    3. third-person limited; 4. Marla's and the spy's

    5. third-person omniscient

Reading: Make Predictions

Practice, p. 8

    1. Student responses may vary but should reflect the use of details from the story to support their predictions. Some students may predict that Kurt will be able to provide a temporary fix to the situation.

    2. Student answers will vary but should contain specific details including the engine sounds, what tools and materials were available to fix the leak, what was leaking, and the weather.

Assess, p. 9

    1. B; 2. A; 3. B; 4. A

Reading: Read to Perform a Task

Practice, p. 10

    1. squirting glue in the holes on the Left Side Piece

    2. *carefully*

    3. *First*

    4. **Sample answer:** If you discover after you start work that you are missing the necessary tools or parts, then you will have to stop working to get them. Interrupting the work is not efficient and could be annoying. If you check the lists first, you can make sure you have all the right tools and parts before you start.

Assess, p. 11

    1. a Phillips screwdriver

    2. *gently*

    3. **Sample answer:** If you do not pull the panel gently, you may break the tabs.

    4. *After the Center Dashboard Panel is removed*

    5. **Sample answer:** If you do not remove the Center Dashboard Panel, then you cannot disconnect the Radio Panel and remove the old radio.

Vocabulary: Prefixes and Suffixes

Practice, p. 12

A 1. B; 2. A; 3. A

B 1. hesitate

    2. distribution

    3. participate

    4. solution

Assess, p. 13

A Sample answers:

    1. T Foreshadowing means a hint of things to come.

    2. F If something is consistent, it holds together well.

    3. F Condolence means sympathy.

    4. F Foresight means seeing the possible results of something.

B 1. conversed; conversation

    2. captivated; captive

    3. locate; location

    4. distraction: distract

Grammar: Common and Proper Nouns

Practice, p. 14

A 1. clouds; common
2. Utah; proper
3. White House; proper
4. Uncle Henry; proper
5. apartment; common

B Sample answers:
1. Garth Brooks
2. South Dakota
3. April
4. Rutgers University
5. Larry
6. Mississippi River

Assess, p. 15

A 1. Margaret Atwood
2. Ireland
3. Johned Road
4. Japanese
5. Empire State Building
6. Florida

B Sample answers:
1. Hemingway; author
2. sights; Indianapolis
3. Stan, sweater
4. Texas; year
5. city; Montana

Grammar: Abstract and Concrete Nouns

Practice, p. 16

1. Helen, wrist, hand, accident
2. Peas, carrots, vegetables, Jose
3. boy, kindness, coach
4. mother, Gus, age
5. Ricardo, hours, day, vaulter, team
6. clock, mantle, minutes
7. season, Jennifer, David, lake
8. Australia, quantity, wool
9. Marblehead, town, Massachusetts, birthplace, navy
10. carpenters, improvements, building

Assess, p. 17

1. car—concrete; garage—concrete; street—concrete
2. Gideon—concrete; Shulamit—concrete; mathematics—abstract; college—concrete
3. Nana—concrete; joy—abstract; song—concrete
4. Joey—concrete; disappointment—abstract; college—concrete

5. Bill—concrete; Sue—concrete; helmets—concrete; motorcycles—concrete
6. ticket—concrete; town—concrete; peace—abstract; quiet—abstract
7. movie—concrete; Linda—concrete; hope—abstract; happiness—abstract

Grammar: Possessive Nouns

Practice, p. 18

A 1. the Smiths' garden
2. men's furnishings
3. the Davises' sons
4. Monopoly's rules
5. Hercules' great strength
6. the games' cards and dice
7. Lawrence High's soccer team
8. Kris's and Sara's contact lenses
9. TV stations' news reports
10. the women's locker room

B 1. Columbus's
2. Hercules'
3. Phyllis's; Barbara's
4. Rome's; Hannibal's

Assess, p. 19

A 1. A; 2. B; 3. C; 4. A; 5. B; 6. C; 7. B; 8. A
B 1. Water's
2. Wells's
3. Julius's
4. people's
5. dog's

Writing: Anecdote

Practice, p. 20

Sample answers:
1. classmates
2. A child receiving his favorite birthday gift—his dog, Charlie.
3. large box—sight; red box—sight; whining—sound; wiggling ball of fur: sight; fuzzy—touch; wet tongue—touch
4. Students' anecdotes should address a particular audience, stay on topic, and provide descriptive details that appeal to the senses.

Assess, p. 21

Student answers should reflect an understanding of anecdotes. Students should choose a topic, identify an audience, write a topic sentence, list three events, identify point of view, and use action verbs and sensory impressions.

Writing: Critique

Practice, p. 22
A 1. B; 2. A
B 1. character development and vivid details
2. Details such as the old man's rough, work-worn hands, his worn and shiny cane, and his careful planting of vegetables help the reader understand and sympathize with the old man.

Assess, p. 23
Sample answers:
1. story line, vivid sensory details, character development
2. The writer creates an interesting story line by making the reader wonder what will happen next. Will the two characters find a safe place from the storm? Will they find their way out of the desert? The writer also uses vivid sensory details, such as pounding thunder and flashing lightning; heavy rain clouds rushing toward them; and rocky, barren landscape. The writer develops the character of the narrator, showing his concern for his little brother and his sense of responsibility for taking care of him.

Writing: Autobiographical Narrative

Practice, p. 24
A Sample answers:
1. The narrative covers one day from early morning until evening. Details include the writer leaving home in the morning still in pajamas and the sun going down and the forest getting dark.
2. a backyard that backs up to a forest; a thick forest
3. The character is six years old; the character likes to watch the deer; the character is afraid and feels cold.
4. The writer faces the problem of being lost in the forest.

B Sample answer:
When my dad brought me home, my mom was waiting for us. She was really happy to see me. I think she was scared, too. She made me some hot soup and gave me some clean, dry pajamas. Then my mom and dad explained what might have happened if they had not found me.

Assess, p. 25
Sample answers:
1. during a basketball game
2. a basketball court in a school gym
3. I was playing on the basketball team against another school; during the game, I became flustered and passed the ball to a member of the other team; our team lost the game, and my team members were angry.
4. The characters include myself, my team mates, and the person on the other team to whom I passed the ball.
5. The events include beginning the game; sitting on the bench; being put in the game by the coach; becoming flustered; passing the ball to the other team; being taken out of the game; my teammates not speaking to me. The problem is solved by my withdrawing from the basketball team and giving up sports.
6. Details include the wooden floor of the basketball court; the colors of the team uniforms; and the walls of the gymnasium.

Literary Analysis: Author's Voice

Practice, p. 26
A 1. A
2. A
B Sample Answers:
1. *my man; look out; sax; joyful jumble; hot*
2. *look out; pour out; joyful jumble; He's so hot, he sizzles!*
3. This sentence-ending adds a casual and energetic quality to the writer's voice. It's as if the writer is talking right to you.

Assess, p. 27
A 1. B
2. B
B 1. **Answers include** *Rain drummed; a crazy map of roads that led nowhere; the rain and the fog and the dark*
2. **Answers include** *I watched the drops of water as they drizzled down the windows; a crazy map of roads that led nowhere; the train would come and take him away to college; the rain and the fog and the dark*
3. **Sample answer** The writer creates a quiet, thoughtful voice. He doesn't say much about how he feels, so he seems quiet, not chatty.

Literary Analysis: Character

Practice, p. 28
A 1. flat; 2. round; 3. round
B 1. static; 2. dynamic; 3. dynamic

Assess, p. 29
A 1. round; 2. flat; 3. flat; 4. round
B 1. dynamic; 2. static; 3. dynamic

Literary Analysis: Theme

Practice, p. 30

A 1. (You can find Nature's beauty in the strangest places.)

2. ("Courage and quick-thinking can help you can get any job done—even the impossible!")

B 1. **Sample answer:** The fact that they have an easy time making up shows the quarrel was not that serious.

2. The theme of the story is that real friends can get over their arguments and that they should not continue arguing out of pride.

Assess, p. 31

A 1. (The main reason to explore outer space is to keep our curiosity and our courage alive.)

2. (Always treat wild animals with caution.)

B 1. C; 2. D

Reading: Author's Purpose

Practice, p. 32

1. B; 2. D; 3. D

Assess, p. 33

1. C; 2. D; 3. A; 4. C

Reading: Analyze Structure and Format

Practice, p. 34

1. the pronunciation of the word

2. *n.*

3. page xiii

4. information about the languages the word came from

5. 2

Assess, p. 35

1. guffaw

2. You can pronounce *guffaw* in two ways; I can tell because the pronunciation has a comma followed by another way to pronounce it.

3. page xiv

4. *Guffaw* can function as two parts of speech. I can tell because there is a dash in the entry. The dash is followed by a second part of speech.

5. To figure out the difference between a "guffaw" and a "chortle," I would look up *laugh.* I know this because the word *laugh* follows the dash and the abbreviation "SYN." The guide says that the dash and "SYN." show which word to look up to find an explanation of synonyms.

Vocabulary: Word Roots and Suffixes

Practice, p. 36

A 1. confined; 2. determined; 3. exterminate

4. final

B 1. instinctive; 2. reliable; 3. portable

4. cooperative

Assess, p. 37

A Sample answers:

1. fin; boundless; Most people believe the universe is *infinite*

2. term; to figure out; I could not *determine* how long the job would take.

3. term; an ending point; The train pulled up to the railway *terminal.*

4. fin; sophisticated; She has very *refined* manners.

5. term; to end; I *terminated* the phone call because I was done talking.

B Sample answers:

1. As a businessman, he was a *respectable* figure in the community.

2. She has an *active* lifestyle and spends a lot of time playing sports.

3. The bright lights and decorations gave the room a *festive* atmosphere.

4. The book was so *predictable* that I saw the ending coming a mile away.

5. I found his meanness and cruelty toward others *despicable.*

Grammar: Personal and Reflexive Pronouns

Practice, p. 38

A 1. We, you; 2. We, you, yourself; 3. He, us

4. herself; 5. I, them, me; 6. they;

7. himself, his; 8. She, she, him;

9. We, them; 10. he, us

B 1. reflexive; 2. personal; 3. personal

4. reflexive; 5. personal

Assess, p. 39

A 1. itself; reflexive

2. her; personal

3. herself; reflexive

4. herself; reflexive

5. your; personal

6. he; personal

7. its; personal

8. himself; reflexive

B 1. her; 2. your; 3. its; 4. their; 5. his; 6. you

7. her; 8. them

Grammar: Relative, Interrogative, and Indefinite Pronouns

Practice, p. 40

A 1. relative; 2. interrogative; 3. relative
4. interrogative; 5. interrogative; 6. relative

B 1. Each; 2. Everyone; 3. Many, any
4. Few, anything; 5. No one, all
6. Some, another

Assess, p. 41

A 1. that; 2. whom; 3. Who; 4. which
5. What; 6. Whom

B Sample answers:
1. None; 2. each; 3. something; 4. several
5. All; 6. everyone; 7. few; 8. Some

Grammar: Pronoun-Antecedent Agreement

Practice, p. 42

A 1. (Victoria) you; 2. (Lydia) her
3. (Roberto) he; 4. I (Sheila)
5. you (David); 6. their (Gina, Trey)

B 1. you; 2. their; 3. its; 4. he; 5. her; 6. they

Assess, p. 43

A 1. its; 2. their; 3. his; 4. their; 5. its; 6. its
7. her; 8. her; 9. her; 10. his

B 1. her; 2. its; 3. my; 4. his; 5. their
6. your; 7. it; 8. him

Spelling: Frequently Misspelled Words

Practice, p. 44

A 1. muscles; 2. metaphor; 3. chord
4. psychology; 5. Arctic; 6. parallel

B 1. psychology; 2. parallel; 3. Arctic

Assess, p. 45

A 1. metaphor; 2. Correct; 3. Correct
4. muscles; 5. Arctic; 6. parallel

B 1. psychology; 2. metaphor; 3. Arctic

C 1. chord; 2. muscles; 3. parallel

Writing: Journal Entry

Practice, p. 46

A Sample answers:
1. Daily
2. The author's feelings were important.
3. new place; very old house; fir trees darkening windows; rain; sun; long green lawn; lake in sunlight
4. wanted to forget where he/she was; eager to go outside
5. author's change of mood and feeling

Assess, p. 47

Answers will vary. If you have elected to review students' journal entries, be sure they understand that your purpose is to offer constructive suggestions only and that all information will be viewed as confidential.

Writing: Character Profile

Practice, p. 48

A 1. Dani has black hair and brown eyes.
2. **Sample answer:** cheerful; freedom-loving
3. **Sample answer:** Dani loves horseback riding.
4. Dani rides easily and well.
5. Dani is having a hard time with math and French.

B Answers will vary. Students should list details about their chosen character, including details about the character's appearance, personality, and achievements.

Assess, p. 49

Sample answers:

A 1. Roberto Gravas, age 15
2. black hair; brown eyes; 5' 2" tall; wears baseball team jacket and jeans
3. Roberto is making jokes all the time, as if he doesn't take life seriously. Inside, though, he is always trying to figure out how things work or how they fit together. He worries about the future. He thinks the best way to make out well in life is to always know what's going on.
4. Roberto is a computer wiz. He makes his own computer games.
5. Roberto is still in high school. He hopes he will be able to work as a programmer someday.
6. Roberto lives with his grandmother. His best friend is Jorge.

B Students' character profiles should incorporate details from their answers to activity A and should focus on a single event demonstrating the character's personality.

Writing: Problem-and-Solution Essay

Practice, p. 50

A 1. A; 2. B

B Sample answers:
1. an old and outdated gymnasium locker room
2. Update the locker rooms with the help of students, teachers, and parents.
3. Parents and teachers could hold bake sales and other types of fund raisers; parents, teachers, and students could donate labor to install new equipment.

Assess, p. 51

Answers will vary. In their answers, students should demonstrate an understanding of the problem and should propose practical, relevant solutions.

Unit 2

Literary Analysis: Conflict

Practice, p. 52

A 1. A. Conflict; B. Resolution
2. A. Resolution; B. Conflict

B 1. External Conflict; 2. Internal Conflict
3. Internal Conflict

Assess, p. 53

A 1. A. Conflict; B. Resolution
2. A. Resolution; B. Conflict
3. A. Resolution; B. Conflict

B 1. Internal Conflict; 2. External Conflict
3. External Conflict; 4. Internal Conflict

Literary Analysis: Irony

Practice, p. 54

A 1. No irony; 2. Irony; 3. Irony

B Sample Answers:

1. **Expectation:** The guard takes a great risk because he thinks he has to protect the money. **Reality:** There is no money in the bank.

2. **Expectation:** Janice is worried about meeting Earl because he seems so great. **Reality:** Earl is nervous, just like Janice.

Assess, p. 55

A 1. Irony; 2. No irony; 3. No irony; 4. Irony

B 1. **Expectation:** Amy thinks Stacy is very adult. **Reality:** Stacy still keeps her old childhood toys.

2. **Expectation:** Matt wants to show off to Sandy. **Reality:** When he tries to show off to her, he makes a mistake that gives her a bad impression of him.

Literary Analysis: Setting

Practice, p. 56

1. the southwestern United States
2. driving to Nevada, desert of sand and sagebrush
3. the present time
4. military watch, driving, secret mission

Assess, p. 57

1. Revolutionary war
2. Redcoats, New Englander, musket, fighting British

3. United States
4. Redcoats, New Englander, British

Reading: Make Inferences

Practice, p. 58

1. It was a cluster of lights moving too fast for a plane.
2. because of their speed
3. Each one wanted to be the first to tell his newspaper of the possible UFO sighting.

Assess, p. 59

1. A; 2. C; 3. B; 4. D

Reading: Critique the Logic of Functional Documents

Practice, p. 60

Sample answers:

1. The sign say that there is danger nearby because of high voltage.
2. The text feature that helped me understand the message is large, bold type.
3. Be careful where you walk because there is a danger of electric shock.

Assess, p. 61

Sample answers:

1. The title shows what the document will help me do.
2. The steps are numbered to show the order in which I should do things.
3. The words in bold type show the actions I should do. The words in bold, italic type show the buttons I should push. Both types of highlighting show me what to do.
4. The drawing helps people find the right buttons.
5. The audience is people who do not know how to operate a DVD player. I know that because the words are simple and do not require technical knowledge.
6. The writer should know the audience to know how much detail to include in the directions and the kind of words readers will understand.

Vocabulary: Word Roots

Practice, p. 62

1. C; 2. C; 3. B; 4. A; 5. C

Assess, p. 63

A Sample answers:

1. reliant; I have always been *reliant* on her advice.
2. Lincolnesque; His way with words was *Lincolnesque*.

3. compliant; I was *compliant* with all their demands.

4. Chaplinesque; He had a *Chaplinesque* gift for using body language.

B Sample answers:

1. N; to demolish something means to knock it down. After *demolishing* the old building, they hauled away the rubble.

2. N; someone who is acquitted is found innocent of a crime. At the trial, the prisoner was *acquitted* and released.

3. Y; to acknowledge means to recognize something.

4. Y; to decelerate means to slow down.

Grammar: Regular Verbs

Practice, p. 64

A 1. (completed for student)

2. stop, stopping, stopped, stopped

3. play, playing, played, played

4. hire, hiring, hired, hired

5. confuse, confusing, confused, confused

B. 1. present; 2. past participle

3. present participle; 4. past participle; 5. past

Assess, p. 65

A 1. contain, containing, contained, contained

2. clap, clapping, clapped, clapped

3. whistle, whistling, whistled, whistled

4. fold, folding, folded, folded

5. practice, practicing, practiced, practiced

6. wiggle, wiggling, wiggled, wiggled

B 1. present; 2. present participle

3. past participle; 4. past; 5. present participle

6. past participle

C Sample answers:

1. The team exercises before practice.

2. My brother can't stop biting his nails.

3. I tripped on the stairs.

4. The animal shelter has rescued many dogs and cats.

Grammar: Irregular Verbs

Practice, p. 66

A 1. running, ran

2. brought, bringing

3. sent, sent

4. cost, costs

5. rise, risen

B 1. knew; 2. hurt; 3. left

Assess, p. 67

A 1. drawn; 2. worn; 3. swam; 4. sunk; 5. frozen

6. taken; 7. rode; 8. taken; 9. fell; 10. drunk

B 1. gave; 2. stung; 3. left; 4. frozen; 5. taught

6. lent; 7. eaten; 8. broke

Grammar: Verb Tenses

Practice, p. 68

A 1. remembered; 2. learned; 3. will live

4. cooked; 5. uses

B 1. expected; 2. are; 3. was

4. arrive; 5. got

Assess, p. 69

A 1. A; 2. D; 3. C; 4. B; 5. D; 6. A

B 1. works; 2. had gone; 3. propped

4. will fail; 5. plans

Writing: Alternative Ending

Practice, p. 70

1. A.; 2. D.

Assess, p. 71

Sample answer:

"Are they your men?" asked Georg. "Are they your men?" he repeated impatiently as Ulrich did not answer.

"Yes," replied Ulrich. "We'll be freed soon." After being rescued, the two men kept their promise. While they did not become friends, they returned to their normal lives. A few years later, Ulrich's son and Georg's daughter married. Their family feud was finally and fully over.

Writing: News Story

Practice, p. 72

A *Who?* the Carpenter family

What? saved from tragedy by their family dog

When? early Tuesday

Where? their family home

Why? Tommy was protective of the family.

How? Tommy woke them when the fire started.

B The first sentence makes the reader want to know what the tragedy was and how the dog saved them.

Assess, p. 73

Sample Answers:

A *Who?* a new student, Jan Golchecki

What? moved to our town from Germany

When? the beginning of the school year

Where? here at Roper High

Why? Her father was stationed in Germany and transferred here.

How? flew from Germany on a military transport

B What is it like coming back to America after living in Germany for three years? Our newest student, Jan Golchecki, can tell you. She just moved to Middleton from Munich, Germany, two days before school started here at Roper High. Her father, a colonel in the army, was stationed in Germany and was just transferred back here. Jan, her family, and all their belongings were flown on a military transport plane to the base here. So when you see Jan in the halls, be sure to tell her, "Welcome home!"

Writing: Short Story

Practice, p. 74

A Sample answers:

1. first person point of view
2. A. She is shy; she is 14 years old; she has long blond hair.

   B. She is shy and feels uncomfortable around the other students.
3. a dense forest of huge ferns; thick fog on the ground; a large, frightening animal

B Sample answers:

Maria grabbed my hand. "What was that?" she said, her voice trembling.

"I don't know, but it sounds big," I answered. "Maybe we should stay really quiet until it passes."

"Is that the best you can think of," she said, her voice rising. "You're the one who got us into this mess. How do you plan to get us out?"

Assess, p. 75

Students should demonstrate an understanding of the characteristics of a short story. Students should provide concrete sensory details that add vividness to the people, place, and events of the story.

Literary Analysis: Character and Characterization

Practice, p. 76

A 1. Direct; 2. Indirect; 3. Indirect

B Sample answers:

1. "Roberto has arrived," said Roberto loudly.; He handed his jacket to Rodney, the friend who followed him everywhere.; a top-brand sports shirt; He flexed his arm muscles so that others could admire them.; The other players looked at each other nervously.; Roberto is full of himself and likes to be the center of attention. He seems to be in shape and a good ball player.
2. Paula called the museum to find out what the hours were.; Then, she dug around in Susan's kitchen until she found the bus schedule.; She got Susan and Janet out the

door; Paula is a leader, the kind of person who takes charge and gets things done. She likes to be active.

Assess, p. 77

A 1. Direct; 2. Indirect; 3. Indirect

4. Direct; 5. Indirect

B Sample answers:

She suspected that, as usual, Jack had gotten distracted and had forgotten all about it.; "Sure," said Jack. "A tiger escaped from the zoo, and the police are out warning people."; "Jack," said his sister, "you aren't telling me one of your stories, by any chance?"; Jack is a dreamer, easily distracted. He tells tall tales and invents excuses for himself.

Literary Analysis: Dialogue

Practice, p. 78

"I'm glad summer is coming."; "I need a break."; "You told me last time I came home that you had a lot of homework."; "What else happened?"; "I joined the basketball team." "Whoah, little brother. You have to make sure you pace yourself."; "I know."; "It's probably even harder in college, right?"

1. Todd: It is almost summer. Todd is glad.
2. Todd: Todd needs a break.
3. Joe: Todd has a lot of homework. Joe is living away from home.
4. Joe: Joe does not talk to Todd every day.
5. Todd: Todd has joined the basketball team recently.
6. Joe: Joe is Todd's older brother.
7. Todd: Todd knows he has to pace himself.
8. Todd: Joe is in college.

Assess, p. 79

A 1. "You are doing a great job!"
2. "Your painting is beautiful."
3. "Let's go back."
4. "Okay, I'll get the car."
5. "Craig is always in a bad mood,"

B Sample answers:

"What was that noise?" "Shhh," "That was just your nerves. Do you want to wake up the guard?" "Okay, Elaine, but I want you to know that I wouldn't be prowling around this museum basement if you were not my friend." "I know, Anna," "and believe me, I appreciate your help." "All right, ladies," "and just what is it that brings you to the museum basement in the middle of the night, might I ask?"

1. Anna: Anna hears a noise.
2. Elaine: Elaine thinks it's Anna's nerves and that she should be quiet or they will wake up a guard.

3. Anna: Anna and Elaine are prowling in the basement of a museum. Anna is there to help Elaine because they are friends.
4. Elaine: Elaine is speaking more kindly to Anna.
5. a voice (probably the museum guard): Someone has caught Elaine and Anna sneaking around.

Literary Analysis: Symbolism and Allegory

Practice, p. 80

A Sample answers:
1. the United States
2. Good job!; Ready to go!
3. a wedding; a bride

B 1. A; 2. D; 3. A

Assess, p. 81

A Sample answers:
1. something forbidden; "do not"
2. a baby on its way
3. autumn

B 1. A; 2. C; 3. C

Reading: Cause and Effect

Practice, p. 82

A 1. B; 2. C; 3. A

B 1. Yusef couldn't ride his bike (because) it had a flat tire.
2. Maria missed the school bus (because) She go up late.

C 1. German submarines sank the Lusitania. Germany tried to get Mexico to fight against the United States. German submarines sank three American merchant ships.

Assess, p. 83

1. D; 2. B; 3. A

Reading: Evaluate Text Format

Practice, p. 84

1. Price of Admission
2. Seasons and Hours of Operation
3. At first a person is more interested in the activities than in the price.

Assess, p. 85

1. Cruise Times and Locations
2. Cruises Run Only When Weather Conditions Permit
3. The list of activities is in larger size type because that is the information most readers will need to know first.
4. You need to call 811-77MUSIC.

Vocabulary: Word Roots and Suffixes

Practice, p. 86

A 1. beneficial; 2. trajectory; 3. projected; 4. benediction

B 1. glorious; 2. complexity; 3. mysterious; 4. possibility

Assess, p. 87

A Sample answers:
1. I was willing to take a job with low pay because the *benefits* were excellent.
2. I felt *dejected* because I was doing so poorly in school.
3. I was disappointed to receive a *rejection* letter from the publisher who had read my book.
4. He was universally loved for his *benevolence* to everybody.
5. The *injection* pumped medicine into the patient's veins.

B Sample answers:
1. sensitivity; I need sunglasses because of my *sensitivity* to bright light.
2. famous; As a child, I dreamed of becoming a *famous* movie star.
3. joyous; Their wedding was a *joyous* event.
4. intensity; I was surprised at the *intensity* of his anger.
5. ridiculous; Her new hairdo was *ridiculous*.
6. eccentricity; She is widely known for her *eccentricity*.

Grammar: Subjects and Predicates

Practice, p. 88

A 1. The angry lion growled at its tamer.
2. Men and women worked side by side on the assembly line.
3. The soldiers were standing at strict attention.
4. Santa Catalina Island lies off the coast of California.
5. The plane landed safely on the runway.
6. Many in the audience laughed at the actor's mistake.

B Sample answers:
1. The Grand Canyon is a great place to go for a vacation.
2. Most science fiction movies have great special effects.
3. The front page of today's paper showed a picture of a flood.
4. The World Series is the most exciting sports event.
5. Fresh fruits are delicious and good for your health.
6. After leaving school, my friends and I practice soccer.

Assess, p. 89

A 1. General Lee surrendered on April 9, 1865.

2. Joseph always stops at stop signs.

3. Deer and other animals roam freely through the San Diego Wild Animal Park.

4. Ernie and his brother often help around the house.

5. Lunch was served promptly at 1:00 P.M.

6. The lawyers in the group had been educated at Southern universities.

7. We climbed to the top of Mount Rainier in Washington.

8. Several huge boulders had fallen onto the highway and shattered.

B Sample answers:

1. The most interesting school club is the Photographers Club.

2. My sister and I raked the leaves yesterday afternoon.

3. A worker in a steel helmet was fixing the railroad tracks.

4. The children jumped into the swimming pool.

5. The class president made a good speech.

Grammar: Active and Passive Voice

Practice, p. 90

A 1. missed; A

2. were arrested; P

3. was ruined; P

4. told; A

5. caught; A

6. will be organized; P

7. has been broken; P

8. will build; A

B 1. Benjamin Franklin invented eyeglasses with bifocal lenses.

2. The mail carrier delivered two bills and a letter.

3. Ginny has just bought a new sports car.

Assess, p. 91

A 1. has read; A

2. are maintained; P

3. chose; A

4. were written; P

5. were stolen; P

6. grew; A

7. were eaten; P

8. visited; A

B 1. Barney hauled the old sofa down to the basement.

2. The boat was tossed and lifted by the sea.

3. David has never understood the way an engine works.

4. Rey suddenly hung up the phone.

Grammar: Subject-Verb Agreement

Practice, p. 92

1. are; 2. seem; 3. have; 4. was; 5. is

6. agree; 7. make; 8. are; 9. does; 10. was

Assess, p. 93

A 1. were; 2. are; 3. was; 4. shovels; 5. is

6. shine; 7. likes; 8. are; 9. scares

10. appears

B Sample answers:

1. are; 2. want; 3. are; 4. has; 5. is

Spelling: Unusual Consonant Groupings

Practice, p. 94

A 1. reminisce; 2. rhythm

3. correct; 4. exhilarating

B 1. brochure; 2. conscientious

3. discipline; 4. correct; 5. silhouette

Assess, p. 95

A 1. reminisce; 2. rhythm; 3. exhilarating

4. unconscious; 5. correct

B 1. brochure; 2. conscientious

3. correct; 4. subtle; 5. discipline

C Students should underline the incorrect spellings of these words and write them correctly on the lines: 1. conscientious

2. exhilarating 3. reminisce

Writing: Written Presentation

Practice, p. 96

A Sample answers:

1. Adding more art classes

2. The audience is the school administration.

3. A. an essay

B. An essay is the best form to address a group of people.

4. Sample: Hiring a part-time art teacher; having one or more qualified parents volunteer to teach one art class a week.

B Sample answers:

1. the lack of school spirit

2. the students

3. Hold pep rallies with entertainment; offer some kind of reward for classes that have the most students attending a game.

Assess, p. 97

A Sample Answers:

1. a personal letter

2. a. —

   b. Keep a calendar with homework assignments and their due dates; ask for my help when you need it.

B Since you're my best friend, I really want you to succeed in school. I want us both to graduate together! I know you've been having trouble in some classes, especially with keeping up with homework. I have some suggestions that might help.

Writing: Informal Letter

Practice, p. 98

Sample Answers:

1. A. to a friend named Jack

   B. Jeremy, a friend to Jack

2. a cabin on a lake; mist rising over the lake in the morning

3. He likes peace and quiet; he likes to fish; he does not like to harm living things.

4. A. He enjoys his visit.

   B. He describes the mist as "spooky," he says that the fish they released was "happy."

Assess, p. 99

A Sample Answers:

1. trip to an amusement park

2. a grandfather who lives far away in a rural area

3. that it was fun, but noisy and crowded

4. the crowd of people pushing and shoving; the screams of the people on the roller coaster

B Sample Answer:

Dear Grandpa Jessie,

   Yesterday I went to the amusement park here with some friends. It was a lot of fun, but really noisy, not quiet like your place on the lake. There was noise everywhere. It was crowded, and it seemed that everybody was pushing and shoving to get in line for the rides.

   The rides were noisy too. The roller coaster sounds like a freight train when it goes by. You can hear the people on the ride screaming all the way across the park.

   When you visit me next month, I'll take you to the amusement park. We'll have a great time.

                        Love,
                        Kendra

Writing: Cause-and-Effect Essay

Practice, p. 100

A Sample Answers:

1. cell phones

2. dangerous driving on the highways

3. studies that show drivers do not perform as well when using cell phones

B Sample Answers:

1. other people being annoyed by someone talking on a cell phone in a restaurant, etc.; cell phones that ring in theaters or in classrooms

2. Another effect on society is that many people become angry at cell phone users. People might go to a nice restaurant, and the person sitting next them may be talking loudly on a cell phone. Many people find that rude to have their meal spoiled by cell phones ringing and people talking on them loudly.

Assess, p. 101

A Sample Answers:

1. Pets are good for children. Caring for dogs, cats, hamsters, fish, and lizards, or any other pet, has positive effects on children.

2. Pets cause children to learn responsibility; they provide companionship for children.

B Sample Answer:

   What child does not want a pet? Almost any animal can become a pet for a child. Dogs, cats, hamster, fish, and birds are some of the common pets. Even though parents might think pets are more trouble than they are worth, caring for pets can have many positive effects on children.

   Caring for pets teach children responsibility. Another living creature is depending on them. The child learns to feed his/her pet the proper amount of food at the proper time. He/she has to brush them, or wash them, and see that the pet has exercise. By taking care of their pets, children get in the habit of doing what they have promised to do or are expected to do.

Unit 3

Literary Analysis: Author's Style

Practice, p. 102

1. A; 2. C; 3. B; 4. A

Assess, p. 103

A 1. A; 2. B

B Sample Answers:

1. Paragraph 1

2. **Answers include** What a weekend; Boy, am I beat!; don't-stop-till-you-drop; rules.

3. **Answers include** recipe for weekend amusement; the presence of Uncle Herman; unique brand; the latest chapter; rounded off; I find I am fascinated.

4. The writer is enthusiastic and positive about his weekend.

Literary Analysis: Expository Essay

Practice, p. 104

1. C; 2. A; 3. A; 4. D

Assess, p. 105

A 1. Answers will vary. Students should name a topic that is suitable for treatment in a brief nonfiction work.

2. Answers will vary. Students should name a purpose that suits the topic they have identified. They should also describe information, explanations, or ideas that are reasonably connected with their topic.

B 1. D; 2. A; 3. B; 4. D

Literary Analysis: Biographical Writing

Practice, p. 106

1. A; 2. D; 3. A

Assess, p. 107

A 1. Answers will vary. Students should name a person who is a suitable subject for a biography.

2. Answers will vary. Students should name a question about the person they have chosen that might be answered in a biography.

3. Answers will vary. Students should give an example of an interpretation of the achievements of the chosen person.

B 1. B; 2. C; 3. C

Reading: Main Idea and Supporting Details

Practice, p. 108

1. The act of laughing is actually good exercise.

2. According to this theory, laughter might actually trigger relief from pain.

3. But instead of dying, Cousins applied a laugh-yourself-to-health approach.

Assess, p. 109

1. D; 2. D; 3. B

Reading: Generate Relevant Questions

Practice, p. 110

Sample Answers:

1. I know that the surface of the Sun is extremely hot and that you should not look directly at it.

2. What is on the surface of the Sun? What are solar flares?

3. What are sunspots? What are prominences?

Assess, p. 111

Sample answers:

1. Three things are on the surface of the Sun: sunspots, prominences, and solar flares. Solar flares are streams of energy that build up, then are released into space.

2. Does the energy from solar flares reach Earth? Where does the gas in the Sun come from?

3. I might find this information in a science book, the NASA Web site, or an encyclopedia.

Vocabulary: Word Roots

Practice, p. 112

A 1. vivid; 2. novelty; 3. tempo; 4. durable

B 1. temporary; 2. endurance; 3. survive; 4. novice

Assess, p. 113

A Sample answers:

1. F Someone who is vivacious is lively.

2. T An extemporaneous speech would be made up on the spot.

3. F Innovative means using a new approach.

4. F Someone who is obdurate will not change his or her mind.

B Sample answers:

1. dur; to last or withstand; I can't endure much more of this annoying hold music.

2. viv; to recover or restore to life; The rescue workers revived the drowning victim.

3. temp; tendency to anger; I often lose my temper with my sister.

4. nov; repairs to restore a building; The library is closed for renovations.

5. temp; something that exists at the same time as something else; The composers Bach and Handel were contemporaries.

Grammar: Direct and Indirect Objects

Practice, p. 114

A 1. performers; 2. lanes; 3. pop-up

4. watermelon; 5. case; 6. flowers

B 1. Nick; 2. Rosie; 3. troops; 4. employees

5. temple; 6. him

Assess, p. 115

A 1. woman; 2. cabin; 3. canoe; 4. mind

5. skates; 6. pie; 7. brother; 8. door

B 1. IO; 2. IO; 3. DO; 4. IO; 5. DO; 6. IO

Grammar: Predicate Nominative and Predicate Adjectives

Practice, p. 116

A 1. PA, <u>empty</u>, (seems)

2. PN, <u>day</u>, (is)

3. PA, <u>fun</u>, (are)

4. PA, <u>hot</u>, (feels)

5. PN, <u>time</u>, (is)

6. PN, <u>Jay and Ari</u>, (are)

B Sample answers:

1. The shells on this beach are beautiful.

2. It is the hot sand that can hurt our feet.

3. The ice cream tastes cool and refreshing.

4. After their long swim, Jessie and Jake appear tired.

5. Tomorrow will be another good day for the beach.

Assess, p. 117

A 1. PA, <u>excited</u>, (seems)

2. PA, <u>calm</u>, (is)

3. PN, <u>pet</u>, (is)

4. PA, <u>cool</u>, (appears)

5. PA, <u>happy</u>, (feels)

6. PN, <u>friends</u>, (are)

B Sample answers:

1. Charlie's new dog bed is soft.

2. However, his favorite place to sleep is still the couch.

3. Chasing rabbits in the field, Charlie never seems bored.

4. His wagging tail tells us that the new treats taste great.

5. Before Charlie, our only pet was a canary.

C Sample answers:

1. This sweater is soft.

2. The newest piece of furniture is the couch.

3. I am never bored playing tennis.

4. Crisp, fresh apples taste great.

5. The prettiest bird in the cage is that canary.

Grammar: Combine Choppy Sentences

Practice, p. 118

1. Our family came from Ireland, so we visited there last year.

2. We will send the boxes today, and you should get them on Friday.

3. I have a new skateboard, but I do not know how to ride it.

4. Kari called yesterday, but Jamie did not call until today.

5. We went to Ronnee and Rick's wedding, and we threw rice on them afterwards.

Assess, p. 119

A Sample answers:

1. The crowd cheered the football team and waved banners in the air.

2. The play was too long and boring.

3. Mr. Lennon is baking chocolate chip cookies and brownies.

B Sample answers:

1. Several of us wanted to see the new horror movie, but it was sold out.

2. In London, tourists can see Big Ben and Buckingham Palace.

3. Joseph's new phone can play music and take pictures.

4. My nephew bought a package of baseball cards and a can of soda.

Writing: Book Jacket Copy

Practice, p. 120

Sample answers:

1. being the first American woman to fly in space

2. This information makes Ride seem like an exceptional person, since it shows that she was selected over so many others for the astronaut program.

3. the fact that she is an athlete and physicist, with a doctorate

4. Students' responses should highlight their subjects' achievements and include some other interesting details.

Assessment, p. 121

Sample answers:

1. the fact that John Glenn was the first American to orbit the earth

2. the long period of Glenn's military service, including his rank of colonel; the fact that he set speed records in flying airplanes; the fact that he served as a U.S. Senator from Ohio; the fact that he returned to space to fly in a shuttle mission in his 70s

3. adventurous, committed, admirable, heroic; Marine, Senator, pilot, astronaut, hero

4. John Glenn made history when he became the first American to see the entire earth from space in 1962. After serving in two wars and developing a record as an outstanding pilot, Glenn joined NASA's astronaut program, being one of the few to pioneer this country's exploration of space. He went on to a distinguished career in the U.S. Senate and returned to space in his 70s as a member of a space shuttle crew.

Writing: Script

Practice, p. 122

Sample answers:

1. to persuade people to spend more time reading

2. anyone who can read but who probably should spend more time reading

3. The script includes images of people reading in different surroundings and then the related images of an early airplane taking off and someone walking on the moon. These images show that reading fits into our daily lives easily but can take us from the past to the future and away from our normal world.

4. Students might propose a likable actor or someone with a friendly yet confident voice.

5. Students might follow the pattern here, in which the visual elements are described—such as images of the people enjoying the activity, followed by the words to be spoken. Students' partial scripts should follow the format shown here.

Assessment, p. 123

Sample answers:

1. to advertise catfood in a somewhat humorous way

2. people who have cats and who watch television

3. The cat owner who has climbed the tree indicates that the catfood brand is his cat's favorite, and that he thinks the cat climbed the tree out of anger about not having its favorite food.

4. The visual elements include the image of the desperate owner, the cat he is trying to persuade, a group of cats apparently wanting the food the owner is carrying, and a tiger who also wants it. These visual elements show in a humorous way how desirable the catfood is.

5. Students might use visual images showing the restaurant filled with happy customers. There could also be sounds of conversation. Or the ad might emphasize how great the food is by showing customers all quiet, concentrating on enjoying their food. The spoken elements could just be one sentence about the place.

Writing: Business Letter

Practice, p. 124

1. inside address; 2. close; 3. heading
4. greeting; 5. modified block style

Assessment, p. 125

Sample Answers:

A 1. B
2. E
3. block style
4. to return a purchase, explain the reason for the return (the dent), and request a refund

B Students should use modified block style, with heading, close, and signature on the right side.

Sample answer:

I'm writing to tell you how much I appreciated the assistance of your employee, Jordan Phillips, when I shopped at your store last week. I was having trouble finding what I needed, but Ms. Phillips listened to me very patiently, asked some helpful questions, and looked very hard to find what I needed. I'm happy to say that she found it. You are lucky to have such a bright, responsible, motivated person working for you.

Literary Analysis: Persuasive Essay

Practice, p. 126
1. A; 2. C; 3. B

Assess, p. 127
1. B; 2. C; 3. C; 4. C

Literary Analysis: Persuasive Speech

Practice, p. 128

(Eating poorly is like pumping dirt into the gas tank of a car.) A gas tank filled with mud is not going to carry you very far, and a body fueled with junk food is not going to serve you very well.; The idea here is simple. People understand it easily. (they forget. They just plain forget.) (You might just as well be pumping dirt into your car.) **Sample answer:** In the analogy, eating junk food is compared to pumping dirt into the gas tank of a car.

Assess, p. 129

A 1. Answers will vary. Students should name an issue that is controversial enough to be a suitable topic for a persuasive speech.

2. Answers will vary. Students should describe a position that someone might plausibly take on the issue they have named.

B 1. repetition; 2. analogy
3. parallelism; 4. restatement

Literary Analysis: Humorous Essay

Practice, p. 130
1. Understatement; 2. Hyperbole

Assess, p. 131

A 1. Answers will vary. Students should name one kind of writing, movies, or television that they find funny.

2. Answers will vary. Students should give examples or descriptions of the kind of humor in works of the type they have named.

3. Answers will vary. In explaining whether a humorous essay could use the same sort of humor as the works they have named, students should take into account the fact that humorous essays are brief works of nonfiction.

B 1. Understatement; 2. Hyperbole; 3. Hyperbole

Reading: Analyze Persuasive Appeals

Practice, p. 132

1. celebrities; perfect, radiant skin; squeaky-clean, fresh, and glowing; Fabu-Face beauty
2. Tired; laboring; Turf-King; Cadillac; power; comfort; work seems like no work
3. Stay Slim; rich and thick and creamy; real homemade; delicious flavors; only a few calories
4. Excelvision; finest quality; highest standards; high-quality; best; you deserve it
5. direct, no-nonsense; honest; real individual; Loner; honest

Assess, p. 133

1. harsh chemicals; nature's own remedies; gently; Herbal Rain: The ad tries to make the buyer believe Herbal Rain is gentle and good for your hair.
2. shamelessly sidestepped; indulged; mud-slinging; cowardly insinuations; patriotism; humanitarian; intelligent; empty; petty: Paragraph tries to make voters believe Jody Pugh is bad and his opponent is good.
3. Rancher; generous; finest; hearty; country flavor; down-home; crisp; super; hungriest: The ad tries to appeal to the consumer's taste buds and persuade the consumer that the Rancher is filling and tasty.

Reading: Evaluate Credibility and Analyze Author's Intent

Practice, p. 134

Sample answers:

1. The speaker does not like horror movies and wants the listener to see a mystery instead.
2. The speaker likes the report, but thinks that the next report could be even better if it had more sources.
3. The speaker wants the listener to take his or her little sister to the playground and offers a later curfew.

Assess, p. 135

Sample answers:

1. The author is saying that designer clothes are not worth their cost. He or she argues that your clothes should be right for you, and that any friends you might make because of your clothes are probably not true friends.
2. The author proves his or her points by saying that people look best if they wear the right clothes for them, not for others, and that it makes more sense to spend less on clothing so you can spend more on other things.
3. I agree with the author because the kids who are only interested in surfaces will probably not value my ideas or feelings.

Vocabulary: Word Roots

Practice, p. 136

A 1. A; 2. A; 3. A; 4. C

B 1. incredible; 2. resumed; 3. introduce
4. details

Assess, p. 137

A Sample answers:

1. He said no to dessert because he wanted to reduce his sugar intake.
2. The room was sumptuously furnished with thick rugs and soft cushions.
3. The retail price of a product is generally higher than what the seller paid for it.
4. Our local government had to curtail its spending because money was tight.
5. The candidate was chosen for the job because she had good credentials.

B 1. A; 2. B; 3. C; 4. A; 5. A; 6. b

Grammar: Adjectives

Practice, p. 138

A 1. little, blue, red
2. last, French
3. Antique, central, rare
4. six, personal
5. quick, many, strange
6. Poor, best, worst
7. double, mysterious
8. sturdy, big, local
9. first, next
10. High, primary

B 1. proud—peacocks; back—garden
2. little—choice; several—people; inexperienced—people
3. major—city; Canadian—city

Assess, p. 139

A 1. <u>restless</u> (crowd); <u>second</u> (race)

2. <u>wet</u> (chipmunk); <u>tiny</u> (hole); <u>old</u> (wall); <u>stone</u> (wall)

3. <u>two</u> (hounds); <u>feeble</u> (hounds); <u>old</u> (hounds); <u>ramshackle</u> (house)

4. <u>That</u> (tie); <u>orange</u> (tie); <u>this</u> (suit); <u>blue</u> (suit)

5. <u>thirsty</u> (athlete); <u>tall</u> (glass); <u>cold</u> (glass); <u>tart</u> (lemonade)

6. <u>airplane</u> (show); <u>one</u> (pilot); <u>young</u> (pilot); <u>several</u> (stunts); <u>risky</u> (stunts); <u>his</u> (biplane); <u>old</u> (biplane)

B 1. Our, fabulous, new, recreation

2. Small, snappish, large

3. Tim's, left, third

4. strong, east, huge, rocky

5. impressive, ancient

6. lecture, four, gold, one, three, large

7. Jeffrey's, old, dusty

8. Italian, splendid, their, magnificent, wall

Grammar: Adverbs

Practice, p. 140

A 1. forcefully; 2. frequently; 3. gracefully

4. there; 5. incorrectly; 6. fully

7. quickly; 8. angrily

B 1. <u>warmly</u> (greeted); <u>graciously</u> (greeted)

2. <u>patiently</u> (waited); <u>carefully</u> (bandaged)

3. <u>threateningly</u> (glared); <u>angrily</u> (growled); <u>then</u> (sprang); <u>forward</u> (sprang)

4. <u>never</u> (will believe); <u>again</u> (will believe)

Assess, p. 141

A 1. <u>Slowly</u> (crept); <u>silently</u> (crept)

2. <u>noisily</u> (stomped)

3. <u>early</u> (rose); <u>halfheartedly</u> (exercised)

4. <u>reluctantly</u> (admitted)

5. <u>up</u> (leaped); <u>deftly</u> (executed)

6. <u>uproariously</u> (greeted)

7. <u>crazily</u> (flashed)

8. <u>Sometimes</u> (means); <u>really</u> (means)

9. <u>calmly</u> (answered); <u>nervously</u> (were moving)

10. <u>hardly</u> (speak)

B Sample answers:

1. loudly; 2. rarely; 3. carefully

4. usually; 5. early

Grammar: Parallelism

Practice, p. 142

1. Correct

2. We will discuss Sandy's proposal and consider alternate plans.

3. Many gases are invisible, colorless, and tasteless.

4. Correct

5. Correct

6. Her aim was teaching college English or becoming a journalist.

7. Eduardo's speech was tiresome, inaccurate, and annoying to a lot of people.

Assess, p. 143

1. B; 2. C; 3. C; 4. A

Spelling: Tools for Checking Spelling

Practice, p. 144

A 1. eliminate; 2. colleagues; 3. illuminate

4. ounce; 5. literally

B 1. incorrect: waist; correct: waste 2. incorrect: ounce; correct: once 3. incorrect: literal; correct: literally 4. incorrect: colleges; correct: colleagues

Assess, p. 145

A 1. illuminate; 2. eliminate; 3. colleague;

4. literally; 5. ounce

B 1. incorrect: Ounce; correct: Once 2. incorrect: colleague; correct: colleagues 3. correct

4. incorrect: eliminate; correct: illuminate

5. incorrect: waste; correct: waist

C Students should underline *illuminate, waist,* and *Ounce.* 1. eliminate 2. waste 3. Once

Writing: Abstract

Practice, p. 146

1. how resourceful Cosby and his friends were in finding ways to play their games in the streets and how much joy they took from these activities

2. details such as the use of manhole covers and cars for bases and the way the boys would play even after dark or when their "bases" would drive away

3. No, because the abstract shows that the writing is a personal memoir about childhood football games, not about the history of the game itself.

4. **Possible questions:** What was the most memorable stickball play? When did the boys feel too old to play in the streets? Was anyone seriously injured by these games?

Assess, p. 147

Sample Answers:

1. The topic is the differences between snakes and lizards.

2. The article gives examples of legless lizards, such as worm lizards and glass snakes.

3. reptiles; lizards; snakes

4. Snakes and lizards are related, and this article explains the real difference between them. Most lizards have legs, while snakes do not. However, the article includes examples of legless lizards. A legless reptile may still be a lizard, according to the article, if it has eyelids it can blink or openings for its ears.

Writing: Proposal

Practice, p. 148
Sample Answers:
1. The clubs are proposing that the school establish an annual Art Fair. The clubs' members would set up the displays and take them down and contribute works and find other students to contribute.
2. the encouragement of creativity; the opportunity to reach out to school parents
3. The school's principal or faculty would be the likely audience for the proposal.

Assess, p. 149
A Sample Answers:
1. A neighborhood association is proposing that the city cooperate and help fund a major restoration of their park. The project would be accomplished by a combination of volunteer and paid professional effort.
2. The park, which is in bad shape, would look significantly better, and people would enjoy visiting it again.
3. The City Council is the audience.
B Sample answers:
Students' proposals should identify and describe the club, indicate how it would operate, and explain how its activities would benefit the community. Since the proposal is being made to a business, it would be especially good if the proposal showed an awareness of the "bottom line"—both the need to economize and the concrete ways in which the action will help the community.

Writing: Editorial

Practice, p. 150
A 1. B; 2. B; 3. A
B Sample Answers:
The school year should be lengthened so that summer vacation is shortened and students go to school year round. *Support:* The current long summer breaks result in students forgetting important material.

Assess, p. 151
1. *Sample thesis statement for cell phone topic:* Cell phones should be limited to use in public since they can also be a nuisance and even a danger.

2. *Sample support for cell phone topic:* People who drive while speaking on cell phones are more prone to accidents than other drivers, since they are distracted.
3. *Sample objection to idea of limiting cell phone use:* Cell phones have certainly added convenience to our lives and have even proven valuable to people in emergencies.
4. *Sample counterargument answering objection in Item 3:* Limiting cell phone use in places like restaurants would not inconvenience people, since they would still be able to use their phones in more private areas such as restrooms.

Unit 4

Literary Analysis: Figurative Language

Practice, p. 152
A 1. L; 2. F; 3. L; 4. F; 5. F; 6. F
B 1. C; 2. B

Assess, p. 153
A 1. L; 2. F; 3. F; 4. F; 5. L
B 1. <u>city</u>, <u>Ice Age</u>; wintry, cold, icy, barren
2. <u>hot dog</u>, <u>charcoal-broiled steak</u>; taste
3. <u>snores</u>, <u>chainsaw</u>; sound
4. <u>park</u>, <u>forest</u>; trees
5. <u>movie theater</u>, <u>sealed tomb</u>; foul-smelling, musty

Literary Analysis: Sound Devices

Practice, p. 154
A 1. B; 2. A; 3. B; 4. C
B 1. B; 2. A

Assess, p. 155
A 1. B; 2. A; 3. A; 4. B
B Sample answers:
1. **onomatopoeia** <u>bang</u> and <u>pow</u>
2. **assonance** <u>chilly</u> and <u>winter</u>
3. **consonance** <u>book</u> and <u>like</u>
4. **alliteration** <u>tree</u> and <u>tremble</u>

Literary Analysis: Imagery

Practice, p. 156
cloudy, torpedo-shaped, floated, deafening, red and yellow, billowing, blazing, flung, odor, intense

Assess, p. 157
1. no
2. distant voices, ice or snow crunching
3. smoke of chimneys; smell of damp, winter forest

4. icy cold

5. heavy insulated winter clothing

Reading: Read Fluently

Practice, p. 158

A 1. C; 2. B; 3. A

B 1. A; 2. E

Assess, p. 159

A 1. C; 2. A; 3. B

B 1. A; 2. B

Reading: Follow Technical Directions and Use Technology

Practice, p. 160

Sample answers:

1. The directions are for a cordless phone.

2. Two technical terms are: LED is a kind of light and the handset is the part of the phone used for talking and listening.

3. The author uses uppercase letters to highlight the features of the phone that are being discussed.

Assess, p. 161

Sample answers:

1. Nintendo Wii is being discussed.

2. Wii is being used in rehabilitation facilities to get patients moving, in nursing homes to give seniors safe ways to exercise, and with injured soldiers to help them continue performing repetitive exercises.

3. Three technical terms are: Wii, which is a gaming system; rehabilitation facilities, which are places where people recover from injuries; and virtual tennis, which is a game in which people play tennis with a computer.

Vocabulary: Word Roots and Prefixes

Practice, p. 162

A 1. transferred; 2. convert; 3. reverted
4. conference

B 1. monologue; 2. anatomy; 3. monorail;
4. analysis

Assess, p. 163

A 1. A; 2. B; 3. A; 4. A; 5. C; 6. B

B Sample answers:

1. The extrovert was very friendly and outgoing.

2. The monotonous melody was very tiresome to listen to.

3. I eat a lot of carrots because I prefer them to other vegetables.

4. She decided to see a psychoanalyst about her nightmares.

5. The fertile land produced a variety of crops.

Grammar: Prepositions and Objects of Prepositions

Practice, p. 164

1. to (store); for (breakfast)

2. of (month)

3. on (floor); in (library); for (librarian)

4. in (wheelchair); up (ramp); into (theater); for (performance)

5. on (patio); until (Tuesday); of (week); after (next)

6. near (door); to (friend); of (mine)

7. At (end); of (quarter); by (points)

8. under (bed); in (hamper); in (dryer); for (sock)

9. in (cabinet); above (stove)

10. During (rainstorm); in (house); near (fire)

Assess, p. 165

A 1. over; Grand Canyon

2. after; lunch

3. toward; destination

4. down; drain

5. between; books

B 1. to (mall); with (mother); for (dress); for (dance)

2. into (friends); in (Robbins Department Store)

3. of (girls)

4. with (it); with (eyes)

5. with (sigh)

6. to (Shana); in (dress); with (buttons); down (front)

7. for (dress); up (escalator); into (department); for (shoes)

8. of (shoes); with (dress)

Grammar: Prepositional Phrases

Practice, p. 166

1. In this city; with crazy ideas; about life

2. At the end; of the Civil War; of the South; by the Union armies

3. with great manual dexterity; in sports; in the arts

4. In the evening; from the southwest

5. of the most unusual animals; in the world; in the Galápagos Islands; off the coast; of Ecuador

6. from the Incanta Manufacturing Company; within an hour

7. among the people; near the bandstand

8. toward his keeper; of the child

9. In the 1800s; with a team; of horses; of land; in a day

10. in the same period; of time

1. of Mrs. Payne's stallions—ADJ; across a busy road—ADV
2. between 1943 and 1945—ADJ; behind enemy lines—ADV
3. in the Revolutionary War—ADJ
4. before my unbelieving eyes—ADV
5. with a limp—ADV
6. over the ridge—ADV; from the cabin—ADJ; in the valley—ADJ
7. behind the others—ADV; with every lap—ADV
8. in the attic—ADJ
9. in bed—ADV
10. beside the puddle—ADV; across it—ADV

Grammar: Vary Sentences With Phrases

Practice, p. 168

A 1. in (P), newspaper (OP)
  2. about (P), pumpkin (OP)
  3. at (P), County Fair (OP)
  4. next to (P), it (OP)

B Sample answers:
  1. In the winter, some birds fly south.
  2. Across the pond, three geese were honking loudly.
  3. On top of the fence, the rooster crowed.

Assess, p. 169

A 1. by (P), roots (OP)
  2. Within (P), minutes (OP); around (P), town (OP)
  3. of (P), fire trucks (OP)
  4. Near (P), garage (OP)
  5. about (P), tornado (OP); for (P), time (OP)

B Sample answers:
  1. For their hit song, the band received an award.
  2. The audience greeted them with loud cheers.
  3. Later, the fans rushed toward the stage.
  4. The limo was waiting in front of the theater.

Writing: Description of a Scene

Practice, p. 170

A 1. sound; 2. smell; 3. sound
  4. sight; 5. touch; 6. taste

B 1. Sample detail: velvety scarlet petal
  2. Sample main impression: dancing flames
  3. Sample main impression: big box filled with happy noise
  4. Sample sensory detail: greenish fluorescent light

C Students should list several details about the sights and sounds of the scene at a particular time of day (e.g., morning, high noon, dusk) in specific weather (such as a rainstorm, snow storm, or bright sunny day).

Assess, p. 171

Sample answers:
  1. feathery snowflakes tumbling down constantly, soft mounds of untouched snow, frosty air, silence, pale gray sky
  2. air filled with snow
  3. Top to bottom: from the pale gray sky, to the snowflakes, to the frosty air, to the piles of snow
  4. Students' descriptions should include at least some of the details they listed, following the order they suggested. The descriptions must begin with or lead up to the overall impression.

Writing: Editorial

Practice, p. 172

A Sample answers:
  1. A
  2. B
  3. Few city projects are as necessary as a new library. OR The city could propose a bond issue, dedicated to funding a new library. OR It should be possible to build a new library without draining money from services such as fire or police.
  4. B

B The students' editorials should take a clear position on an issue about which there can be discussion. They should include several items of support and use language that is persuasive without being antagonistic or insulting to the opposing point of view.

Assess, p. 173

Sample answers:
  1. A new bridge must be built to replace the old one on Samson Street.
  2. An engineer's report indicated that the old bridge was so low that it contributed to the recent flood.
  3. There is no guarantee that the bridge will solve the problems from the creek's overflow.
  4. No prediction about the future can be certain, but it is clear that the old bridge creates problems and that any new bridge will be designed to avoid those problems.

Writing: Descriptive Essay

Practice, p. 174

A Sample Answers:
  1. wet hair plastered to a face

2. continuous, smooth movement

3. deep shade and silence

B Sample Answers:

Sentence 5 presents the overall impression, and it should come last in the order. The sentences could be arranged from near to far (2, 3, 6, 4, 1, 5) or far to near (1, 4, 6, 3, 2, 5).

Assess, p. 175

Sample answers:

1. *Sample details for a performer:* black velvet sleeveless dress; sleek silver jewelry; long straight red hair swinging from side to side; tall, thin body swaying to the music; eyes closed; rich, expressive voice; flashing violet and gold lights onstage; rhythmic backup band; rich, expressive voice

2. *Sample main impression:* Her body was an extension of her voice—expressive, soulful, elegant.

3. *Sample organization:* From far to closeup— from a view of the flashing lights and the singer's body to her hair and face, and finally her voice.

4. Students' descriptions should include at least some of the details they listed, following the order they suggested. The descriptions must include an overall impression.

Literary Analysis: Narrative Poetry

Practice, p. 176

A 1. A; 2. D; 3. C; 4. B

B 1. C; 2. A; 3. D

Assess, p. 177

A 1. "Of the midnight ride of Paul Revere"

2. "On the eighteenth of April in Seventy-five"; "North Church"; "Middlesex"

3. Paul Revere will ride through every Middlesex village and farm and warn the colonists that the British are coming.

B Sample answers:

The mood may be described as dramatic, exciting, intense, heroic, or patriotic.

Literary Analysis: Rhyme

Practice, p. 178

1. hands/lands/stands; crawls/walls/falls

2. hands/lands/stands; crawls/walls/falls

3. *aaa bbb*

Assess, p. 179

1. March/larch; before/door; air/bare; yield/field

2. March/larch; before/door; air/bare; yield/field

3. The poem does not use any slant rhymes.

4. The poem does not use any internal rhymes.

5. *abab cdcd*

Literary Analysis: Lyric Poetry

Practice, p. 180

A Sample Answers:

1. "No one but Night . . . watches beside me"

2. "<u>N</u>o one but <u>N</u>ight"; *face* rhymes with *place*; *dark* is repeated

3. "Night, with tears on her dark face, / Watches beside me"

4. "No one but Night"; "tears on her sad face"; "this dark place"

B Sample Answers:

1. 5; 2. 7; 3. 5; 4. "crickets sing"

Assess, p. 181

A Sample Answers:

1. "And sob and curse and fall and weep and rise"; "Miserable and lost, with stinging eyes"

2. "<u>w</u>iser in no <u>w</u>ise"

3. "I chase your colored phantom on the air"; "sob and curse and fall and weep and rise"; "Once more I clasp,—and there is nothing there."

4. "And sob and curse and fall and weep and rise"; "Miserable and lost, with stinging eyes"

B Sample Answers:

1. The first line has 14 syllables. The second line has 21. The third line has 13. None of the lines has the same number of syllables as any other.

2. "else," "friendly," and "songs" do not rhyme.

3. "<u>S</u>inging with open mouth<u>s</u> their <u>s</u>trong melodiou<u>s</u> <u>s</u>ong<u>s</u>" repeats the *s* and *g* sounds.

Reading: Paraphrase

Practice, p. 182

A 1. *met; didn't*

2. Isabel met an enormous bear. Isabel didn't care.

B Sample Answer:

Isabel met a huge bear. She didn't care. The bear was very hungry. The bear's mouth was cruel and enormous.

Assess, p. 183

A Sample Answers:

1. **Subject 1:** they; **Subject 2:** they; **Verb 1:** built; **Subject 1:** built

2. And so they built a glider, first. Then, they built another.

3. *ran*

434 Reading Kit Answers

4. *bought*

5. *praised*

6. They ran a dusty little shop for bicycle repairing. They bought each other soda pop. They praised each other's daring.

B First, they built one glider. Then, they built another. They were two devoted brothers. They ran a bicycle-repair shop. They were supportive and affectionate with each other.

Reading: Paraphrase a Text and Find the Main Idea

Practice, p. 184

Sample answers:

1. I found that the text would be about why some dogs behave in a dominant way.

2. The text is about the link between wild dogs and domestic dogs. It says that domestic dogs act like wild dogs, so it is important for dog trainers to understand the rules of life in a dog pack.

Assess, p. 185

Sample answers:

1. The headlines say that the case study will be about how to become a dog trainer.

2. The case study discusses what dog trainers need to learn about dogs and dog training. They should learn with an experienced trainer, and they should realize that although the rewards of dog training are great, trainers must avoid getting emotionally involved with their clients.

B Sample answers:

1. You need to evaluate Web sources because the information on different Web sites is not equally reliable.

2. You need to figure out why the sponsor runs the site, and whether the sponsor has a reason not to give you good information.

Vocabulary: Prefixes and Suffixes

Practice, p. 186

A 1. predated; 2. immature; 3. immeasurable

B 1. B; 2. A; 3. A

Assess, p. 187

A Sample answers:

1. She stumbled through her class presentation because she was not prepared.

2. His neighbors all condemned him for his immoral behavior.

3. I need this done immediately, so please start right now.

4. The preface to a book is found at the beginning.

B Sample answers:

1. amusement; amused

2. reflected; reflection

3. completion; complete

4. puzzling: puzzlement

Grammar: Appositive Phrases

Practice, p. 188

A 1. a lightweight streamlined canoe

2. a new department store

3. the temporary bookkeeper

4. the student I am tutoring

5. the patron saint of Ireland

B 1. This novel is from the north branch of the library, the building on Central Street.

2. Jamestown, the first permanent English settlement in the New World, was founded in 1607.

3. The harpsichord, a stringed musical instrument, is the predecessor of the piano.

Assess, p. 189

A 1. the state bird of North Carolina

2. my best friend since second grade

3. sometimes called the northern lights

4. a derivative of soybeans

5. the earliest surviving system of civil laws

B 1. Next Friday Bill has a date with Keisha Lewis, the new girl in our class.

2. Mrs. Franks, a close friend of Mom's, teaches sculpture three evenings a week.

3. Hogans, the traditional dwellings of the Navajos, always face east.

4. Burke Hollow, my favorite Vermont village, is especially pretty this time of year.

Grammar: Infinitives and Infinitive Phrases

Practice, p. 190

A 1. to wait here for Mary

2. to win

3. to be sure

4. To accept stolen goods

5. to get seats near the stage

6. to stay on the team for one more year

B 1. <u>to beat</u>; ADJ
2. <u>to eat</u>; ADJ
3. <u>to learn</u>; ADV
4. <u>to help</u>; ADV
5. <u>to play</u>; noun

Assess, p. 191

A 1. To plan a successful vacation
2. to be ill
3. to recommend new products
4. To fish for trout
5. to live in this community
6. To argue with Neil; to ask for trouble
7. to open a new office
8. to see the memorial
9. to hear from the voters
10. to play in the finals

B Sample Answers:
1. It is important to help others.
2. Uncle Simon's dream is to travel across Africa.
3. The contractors were unable to finish the job on time.
4. Janice decided it was time to relax in the pool.
5. Sam's grandmother taught him how to set the table.

Grammar: Common Usage Problems

Practice, p. 192

A 1. between; 2. among; 3. among; 4. between
B 1. as if; 2. as; 3. like; 4. as if

Assess, p. 193

1. B; 2. C; 3. B; 4. A; 5. A

Spelling: Words with Affixes

Practice, p. 194

1. spontaneity; 2. pretentious
3. ecstatic; 4. maintenance

Assess, p. 195

A 1. ecstatic; 2. maintenance; 3. spontaneity
4. pretentious; 5. wisdom
B 1. pronounceable; 2. accompaniment
3. generosity; 4. proclamation
C 1. proclamation; 2. consumption
3. accompaniment; 4. maintenance; 5. ecstatic

Writing: Description of a Movie Scene

Practice, p. 196
Sample Answers:
1. late spring; morning
2. a two-story, dark-green shingled house surrounded by blooming azalea bushes, with tall trees on either side of it; a heavy rainstorm
3. Jeremy (9 years old) and Kate (5 years old), dressed for school, each struggling with a backpack and small umbrella, walking down the front path, reluctantly, looking at the pouring rain around them
4. Begin with a close-up shot of Jeremy and widen it to include Kate. Open up to show that it is raining. Keep pulling back to show how heavy the rain is and how slowly the children are walking. End with Jeremy's umbrella blowing inside out.

Assess, p. 197

A Sample Answers:
1. Washington at Valley Forge: Inside a soldier's tent at Valley Forge during the Revolutionary War, 1776, winter.
2. It is night. Snow can be seen outside the tent opening; we hear the wind howling. The tent is low and dark inside. One candle is burning, which is the only source of light.
3. Two scruffy-looking soldiers sit near the candle and as far from the opening as possible, wearing as many clothes as they can. Their clothes are ragged. One is trying to write a letter, and the other is trying to read. Both are shivering.
4. The camera begins on the soldiers' faces and then pans so that we see the rest of the tent and finally the opening to the dark cold night and patches of snow.

B Students' paragraphs should include the information they generated for Items 1–4, but should be written in a continuous way, with transitions.

Writing: Poem

Practice, p. 198

A Sample answers:
1. floor; roar
2. "Have a seat"
3. crayon-melting warmth; cobalt-blue sky
4. The alarm clock sat as alert as a soldier, guarding the night table.

B Students' poems can take any form, rhymed or unrhymed. But the poems must focus on an object; the poems' lines must be of a definite length; and the poem must include more than one image.

Assess, p. 199

A Sample answers:

1. loud bursts of laughter; smiling until your face aches

2. Memory is an eye that never closes. Memory is a companion in old age.

B Sample answer:

1. There it sits / until I turn it on. / What sounds & sights now fill the screen!

2. I am the refrigerator. / I am taller than anything else in this house. / I am the king of the kitchen. / The oven envies me. / I see his red eye glow. / I give him the cold shoulder.

C Sample Answer:

Students' poems should tell a story of any sort. Each poem should have lines that begin and end in a definite place, rather than running on like prose.

Writing: Response to Literature

Practice, p. 200

A Sample Answers:

1. "The Breaks" is a story filled with great characters, such as Nick, the fascinating main character.

2. The focus of my response would be the characters in the story.

B 1. B; 2. A

Assess, p. 201

A Sample Answers:

1. temple bells; fragrant blossoms

2. In just a few words, this poem re-creates the feeling of absolute peace and harmony.

3. Like all haiku, this is a beautiful and simple poem. It says a lot in just seventeen syllables, using simple words and images that everyone can appreciate.

B Students' paragraphs should include a thesis statement (probably one of those written for Section A), with supporting evidence that interprets the poem according to the thesis.

Unit 5

Literary Analysis: Dialogue and Stage Directions

Practice, p. 202

A 1. Jen; Monty is Jen's uncle; Jen is worried about why Rohan is sad.

2. Monty; He has tried to get Rohan to tell him why he is sad but without success.

3. Jen; She wants to know if Monty has really questioned Rohan.

4. Monty; Monty insists that he and other friends have questioned Rohan.

B Sample answer:

[*Early morning, in the kitchen of Elijah's house. Kitchen painted bright yellow. Enter Elijah, fourteen, dark-haired, dressed in green pajamas. He yawns sleepily as he walks over to the refrigerator and opens the door.*]

Assess, p. 203

A 1. Cal; A ship has arrived, bringing a prince and his new wife. Cal seems excited.

2. Lucia; The prince has a palace and a country estate, and Lucia wonders where they will live.

3. Cal; He gives some information about the princess—that she prefers the city.

4. Lucia; Lucia assumes that the couple will stay in the city and do lots of entertaining.

B 1. D; 2. SD; 3. SD; 4. D; 5. SD

Literary Analysis: Blank Verse

Practice, p. 204

A 2. When you are young, your life is full of fun.

3. The clock struck nine when I did send the nurse.

4. She rests at ease beneath some shady tree.

B L; the character is speaking in prose instead of verse.

Assess, p. 205

A 1. B; 2. C; 3. A

B 2. More lovely are you than a velvet rose.

3. We met, we wooed, and made exchange of vow.

C 1. H; 2. L

Literary Analysis: Dramatic Speeches

Practice, p. 206

A 1. A; 2. B

B 1. monologue; 2. soliloquy; 3. aside

Assess, p. 207

A 1. A; 2. C; 3. B

B 1. monologue; 2. soliloquy; 3. aside

Literary Analysis: Dramatic Irony

Practice, p. 208

A 1. NDI; 2. DI

B Sample Answer:

I know that Linda's sister is on the other side of the door. Linda does not realize that her sister is there, so she lets herself be distracted.

Assess, p. 209

A 1. B; 2. A

B 1. DI; 2. NDI

C Sample Answer:

1. I know that Karen is actually the princess. The prince thinks that she is the maid, and he is worried that he has fallen in love with the wrong person.

Literary Analysis: Tragedy and Motive

Practice, p. 210

A 1. NT; 2. T; 3. T; 4. NT

B Sample answers:

Students may list any three of the following: *fatal; foes; star-crossed; piteous overthrows; death; their parents' strife.*

Assess, p. 211

Sample answers:

1. Yes, it would be a tragedy because the main characters meet with disaster, and the ending is tragic.
2. "their meeting was fate"; "killed in battle"; "vowed never to marry"; "died alone"
3. She was probably worried that she would not see Javier again.
4. Yes, in vowing never to marry again, Isabella gave up her chances for a happy life.

Literary Analysis: Archetypal Theme

Practice, p. 212

Check marks should be placed against items 1, 2, 3, 4, 5, 9, and 10.

Assess, p. 213

A Sample answers:

1. Character: the hero, the evil stepmother, the wise prophet
2. Plot Type: the quest, the birth of the hero, the triumph of good over evil
3. Symbol: rose as a symbol of love, water as a symbol of life
4. Theme: ill-fated love, coming of age

B Check marks should be placed against items 1, 2, 5, 7, 8, and 10.

Reading: Summarize

Practice, p. 214

1. B; 2. C; 3. B; 4. D

Assess, p. 215

Sample answers:

1. In space, the weaker gravity causes changes to occur in the human body.

2. Our bodies are adapted to Earth's gravity; in space, your blood is rerouted.
3. In space, the weaker gravity causes changes to occur in the human body. Weak gravity makes blood flow from the legs to the head. Because we are used to Earth's gravity, humans in space notice many strange sensations.

Reading: Analyze Text Information

Practice, p. 216

Sample answers:

1. The main idea is that Mexico is a great place to visit.
2. The supporting details describe Mexico's attractions: beaches, mountains, history, culture, and Aztec pyramids.
3. The author's purpose is to persuade people to visit Mexico. I determined this because of the title and the excited tone of the excerpt that highlights Mexico's attractions.

Assess, p. 217

Sample answers:

1. The main idea is to tell readers about Mexico's geography.
2. The supporting details describe the location, place, and region of Mexico.
3. The author's purpose is to inform readers about the geography of Mexico. I determined this because it presents facts about Mexico, not the author's opinions.
4. I would expect the rest of the entry to have more facts about the geography and culture of Mexico.

Vocabulary: Word Roots and Prefixes

Practice, p. 218

A 1. B; 2. B; 3. A; 4. A; 5. A

Assess, p. 219

A 1. loquacious; 2. transmit; 3. propelled
4. entangled; 5. amitious

B Sample answers:

1. I was uncertain of his intentions because he answered all my questions ambiguously.
2. The audience was very moved by the politician's eloquent speech.
3. The teacher said to proceed with our experiment, so we got started.
4. I was enraged by her insulting remarks about my family.
5. The vegetables were all home-grown, so we did not need to transport them to our house.

Grammar: Participles and Participial Phrases

Practice, p. 220

1. <u>Dressed in his old uniform</u> (Dad)
2. <u>Working hard for six months</u> (Gladys)
3. <u>reading a newspaper</u> (man)
4. <u>parked illegally</u> (car)
5. <u>held at Stanley Park</u> (concert)
6. <u>Gasping for breath</u> (swimmer)
7. <u>left in the playroom</u> (toys)
8. <u>driven safely to the range</u> (cattle)
9. <u>approaching</u> (storm)
10. <u>announcing my prize</u> (letter)

Assess, p. 221

1. roaring lion; 2. broken pipe; 3. torn shirt
4. talking parrot; 5. depressed person
6. soaring condor; 7. exciting idea
8. depressing movie; 9. crying children
10. shining stars

Grammar: Gerunds and Gerund Phrases

Practice, p. 222

1. returning your ring
2. Jousting in tournaments
3. giving them bonuses
4. Hunting on these premises
5. raking leaves in the fall
6. Decorating our new apartment
7. listening to the announcer
8. studying
9. opening the cellar door
10. Hearing people shout

Assess, p. 223

1. becoming a successful writer; PN
2. paying ten dollars; DO
3. forgetting his homework; Obj. of Prep.
4. waiting for anyone; DO
5. quitting her job; PN
6. sitting around the snack shop; PN
7. Frightening the neighbors; S
8. postponing the tournament; Obj. of Prep.
9. leaving early; Obj. of Prep.
10. painting the dock; PN

Grammar: Combine Sentences With Phrases

Practice, p. 224

A Sample answers:
1. The breeze, coming in from the north, cooled the sweltering island.

2. Robert Frost, a New England poet, wrote "Birches."
3. Ted, worried about spraining his back, refused to put up the tent.
4. The council will meet in Frankfort, the capital of Kentucky.

B 1. that you sent him
2. badly
3. with a stubby tail
4. After they had been sharpened
5. staying at the lodge
6. with bared teeth

Assess, p. 225
Sample answers:

A 1. Sarah, blinking continuously, said she had something in her eye.
2. Al, sipping a glass of tea, daydreamed peacefully.
3. Mr. Taylor, my neighbor, is a famous civil rights lawyer.
4. Bonnie, hoping to get a chance to speak to Mrs. Gleason, waited around until five o'clock.
5. Earthquakes and volcanic eruptions can cause tsunamis, large, rapidly moving waves.

B 1. Because it was burnt to a cinder, I could not eat the marshmallow.
2. The actor in faded blue jeans saddled his horse.
3. The pears that had been left on the kitchen table were eaten by the children.
4. The woman informed the police by phone that the thief had escaped.

Writing: Letter to an Advice Columnist

Practice, p. 226
Sample answers:

1. John is a sixteen-year-old boy who has an after-school job.
2. A coworker has been saying things that are not true, and John fears his boss believes these lies.
3. Talk to the boss and ask her to watch John work to see for herself that he is a polite and hard worker. Confront the coworker and ask him to stop spreading lies.

Assess, p. 227
Sample answers:

A 1. My parents do not like my friends.
2. I will describe myself so the columnist knows what kind of person I am. Then, I will explain my problem clearly and briefly. Finally, I will ask for advice.

3. Dear Marilyn, I am a seventeen-year-old girl. I have a great group of friends, but my parents do not like them at all. My mother thinks they are a bad influence on me, but they really aren't. When I get in trouble, it is usually my fault. I don't do things because my friends tell me to. How can I convince my parents that my friends are okay? —Lora J.

B Dear Lora, I suggest that you stop doing things to get in trouble. When your parents can trust you, they will be more likely to trust your choice of friends. —Marilyn

Writing: Parody

Practice, p. 228
Sample answers:

1. a. Bruno talks like a real smoothie about how much he loves Marta. "My love for you is far, far deeper than the ocean!"
   b. Bruno and Marta act cute and lovey-dovey with each other. Bruno helps her on with her coat.
2. Students' parodies should refer to and make fun of at least two of these elements: Bruno's way of talking; Bruno and Marta's way of acting with each other; Bruno and Marta's lifestyle.

Assess, p. 229
Sample answers:

1. a. Commander Spackle is shouting all the time, it seems. She gives orders in a tough way. She slams her fist in her palm. "Now, move!"
   b. The commander orders the crew around. They obey her and are probably scared of her. When Officer Yurt points out that the commander might be doing something wrong, he shouts at her. She says "Aye, aye!"
   c. The commander faces problems such as attack by alien spaceships. The ship is hit by a pulse bomb, and the commander thinks it was fired by the Zone.
   d. The story talks about starships, pulse bombs, and Draconic Shields. The technology is from the imaginary future.
2. Students' parodies should continue the story of Commander Spackle and the Starship *Excel*. In their parodies, they should refer to and make fun of at least three of these elements: Commander Spackle's way of talking and gesturing; her interactions with Officer Yurt and the rest of the crew; the type of problems the Commander faces; and the technology they use.

Writing: Editorial

Practice, p. 230
Sample answers:

1. safety in the school's parking lot at lunchtime
2. Closing the campus for lunch would not be the best way to make the parking lot safer.
3. an alternative suggestion and supporting details
4. Closing the campus would upset many students and the restaurants that rely on their business; local police or volunteers could help monitor the parking lot to discourage unsafe driving; there was just one incident, so it is not a pattern calling for drastic action.

Assess, p. 231
Sample answers:

1. funding for extracurricular activities such as music, art, and athletics
2. I believe the state should provide more money for extracurricular activities.
3. Extracurricular activities such as music, art, athletics, clubs, and others keep students out of trouble after school; after-school activities help build students' creativity, physical fitness, and group skills; competitions increase school spirit.
4. In recent years, our state has had problems paying for schools. However, cutting funding to extracurricular activities is not the way to solve this problem. After-school activities such as band, clubs, athletics, and others give many students a chance to do something they would not be able to do otherwise. These activities keep students out of trouble. They build school spirit and keep students excited about school.

Writing: Abstract

Practice, p. 232
Sample answers:

A 1. *Star Wars: A New Hope*
   2. A young man joins the fight to save the galaxy from an evil empire.
   3. The hero learns he has special powers; he helps save a princess and joins the rebellion; the rebels win an important battle against the evil empire.
   4. Good triumphs over evil.

B In the movie *Star Wars: A New Hope*, a young man named Luke Skywalker joins the fight to save the galaxy from an evil empire. He learns he has special Jedi powers. Luke helps save a princess and joins the rebellion against the evil Empire. Luke, his friends, and the rest of the rebels win an important battle when they blow up the Death Star and good triumphs over evil.

Assess, p. 233

Sample answer:

Most of Shakespeare's plays were performed in the Globe theater. The Globe was a round or octagonal public theater that was open to the sky. Audiences were treated to fast-paced, colorful performances there. Seeing a play at the Globe must have been fun.

Writing: Persuasive Letter

Practice, p. 234

Sample answers:

1. extend her curfew; 2. D; 3. D

Assess, p. 235

Sample answers:

Topic: Music piracy

1. teens and young adults
2. People should not pirate music because it is illegal and hurts musicians.
3. If musicians do not make money, they cannot afford to make more music; if you get caught, you can be fined or even jailed; it is not very expensive to pay for most song downloads.
4. Many young people think there is nothing wrong with downloading songs without paying for them. However, music piracy is clearly wrong. It is illegal and hurts musicians. If musicians do not make money, they cannot afford to make more music. It is not very expensive to pay for most song downloads, so music lovers should just go ahead and pay. This rewards artists for their talent and effort and makes it more likely that they will make more music.

Writing: How-to Essay

Practice, p. 236

Sample answers:

1. a card trick
2. before, then, when you come to it, when all the cards have been turned over, after the cards have been shuffled, until
3. Your friend will surely be amazed since this trick never fails to impress an audience.

Assess, p. 237

Sample answers:

Topic: how to make a hamburger

1. hamburger meat, buns, vegetables, condiments, plate, skillet or grill, spatula
2. form the meat into a patty; cook the meat; place the meat on the bun; add favorite vegetables and condiments; place burger on a plate and serve

3. Readers might not know how to cook the meat or that undercooked meat can be dangerous; they can cut the patty open in the center to see if it is brown or still pink.

Literary Analysis: Comedy

Practice, p. 238

Sample answers:

1. Bob is hiding in the closet and hears every word. Jane thinks she is fooling him, but the audience knows better.; comic situation; dramatic irony
2. **Professor Humphrey Wheezer:** Lance Dashboard; Professor, I don't see even one sock. Are you feeling OK?; funny names; witty dialogue
3. The elevator breaks down, and the two are stuck together for an hour; comic situation

Assess, p. 239

A 1. D; 2. A

B Sample answers:

1. He complains about Jeff's cousin to her. Neither Sam nor the audience know that Sally IS Jeff's cousin.; comic situation
2. **Dr. Prod; Harry Clunker;** You're already taking my money. Sure, take my pulse, too.; funny names; witty dialogue

Literary Analysis: Satire

Practice, p. 240

1. No satire
2. **Sample answers:** Satire; Target of satire: fancy jogging sneakers and suits; (Hopefully, the people at Atomic will add even more power to their next model of sneaker.); these sneakers now come equipped with a "rocket-assist" feature

Assess, p. 241

1. A; 2. B
2. No satire
3. **Sample answers:** Satire; Target of satire: small, powerful computers; (I don't know how I'll live without it.); I hit a wrong key and turned on all the television sets in my neighborhood.

Reading: Draw Conclusions

Practice, p. 242

1. D
2. Ben
3. Tanya asks Ben for a ride. Ben probably has his license, and Tanya does not.
4. A

Assess, p. 243

1. A
2. "We could see all the way to the mainland"; "the boats below us"
3. The writer thinks the setting is beautiful.
4. B
5. The writer uses the words *we* and *us*.

Reading: Evaluate the Author's Credibility

Practice, p. 244

A 1. Knowledgeable; 2. Lacks Knowledge

B 1. Bias; 2. Unbiased

Assess, p. 245

A 1. B 2. B

B 1. Knowledgeable; 2. Lacks Knowledge

C 1. Biased; 2. Biased

Vocabulary: Prefixes and Word Roots

Practice, p. 246

A Sample answers:

1. Y; the denomination of money is the value shown on the bill.
2. N; a synonym is a word with a similar meaning to another word. The students used synonyms to give their writing more variety.
3. Y; a misnomer is an inaccurate name.
4. N; to nominate someone means to name him or her for a position. We nominated her to head the environmental committee because she knew a lot about that field.

Assess, p. 247

A 1. antonyms; 2. nominees; 3. nomenclature
4. anonymous; 5. nominal

B Sample answers:

1. The police got a tip from an anonymous informant.
2. The word *full* is an antonym for *empty*.
3. I find scientific nomenclature hard to use.
4. I gave the waiter only a nominal tip because I was displeased with the service.
5. The two parties' nominees faced each other in the general election.

Grammar: Main and Subordinate Clauses

Practice, p. 248

A 1. M; 2. S; 3. S; 4. M; 5. M; 6. S; 7. M

B Sample Answers:

1. Patrice found the perfect costume after looking in numerous stores.

2. We tried to eat with chopsticks but ended up dropping most of our food.
3. The tomatoes were ripe and were ready to be eaten.

Assess, p. 249

A 1. (When Allison called me on the phone); I was not at home
2. Grandpa led an active life; (until he hurt his hip while skiing)
3. People should turn off their cell phones; (when they go to the movies)
4. (If you are careful); you can make a beautiful vase on the potter's wheel
5. Alfred cannot go to the movies; (unless he does his work first)

B Sample answers:

1. main; A show always entertains.
2. subordinate; I went to see the play because a friend recommended it.
3. subordinate; I would not pay that much for a ticket again, though the show was great.
4. main; I kept quiet.
5. subordinate; My friend Lisa cried if it was a sad scene.

Grammar: Adverb Clauses

Practice, p. 250

A 1. (When) the weather is hot
2. (until) I have finished it.
3. (unless) it rains.

B 1. Until the bus arrives, the campers will wait in the gym.
2. If there is a long period without rain, many plants will not survive.
3. Although Miami is a large city, Los Angeles is even larger.
4. The Jackson's moved to Charlotte because Mr. Jackson got a new job.

Assess, p. 251

A 1. A; 2. B

B 1. (Until) the prices go down
2. (unless) there is a rain delay.
3. (After) the icebreakers open the channel
4. (before) he sent in his report.

C Accept adverb clauses at the beginning or at the end of the sentences. Those beginning sentences should be followed by a comma.

1. Unless he has soccer practice, Steve goes to the library after school.
2. A fox lives in the woods nearby although the farmer rarely sees it.

Although a fox lives in the woods nearby, the farmer rarely sees it.

3. Many good-hearted people volunteer when disasters occur.

4. Because the price of gas has risen, airfares have also risen.

Spelling: Using Silent *e*

Practice, p. 252

A 1. alternatively; 2. revision; 3. involving; 4. density

B 1. college; to turn a hard *c* or *g* into a soft *c* or *g*
2. rectangle; to avoid a syllable with no vowel
3. revise; to turn a short vowel into a long vowel
4. dense; to avoid being confused with a plural

Assess, p. 253

A 1. resourceful; 2. revising; 3. involvement; 4. densely

B 1. resource; to turn a hard *g* into a soft *g;*
2. credible; to avoid having a syllable with no vowel; 3. remote; to turn a short vowel into a long vowel; 4. tense; to avoid being confused with a plural

C Students should underline the incorrect spellings of these words and write them correctly on the lines: 1. revising; 2. college; 3. Involvement

Writing: Play

Practice, p. 254

1. The writer identifies the speakers in boldfaced all-capital letters before their lines.

2. The narrator tells us.

3. Alicia speaks as if winning the lottery is a fantasy. Mom tells Alicia it will not happen.

4. The audience knows that Alicia is going to win the lottery and that it will cause problems; Alicia and her mother do not know this.

Assess, p. 255

Sample Answers:

A The football player thinks he has scored a touchdown, but the spectators know he has not. He has no idea he is about to get tackled.

B **KATIE.** Hi! You're Steve, right? I think you're in my math class.

STEVE. [*nodding*] Yeah. That's right.

KATIE. Hey, have you seen the latest Katy Zed music video? That woman is clueless. She thinks everyone loves '70s R-and-B like she does! Her hair and clothes are straight out of the 1970s, too. She has no idea how goofy she looks.

STEVE. [*smiling to hide his irritation*] What would you say if you found out that Katy Zed is my aunt?

KATIE. [*laughing*] Yeah, right!

Writing: Research Report

Practice, p. 256

Sample answers:

1. narrow the topic by writing a question that guides the research

2. a topic sentence that clearly states what one intends to prove in the report; it is important because it gives the report a focus

3. gives proper credit to sources

4. elaborate and revise; proofread for correct grammar, spelling, and punctuation

Assess, p. 257

Sample answers:

1. drafting the Constitution, the Civil War, the New Deal, 9/11

2. How are New Deal policies still affecting people in the United States?

3. Many New Deal policies, such as Social Security, are still in place in the United States. Some people believe that these policies are no longer necessary and will eventually collapse under their own weight.

4. write rough draft; elaborate and revise; proofread; write final draft; include bibliography or works-cited list

5. encyclopedias, books about history written by reliable historians, government Web sites showing statistics on New Deal programs, etc.

6. include a properly formatted bibliography or works-cited list

Unit 6

Literary Analysis: Epic Hero

Practice, p. 258

1. D; 2. C; 3. A; 4. B

Assess, p. 259

1. B; 2. C; 3. B; 4. C

Literary Analysis: Epic Simile

Practice, p. 260

1. C; 2. B; 3. C

Assess, p. 261

1. B; 2. D; 3. A; 4. A

Literary Analysis: Contemporary Interpretations of Classical Works

Practice, p. 262

1. C; 2. B; 3. A

Assess, p. 263

1. C; 2. C; 3. B

Reading: Analyze Cultural and Historical Context

Practice, p. 264

1. B; 2. C

Assess, p. 265

A 1. A; 2. A; 3. B

B Sample answers:

Context: In King Arthur's time, people thought it was important to be brave and fight for honor.
What the context helps me understand: why Gawain volunteers to fight the giant green knight

Reading: Identify Characteristics of Various Types of Texts

Practice, p. 266

Sample answers:

1. The main idea is that the author loves superheroes.
2. The author likes superheroes because he or she loves their optimism and thinks the world would be dull without them.
3. The purpose of the commentary is to persuade others that superheroes are not only for children.

Assess, p. 267

Sample answers:

1. The main idea of the article is that Superman is a very popular character who started the superhero trend.
2. The author supports the main idea by stating that the character has appeared in countless comic strips, radio serials, TV series, and movies.
3. The purpose of the article is to describe Superman and guess at why he might appeal to so many people.
4. The difference between the two texts is that the commentary expresses an opinion, but the article explains who Superman is and what he does.

Vocabulary: Prefixes and Suffixes

Practice, p. 268

A Sample answers:

1. disrespect; Teachers disliked him because he treated them with *disrespect*.
2. befriend; I made an effort to *befriend* the new student.
3. discharged; The soldiers *discharged* their guns toward the enemy.
4. becalm; The ship was *becalmed* for two days.
5. bedew; His tears *bedewed* his cheeks.

6. disorganized; My parents think my room is too *disorganized*.

Assess, p. 269

A 1. dismissed; 2. betrothal; 3. bereaved
   4. dispensed; 5. disposal; 6. bedraggled

B 1. belied; 2. disembarked; 3. dislocated
   4. besprinkled; 5. bemused; 6. dislodge

Grammar: Simple and Compound Sentences

Practice, p. 270

A 1. "The Gift of the Magi" has a surprise ending, (and) "The Necklace" also has one.
   2. Poetry is often beautiful, (but) sometimes it is difficult to understand.
   3. You can explain the directions, (or) you could draw me a map.
   4. Pears and apples are good, (but) I prefer peaches and plums.

B 1. Enjoy watching the animals, but do not feed them.
   2. Carl and Jane work hard all week, and they relax on the weekend.
   3. The trains have stopped running, so we will take a bus.

Assess, p. 271

A 1. On Saturday we will have a party, (and) we will invite the whole neighborhood.
   2. David and Daniel are twins, (but) they don't look anything alike.
   3. You can watch the news on television, (or) you can read it on the Internet.
   4. Jay's family rents DVDs online, (so) they don't have to go to the video store.

B 1. Read the poem out loud, and you will really appreciate the images.
   2. Do come again, for it is always a pleasure to see you.
   3. Turn down the air conditioner, or we will all freeze!

C 1. Birds and hamsters make good pets, but dogs and cats make better ones.
   2. You may sell tickets at the door, or you may hand out programs.
   3. Please remember to turn off your cell phone, so the ringing does not disturb the audience.

Grammar: Complex and Compound-Complex Sentences

Practice, p. 272

A 1. C; (When)
   2. C-C; (which); (and)
   3. C; (Because)

4. C-C; (that); (and)
5. C; (Before)

B Sample Answers:

1. <u>if</u> you will clean up
2. <u>which</u> are more exciting
3. <u>After</u> I finish my homework

Assess, p. 273

A 1. C; (When)
2. C-C; (and); (because)
3. C-C; (who); (but)
4. C; (Before)
5. C-C; (that); (but)
6. C; (When)
7. C-C; (or); (that)

B Sample Answers:

1. <u>if</u> it rains
2. <u>which</u> is more mellow
3. <u>because</u> it hasn't rained

C Sample Answers:

1. <u>and</u> the days get cool
2. <u>but</u> it was too small
3. <u>or</u> I will

Grammar: Fragments and Run-ons

Practice, p. 274

A 1. F; 2. F; 3. S

B Sample Answers:

1. The new store is located on the corner.
2. By the time the show ended, the rain had stopped.
3. We saw the toad hopping in the grass.

C Sample answers:

1. The rain has stopped, but the trees are still wet.
2. We painted the walls blue. We painted the ceiling white.

Assess, p. 275

A 1. F; 2. F; 3. S

B Sample Answers:

1. I like staying up past 11:00 P.M. to watch the talk shows.
2. Our family watches football on the weekend.
3. correct
4. Hockey playoffs begin tomorrow at 4:00 P.M.

C Sample Answers:

1. Our friends came over. Some brought refreshments.
2. Amy made the popcorn, and Manuel poured the drinks.
3. I started the movie, but everyone kept talking.

Writing: Everyday Epic

Practice, p. 276

1. Reno is heroic because he has a dangerous job.
2. The writer describes Reno as *brave* and *modest.*
3. A. A short boy would face many challenges on a basketball team. It would be harder for him to sink a basket; he might not run as fast as players with longer legs; he could be injured in a collision with bigger boys on the team.

   B. A student from another country might have difficulties with the language; might not understand the culture; might feel awkward or shy; might find it difficult to make friends.

   C. Someone training for a marathon would face the physical challenge of getting in shape and would need strength and determination to achieve his or her goal.

Assess, p. 277

A 1. Students should name a real person from their everyday lives.
2. Students should provide at least one clear reason why the person is heroic.
3. Students should supply three words that describe heroic qualities. Examples include *fearless, strong, caring, selfless, motivated, reliable,* and *inspiring.*
4. Students should clearly explain why they consider the person inspiring.

B Students' epics should describe a real person whom they know and should provide details about why the person is heroic.

Writing: Biography

Practice, p. 278

1. Students should list three of the following: Ali plays the drums; Ali has always had rhythm; Ali's parents bought him his first drum set when he was six; Ali formed his first band when he was in seventh grade; Ali's music teacher introduced him to a jazz musician; Ali plays in a jazz band with older musicians.
2. Ali's teacher introduced him to a local jazz musician.
3. B; 4. Neither A nor C focus on Ali, the subject of the biography.

Assess, p. 279

1. Students should name the subjects of their biographies.
2. Students should list facts that relate specifically to their subjects.

3. Students should choose events that are significant in their subjects' lives and that will be of interest to readers.

4. Students' biographies should describe a real person and should provide important information about the person.

Writing: Timed Essay

Practice, p. 280

A Students should choose one of the topics given.

B Sample answers:

1. Computers have changed the way people work and play.

2. People use computers to get work done faster than ever before. When people use computers for entertainment, it can cut them off from other people.

3. A. Using a computer, a person can run complicated machinery easily. Computers let office workers store and find information efficiently.

   B. People spend too much leisure time indoors, surfing the Internet and playing games. Chat rooms help people talk to other people, but the experience is not the same as having friends you go out and do things with.

Assess, p. 281

A Students should choose one of the topics given.

B Sample answers:

1. Big cities may be crowded and dirty, but the freedom and all the activity there makes me feel really alive.

2. In a big city, you can feel free to move around and explore as you please. In a small town, you may feel that you always need a reason to be where you are. In a big city, you can find something to do, even late at night. In a small town, the streets are empty, and everyone is home after a certain time.

3. a. I once took a long walk with friends in a big city. We walked from rich neighborhoods to poor neighborhoods. We went from streets full of big shops to streets where kids were out playing. If you took a similar walk in a small town or in the suburbs, you would see less variety. More importantly, you might feel that you were trespassing or going to places where you did not belong.

   b. I once went to a restaurant in a big city after seeing a play. We ate dinner at 11:00! Most restaurants in a small town are closed by then.

4. Students' opening paragraphs should incorporate their thesis statement and introduce the two main points they will make. They may also indicate the type of support they will use in the body of the essay.

Literary Analysis: Protagonist and Antagonist

Practice, p. 282

1. B; 2. D; 3. D

Assess, p. 283

1. A; 2. A; 3. C

Literary Analysis: Author's Purpose and Philosophical Assumptions

Practice, p. 284

1. B; 2. D; 3. C

Assess, p. 285

1. B; 2. D; 3. B

Literary Analysis: Tall Tale and Myth

Practice, p. 286

A 1. hyperbole and humor

   2. hyperbole; larger-than-life character; amazing deeds that are hard to believe

B 1. tells the actions of a god; explains the beginnings of a tradition

   2. has a parent who is a god; faces impossible tasks; has special gifts

Assess, p. 287

A 1. humor; larger-than-life hero; amazing deeds; hyperbole

   2. humor; hyperbole

   3. hyperbole

B 1. actions of a god; why life is the way it is

   2. why a natural event occurs

Reading: Compare and Contrast

Practice, p. 288

Sample Answers:

1. background; Sally and Beth are similar because they come from the same wealthy family.

2. actions/feelings; Sally and Beth are different in the way they act. While Sally invents a new medicine to help other people, Beth steals the formula.

3. fate: What happens to Sally and Beth is very different: Sally wins a prize, but Beth goes to jail.

Assess, p. 289

A Sample answers:

1. appearance/personality; Richard is different from Ralph because Richard is friendly and outgoing while Ralph is shy.

2. motives; Richard and Ralph have different goals. Richard wants to be popular at school, while Ralph wants to win a prize at the Science Fair.

3. actions/feelings; Richard and Ralph are different in how brave they are. Richard just goes along with the crowd when he makes fun of Ralph, but Ralph is brave and stands up for himself.

4. actions/feelings; Richard apologizes to Ralph for making fun of him, and Ralph accepts the apology. These actions are similar because they show that the characters care about doing what is right.

5. fate; Ralph and Richard both end up happy, but Ralph is happy because he gets what he wanted. Richard is happy because he changes what he wants.

B In their paragraphs, students should draw on the details in activity A to compare Richard and Ralph with respect to their personalities, motives, actions, and fate. Students should conclude their paragraphs by stating the lesson presented by their comparison. They should note that the comparison suggests that the desire to be popular can lead to bad behavior and that popularity is not the only means to happiness.

Reading: Analyze Primary Sources

Practice, p. 290

Sample answers:

1. Does the photograph represent the entire event or only a minor part of it? Was the photograph altered in any way?

2. Does the article report on all sides of the story? Is the reporter biased?

3. Did the person actually witness the event or is he or she describing something that someone else saw? Is the person's view biased?

Assess, p. 291

A Sample answers:

1. The topic of this excerpt is a captain describing his experiences in the air force during a war.

2. He probably wrote it to show what it felt like to be in a war.

3. The topic of this excerpt is the changes Momaday's grandmother saw during her life in the way people observed the traditional ways.

4. The author probably wrote it to preserve a sense of the traditional ways and to honor his grandmother.

5. These primary sources offer insight into people's hopes and fears at a particular point in history. They give a personal view of events, rather than a strict list of facts.

B Sample Answers:

1. Zebra

2. Mail (also accept Postal Service and Communications)

3. Medicine (also accept Disease)

C 1. C; 2. C; 3. B

Vocabulary: Word Roots

Practice, p. 292

A 1. diminished; 2. emerged; 3. fertile; 4. inspected

B 1. transfer; 2. emergency; 3. minority

4. spectators

Assess, p. 293

A Sample answers:

1. The cars on the road merged from two lanes to one.

2. I took a ferry to get from one side of the river to the other.

3. I thought the simple task could be carried out with minimal effort.

4. If he weren't so introspective, maybe he'd talk more instead of just thinking.

B Sample answers:

1. -spec-; what can be seen by looking forward. I think my prospects of getting into my chosen college are very good.

2. -merg-; to go below the surface. The toddler submerged his toy boat in the bathtub.

3. -min-; small, trifling details. Let's not let our project get bogged down in a lot of minutia.

4. -fer-; to give or bestow. My new position confers a great deal of responsibility on me.

Grammar: Commas

Practice, p. 294

1. The ocean is calm in summer, rough in winter, and beautiful all year.

2. The lobster boats will return soon, so we are watching for them.

3. Portland, Maine, has many great seafood restaurants.

4. We visited cousins in New Orleans on February 12, 2005.

5. The island, which is in the middle of the lake, has a sandy beach.

6. Kyle said, "Let's row the canoe over tomorrow for a swim."

7. They decided to invite Luis, who is Juan's younger brother.

8. In addition, they decided to pack a lunch to take with them.

9. When he heard about the plans, Juan shouted, "I'm ready!"

Assess, p. 295

A 1. Gregory wants eggs for breakfast, soup for lunch, and spaghetti for dinner.

2. Kate also likes eggs for breakfast, but she wants a sandwich for lunch.

3. On Monday, October 8, the new cafeteria opened.

4. C

5. Kate loves the sandwiches, but Gregory does not like the soup.

B 1. The gray fox, which is a member of the dog family, can climb trees.

2. Although mostly active at night, this fox sometimes hunts during the day.

3. John, who was riding his bike on a desert path, spotted a gray fox.

4. He said, "I thought there was a coyote in front of me."

5. C

C On July 4, we are having a barbecue. Jane will bring hot dogs, salad, and corn. Becca will supply napkins, cups, and plates. Pam said, "I will make brownies, which are my specialty." As always, Ty will bring the charcoal and do the grilling.

Grammar: Colons, Semicolons, Ellipsis Points

Practice, p. 296

A Sample answers:

1. I want to visit these three cities: Miami, Louisville, and San Diego.

2. Here are two rules for bicycle safety: Wear a helmet and use reflectors at night.

3. Pack these things for the hike: water, trail mix, and a compass.

4. Original sentences should mimic correct colon usage as in the three preceding items.

B 1. Ashville;

2. May 2; May 4;

3. Erie; Michigan;

C 1. wondered . . .

2. waterfront . . . we

3. greasy fries . . .

Assess, p. 297

A Sample answers:

1. This cell phone comes in three colors: red, blue, and black.

2. I'll give you one reason to see the movie: The special effects are fantastic.

3. We have band practice three days a week: Monday, Wednesday, and Saturday.

4. and 5. Original sentences should mimic correct colon usage as in the three preceding items.

B 1. sings;

2. bass; guitar;

3. 7:00 P.M.; 9:00 P.M.;

4. and 5. Original sentences should mimic correct semicolon usage as in the three preceding items.

C 1. thing . . . (*Also acceptable:* couldn't be sure . . .)

2. favors and . . .

3. seven years ago . . . "

4. ticking sound could be . . .

5. "You . . . you

Grammar: Sentence Structure and Length

Practice, p. 298

A 1. Wherever they looked, the divers saw colorful fish.

2. Surprised were they to find an old sea chest.

3. The treasure they would divide among themselves.

B Sample Answer:

The discovery of the treasure made the evening news. Suddenly, the divers became famous. Some people even declared that they were the rightful owners of the treasure.

Assess, p. 299

A 1. The nuts Ann gave to her brother.

2. The chocolates she saved for herself.

3. The most delicious were the caramel-filled, and she ate them first.

4. If the whole box were filled with caramel-filled chocolates, Ann would be happy.

5. Before the evening was over, Ann's brother had finished the nuts.

B Sample Answers:

1. When volcanoes erupt, lava streams down the mountainside, and nearby residents flee.

2. When we went to Italy, we visited the ruins of the ancient city of Pompeii. The city was destroyed during an eruption of the volcano Mount Vesuvius in A.D. 79. However, the molten lava preserved many of the buildings.

Spelling: Spelling on College Entrance Exams

Practice, p. 300

A 1. misshapen; 2. preceding
3. courageous; 4. occurred
B 1. correct; 2. sophomore
3. acclaim; 4. parentheses

Assess, p. 301

A 1. account; 2. occurrence; 3. preferred
4. preceding; 5. courageous
B 1. preference; 2. correct; 3. occurring
4. misshapen; 5. parentheses
C 1. adapt; 2. adopt; 3. parenthesis

Writing: Journal Entries

Practice, p. 302

1. The author describes getting a much smaller role than she had hoped for in the Drama Club play.
2. The author is disappointed.
3. Students should list events that happened recently and that involved themselves.
4. Students should record their own thoughts or reactions to the events.

Assess, p. 303

A 1. Students should choose one event in their own lives.
2. Students should record specific details in chronological order.
3. Students' journal entries should describe events in chronological order, should include their own thoughts or reactions to the events, and should be written in from the first-person point of view.
B 1. Students should choose a fictional character from literature.
2. Students' journal entries should be written in the character's voice, using the pronoun *I*. The entries should describe events in chronological order and should include the character's thoughts or reactions to the events.

Writing: Letter

Practice, p. 304

1. friendly letter
2. B
3. Students should list three people with whom they have personal relationships.
4. **Sample Answers:** a recent movie or concert; family news; an invitation to an upcoming event.

Assess, p. 305

1. Students should name people with whom they have personal relationships.
2. **Sample Answers:** an expression of thanks for a gift; news about mutual friends; a description of a recent event in the writer's life.
3. Students should follow the standard format for a business letter and write in a friendly, informal tone.

Writing: Comparison-and-Contrast Essay

Practice, p. 306

Sample answers:

1. subject-by-subject organization
2. the animals' responses to being left alone; the animals' ability to be trained
3. the animals' eating habits; their sizes; their sleeping habits; their life spans
4. Students' paragraphs should point out clear similarities and differences and should include accurate facts and details.

Assess, p. 307

Sample answers:

1. Students should name a specific topic for comparison.
2. Students should list at least three accurate facts or details about each subject.
3. Students should list both similarities and differences
4. Students should choose one of the two organizations.
5. Students' paragraphs should point out clear similarities and differences and should include accurate facts and details. Students should use their chosen organizations throughout their paragraphs.